Acclaim for
The Uncrowned King of Swing:
Fletcher Henderson and Big Band Jazz

"Excellent." — Alex Ross, *therestisnoise.com*

"An invaluable survey of Henderson's life and music. Detailed analyses of numerous musical scores are juxtaposed against a view of the roller-coaster progress of Henderson's career in the midst of the Harlem Renaissance. Perhaps most important, Magee deals with the complex issue of Henderson's identity as both a creative facilitator of other musicians' efforts and the frustrated composer-arranger of music that was a foundational element in the Swing Era— bringing triumphs that had eluded his groups to leaders such as Goodman, the Dorsey Brothers and Isham Jones." — Don Heckman, *Los Angeles Times*

"The definitive biography of this musical legend. Magee's argument is well laid out and his writing style inviting." — *Popular Music and Society*

"Excellent. . . . Well researched and highly readable." — *Library Journal*

"Nobody—not Ellington, nor Basie, nor Goodman—was more thoroughly involved with the beginnings of the Swing Era than Fletcher Henderson. Jeff Magee's book gives this jazz giant what he deserves: a sensitive and balanced examination of the pianist and arranger's personal history as well as a judicious evaluation of his music." — Scott K. Deveaux, author of *The Birth of Bebop: A Social and Musical History*

"Magee's treatment of Henderson and jazz music here is a loving, erudite and welcome one on a giant of the form." — *Charleston Post & Courier*

"Magee paints a vivid portrait of the central figures of early jazz and swing (Louis Armstrong is a 'strong streak of color in a crazy quilt') as well as the business of recording and touring in the 1920s and '30s. While Benny Goodman is lauded as the major force behind the Big Band sound, Magee argues convincingly that Henderson was equally important in 'building the kingdom of swing.'" — *Publishers Weekly*

"Fletcher Henderson occupies such a vital role in the evolution of American music that it comes as a shock that we had to wait this long for a superlative biography such as this. Jeff Magee has not only discovered hitherto unknown connections between Henderson's life and music, but has also linked them to the cultural scene in which they existed. The jazz world owes Jeff Magee a big thank-you for undertaking such a massive project and for doing it so well." — Loren Schoenberg, Executive Director, The Jazz Museum in Harlem

The Uncrowned King of Swing

Fletcher Henderson and Big Band Jazz

Jeffrey Magee

OXFORD
UNIVERSITY PRESS

Oxford University Press, Inc., publishes works that further
Oxford University's objective of excellence
in research, scholarship, and education.

Oxford   New York
Auckland   Cape Town   Dar es Salaam   Hong Kong   Karachi
Kuala Lumpur   Madrid   Melbourne   Mexico City   Nairobi
New Delhi   Shanghai   Taipei   Toronto

With offices in
Argentina   Austria   Brazil   Chile   Czech Republic   France   Greece
Guatemala   Hungary   Italy   Japan   Poland   Portugal   Singapore
South Korea   Switzerland   Thailand   Turkey   Ukraine   Vietnam

Copyright © 2005 by Jeffrey Magee

First published by Oxford University Press, Inc., 2005
198 Madison Avenue, New York, NY, 10016

www.oup.com

First issued as Oxford University Press paperback, 2008.

Oxford is a registered trademark of Oxford University Press

Library of Congress Cataloging-in-Publication Data
Magee, Jeffrey, 1961–
The uncrowned king of swing : Fletcher Henderson
and big band jazz / Jeffrey Magee.
p. cm.
"Henderson's arrangements for Benny Goodman": p.
Includes bibliographical references (p.   ) and index.
ISBN: 978-0-19-534065-5 (pbk.)
1. Henderson, Fletcher, 1897–1952.
2. Jazz musicians—United States—Biography. I. Title.
ML422.H44M34 2004
781.65'092—dc22

Design and composition: Jack Donner, BookType

To Gayle

CONTENTS

PREFACE
Crossing the Tracks in Cuthbert

Y OU'RE NOT LIKELY TO PASS THROUGH CUTHBERT, GEORGIA, on the
way to somewhere else. To see the town and its modest memorials to
a famous native son you must decide to go there. Following Interstate
75 from Michigan to Florida in the summer of 1992, I took a long detour
south from Atlanta through Columbus to Cuthbert, which lies just twenty-
five miles east of the Alabama state line formed by the Chattahoochee River.
Route 27, the two-laner leading down to Cuthbert, is a dream of a road on
a bright summer day. The road is dark, smooth, and sparkling, its broad
shoulders orange-red with rich Georgia clay, and the foliage beyond thick
and green. Along the way stands a sign that says "Westville—Where it's
always 1850," and the traveler crosses many creeks—the Upatoi, the
Hitchitee, the Pataula, and other tributaries of the Chattahoochee—on the
way to the quiet town where Fletcher Henderson was born more than a
century ago.

Having devoted years of research on Henderson, his career, and his
music, I was now able to ground my perspective in a sense of place. It
occurred to me that the resonance I felt in that town might begin to match
what my colleagues in European music studies experience in places like Eise-
nach, Salzburg, and Bonn, the birthplaces of Bach, Mozart, and Beethoven.
Yet those hallowed grounds lack one particular dynamic that strikes a visitor
in Cuthbert. Like many small southern towns, and some farther north,
Cuthbert is divided literally and symbolically by railroad tracks. On one
side lies downtown Cuthbert, anchored by the town square with its tall
statue of a Confederate soldier and Andrew College, a small, two-year
Methodist college, founded in 1854 and named after Bishop James O.
Andrew. On the other side lies Cuthbert's black community, which used to
be called "Andrewville," with Andrew Street, its main street, running at a
right angle away from the college. As one resident avows, the neighborhood
"suffers from benign neglect." Walking down Andrew Street on a searing
August afternoon, I sensed an eerie calm in the neighborhood. Hardly any
cars drove the streets. A few residents sat on their front porches or on metal
chairs in their yards of hard clay. They stared silently at me, a white
passerby. A couple of young boys chattered something (of which I discerned
only the words "beat you up"), and I walked on with the sharp impression
that Cuthbert's whites do not, as a rule, cross the tracks.

At 1016 Andrew Street stands Fletcher Henderson's boyhood home. It is a white, one-story Victorian cottage with an air of faded distinction. An awning-shaded porch stretches across the front. Tall windows framed by green shutters line the facade. Behind one of the windows is the room where young Fletcher's parents locked him up and enforced regular piano practice. On the day I visited, I saw a red Lawn Chief riding mower and plastic chairs on the porch, and a big, rusty 1970s-model car on cinder blocks in the dirt yard. Closed to the public, the house was still occupied.

More accessible than the house itself is a plaque, set on a post a few feet from the street, that describes its historical importance. It reads:

HENDERSON HOME
Fletcher H. Henderson (1857–1943), pioneer Georgia
educator, built this home in 1888 and lived here
until his death. Principal of nearby Howard Normal-
Randolph School 1880–1942, his contributions to
education won professional recognition and enriched
the lives of a multitude of students. Fletcher
Henderson, Jr. (1897–1952), born here, developed
one of the earliest "Big Bands." A pianist and
composer, he was a pioneer in "swing" music.
He was Down Beat Magazine Arranger of the Year
in 1938 and 1940. The Hendersons are buried
near here in Greenwood Cemetery.

Erected by the Historic Chattahoochee Commission
and Friends of the Henderson Family
1986.

For a jazz aficionado the sign is a minor revelation. Clearly, Cuthbert values the contributions of the founder and principal of its black school as much as, and perhaps more than, those of his more famous and influential musical son.

Enticed by the sign's last line, I found nearby Greenwood Cemetery ensconced obscurely along an alley just off Andrew Street. The entire Henderson family now rests there, except for Fletcher's younger brother, Horace, a fine arranger and bandleader in his own right who died in 1989 and is buried in Denver. Henderson's headstone refers only to his modest military service, not his major musical contributions:

FLETCHER H.
HENDERSON
JR
GEORGIA PVT
STU ARMY
TNG CORPS
WORLD WAR I

DECEMBER 18, 1897
DECEMBER 29, 1952

To the right are the graves of his mother and father respectively. And several feet beyond them is the stone of Charlotte Boozer, the mother of Fletcher, Sr., who supposedly covered some two hundred miles on foot with her son to ensure his education. The ashes of Leora, Fletcher's wife, are also said to be buried in the family plot, though their presence remains unmarked.

A helpful clerk at the post office had referred me to a Mr. Muse as a source of information on the Henderson family. Muse, himself a resident of Andrew Street, had played a large role in getting the plaque erected. He is a retired U.S. Defense Department employee, a former Randolph County commissioner and self-described "minority historical preservationist" who has been ineluctably linked to the two Henderson men since birth by his Christian names: Fletcher Henderson. Born in 1920, the year young Fletcher, Jr., went to New York City to seek his musical fortune, Fletcher Henderson Muse was named after Fletcher, Sr., the pillar of Cuthbert's Negro community for over half a century. Although I hadn't even called in advance, he welcomed me into his house that day, sat me down in his living room, and asked me what I was "about." After I told him a little about my research, Muse produced a file of clippings he had compiled over the years, including programs of the "Annual Fletcher Henderson, Jr., Jazz Festival" held at Andrew College in 1987, 1988, and 1989. I noted that one of the festivals had featured Lionel Hampton, the great vibraphonist with whom Henderson played in Benny Goodman's sextet a half-century earlier. Muse also shared memories of his namesakes, particularly of his former teacher, Fletcher Henderson, Sr. His observations have filtered into my narrative of Fletcher, Jr.'s, early years, in chapter 1 of this book.

At the end of the day, Muse drove me in his pickup back to campus, where I had parked the car. As I got out he gave me his business card. It read, in part: "Fletcher Henderson Muse, Sr. 'The Commish'—Culinary Consultant, Political Analyst and 'sociation Member." "Next time you're in town, stop in," he said. Then with a twinkle in his eye, he added, "We even sleep on white sheets," which reminded me that in walking across the railroad tracks and down Andrew Street, I had covered a good distance that day.

Since my visit, Fletcher Muse has passed away. But his legacy lives through ongoing efforts to establish a Fletcher Henderson Museum and a historic trail that will lead other visitors to cross the tracks.

The Uncrowned King of Swing

Introduction
Out of the Jazz Tradition

N HIS CLASSIC BOOK of criticism, *The Jazz Tradition*, Martin Williams explored the work of individual musicians who, in his view, constructed a continuous artistic lineage and collectively ensured the survival and development of the music. Williams's work served a crucial function in the discourse on jazz and has been a controversial touchstone for jazz writing ever since. First published in 1970, it insisted on the music's artistic legitimacy and historical breadth at a time when music loosely identified as "jazz" seemed virtually eclipsed between the popularity of rock and the artistic crucible of classical music. Since then, the phrase *jazz tradition* has assumed a life of its own and come under attack, as Scott DeVeaux has vividly demonstrated, distilling a set of assumptions in which jazz appears to be "an autonomous art form ... subject to its own aesthetic principles and laws of development rather than to forces of the marketplace." As a result musicians are portrayed as "similarly high-minded, pursuing their artistic vision in serene disregard of commercial considerations."[1] Musicians in the jazz tradition, then, form a pantheon of artists.

I'm sorry to report that the subject of this book, Fletcher Henderson, did not quite make the cut. But in the preface to the expanded 1983 edition of *The Jazz Tradition*, Williams wrote that with more time and space, he would have devoted a chapter to Henderson's work. So, instead of invoking the familiar trope of unjust neglect, I will state at the outset that Henderson needs no special pleading as a key figure in the jazz tradition. Henderson's position in jazz history has been well established for some time. After a tentative start in which his band attempted to imitate the popular dance orchestra of Paul Whiteman, so the story goes, Henderson hired Louis Armstrong, who taught the band—and the rest of the world—to swing. It thus became a progenitor of big-band jazz in the 1930s and beyond. In the mid-1930s, Henderson wrote arrangements for Benny Goodman, and his style established a standard for big-band writing that helped set the stage for jazz's next important phase: bebop. Underlying this narrative is the notion that Henderson steered jazz away from its links to dance and popular music and toward a more artistic expression. In this view, Henderson represents a crucial link between early New Orleans jazz and modern jazz who helped preserve jazz's purity in the face of commercial corruption, a view summed up by the historian and critic Ross Russell: "The war against the horrible products of the tunesmiths, which began with Fletcher Henderson in the 1920s, has been brought to a successful conclusion only by the beboppers."[2]

In Russell's statement, Henderson stands as the key agent in a teleological evolution. No wonder Martin Williams believed that Henderson deserved a place in the jazz tradition. From a later vantage point, however, the "jazz tradition" itself may be a problematic framework through which to understand his musical activities and significance, for Henderson's entire career depended on the very things he is assumed to have transcended: popular music and dance. Henderson's career illustrates that "jazz" remains inseparable from the matrix of popular music styles, commercial circumstances, and social activities that the concept of the "jazz tradition" segregates from musical artistry.

While complicating the consensus view of Henderson's role in jazz history, this book also aims to address a remaining controversy over how much to emphasize that role. Two perspectives on Henderson may be summarized as the Frustration thesis and the Inflation thesis. The Frustration thesis portrays Henderson as overshadowed by musicians who went on to greater fame after playing in his band, such as Armstrong and Coleman Hawkins. As he shifted his sights from bandleading to arranging, Henderson remained overshadowed by the bandleader who became famous playing Henderson's arrangements: Benny Goodman. In addition, his ideas got taken up by so many others that they lost their identity as Hendersonian. As Duke Ellington put it, Henderson "was liberal in giving away his ideas to people. So liberal, in fact, that it is difficult to recognize the original Fletcher Henderson through his flock of imitators."[3] The Frustration thesis received its most powerful articulation by John Hammond, the record producer who became Henderson's chief advocate in the early 1930s:

> In the '20s, the Fletcher Henderson Orchestra was musically the most advanced in the land, but it was revered by a very limited public. He developed musicians who went on to much greater fame on their own, and devised the arranging formula that made Benny Goodman the "King of Swing" in the '30s and '40s. He made great recordings of his own compositions which sold a minimal number, only to have the same tunes and arrangements cut by Benny Goodman with astronomical sales. No question about it; he was frustrated.[4]

The Inflation thesis offers a contrasting view. It holds that historical accounts have overcompensated for Henderson's "frustration" by exaggerating his importance at the expense of others. The Inflation thesis contends that Henderson receives more credit than many equally talented peers, especially in the realm of arranging, where the likes of Don Redman, Benny Carter, Jimmy Mundy, and Henderson's own brother Horace made innovative contributions that Henderson absorbed and got credit for while working with Goodman. Mundy, for example, was "extremely talented," wrote pianist Teddy Wilson, "but he never got the recognition and publicity that Fletcher Henderson did." The larger quest behind such statements is to give arrangers the credit they deserve, since they tend to be de-emphasized in jazz, where solo instrumentalists claim pride of place, and in classical music, where composers are assumed to be the chief agents of music history. Complicating Henderson's role, and augmenting the Inflation thesis, are observations by sidemen that Henderson's arranging style grew out of his tendency to put into written form arrangements that he and his sidemen had worked out orally and collectively—that is, "head" arrangements. "Fletcher'd take these heads and write 'em down," Coleman Hawkins recalled. "That was all the stuff he sold to Benny Goodman." Rex Stewart likewise claimed Henderson's special talent as the ability "to take improvised licks he'd heard the guys playing, and harmonize and orchestrate them into an arrangement." What came to be known as "Henderson's" style, then, comprises a written synthesis rooted in oral exchange. In Henderson's own terms, the transference from oral to written marks the distinction between "jazz" (connoting "spontaneity") and "swing" (connoting "premeditation"). Meanwhile, as a corollary to the Inflation thesis, there exists a subcategory of reaction against a perceived "crow-jim" tendency to emphasize black contributions at the expense of white musicians.[J]

Such conflicting interpretations flourish, in part, because conventional musical terminology does not have an apt way to describe Fletcher Henderson's work. To be sure, he was a bandleader, arranger, and pianist whose work profoundly shaped American jazz and popular music during the 1920s and 1930s. But the terms unnaturally segregate his activities into categories that obscure as much as they reveal. To get at what Henderson did, it might be best to describe him as a musical catalyst, facilitator, collaborator, organizer, transmitter, medium, channel, funnel, and "synergizer," if such a word existed. Then again, there is another term for his musical role that also describes him accurately. The *Oxford English Dictionary*'s first definition of composer is: "One who puts together or combines into a whole; one who fashions or constructs." The description fits, as long as we can strip the term of the exalted, romanticized aura of redemptive individual genius that accrued around it as part of Beethoven's legacy to Western civilization, and of the connotations of legal ownership it holds for a creator earning income from copyrighted work that bears his or her name on publications, sound recordings, or other material or electronic forms. Henderson was a member of ASCAP, the American Society for Composers, Authors, and Publishers, but while earning royalties on a few of his published works, Henderson sold most of his arrangements for a one-time flat rate. Nevertheless, Fletcher Henderson was a composer, and the word fits in two ways: Henderson composed musicians as well as music. Any discussion of Henderson's work, then, would not be complete without an exploration of the musical company he kept. This book is not a biography but a portrait of musical collaboration with Henderson at the center.

Henderson was able to stake and sustain his position by assembling some of the era's best jazz musicians, a Who's Who of pre-modern jazz. Some created artistic lineages on their respective instruments. A substantial history of jazz trumpet, for example, could be written using only musicians who passed through Henderson's band: Louis Armstrong, Joe Smith, Tommy Ladnier, Rex Stewart, Bobby Stark, Red Allen, Roy Eldridge, and, subbing in the band for about two weeks, Dizzy Gillespie. The same could be said of reed players Coleman Hawkins, Buster Bailey, Benny Carter, Russell Procope, Hilton Jefferson, Lester Young, Ben Webster, Chu Berry, and Dexter

Gordon. In Henderson's prime, the only other comparable group of stars performing in public at such a consistently high level was the New York Yankees. The comparison is apt in more ways than one. The baseball team began playing in Yankee Stadium in 1923, the same year that Henderson began leading a band under his own name. Moreover, jazz bands competed—in events called "cutting contests," or sometimes simply "battles"—as fiercely as sports teams. No one kept score, but dancers and musicians always knew the winner, and it was usually Henderson. Henderson's most famous collaboration came after his own orchestra disbanded. Writing arrangements for Benny Goodman's band, Henderson became the power behind the throne of the "King of Swing."

Henderson's character seemed ill-suited for an influential position in a competitive field. "Easygoing" is by far the most frequently used word to describe his personality. By the early 1930s, musicians who showed up late for a job received no penalty; one of them recalled Henderson's tendency to start off a piece "while half the band was looking for the music." A band member called Henderson "aloof" and not much of a mixer. Another observer found him "removed" and "inaccessible" on the bandstand. Henderson's "Mona Lisa smile" rarely revealed the thoughts and feelings behind it. By the mid-1930s, when he was struggling as a bandleader but his arrangements had made a national impact through Benny Goodman, a musician recalled that Henderson's manner suggested "depression."[6]

Thin and almost gangly in childhood, Henderson as an adult was tall and lean, gradually filling out with age, a process documented in photographs. He stood over six feet tall, and in his prime weighed about 170 pounds. A well-trimmed, pencil-thin mustache—extended from the clipped configuration he'd sported as a young man (a style later associated with Adolf Hitler)—enhanced his image of quiet elegance. The nickname "Smack," apparently acquired in his youth, stuck with him throughout his career, though its origins remain unclear.[7] As Rex Stewart writes, in the most vivid and sustained description of Henderson:

> Smack was a man of imposing stature.... His complexion was that of an octoroon, and in his youth he could have been mistaken for an Italian, as long as he was wearing his hat, because his hair was on the sandy side for his skin color. He was a pleasant man, gentle and thoughtful. He could be frivolous or serious, according to his mood. However, even in his zany moments, there would be overtones of gentility.... He was just too gentle for his time. In my mind, he was the Mahatma Gandhi of the jazz age.[8]

Henderson's calm, smooth exterior concealed several passions. One colleague described him as "car crazy," buying a new Packard every year and driving it sometimes over a hundred miles an hour on the band's road trips. He had "a predilection for rose," as Stewart put it, wearing "rose-colored shirts and ties" and even ordering a rose-colored Packard. He relaxed by playing pool; and he developed a reputation as a ladies' man, though he remained married to his wife, Leora, from 1924 to his death.[9]

When he first started out in the early 1920s, Henderson was rather more conventionally responsible, exacting, even fastidious, inspecting every detail of his sidemen's appearance before a public performance. By several accounts, including his wife's, a change happened in 1928, after Henderson suffered injuries in a car accident in Kentucky, and he developed a bemused detachment from his affairs. John Hammond believed that by the time he met him in the early 1930s, Henderson had become distrustful of music agents, and passive resistance became his response to potential exploitation.

Whether the fastidious young man of the 1920s or the "easygoing" bandleader of the 1930s, Henderson was by all accounts an excellent musician who challenged those around him. He forced his sidemen to play in "hard" keys—going beyond the familiar F, B♭, and E♭ that formed the common ground for most brass and reed players, whether improvising or reading music. Once he began writing arrangements in the 1930s, musicians were astonished with the speed and fluency of his writing. He was also among the most versatile American musicians of the 1920s and 1930s. When he came to New York, his musical pedigree recommended him more for work in classical music than in jazz. Clarinetist Russell Procope, whose oral history stands among the most valuable eyewitness accounts of Henderson's band in the early 1930s, singled out Henderson's band for playing a varied repertoire that went far afield from jazz and conventional dance music. And Procope remembered with awe how Henderson reassured a white opera singer that he could play her accompaniments on short notice—and did so. Benny Goodman recognized Henderson's big-band arrangements as a kind of "art."[10]

Such accounts suggest that the story of Fletcher Henderson challenges the persistent image of the black early-jazz musician as a "natural" talent spawned by the urban ghetto. The image inspired Ted Gioia to attempt to debunk it as late as 1989 in an article "Jazz and the Primitivist Myth." Before that, social historians of early jazz had already begun to point to the rise of a group of black musicians from middle-class backgrounds who helped professionalize and expand the role of black musicians in 1920s New York jazz, a group in which Henderson holds pride of place. Yet the phrase "middle-class backgrounds" needs further explanation, for the black middle class has occupied an uneasy niche in historical writing. On one hand, its members demonstrate the power to break through racial barriers to achieve prestige and economic stability. On the other hand, they have been criticized for aspiring to imitate and adopt the codes and behaviors of white society. Scott DeVeaux has noted that "middle-class" meant something different in black and white cultures. African Americans, able to earn only "a fraction of what their white counterparts earned," defined middle-class privilege not through income but "more by skin color, family background, and educational attainment." Henderson, a light-complexioned Atlanta University graduate whose parents were prominent school teachers in southern Georgia, had the chief attributes of black middle-class status in the early twentieth century.[11]

With that pedigree, Henderson arrived in New York in 1920 on the doorstep of Harlem's cultural reawakening and became a conduit for musical renaissancism. Literary critic Houston A. Baker, Jr., has defined "renaissancism" as an artistic reformulation of black folkways—"the blending ... of class and mass—*poetic* mastery discovered as a function of deformative *folk* sound."[12] Henderson's music does show a unique, savvy synthesis of contemporary urban popular music, classical gestures, and blues, ragtime, and jazz. His blues compositions—such as "Dicty Blues," "'D' Natural Blues," and "Just Blues"—provide one good analogy to the literary work that Baker describes.

Renaissancism, however, extends beyond artistic content. It also encompasses two other impulses in Henderson's career: versatility and professionalism. Versatility emerges in every aspect of Henderson's music making: in the repertory his band played; in the stylistic hybridity it brought to custom-made arrangements of that repertory; in the mixture of music reading and music improvisation it deployed; and in the multiple musical roles Henderson and many of his sidemen played. Professionalism also pervaded Henderson's musical activity. It revealed itself in everything from finding and keeping a nightclub or ballroom job, to scheduling a logical sequence of engagements on tour outside of New York, to making records and maintaining links with record companies, and in showing up for a job on time, wearing a clean, pressed tuxedo, shined shoes, and a shaven face.

The two impulses are linked in the sense that versatility formed the bedrock of professional survival. As Gunther Schuller has put it, "survival ... depended not on how much jazz or sweet style you could play but how well you could fit—on a moment's notice—into the various precisely defined musical slots."[13] For black musicians, however, versatility and professionalism also served another purpose: they foiled the stereotypes in which white listeners, dancers, critics, record producers, and nightclub managers trafficked. A vivid example of that effect appears in the writing of dancer and music critic Roger Pryor Dodge, one of the most astute early observers of the New York jazz scene. Dodge heard Henderson's orchestra play at the Roseland Ballroom in the "winter of 1924–25" and witnessed improvisation and heard a dance arrangement of Gershwin's *Rhapsody in Blue*. Dodge disdained Gershwin's music as ersatz jazz, but on that night, Dodge "learned two things at once: that all the good music was improvised and that the scorn I felt for Gershwin ... wasn't even completely shared by Henderson. At the time it was quite a jolt to find out the solos which seemed so inventive and comparable to the great written music of other periods were not consciously plotted and composed, but were simply played ad lib by players who thought that Gershwin was a great composer."[14]

Henderson's players did not "ad lib" all the music, of course. Indeed, their ability to read music reinforced an image of versatility and professionalism. Most accounts of Henderson's band emphasize its spectacular and influential soloists. But equally remarkable in the 1920s and 1930s was Henderson's use of written music, for it represents an important musical *and* social dimension of his work. "Jazz" that was written down and played from parts on music stands forged a social consensus: it both suited the black assimilationist agenda and assuaged white panic about the increasing pervasiveness of black music through the media of radio and recording. Some of the earliest commentary on jazz—by both white and black writers—describes it as an arranged, written-down, stylized dance music, not the chiefly improvisatory, solo art that solidified as the interpretive paradigm from the bebop generation onward.[15]

The stakes now seemed higher because a variety of new media disseminated the music. Indeed, Henderson's career coincides precisely with the advent and development of radio as the leading disseminator of music. He arrived in New York in 1920, the year that KDKA began broadcasting in Pittsburgh. His band's residency at the Roseland Ballroom in midtown Manhattan not only carried the prestige of a midtown address, where white bands predominated, but also commanded respect for its radio wire, which broadcast the band's performances on WHN. These "sustaining" or "on-location" programs helped extend the band's popularity and influence beyond its immediate milieu. Henderson enjoyed even greater prominence on network broadcasts from Connie's Inn in 1930–31. Within five years, Benny Goodman began performing Henderson's arrangements on a commercially sponsored network broadcast—the cream of radio jobs in the 1930s. From local sustaining programs, to network programs, to commercially sponsored network programs, Henderson's career tracks the development of radio in its crucial first two decades.

Henderson's career also neatly coincides with a paradigm shift in the record industry. The year 1920 marked the beginning, when music industry executives began to realize that record sales had become a better measure of success and popularity than sheet music sales. The same year also marks the moment when white record company owners recognized a substantial market for black performers singing and playing black music for black record buyers. Because the whole enterprise was saturated in racial difference, such records came to be known as "race records," a distinction that remained a characterization of black music making for more than two decades, until being replaced by the new marketing label "rhythm and blues." What made Henderson remarkable was that he made both "race records" and "general records," the industry's term for disks appealing to the white mainstream.

By the end of the 1920s, radio, records, and touring had developed a feedback loop that enhanced a band's reputation. "The radio made audiences for you when you went on tour," recalled bandleader Claude Hopkins. "Tours produced new markets for the music," wrote Rex Stewart. "[T]here would always be a lot of record dates for us because of the snowballing of popularity on the road." And recordings, in turn, were a band's "best advertisement," according to John Hammond. Benny Goodman became "King of Swing" in 1935 by playing the arrangements of Henderson and others within a consolidated industry that systematically exploited the interdependence of what can be called the three R's: Road, Radio, and Records.[16]

Records are the chief material legacy of all this musical activity and they comprise a crucial primary source for this book, but they occupy a para-doxical position in Henderson's career. If records were a band's best advertisement, then Henderson did not get consistently good advertising. Indeed, critics and musicians alike have repeatedly testified that there was both a quantitative and qualitative difference between the way Henderson's band played in public and in the record studio. In public, the band could extend a piece indefinitely with a long sequence of solos, but in the studio, it had to confine itself to the approximately three-minute limit of one side of a 78-rpm record. What critic Wilder Hobson called "the golden, seething spirit of a Fletcher Henderson occasion" does not come forth on record for those who witnessed the band in public. On top of that, Henderson's re-cordings offer only a slice of his band's repertoire. For example, Henderson's band was admired by some for playing arrangements of the classics and especially for waltzes. But governing racial stereotypes forced Henderson to suppress this repertory when he entered the recording studio. Moreover, from 1935 onward, Henderson wrote hundreds of arrangements for his own band and Benny Goodman's, and while many of them were recorded, many others never made it to disk. Meanwhile, jazz scholars have challenged the traditional emphasis on sound recordings as the primary source material for the telling of jazz history, raising thoughtful questions about the recording bias of the jazz canon, and about how the "seductive menace" of records leads historians to construct artifices of musical evolution. Henderson's career offers a case study in the limitations of sound recording.[17]

Yet we have the records—hundreds of them. Henderson was the most frequently recorded black musician in the first decade of jazz's recorded history, outdistancing Louis Armstrong, Duke Ellington, and even the omnipresent pianist-composer-bandleader-entrepreneur Clarence Williams. Therefore, sound recordings provide a reliable indicator of his work, especially in its ascendency in 1923–27. After that, he made fewer recordings, but they still offer valuable glimpses of his band in action during the crucial period just preceding the swing era. From 1935 onward, when his association with Benny Goodman catapulted his music to unprecedented national recognition and popularity, Henderson's arrangements had a regular outlet thanks to Goodman's long-term contract with Victor Records. And Goodman aficionados preserved many public appearances and radio broadcasts that have been disseminated on compact disc since Goodman's death in 1986. But the records do need to be put in context, not treated as transparent media for musical artistry. As Scott DeVeaux has noted, "[o]ne of the most striking aspects of the writing on jazz is a reluctance to relate the history of the music to the messy and occasionally sordid economic circumstances of its production."[18] So my discussions of records include, when possible, information on record companies and record producers that impinge on the musical choices inscribed on the disk.

Two other kinds of primary source material have emerged as essential complements to recordings: "stock," or published, arrangements adapted by Henderson's band, and original manuscript scores and parts (many of them holographs, signed by Henderson) of orchestral arrangements held in the Benny Goodman Collections at Yale University Music Library and the New York Public Library for the Performing Arts. Only recently have scholars begun to mine written music as a viable and revealing source for jazz research. Stock arrangements have been problematic because they are traditionally dismissed as simple and commercial: when Steve Allen, in the title role of *The Benny Goodman Story*, complained about "the same old stock arrangements," no further explanation was necessary. But Henderson's 1920s work is unintelligible without seeing how the band, especially its first arranger Don Redman, creatively adapted published music to develop the band's style. And for the 1930s and 1940s there are nearly three hundred folders of Henderson's scores and parts—most, though not all, of Henderson's arrangements that Goodman played. These arrangements, accessible to scholars only after Goodman's death in 1986, are therefore ripe for analysis and interpretation.

Recordings and scores alike, however, leave out a crucial dimension of the music's social milieu: dancing. Some of the earliest sophisticated jazz criticism took great pains to remove the music from its links to dance. As the influential French critic Hugues Panassié put it in 1936, "the public in general treats jazz as mere dance music and never listens to it carefully." (The writer, stricken with polio as a teenager, encountered jazz when he could not treat it as dance music even if he had wanted to.) Yet the period of Henderson's most intensive and innovative work, the 1920s and 1930s, encompasses a peak era of social dancing, and Henderson's music was designed for dancers. Danceability has a long history of underemphasis in studies of western music, including jazz, a reflection of western culture's tendency to distinguish music-making from movement—impulses so intertwined in African cultures that they comprise a single, integrated activity that Samuel A. Floyd, Jr., has called "the artistry of ritual." The bromide that jazz became "art music" with the advent of bebop thus carries with it the assumption that "pure" listening is a higher value than virtuosic dancing. That bias is a particularly crucial one to note in the swing era, a time when racial segregation in the social realm obscures the Africanized links between music and dancing that pervaded both white and black culture. That the Lindy Hop was "choreographed swing music," as Marshall and Jean Stearns have put it, lends force to the notion that music and dance form parts of the same activity. Considering swing from that point of view, it should be viewed without qualification as an "art form," using the term with which Olly Wilson redefined musical artistry from an Africanist perspective. Dancing must be kept in mind as the foundation of musical style, from Henderson's earliest jobs in ballrooms and dance halls; to his records, often labeled "fox trot" or "for dancing"; to his arrangements for Benny Goodman, which were custom-made for performance on a radio show called *Let's Dance*. That Goodman recognized Henderson as a dance-music arranger par excellence is the highest praise from a musician who spent thousands of nights on the bandstand.[19]

This study may fill a gap that Martin Williams perceived in his own book, but it is intended to be more than a monograph on a key figure in the "jazz tradition." It aims to redefine Henderson's role in American music through an analysis of the primary source materials embedded in the historical circumstances of their creation, including the Great Migration of African Americans from the rural South to the urban North, the Harlem Renaissance, the dissemination of jazz and dance music through radio, records, and touring, the consolidation of the music industry in the hands of white agents and bookers, and American popular music and culture of the 1920s and 1930s.

Several writings and interpretive approaches proved indispensable for my work. Among them, Gunther Schuller's magisterial studies of *Early Jazz* and *The Swing Era,* for example, laid the foundation for any musical study of the period, and my account frequently addresses issues and details that Schuller raised. But there is one book without which this study would never even have been undertaken: Walter C. Allen's *Hendersonia: The Music of Fletcher Henderson and His Musicians: A Bio-Discography*. Self-published in 1973, Allen's work is still regarded with respect, even awe, by scholars, enthusiasts, and musicians. The 651 pages of Allen's work comprise a portable archive, listing all of the records on which Henderson ever appeared, the personnel involved, and complete information from the record labels. It also includes lists of known public appearances by the band. Together, the lists of recordings and live performances provide an almost daily log of the band's activities, imparting an unparalleled intimacy with the professional lives of one ensemble of musicians. The lists appear between longer segments of narrative, highlighting the band's activities and providing extensive quotations from the contemporary press. Along the way, Allen furnishes much information about publishers, songwriters, record companies, and many other aspects of the music business in the 1920s. As Allen concedes, however, his book is neither musically analytical nor interpretive. In his preface, Allen writes that "perhaps others will find here the necessary facts for a more interpretive book in times to come."[20] Three decades after the publication of *Hendersonia*, my work attempts to answer Allen's invitation.

A Note on Transcriptions

Much of this book relies on musical transcriptions from recordings, which are scattered liberally throughout the text. Although musical examples may make a book appear forbidding to nonmusicians, many of them help to make a point at a glance. These transcriptions are descriptive, not prescriptive, to use a distinction sometimes made in the jazz literature. In other words, most of the examples include only voices and indications that I have deemed necessary to illustrate a point; they cannot be played with the expectation of recreating the original sound.

Transcribing the music of large dance and jazz orchestras in the 1920s and early 1930s presents a special set of problems. Inner voices of chords are often difficult to hear below the ubiquitous surface noise of old disks and their reissues. As a result, I include only the full voicing of multiple-voice examples when I deemed it essential to the point under discussion, or when it was relatively straightforward. Otherwise, and more frequently, I offer the top line of the ensemble and the underlying chord symbols.

Another problem that faces a transcriber, however, is that recordings often distort the tempo and pitch of the performances. James Dapogny first warned me that early jazz recordings tend to play (or be reissued as) fast and sharp. A comparison of stock arrangements and recordings often confirmed the warning. To cite just one example of this phenomenon, "T. N. T." is in a key that matches D♭ (A=440) on the reissues I have heard of this 1925 recording. Yet the stock arrangement, which the Henderson band clearly used, is in the key of C. Reduced to C on a variable speed cassette player, the performance slows about ten beats per minute, from ca. 234 to 224, a change that alters the character of the performance.

I have found plenty of exceptions to the "fast-and-sharp" tendency, and many recordings deliver the actual tempo and pitch of the performance. There was one case, however, in which a recording was slow and flat—the October 1927 recording of "Hop Off" by the pseudonymous "Louisiana Stompers." In this case, a performance read from an A♭ stock arrangement sounded as if it were in the key of G.

How does one determine pitch and tempo when there are no printed sources to consult? Because no definitive answers exist, common sense must be a guide. If a recording, checked against a tuning fork, appeared to be in an unusual key such as B or F♯ major, the choice was simple: the actual key was almost certainly a half-step lower. Indeed, the fact that guided most of my choices was that to musicians playing E♭ alto saxophones, B♭ trumpets and tenor saxophones, and trombones as well, pieces in flat keys were easier to play than those in sharp keys. Therefore, keys sharper than D major were immediately suspect. Of course, that assumption creates problems because of Henderson's well-documented penchant for arranging in unusually sharp keys during the 1930s. The 1920s, however, appear to tell a different story. That Henderson entitled one of his pieces "'D' Natural Blues" (1928) suggests that D major, even with only two sharps, was unusual for its time.

1

A New Negro
from the Old South

FLETCHER HENDERSON CAME TO NEW YORK in the summer of 1920 intending to earn a master's degree in chemistry at Columbia University. When he stepped off the train from Atlanta at Pennsylvania Station, he was met by the young clarinetist Garvin Bushell and a woman Bushell later described as Henderson's aunt, who rented a room on the top floor of the Bushell's townhouse on West 136th Street in Harlem. Although far from his Georgia home, the city offered prospects familiar to Henderson: an urban university environment, continued academic emphasis in the sciences, and a family friend only fifteen blocks north of the campus.[1]

As a young black man seeking graduate education, Henderson stands out as a virtual anomaly in the story of the Great Migration, yet the journey from his home town to the big city traced a well-worn path from the rural South to the urban North. Henderson arrived in New York at an auspicious moment. Northern cities had witnessed an unprecedented influx of black migrants from the South between 1890 and 1914, a quarter century marking the "formative years" of urban black communities. By 1920 those communities had solidified, and Harlem had become the site of the largest and most concentrated black urban population in the country, the "Mecca" of New York's black residents. Only thirty years earlier, Harlem had been a "genteel community" for "older and wealthier New Yorkers" of European extraction; by the time Henderson arrived there, Harlem was a "neighborhood transformed."[2]

The population influx created the conditions for a cultural transformation as well. In 1920, Harlem's new residents were redefining the place of African Americans in American life. W. E. B. DuBois believed that a "Talented Tenth" of the black population would guide the rest "into a higher civilization"; seeing the growing number of educated men and women gathering around him in Harlem during the second decade of the twentieth century, he must have sensed that his vision had come to pass. These cosmopolitan men and women embodied the "New Negro," as Alain Locke referred to them in the title of his landmark anthology published in 1925. Young Fletcher Henderson, with his college education, middle-class background, and cultivated mien, embodied key traits of the New Negro.[3]

Redefining black American cultural identity necessarily affected—and was shaped by—the response of New York whites. Henry F. May and Ann Douglas have shown how many whites, restless with the cultural ideals of

Victorianism, embraced black culture as one means of both resisting the old ways and celebrating a new and distinctively American identity. The Harlem Renaissance, as it came to be known, was not just an isolated development within black culture, then; it also stands as a historical episode that irrevocably shaped America. As Douglas has written, "the 1920s were the decade in which the Negroization of American culture became something like a recognized phenomenon." That phenomenon opened up unprecedented opportunities for African Americans with ambition and talent.[4]

In music, the city offered more opportunities than Fletcher Henderson had ever known. For as a young black pianist, Henderson could hardly have chosen a better time to arrive in the city. Black achievements in music were growing ever more conspicuous, as two events in 1919 and 1920 symbolized. The first, in 1919, was the celebrated march of the 369th ("Hell Fighters") Regiment—with its band led by James Reese Europe—up Fifth Avenue from downtown Manhattan to Harlem. With their many successes in the war, the men in his all black infantry had shown exceptional courage and talent. The band itself had become a crack, disciplined outfit under its leader, and its solid reading ability could be supplemented by unusual instrumental effects and syncopated paraphrase, when Europe allowed it.

The march, however, was just one of Europe's most conspicuous feats as a musical leader and organizer. A decade earlier, Europe had practically invented the structure of black professional music making in New York, a system whose beneficiaries would include Fletcher Henderson and many of his early sidemen. In 1910 Europe had become founding president of the Clef Club, an employment and booking agency for black musicians in New York. Over the next decade, the Clef Club, promoted most notably through concerts led by Europe himself at Carnegie Hall, extended opportunities and raised the prestige of black musicians throughout the city. Testimony from people who knew Europe suggests the extent of his influence. Tom Fletcher, a traveling entertainer based in New York, recalled that in the 1920s black orchestras with ten to twenty musicians, led by such men as Tim Brymn, William Tyers, Ford Dabney, and Europe himself, played in "all of the big hotels, restaurants, clubs, private homes and resorts" thanks to the Clef Club's connections. In the view of composer-pianist Eubie Blake, who had played in Europe's band, "he did as much for [black musicians] as Martin Luther King did for the rest of the Negro people. He set up a way to get them jobs—the Clef Club—and he made them get paid more.... And all the rich white people loved him." Linking Europe and King, Blake conjures an image of Europe as the figurehead of a musical civil rights movement, and it's tempting to view the Clef Club as an outgrowth of the same organizational impulse that led to the founding, a year earlier, of the National Association for the Advancement of Colored People. Thanks to his performances and organizational enterprises, Europe instilled widespread respect for the professionalism of black musicians. Stabbed to death by a troubled band member in 1919, Europe did not live to see all the fruits of his labor, but other leaders such as Brymn, Dabney, Tyers, Will Vodery, and Europe's assistant, Eugene Mikell, continued on. Henderson and many of his musicians benefited from their influence and collective achievements.[5]

The second development in black music that shaped Henderson's future was Mamie Smith's recording of "Crazy Blues," on August 10, 1920—within weeks after Henderson's arrival in New York. Before this recording, record company executives doubted the potential of black music on disk. But "Crazy Blues," backed with "It's Right Here for You," sold 75,000 copies within the first month of its release in November and became the "first record to find a chiefly black audience." When it sold over a million copies within seven months, the bottom line began to change some minds. Young Fletcher Henderson unquestionably knew of the success of "Crazy Blues," for the publishing company that employed him brought out the song. Yet he could have hardly realized the full implications of the "Crazy Blues" phenomenon for his own career. The countless black women singers who quickly found their way to New York recording studios—whose white executives were now anxiously searching for "race" talent—would need a pianist, and dozens would sing to Henderson's accompaniment. Almost accidentally, Henderson would find himself a key figure in the "blues craze." It was not quite what his parents had hoped for him when they bid him goodbye after his college graduation. To understand that Henderson's new line of work was both inevitable, given his musical talent, and unlikely, given his upbringing, one needs to know more about the family from which he came.

Up From Slavery

Henderson's parents were unusually well educated and respected for a black family in late nineteenth-century Georgia after Emancipation. His grandfather, James Anderson Henderson, and his father, Fletcher Hamilton Henderson, were both prominent public servants. The story of James (1816–ca. 1885) is especially remarkable for a man who lived most of his life in slavery. A farmer and carpenter, he became well known in Newberry County, South Carolina, for his "strong personality and reputation as an accomplished craftsman." These qualities—and probably his light skin— recommended him for the job of delegate to the South Carolina Constitutional Convention in 1868. He then served for two terms as the county's representative in the state legislature. He was later elected county coroner and before his death had accumulated 373 acres of land.[6]

In his memoir *Up From Slavery*, Booker T. Washington wrote that two ambitions "were constantly agitating the minds of colored people" during Reconstruction: to hold political office and to master Greek and Latin learning. The Henderson men were unusual in realizing these precious goals. The father held office; the son learned Greek and Latin. James's son Fletcher Hamilton Henderson (1857–1943) became a widely noted educator, serving for over sixty years as teacher and principal of Howard Normal School (renamed Randolph Training School in 1919) in Cuthbert, Georgia. Henderson also became a church leader who held local and state positions in the African Methodist Episcopal Church.[7]

Cuthbert was a good place for Henderson, Sr., to apply the full range of his training and talent. After the Civil War, Cuthbert had blossomed into a progressive community of upstanding citizens where children could get a solid education. It would become what a local historian has called "a cultural anomaly—a well-educated, middle-class area within a tiny black community in the early 1900s." The black community had benefited considerably from Henderson's predecessor, Richard Robert Wright. An 1876 graduate of Atlanta University, Wright was a trained teacher and political activist. As August Meier has written, "in what was later good Booker T. Washington fashion, he [Wright] began without even a building and created a school [in Cuthbert] with the aid of the community, developed a Farmer's Institute, and demonstrated to farmers how to market co-operatively—all before Tuskegee was founded." Wright's political activities were deemed inappropriate for an educator, however. In 1879 he was asked to leave his job, thus opening the door for Henderson.[8]

The road to Cuthbert had been a rough one for Henderson, but he seems never to have wavered in his goal to improve his circumstances through education. Born into a separated slave family, he grew up alternately under the care of his father and mother, Charlotte Boozer, who continued to live apart after Emancipation because James had begun another family. Entering adolescence during a brief, progressive period of Reconstruction, he attended the integrated preparatory high school of the University of South Carolina. A letter exists among the Henderson family papers in the Amistad Research Center at Tulane University testifying to Henderson's higher education. Dated June 15, 1877, the document boasts the letterhead of the University of South Carolina and certifies that Fletcher Hamilton Henderson "of the sophomore class" had passed his Greek examination. Despite his academic accomplishments, Henderson would not continue at the University of South Carolina. Racist retrenchment led to repeals of integration laws in 1877, and he was forced to leave the school.

At that point, Fletcher and his mother took drastic measures. In a story reminiscent of Booker T. Washington's arduous journey to Hampton Institute, they traveled to Atlanta, nearly two hundred miles from Columbia—and "largely on foot," according to the family legend—in hopes of continuing Fletcher's education at Atlanta University. The Hendersons' high hopes had solid foundation. Atlanta University's president, Edmund A. Ware, had established the school after Emancipation with a mission to educate blacks. Ware became Henderson's mentor and exerted profound influence on his life. After Henderson graduated from Atlanta University, Ware helped establish him in 1880 as principal of the Howard Normal School in Cuthbert. By 1905, the school was considered the "leading colored school" in Randolph County, representing "all that is best in the training of the race." In the 1920 *Atlanta University Bulletin* Henderson again won praise for graduating students who stood "among the better class in the colored race." In 1932, the Georgia Department of Education cited Randolph Training School one of the best black schools in the state.[9]

That Henderson also took an active role in the A. M. E. Church further reveals his character and ideals. Black churches served as "battlegrounds for rival forces," and a key point of conflict was the extent to which black folk practices such as the ring shout and spiritual singing might be incorporated, albeit in modified form, into the church. By the time Henderson came to Cuthbert, the A. M. E. Church had become a leading force in eradicating such "heathenish" and "disgusting" worship styles, as they were called by one of their most zealous opponents, A. M. E. Bishop Daniel A. Payne. If many A. M. E. leaders and congregations failed to share Payne's "disgust," the church nevertheless provided a forum for black religious expression that suppressed Africanisms in favor of what its members believed to be more civilized and respectable forms of worship. By separating from white churches but adopting many white religious practices, it was thought, the A.M.E. Church would accomplish a great deal for racial equality. Such ideals suited the temperament of Fletcher Henderson, Sr., who served as a deacon and superintendent of Sunday school in Cuthbert's Payne Chapel and was appointed "State Education Evangelist" by the A.M.E. Church.[10]

In his dual role as educational and religious leader, Henderson embodied what W.E.B. DuBois would later call an "ideal maker" in the black community: a model of upright living. Born within a year of Booker T. Washington, Henderson absorbed and taught the same values of thrift, industry, self-reliance, and Christian living that Washington promoted from the founding of Tuskegee Institute in 1881 until his death in 1915. Henderson's towering presence in Cuthbert even led one visitor, trombonist J.C. Higginbotham, to believe that Henderson was the mayor. "He was the boss of everything," Higginbotham recalled.[11]

Henderson's namesake, Fletcher Henderson Muse, attended Randolph Training School in the 1930s and evokes a more nuanced and vivid picture of its principal. In the black community, Henderson was known as "Fess," for professor. "Anybody who thought Latin was a dead language changed their minds when Fess walked into the classroom speaking it fluently," said Muse. Henderson's model of learning and discipline inspired generations of students, many of whom went on to college and became teachers themselves. At many state colleges and universities in Georgia, "when you told them you graduated from Randolph they knew you could cut it, and you were exempted from certain courses." Muse grew up in a house on Andrew Street between the Henderson home and the A.M.E. Church. Every Sunday, Muse could look out his window and see "Fess" walk past. He always wore a crisp suit. "I never saw him in what people would call 'work clothes'—never ever."[12]

Just as Muse had been named after a community "ideal maker," so too had Henderson named his own sons: James Fletcher (1897–1952), after Henderson's father and himself; and Horace Ware (1904–89), most likely after the great nineteenth-century educational reformer, Horace Mann (or perhaps after the great Roman poet), and the Atlanta University president, Edmund Ware. The Hendersons also had a daughter, Irma Belle (1907–76), who became a school teacher. Their mother, Ozie Lena Chapman (1865–1937), had graduated from Howard Normal School, married Henderson, and began teaching in the school in 1883. If the parents were to have their way, the children were destined for success through education.

From Cuthbert to Atlanta

Fletcher Hamilton Henderson, Jr., was born James Fletcher Henderson on December 18, 1897. In keeping with their value of a well-rounded education, the parents emphasized musical training for all three children. Everyone in the family could read music and play the piano. Throughout the nineteenth-century and into the twentieth, the piano had symbolized middle-class respectability. For black families, struggling to prove their worth in a white world, possessing such symbols could become a mission. Booker T. Washington tells a tale of sitting down to dinner with a family whose table was set with a single fork, while across the room stood an organ for which the family paid monthly installments. Although not so desperate, the Hendersons bought their piano at considerable sacrifice. They mortgaged their house for $133, but the piano cost $275, which, according to Margery P. Dews, "represented more than a half-term's salary for both parents." In the Henderson family the piano stood for more than respectability. It had to be used as another means of instilling the importance of education through discipline. Young Fletcher reacted with passive resistance. According to Horace, his parents "used to lock Fletcher up when he was six or seven years of age in the front room and make him practice, and they would hear the noise [of the piano] ... and after a while there was silence. They'd open the door and there he was curled up in the middle of the room asleep." During their childhood years, the children heard and played only "classical and church music."[13]

Fletcher attended Howard Normal School, and, like his father, Atlanta University (1916–20). Apparently, Fletcher, Sr., saw his son's early move to Atlanta as crucial, for to finance the prep school education he had to mortgage his home again. If Cuthbert was a progressive community, it could hardly compare with the advanced culture of Atlanta. With its "phoenix-like" rise from the ashes of the Civil War, Atlanta had enjoyed a unique prosperity among southern cities. And in the years before massive migration established significant black communities in northern cities, Atlanta stood among the elite centers of black culture. By the early 1900s the city had developed a critical mass of black entrepreneurs rivaled only by that of Durham, North Carolina. These entrepreneurs not only filled high-level roles in black business, they also began to transform the nature of black business itself to an enterprise serving other blacks rather than catering to whites. Fletcher Henderson's future employer Harry Pace worked for one of those pioneering businesses.[14]

Atlanta also boasted more predominantly black colleges than any other city in the country, all founded within two decades after the war, including Atlanta University (1865), Morehouse College (originally Atlanta Baptist College, 1867), Clark University (1869), Morris Brown College (1880), and Spelman College (originally Atlanta Baptist Female Seminary, 1881). These schools offered a wide range of educational services, from academic courses reflecting the ideals of a classical education to the kind of practical skills training advocated by Booker T. Washington.

By the early 1900s, socially conscious blacks had organized protests and had openly opposed Washington's accommodating style and vocational emphasis. Ironically, Atlanta had been the site of one of Washington's finest moments, in September of 1895, when he delivered the speech at the Cotton States and International Exposition that catapulted him into a position of national leadership. Soon after that, W. E. B. DuBois joined the faculty of Atlanta University. He taught there from 1897 to 1910, a fruitful period in which he laid the foundation for a career as the most influential black intellectual of the first half of the twentieth century. DuBois's years in Atlanta saw the publication of his seminal work, *The Souls of Black Folk* (1903), as well as the annual Atlanta University Publications, a series of sociological reports on black society that DuBois edited from 1896 to 1906. One of DuBois's most outstanding students during this period was Harry Pace.

Atlanta also witnessed racial unrest, which came to a head in the riot of 1906, when a white mob swept through a predominantly black neighborhood, destroying property and attacking black residents. DuBois cut short a trip to return to his family and "bought a Winchester double-barrelled shotgun and two dozen rounds of shells filled with buckshot" in case the mob reached campus. It did not, but the riot gained national attention. A sociological study in its aftermath focused more on the black community than the white mob, dramatizing the discrepancy between "negroes of the criminal type" and the "best class" of Negroes. Such sharp distinctions separated the black community as much as they shaped white perceptions. With such a vivid line drawn between social categories, no wonder Henderson's parents did all they could to guide their children to the right side of it. Sending their elder son to Atlanta, despite the city's occasional troubles, must have seemed like the best guarantee of his future.[15]

For a glimpse of the other side of the divide, one need only consider the case of the influential gospel composer, Thomas A. Dorsey (1899–1993). Like Henderson, Dorsey was born in a small Georgia town (Villa Rica) just before the turn of the century and spent several years of his youth in Atlanta. Yet the two young black musicians could hardly have had more dissimilar experiences in the city. Michael W. Harris poignantly conveys the Dorsey family's dislocation there and how a cruel black caste system separated the black community socially, economically, geographically, and musically. Harris argues that Dorsey's parents "represented archetypal black Atlantan immigrants," living "in the squalor of the side streets of the West Side" and performing "domestic and personal services for whites," the kind of jobs held by almost one-third of Georgia's black workers. Young Thomas, unable to adjust to his new surroundings, dropped out of school by the age of twelve. He began to make his way in the world only when he learned to play the piano blues by ear. Yet even then, as Harris points out, "his accomplishment meant playing mainly on the rent-party circuit and in Atlanta's red-light district, places most professional pianists avoided." Finding little opportunity to sustain a living in such conditions, Dorsey went north in 1916, working in the Gary, Indiana, steel mills and as a railroad dining-car cook in the warm months and returning to Atlanta in the winter. He finally settled in Chicago in 1919.[16]

While Dorsey shuttled between Atlanta and Chicago to pick up work, Henderson finished prep school, entered Atlanta University, and thrived. The first thing he did upon matriculation in 1916 was change his name. Such an act by a young man beginning college might be regarded as a personal declaration of independence. But for Henderson, who from now on would be known as Fletcher Hamilton Henderson Jr., the change allied him more strongly with his father. James carried for him the connotation of domestic service. He used his name throughout college; yet the news was apparently slow to circulate beyond the campus, or at least to the family friend with whom Bushell met Henderson at Penn Station. Recalling Henderson's arrival in New York, Garvin Bushell said, "At the time his name was James, and we called him Jimmy. When people first started talking about Fletcher Henderson, I didn't know who they meant."[17]

Having been "brought up in the small-town tradition of taking part in all activities of the community," as Margery P. Dews has put it, Fletcher made the most of his college experience. He majored in chemistry, played football and baseball, acted in theatrical productions, and joined the debate team. According to Horace, Fletcher also "had a little band" in which he probably got his first extensive exposure to popular music. Horace looked forward to Fletcher's return home "about twice a month," because "he would just sit down and play, and we would have selections to call, and he would just play anything—anything that we asked for ... this just amused me to no end."[18]

Atlanta opened up musical and social opportunities that Cuthbert did not offer. For four years, Henderson served as university organist and played for "the mandatory-attendance chapel services." He studied music under Professor Kemper Harreld, a violinist and conductor who stood among the leading black classical musicians of the city. Under Harreld's direction, university musical groups combined to present a pageant tracing black history called *The Open Door*, which Henderson accompanied on the piano. Such programs and other formal recitals offered Henderson the chance to display his training, but parties allowed him to combine his musical and social interests. Henderson was always willing to play upon request at social functions. "He was a naturally friendly and accommodating person, very, very popular," a close friend later recalled. His musical skills and social grace made him the center of attention. Another friend noted that Henderson "used to have eight or ten of the most beautiful girls ... at his beck and call." In the senior yearbook, Henderson was noted above all for his musical ability and his potential for a great musical career. "He is destined ... to become an eminent authority," a classmate wrote in 1920, "classed with Rachmaninoff and other noted musicians."[19]

Harlem: High Ideals and Low Down Blues

The prophet saw Henderson's future more clearly than Henderson himself. Although he never enrolled at Columbia, Fletcher apparently did try to continue his study of science in New York City with a part-time job in a chemical laboratory. But almost in spite of himself he began getting musical jobs. He shared an apartment with a pianist, and when the man came down with an extended illness, Henderson sat in for him in a riverboat orchestra that played on the Hudson. Fred "Deacon" Johnson, a music contractor and former president of the Clef Club, soon hired Henderson as a permanent replacement. The job proved auspicious in more ways than one. One of the trumpet players in the riverboat orchestra was his future wife, Leora Meoux, whom he would marry on Christmas Day 1924.[20]

Around the same time, in the fall of 1920, Henderson also became a song plugger for the Pace and Handy Music Company. Though a fresh face in New York, Henderson had much to recommend him for the job. For one thing, he had already proven himself to a valuable contact, Deacon Johnson, who knew W. C. Handy through the Clef Club. For another, as an Atlanta University alumnus, Henderson also would have found favor with Harry Pace. Pace, then thirty-six, had graduated from the university in 1903 and returned to Atlanta as an insurance executive from 1913 to 1918, while Henderson was there. Even if Henderson and Pace had never met, the close-knit spirit of Atlanta alumni must have helped Henderson get the job.[21]

Within a few months of his arrival in New York, then, Henderson had won access to the city's black musical elite. His budding musical career appears to be a sharp turn in professional aspiration. Henderson broke with the future he had prepared at college and which his parents had imagined for him. He had abandoned science for music, now working at what had been an extracurricular activity instead of building on his major field of study.

While the career shift might have seemed drastic, Henderson held onto the middle-class values his parents had instilled in him by placing his trust in the hands of men who in many ways resembled his father. Indeed, Handy really did resemble Fletcher Sr.: photos show both men as stout, bald, dignified men wearing dark suits. Like Fletcher Sr., in Cuthbert's black community, Pace and Handy stood among the "ideal makers" of the burgeoning Harlem music scene. By the time W. C. Handy (1873–1958) moved to New York, he had already composed and published several songs that would become standards, most notably "Memphis Blues" (1912), "The St. Louis Blues" (1914), and "Beale Street Blues" (1916). With such pieces, Handy captured and circulated a fresh alternative to ragtime, the style that had animated popular music since the turn of the century. What Handy produced is best summed up by the title of chapter 10 of his autobiography, *Father of the Blues*: "Blue Diamonds in the Rough[,] Polished and Mounted."

Handy aimed to take what he regarded as a "primitive" music with "folk ancestry" and transform it into art. His story of composing "The St. Louis Blues" from remembered fragments of personal encounters in the South offers the most vivid testimony to how he viewed his artistic method. After a few years in New York, he had produced enough such pieces to compile his landmark songbook, *Blues: An Anthology* (1926). The book won widespread attention, including favorable reviews by literary critic Edmund Wilson and Harlem poet Langston Hughes. Literary men agreed that Handy had taken a musical idiom once thought to be lowly and elevated it into respectable form.[22]

Handy's partner had similar goals. Harry Pace (1884–1943) had graduated as valedictorian of the Atlanta University's Class of 1903. According to one who knew him, he had remained a "devoted disciple" of W. E. B. DuBois since studying with him at the university. Pace was a multifaceted figure who combined a poetic sensibility with a "sharp business side." After graduation he had taught Greek and Latin at Lincoln Institute in Jefferson City, Missouri, and he began collaborating with Handy in 1907. With "Memphis Blues" (1912), Handy began publishing under his own name, and together Pace and Handy began their joint venture the following year. Although the partnership allowed him to fulfill both his poetic impulse and his business talent, Pace left Memphis soon thereafter to become secretary-treasurer of the newly formed Standard Life Insurance Company, "an unusually progressive black enterprise," which became a model for the new "cooperative" business methods. As the publishing firm prospered with Handy's hit songs, Handy moved it to Chicago in 1918. Pace insisted on moving the business to New York, and the partners were rejoined. The company began compiling a talented staff, including a young William Grant Still, who, according to Handy, "took charge of the arranging department," and Henderson, one of three new pianists hired in 1920. Much later, Handy recalled that pianists Georgia Gorham and Artemus Stevens specialized in jazz and blues, "while Henderson played ballads."[23]

Just as Henderson began making his mark on New York's black music scene, record companies began to realize that an untapped market existed for "race records," that is, recordings by black musicians intended for black consumers. Pace and Handy had published "Crazy Blues," so when Mamie Smith's record soared in popularity in late 1920, Henderson would have been among the first to hear the sheet music being plugged for prospective buyers. As a piano accompanist, Henderson also made his first record in the wake of Mamie Smith's success, on October 11, 1920, on a tune called "Dallas Blues" with Lucille Hegamin, a singer with a pretty, refined voice who would become known as "Harlem's Favorite." The record, an audition for Victor records, was never issued and only the Victor files document its existence.[24]

By this time, perhaps, Harry Pace had begun planning his new business, the Pace Phonograph Corporation. Anxious to capitalize on the growing race-record market, he left the publishing firm in Handy's care, and, in January 1921, took Henderson with him as music director. The company started operating the next month. Commercial success had changed attitudes toward black music making so markedly that Pace confidently stressed the company's uniqueness as the first black-owned record company. Its label, "Black Swan," borrowed the elegant nickname of the famous nineteenth century concert singer Elizabeth Taylor Greenfield. The company's advertising slogan—"The Only Genuine Colored Record. Others Are Only Passing for Colored"—signified an ironic reversal of the familiar notion that light-skinned blacks could "pass" as white to get ahead in society.

Pace assembled a board of directors that reflects the prestige and respectability that he wanted to impart to the company. The most renowned board member was Pace's former teacher, W. E. B. DuBois, who had left Atlanta in 1910 to become cofounder of the National Association for the Advancement of Colored People. In the third volume of his Atlanta University Publications, DuBois had written that racism created the need for the black community to take "the responsibility of evolving its own methods and organs of civilization." Pace must have believed that, in founding Black Swan Records, he had personally fulfilled his mentor's directive.[25]

Pace's board also included at least three other prominent black leaders: John Nail, Emmett J. Scott, and Lester Walton. Nail (ca. 1884–1947), brother-in-law of the multitalented and omnipresent James Weldon Johnson, had been perhaps the most successful businessman in Harlem— and "one of the few black men to profit from the creation of black Harlem"—since opening his real estate office in 1907. Emmett Scott (1873–1957), a close associate of Booker T. Washington until Washington's death in 1915, had been secretary of Tuskegee Institute since 1912, and served as assistant to Secretary of War Newton D. Baker. Scott sat among the notables on the official reviewing stand on Sixtieth Street when the 369th ("Hell Fighters") Regiment marched through Manhattan to Harlem on February 17, 1919.[26]

Lester Walton (1882–1965), another influential associate of Pace, was a prominent Harlem journalist and theater manager and, as such, knew more about performing than the other board members. According to Garvin Bushell, who played on some of the early Black Swan recordings: "I never saw Pace; he had nothing to do with recording. But Lester Walton used to come in all the time." William Grant Still, Black Swan's arranger, recalled that Pace played a more active role in musical decisions, coming to the studio "to listen to the singers and pass on the choice of music for recordings ... though he did not ride herd on his employees in a restrictive way."[27]

Befitting the prominence of its board members, Black Swan's choices of artists and repertory—choices that Henderson would have played a role in making—reveal a striving for cultural respectability. As its name implied, Black Swan would record concert music. The company issued records by classically oriented black singers such as C. Carroll Clark, Revella Hughes, and Antoinette Garnes. They usually performed with the accompaniment of a small group of three to seven musicians, including Henderson, or the "Black Swan Symphony Orchestra," a slightly larger ensemble that included a couple of stringed instruments. Much of the repertory comprised music that might be on any black concert singer's recital program. It included spirituals ("Nobody Knows De Trouble I've Seen," "Swing Low Sweet Chariot"); other religious songs ("Thank God for a Garden," "Christians Awake"); high-class ballads ("The Rosary," "By the Waters of Minnetonka"); and standard opera excerpts ("Caro nome" from *Rigoletto*, "Ah fors' è lui" from *La Traviata*).

C. Carroll Clark's rendition of "Nobody Knows De Trouble I've Seen" (ca. April 1921), with Henderson at the piano, illustrates the cultivated side of Black Swan's offerings. Clark communicates the song as if he were the poem's persona. He delivers a "tired" performance in an extremely slow tempo and with broad rubato. The refrain climaxes with "Glory Hallelujah," and each one becomes more dramatic as Clark sustains them with longer and longer fermatas. Henderson sensitively follows every nuance of the singer's performance. A similar mood pervades another refined record in Black Swan's catalog. Kemper Harreld, Henderson's music teacher at Atlanta University, came to the studio to perform with his protégé a pair of cameos for violin and piano.[28] Their recording of Stephen Foster's "Old Folks at Home" (called "Swanee River" on the record label) displays a gentle performance sweetened with portamento and a perfectly synchronized rubato that suggests a strong musical affinity between teacher and former student.

DuBois, for his part, favored the European tradition and black spirituals over jazz, and must have approved of *his* former student's cultivated aims. But now Pace's artistic ideals and pragmatic business sense came into conflict. In order to keep the company afloat Pace had to admit a greater stylistic range into the Black Swan repertory. Indeed, in practice, the company's chief characteristic—and probably the reason for its ultimate demise in 1923—was its inclusiveness. To support its potpourri of concert-oriented offerings, Black Swan also issued recordings of more recent tunes by popular songwriting teams like Creamer and Layton, Higgins and Overstreet, and Sissle and Blake.

Black Swan also produced blues. Its large stable of blues singers included young women who would soon become famous, such as Alberta Hunter, Trixie Smith, and Ethel Waters. The company also hired many blues singers who enjoyed modest success during the 1920s but who mostly disappear from the annals of recorded sound after 1925: Katie Crippen, Lulu Whidby, Etta Mooney, Josie Miles, Julia Moody, Mary Straine, Lena Wilson, Inez Wallace, and Maud De Forrest. Notably absent from this roster is a singer who auditioned for Black Swan but got rejected as too earthy: Bessie Smith.[29] The New York race-record market could not yet absorb the singer who would soon become its greatest asset and be dubbed "the Empress of the Blues." (OKeh Records, which had issued Mamie Smith's breakthrough

"Crazy Blues," would also reject Bessie, who finally signed with the more prestigious Columbia and began making records for it in early 1923.) Nevertheless, with its ample supply of singers, Black Swan made more blues records than anything else. And in spite of Pace's hopes, the blues recordings far outsold the other repertories. Revella Hughes, a conservatory-trained concert singer who went into musical comedy soon after coming to New York, made four or five records for Black Swan in early 1921. She recalled that "the Black Swan company hoped to give colored artists who sang classical music as much opportunity to record as the blues singers had been given by the white companies. But the classical artists did not sell well."[30]

The blues singers sold more. Ethel Waters's recording of "Down Home Blues" and "Oh Daddy" became Black Swan's biggest hit. "It proved a great success and a best seller among the white and colored," Waters noted later. Waters's account of the recording session reveals a telling incident. "There was much discussion of whether I should sing popular or 'cultural' numbers," she recalled. Apparently, Pace's ideals had instilled a dilemma in Henderson and his associates who chose the repertory. On one hand, the Black Swan staff wanted to do whatever it took to sustain its pioneering enterprise, which stood as a symbol of black achievement. On the other hand, recording "popular" numbers and the blues would link Black Swan to the very musical styles that it was trying to rise above by promoting "classical artists," as Revella Hughes had put it.[31]

Not surprisingly, Waters and Henderson had to work hard to develop some personal and musical affinity. The strong-willed cabaret singer and the gentle college-educated pianist stood on opposite poles of the social and musical spectrum in New York. Waters seems to have recognized this immediately. "Remember those class distinctions in Harlem," she writes, "which had its Park Avenue crowd, a middle-class, and its Tenth Avenue. That was me, then, low-down Tenth Avenue." If Waters saw herself as "low-down," she must have considered Henderson to be at least middle class, or maybe even "Park Avenue." Entering the Black Swan studio for the first time, she recalled, "I found Fletcher Henderson sitting behind a desk and looking very prissy and important." At this point, Henderson held much more in common with classically trained musicians like Clark and Harreld. But circumstances would lead him away from that "respectable" milieu; he would have to begin to embrace the other side of the black social divide. To capitalize on the success of "Down Home Blues," Ethel Waters and her "Jazz Masters," with Henderson on piano, went on tour. But, as Waters recalled in her autobiography, "Fletcher Henderson wasn't sure it would be dignified enough for him ... to be the piano player for a girl who sang the blues in a cellar. Before he would go out [on tour] Fletcher had his whole family come up from Georgia to look me over."[32]

The collaboration of Fletcher and Ethel Waters ultimately received the family's "stamp of approval," as Waters called it, but an intriguing document from this period written by Henderson Sr. suggests that the trip may not have allayed all of his worries. In it, one may read a father's hope, if not his expectations. Titled "Silas Green in the Kid Glove Church," the document exists in a file labeled "Speeches" in the Fletcher Henderson Family Papers in the Amistad Research Center at Tulane University.[33] Yet it lacks the functional tone of direct address that mark the other speeches in the file. It tells the story of a young man who leaves his family farm to take a job in the big city. Once there, Silas seeks membership in a church and, despite his humble "rube" appearance and dialect, ends up teaching the minister and "richly dressed congregation" about being "pure in heart," including abstinence from card-playing, dancing, and drinking—"because you just can't do them things and be like Jesus wants you to be." But Silas is not welcomed into the church, where the minister tacitly accepts such behavior. Having held his principles, Silas accepts his fate philosophically. The parable is dated "Jan. 26, 1922," just two or three months after Henderson's parents came to New York to "approve" Fletcher's new enterprise.

Fletcher may have won his father's stoic "approval," but Waters proved even tougher to please, and for entirely different reasons. "I kept having arguments with Fletcher Henderson about the way he was playing my accompaniments," Waters wrote. She urged him to learn from the great stride pianist James P. Johnson. Her colorful observations on young Fletcher dramatize better than any other first-hand account that, for Henderson, playing jazz was an awkwardly acquired ability. They also reveal something usually overlooked, something that would serve Henderson well in his musical career: that he was a quick study.

> On that tour Fletcher wouldn't give me what I call "the damn-it-to-hell bass," that chump-chump stuff that real jazz needs. All during the tour I kept nagging him. I said he *couldn't* play as I wanted him to. When we reached Chicago I got some piano rolls that Jimmy Johnson had made and pounded out each passage to Henderson. To prove to me he could do it, Fletch began to practice. He got so perfect, listening to James P. Johnson play on the player piano, that he could press down the keys as the roll played, never missing a note. Naturally, he began to be identified with that kind of music, which isn't his kind at all.[34]

"Down Home Blues," recorded about April 1921, provides a glimpse of an early stage of commercial blues performance. The song, by Tom Delaney, has a sixteen-bar verse and two twelve-bar choruses. The lyrics tell a typical blues love story of lost love and nostalgia for the South. For all her claims of being "low-down," however, Waters actually sounds quite polished, at least to listeners familiar with the raw power of Bessie Smith. Waters's singing blends elements of the popular crooning typical of white and northern black singers and the blues "shouting" popularized by Mamie Smith a few months earlier. Garvin Bushell, who played on several of Waters's Black Swan sides, recalled that Waters "didn't sing real blues," but she "literally sang with a smile, which made her voice sound wide and broad."[35]

A six-piece group called Cordy Williams' Jazz Masters, with Henderson at the piano, accompanies Waters. They play in a style reminiscent of James Reese Europe's band, featuring a brass-dominated sound with heavy, even eighth notes; composed breaks; and blunt, forthright cadences. The third chorus, which the band plays without Waters, spotlights an unknown trumpeter with a clean tone and smooth, legato phrasing. The last two choruses form the recording's climax. In the fourth chorus, Waters reenters, singing a variation of the melody at a higher pitch, and louder than before. In the final chorus, she ascends higher, raising tension and excitement. The last two choruses suggest the chief musical appeal of the earliest blues recordings:

exuberant abandon, or at least the impression of it, and sheer volume. Even through the scratches of a worn record, a listener can imagine why the group chose to end its tour performances with "Down Home Blues," night after night. The finale became so familiar even a dog could recognize it: Waters recounts how her Pekinese, Bubbles, would hear the song and "know it was time for me to come off. He'd trot out of the dressing room and onto the stage, pawing at my dress to be picked up."[36]

The tour proved to be very successful. The Black Swan Troubadours, as they were known, covered eighteen states in seven months and went as far afield as Texas. Although touring black performers experienced daily hardships, the young troupe didn't seem to mind. "Conditions of traveling didn't bother us too much," clarinetist Garvin Bushell recalled. "If you had to walk the streets all night or sleep in a church, you did it." Sometimes they'd find a black hotel or an accommodating local family to stay with, but "accommodations in Negro neighborhoods could be lousy—with bad food and a lot of bedbugs. But being young, we didn't care." They played in black theaters for black audiences, and the black press paid close attention to the tour. Thanks to reports from Lester Walton, the group's advance man, the *Chicago Defender* seems to have recorded the Troubadours' every move with pride.[37]

For Henderson, the tour did more than confer money and notoriety. It also led him to meet a few men who would later join the band. In Chicago, his future clarinetist William "Buster" Bailey substituted for Bushell, who had gotten jailed on dubious charges. Then, just before the group headed south, four musicians quit. Bushell was one of them. "In those days you went South at the risk of your life," Bushell later explained. "It would be very uncomfortable, very miserable ... So many incidents occurred; you weren't even treated as a human being." One replacement turned out to be another future Henderson sideman, trumpet player Joe Smith. "Fletcher Henderson was very impressed with Joe's sound," Bushell recalled, "and he never forgot it." In New Orleans, Henderson met another trumpet player. As he recalled in *Down Beat* magazine years later, "I heard this young man playing trumpet in a little dance hall ... [who] would be great in our act. I asked him his name and found he was Louis Armstrong." But Armstrong wouldn't go on tour without his drummer, Zutty Singleton. "The next day," Henderson continued, "Louis was backstage at the theater to tell me that he'd have to be excused, much as he would love to go with us, because the drummer wouldn't leave New Orleans." Two years later, in 1924, Armstrong would join Henderson in New York—without his drummer.[38]

Upon his return to New York in July 1922, Henderson gained a name as organizer of recording sessions and as an able accompanist to blues and popular singers. Although Black Swan was about to go out of business, Henderson had gained valuable contacts as part of Pace's enterprise. By 1923 he was the most widely recorded accompanist in New York, playing regularly with such leading black singers as Waters, Bessie Smith, Clara Smith, and many others for a variety of record companies. In a little less than three years—from early 1921 to late 1923—Henderson played on more than 150 records as an accompanist for singers. By 1923, he had already appeared on more sides than any other black musician in the short history of recorded sound. Meanwhile, Henderson continued to earn work among Clef Club musicians. In early 1923, the eminent black composer-conductor

Will Marion Cook formed the "Clef Club Orchestra," including "F. Henderson, Paramount Recording Wizard, At the Piano," as one advertisement noted. The orchestra performed a potpourri of black show tunes, spirituals, and concert pieces, with a number of guest performers, including the young actor-singer Paul Robeson.[39]

Within three years of his arrival in New York, then, Henderson had formed connections among musicians and within the blossoming record industry that put him in a promising professional position. At this point Henderson was not a jazz musician; as an organizer of recording sessions, however, he had already begun to surround himself with a group of musicians who could play jazz. Some of these musicians would form the core of Henderson's first regular band. He had come a long way from Georgia. Two years in Harlem and seven months on the road had enlarged his social and musical purview. A "respectable," middle-class, college-educated young man had absorbed elements of black culture that had existed outside his privileged domains in Cuthbert and Atlanta.

In *The Autobiography of an Ex-Colored Man* (1912), James Weldon Johnson tells the story of a light-skinned black musician who decides to "pass" as white, ultimately renouncing his background as a ragtime pianist and his interest in the music of ordinary southern black folk. In some ways, Fletcher Henderson's early years tell the story in reverse. Raised and educated in a milieu that cherished concert music, Fletcher Henderson had to be forced to study and practice the musical idioms that many whites assumed to be the Negro's natural heritage. As Ethel Waters had said, that kind of music "isn't his kind at all."

Yet in an important way, Henderson's story does not represent Johnson's novel in "reverse," for Henderson never passed. It is a more complex story than that, one that illuminates a world in which the term *black culture* connotes a multifaceted, and even contradictory, culture that both absorbs and reshapes elements of white culture, and that is no less "authentically" black for doing so. Like Scott Joplin, Will Marion Cook, and James Reese Europe before him, Henderson was wrestling to bridge a respectable but restricted past with a more cosmopolitan and liberated outlook. And like his contemporary Edward Kennedy "Duke" Ellington, two years his junior, Henderson faced both advantages and setbacks in his effort to parlay a cultivated upbringing into a musical career. Meanwhile, Henderson's feet remained firmly in a world created by black citizens from a variety of backgrounds, whether he was studying Latin at prep school or playing blues in Harlem. He grew up in Cuthbert's black community, attended its black school, graduated from a black university in Atlanta, and then moved to black Manhattan. Moreover, many of his important models and contacts were black "ideal makers": Fletcher Sr., Kemper Harreld, Deacon Johnson, W. C. Handy, and Harry Pace. He would not have considered his formative years to have been in emulation of white culture. Nor did coming to Harlem and learning blues represent his passing over into an "authentic" black culture. Rather, living in Harlem helped Henderson begin to integrate his identity as an American musician.

2.

The "Paul Whiteman of the Race"

O N FEBRUARY 22, 1924, the *New York Clipper* published an advertisement for the Roseland Ballroom announcing "an opening for TWO VERSATILE BANDS. Two high-grade Dance Orchestras ... wanted for the evening sessions. Jazz bands will not be considered."[1] Fletcher Henderson's orchestra already met the qualifications for the job it would begin in July: "versatile," "high-grade," and mostly nonjazz. Whatever the Roseland managers meant by "jazz" in 1924—probably a boisterous, undisciplined, and semi-improvised music they associated with the seedier cabarets—they must have been pleased to find that, to their ears at least, the Henderson band did not play it.

Historical accounts of Henderson's early band tend to disparage it for the same reason the Roseland management embraced it—for not playing jazz. Writing in the 1940s, the influential French critic Hugues Panassié found the band making "commercial concessions, especially at its debut when it attempted to be the 'Paul Whiteman of the race.'" Gunther Schuller extended this line of criticism in the late 1960s when he wrote of the band's "erratic path, inevitably vacillating between opposing pulls, catering on the one hand to the tastes of their [*sic*] white dancing audience, trying on the other to deal with new musical problems in an original and honest way." Even after hiring Louis Armstrong in late 1924, Henderson continued to manifest this "problem," which in the view of most historians was only exacerbated by Armstrong's presence. That presence, indeed, has made it difficult to recapture the early 1920s as experienced by musicians and audiences of the time.[2]

The binary perspective manifested in Panassié's and Schuller's critiques has a long history in jazz criticism, but it should have no place in efforts to understand the musical activities of the early Henderson band. Coming to terms with this music calls for looking beyond the traditional dichotomies of jazz criticism: between "true and false jazz" as Panassié so baldly put it, between "hot" and "commercial" jazz, and between "black" jazz, "the primitive art of Negroid improvisation," with its associations of "natural," "vibrant, spirited playing," and "white" jazz, which usually connotes "clean" and "carefully rehearsed" commercial arrangements.[3]

Taken together, these writings have constructed a clear message linking race, musical style, and commercial inclination: black jazz is improvisatory, authentic, and non-commercial and therefore "true," and white jazz is written down, diluted, and commercial, and therefore "false." This rigid dichotomy, which still resonates in jazz criticism, diminishes the achievements of black and white musicians alike. Particularly vulnerable are black musicians like Henderson, whose early professional activity and stylistic leanings link him to "false jazz." In fact, the dichotomy leaves young Fletcher Henderson guilty on two counts: of making "commercial concessions," and of abandoning the "true" musical heritage that presumably was his birthright. Economically and racially, then, the early Fletcher Henderson band appears to have sold out, and Panassié crystallized that double-edged critique with his label the "Paul Whiteman of the race," which linked Henderson's name with the most successful white dance bandleader of the 1920s. Henderson's youth and early adulthood, however, have already challenged the conventional racial dichotomies that later jazz criticism would impose on his music.

In fact, Henderson's early efforts represent one particularly effective way for an African American to have made a life in music in 1920s New York. How might Henderson's early career be reinterpreted within that context? What do Henderson's varied recordings reveal about the scope of black music in the 1920s and its viability as a means of making a living? If Henderson's early band was as misguided as most later critics suggest, why did Duke Ellington claim that "when I first formed a big band in New York, [Henderson's] was the one I wanted mine to sound like"? Considering that Henderson stood among the most successful black musicians in 1920s New York, what does his music reveal about the possibilities for a black man to have a successful musical career at the time?[4]

There are several perspectives from which to consider Henderson's early work. Together they help illuminate the structure of his professional activity, what Scott DeVeaux has termed the "disciplinary matrix" of jazz, which he defines as "the sum total of practices, values, and commitments that define jazz as a profession." In reconstructing Henderson's musical world of 1923–24—specifically, the eighteen months immediately preceding Louis Armstrong's arrival in the band—the "disciplinary matrix" can be illuminated through: (1) the backgrounds of the musicians he led, (2) the media that disseminated their music, (3) the public venues in which they performed, (4) the repertory the band played, and (5) the styles in which they played it. In their focus on cultural context, the first three subjects typify the "new jazz history," as it has been dubbed. The last two subjects, repertory and style, focus more on musical texts and tend to be underestimated in "new" jazz histories, where the sound recording or score is "merely the sign of a large field of social forces." Yet only by considering all of these angles—that is, by combining "new" and "old" approaches—can a historian clarify the working life of a band whose early activities have been muffled by the overpowering impact of Louis Armstrong on jazz and on jazz historiography. This chapter will survey the first four elements; the band's style will form the subject of the next chapter.[5]

Renaissance Men

A survey of the backgrounds of the musicians in Henderson's first band reveals strong connections between them and the emerging New Negro of the Harlem Renaissance. For upwardly mobile African Americans in 1920s New York, racial empowerment came through assimilation. This did not mean a self-effacing denial of uniqueness, but rather a cultural mastery demonstrating that African Americans could make a contribution to the cultural mainstream. This theme arises repeatedly in Alain Locke's landmark anthology of 1925, *The New Negro*. Essays by Locke, James Weldon Johnson, Melville J. Herskovits, and others elaborate on it in various ways. Johnson and Herskovits, for example, both saw Harlem as a paradigm of cultural integration. "Harlem talks American, reads American, thinks American," wrote Johnson. And for Herskovits, Harlem represented "a case of complete acculturation." Nathan Irvin Huggins later summed up the book's guiding logic when he wrote that "inequities due to race might best be removed when reasonable men saw that black men were thinkers, strivers, doers, and were cultivated, like themselves." In its early manifestations, the effort demonstrates the calculated strategy that Houston A. Baker, Jr., has described as "mastery of form." In Henderson's case, "mastery of form" pervades every aspect of his band's disciplinary matrix; musically, it means versatility, which in turn brought a measure of prominence and financial security in New York's musical culture. The idea of playing jazz exclusively did not yet hold the cultural power to attract ambitious black musicians who sought professional respectability and financial security.[6]

Unlike many black musicians of the period, Henderson and his sidemen comprised an expert reading band, a band that could play arranged dance music comparable to that of the leading white society orchestras like Paul Whiteman's and Vincent Lopez's. The mere sight of a black band reading from parts had a vivid impact on musicians and audiences of the early and mid-1920s. Recalling Henderson's band in the period 1924–26, trumpet player Louis Metcalf noted that "the sight of Fletcher Henderson's men playing behind music stands brought on a learning-to-read-music kick in Harlem which hadn't cared before for it. There were two years of real concentration. Everybody greeted you with 'How's studying?'"[7]

Playing in the white-dominated Times Square area, Henderson's men had to look the part of a downtown orchestra, and they cultivated an immaculate appearance with tuxedos, shined shoes, and shaven faces, always examined by Henderson himself before every performance. As trumpeter Howard Scott recalled,

> He was a very strict leader. Every night you had to ... stand inspection. He'd look at your hair, your face, see if you shaved, your shoes, see if they're shined. You had to be perfect to suit him.... He was strict and nice and exact in everything he did.[8]

That careful concern for appearance reflects a larger impulse to see music making as a dignified profession. Cultural historians such as Hsio Wen Shih and Thomas J. Hennessey have argued that, in its professional approach to music making, the Henderson band comprised the vanguard of a new generation of jazz musicians. Shih has suggested that in the early years of big-band jazz, a kind of selection pressure favored well-educated musicians born around the turn of the century and raised in middle-class families. Music making in the popular music idioms of which jazz was a part had been transformed from an avocation to a profession. Middle-class and well-educated musicians such as Fletcher Henderson and Don Redman approached music as a competitive job, and they saw their domain as popular entertainment.[9]

They ranked high in that domain, as the perspective of a reliable insider testifies. Recalling a period around early 1924, trumpeter Rex Stewart outlines what was, in effect, a four-tiered caste system among black musicians. On the top was the Clef Club, the union of black musicians founded by James Reese Europe. Its musicians played the "society" jobs in mostly whites-only ballrooms, hotels, and restaurants. On the next rung down were the "burlesque musicians." These were touring troupes with a single star attraction, such as Mamie Smith, who mixed music and vaudeville skits. "They were very important," writes Stewart, "due to their year long contracts traveling all over the country." Next were "the newer members of that select fraternity," the large bands led by Henderson, Sam Wooding, and Billy Fowler, and their Chicago counterparts Doc Cook, Dave Peyton, and Erskine Tate. On the lowest level of the hierarchy were musicians playing in "small clubs, neighborhood joints, the Penny-a-dance halls, etc." Stewart spent his early years in that milieu, and he claims that musicians in the large orchestras "had little to do with the rank and file such as us."[10]

From this perspective, the musicians under Henderson's leadership in January 1924, when they began performing regularly in public, were a select group; and the image of the floundering, motley pick-up band constructed in later histories misrepresents it. In fact, a regular job in the heart of Manhattan, although extremely rare for black musicians, would have seemed a natural extension of the careers of Henderson's sidemen. Most of them already had connections in the upper strata of the black music hierarchy outlined by Stewart, and many had played with some of the well-known leaders and stars of black music in the early 1920s. Yet they were all still young. The oldest of them were twenty-six years old (Henderson himself had turned twenty-six in December 1923); the youngest, Coleman Hawkins, was nineteen.

Several members of the band enjoyed Clef Club membership and contacts: the "top" of Stewart's hierarchy. For example, three musicians who joined Henderson's band in 1923—banjo player Charlie Dixon, drummer Joseph "Kaiser" Marshall, and saxophonist Coleman Hawkins—had played as sidemen in the orchestra of Ralph "Shrimp" Jones, a Clef Club violinist-bandleader. Dixon in particular would rise to importance as a leader within the band, doing some arranging and acting as a "straw boss—and a worrier" when Henderson later grew lax.[11] As we've seen, Henderson himself had gotten his first New York musical job as the result of a Clef Club contact, Fred "Deacon" Johnson, and thereafter toured with a star attraction, Ethel Waters. Henderson thus had experience on the top two strata of Stewart's hierarchy.

Other sidemen also enjoyed a network of valuable connections. The Puerto Rican tuba and bass player Rafael "Ralph" Escudero had gotten regular and varied work in theater, symphonic, and dance orchestras thanks to his Clef Club affiliation. In a small band that also included Kaiser Marshall, Escudero had accompanied Lucille Hegamin on her first issued record (a month after the Victor test with Henderson), and he continued to play behind her in 1921. Later that year he toured in the pit orchestra of the all-black musical comedy *Shuffle Along.* In early 1923, he played in the pit of the Howard Theater in Washington, DC, and performed in a week-long engagement under the popular clarinetist-bandleader Wilbur Sweatman in a band that included Duke Ellington and his cohorts Sonny Greer and Otto Hardwick. Back in New York by late 1923, Escudero joined Happy Rhone, a major figure among Clef Club bandleaders who had opened an elite, integrated Harlem nightclub the previous year. When Escudero joined Henderson's band in January 1924, few black brass players could rival him in the range of his professional experience and contacts.

If Escudero had the best resumé, trumpet player Howard Scott had the most compelling story, linking him to the Clef Club's founding father. In fact, as Scott himself recalled, the course of his musical life became clear on the day in 1919 when James Reese Europe's band, just home from the war, paraded through New York City with the renowned 369th Regiment. Scott recalled that, in the excitement of watching these famous uniformed musicians, he walked all the way to Harlem with the band. Eventually he got to know Cecil Smith, a saxophone player in that band who helped Scott get a job in an ensemble led by a pianist named Honey Potter. Potter, according to Scott, "had most of the work out there in Long Island," suggesting that Potter enjoyed high status in the community of black musicians. Having learned to read music as a boy, Scott could also pick up tunes quickly from sound recordings—"new records from the shows and things"—and he became a valuable sideman, impressing his leader by learning the songs before Potter's band even got the music sheets. When Henderson hired Scott in late 1923, then, he got a talented, experienced young musician of twenty who could read and play by ear with equal facility.[12]

Coleman Hawkins's tours with Mamie Smith's Jazz Hounds in 1922–23 placed him high in Stewart's second tier. In 1921, at seventeen, Hawkins was already an excellent reader and improviser who knew his own worth. According to clarinetist Garvin Bushell, who heard him as early as 1921, Hawkins was "a cocky youngster who realized he was head and shoulders above anyone of his age, anywhere. But he was a very knowledgeable young man, highly intelligent, with none of the common ways that some touring musicians had."[13]

Perhaps Hawkins did not seem "common" because he had been raised in a family similar to Henderson's. Biographer John Chilton stresses several aspects of Hawkins's background in St. Joseph, Missouri, that reflect the Henderson-model musician that Shih and Hennessey noted: he grew up in a middle-class family, had thorough musical training from an early age, was exposed to a wide variety of music, and developed a broad musical taste. Hawkins's parents, like Henderson's, emphasized musical education and began his piano lessons at age five. With the encouragement and discipline of his mother, Hawkins also studied cello. His recollection of being locked up in a backyard shed for practice sessions recalls Horace Henderson's story of how his parents enforced Fletcher's early piano studies. Moreover, both Henderson and Hawkins faced a pivotal professional moment when they went on tour with a female singer in the face of parental worry. For Hawkins, a tour with a headliner such as Mamie Smith proved irresistible, especially when the singer gave him special billing as "Saxophone Boy." Henderson first heard Hawkins play in 1923 at Connie's Inn, then a sophisticated new Harlem club. Later that year, when Hawkins joined Henderson at age nineteen, he already enjoyed renown and prestige among New York's black musicians.

Several other sidemen in Henderson's first band had experience in the third stratum in Stewart's hierarchy: the large bands whose leaders comprised "the newer members of that select fraternity." Charlie Dixon and trumpet player Elmer Chambers, for example, both served as sidemen in the orchestra of Sam Wooding before joining Henderson. In Wooding's seven- or eight-piece orchestra, both musicians tasted the life of an elite black musician playing in a prestigious venue. From 1920 until early 1923, Wooding's base was Harlem's posh Barron's club, where a musician could make important professional connections in a sophisticated milieu.

Two outsiders completed the band: Don Redman and Charlie Green. Don Redman, the multi-reed player and sometime singer who would serve as Henderson's principal arranger from 1923 to 1927, was a newcomer to New York when he joined Henderson. In the early 1920s the West Virginia native joined Billy Paige's Broadway Syncopators, a Pittsburgh-based band in which Redman played reeds and did some arranging. In early 1923, Paige's band went to New York. By late February, Redman was making records with Henderson. Redman, in the words of Rex Stewart, "played a most important role in the Henderson band," which "assumed another dimension" with his arrangements, which will be explored in the next chapter.[14]

One additional musician played a key role in Henderson's early band: trombonist Charlie Green, who was hired in July 1924 about the time Henderson began playing at the Roseland Ballroom. Nothing about Green recommended him for work at the Roseland, and he certainly cut a distinctive figure among Henderson's elite sidemen. "Big Green," as the musicians called him, was a formidable fellow from Omaha, Nebraska. In his home town he had played in brass bands; he had left at the age of twenty with a traveling carnival show. Rex Stewart has written a vivid portrait of Green, having suffered the trombonist's "devilish tricks" and threats as an eighteen-year-old replacement for Louis Armstrong in 1925:

> Now Big Green was a big bruiser and it took some courage to joke with him. He was 6 foot plus, his manner was rough and loud, and he always appeared ready for a fight at the drop of a wrong word. Charlie was slightly cockeyed, and the more saturated he was with his bathtub gin, the more his eye seemed to move all around in his head. He became even more frightening when he'd brandish his six shooter, which kept company with his gin in his trombone case.

Among all of Henderson's early sidemen, Green came closest to the lowest stratum of Stewart's hierarchy. Yet Green, like his fellow band members, was a versatile musician who could both read and play by ear, and his early solos demonstrate an astonishing variety of sound and style.[15]

Thus, by early 1924, when Henderson's band began its first steady job at the Club Alabam, on West Forty-Fourth Street just off Times Square, its nine members were young but experienced musicians accustomed to both reading and improvising. As a recording unit with slightly varying personnel, the band had made some two dozen records since early August 1923. At least three of the musicians (Elmer Chambers, Charlie Dixon, and Don Redman) had been working with Henderson for almost a year. Ralph Escudero, the tuba player, was apparently the only musician drafted especially for the Club Alabam opening in January 1924. Most of the others (including Coleman Hawkins, Kaiser Marshall, and Howard Scott) had been hired for studio work since late spring 1924, and Green joined them around the time the band became the Roseland's house orchestra.

By 1925, black critics were pointing to Henderson's band as a model for the future of jazz. From his powerful base in Chicago, Dave Peyton, for example, praised Henderson for developing a cultivated strain of jazz. Peyton's voice carried authority. He led a dance orchestra that played for Chicago's white society; he was an influential member of the musicians' union Local 208; and he wrote a column on music for the *Chicago Defender*, the city's leading black periodical. One of the recurring themes in Peyton's column, "The Musical Bunch," was that black musicians should project a sophisticated personal manner that countered the primitive stereotype held by whites. Henderson's sidemen embodied Peyton's image of the ideal jazzmen.[16]

Peyton's attitude reflected the assimilationist, achievement-oriented outlook voiced in Alain Locke's *The New Negro*. In the essay "Jazz at Home," J. A. Rogers defends jazz against critics who hear the music as morally suspect. Rogers echoes their concerns but concludes that jazz "has come to stay, and they are wise, who instead of protesting against it, try to lift and divert it into nobler channels." Rogers names several bandleaders whom he believes to be exerting this ennobling force: "famous jazz orchestras like those of Will Marion Cook, Paul Whiteman, Sissle and Blake, Sam Stewart, Fletcher Henderson, Vincent Lopez, and the Clef Club units," which have expunged the "vulgarities and crudities" from jazz. These writings name only bands and bandleaders, not improvising soloists. Peyton, Rogers, and other members of the black press and intelligentsia were not interested in improvised solos; they cared about arrangements, which revealed the values such critics promoted: discipline, order, sophistication, and music literacy. In later decades, white jazz critics, listening back through the legacy of Louis Armstrong, did not appreciate these qualities. There's an obvious paradox here: the qualities of the Henderson band that black critics tended to praise in the mid-1920s were precisely the qualities that later white critics would condemn. But in their image and their musical style, Henderson and his musicians showed that, in the musical world, the New Negro ideal had become reality.[17]

On "General" Records and "Race" Records

Henderson's band first took shape as a group of working musicians assembled to make records. Before it began working at the Club Alabam in January 1924, it was strictly a recording group that did not yet exist outside of the studio. From early spring 1923 to October 1924 (when Armstrong made his first records with Henderson), Henderson's orchestra made nearly one hundred recorded sides, a quantity that testifies to the band's high standing among its peers. (This total does not include dozens of other records that Henderson made as an accompanist to blues singers, sometimes in the company of one or more sidemen.) No black band had ever been so active before. Up to now, recording had been merely a sideline for the established black orchestras led by such men as James Reese Europe, Tim Brymn, Ford Dabney, and W. C. Handy—leaders who made their mark on the music world chiefly through public performances, composing, and publishing. Likewise, by the end of 1923, small groups of jazz musicians led by Johnny Dunn, Edward "Kid" Ory, King Oliver, and Jelly Roll Morton had made a few recordings, but their fame too lay chiefly in public performing. Henderson, in contrast, was at first known primarily as a recording musician. The 1923 Henderson band was the first black orchestra to make recording the central focus of its work.

A combination of factors made this activity possible. One well-documented factor was that the music business was just beginning to realize the commercial potential of recording. Until the early 1920s, the industry measured the success of a song primarily by the sales of its sheet music. But the combined force of a printers' strike, a paper shortage, and the resulting price rise, followed by the phenomenal success of such recordings as Ben Selvin's "Dardanella" (1919) and Paul Whiteman's "Whispering" and "Japanese Sandman" (1920) caused music publishers to shift their focus from sheet music sales to "mechanical royalties." Meanwhile, the wave of interest in black music following Mamie Smith's first recordings made the early 1920s an especially good time to be a black musician making records. The recording studio therefore had become a lightning rod for currents in popular music, and Henderson's band stood in a prominent position to transmit those currents.[18]

Despite Henderson's uniqueness as the leader of a black recording band, evidence suggests that record companies suppressed the racial aspect of his instrumental recordings. Most black musicians in the early 1920s made "race records," that is, black music in which racial difference was emphasized—indeed, *advertised*—in order to appeal to black consumers. Exotic band names, such as the Creole Jazz Band and the Jazz Hounds, highlighted their racialized appeal. But while Henderson and his sidemen made many race records as accompanists to blues singers, they were also making instrumental records under the dignified name "Fletcher Henderson and His Orchestra" marketed as part of the "general" series of several record companies, that is, records designed to appeal to white listeners.

Indeed, the amount and nature of the Henderson band's recording activity suggests that, far from competing with other black musicians in the race record market, Henderson sought to appeal across racial boundaries. The sheer quantity of his band's recorded work in 1923–24 put it in a league with major white dance bands of the day, those of Paul Whiteman, Vincent Lopez, Sam Lanin, and the California Ramblers. All of these bands were well established before Henderson. They had been recording regularly since at least 1921, and except for Lopez's orchestra, their recorded output had exceeded two hundred sides *each* by the end of 1924. By making approximately one hundred records in an eighteen-month period of 1923–24, Henderson's band maintained a similar pace. No other black band came close.[19]

Like most dance orchestras the group made records for several companies. (Whiteman's was unusual for working exclusively with one company, Victor.) The variety of record companies reflected the diversity and commercial potential of the Henderson band's early style and repertory. In 1923 and 1924 the band made at least a dozen sides each for Vocalion, Columbia, Plaza, Pathé, and Ajax, plus a few for other companies. The disks for

Vocalion and Columbia signify the band's early success. Both were established major companies issuing everything from opera to blues by an equally wide range of musicians. Vocalion released at least twenty-six sides by Henderson's band in this period, far more than any other company. Columbia was, and would remain, a particularly prestigious company. Don Redman later spoke of having "graduated to Columbia" in 1923. Vocalion and Columbia fostered variety in the band's style and repertory, recording blues and jazz-oriented material as well as straitlaced dance arrangements of Tin Pan Alley songs. In contrast, Plaza and Pathé released mainly the latter. Banner and Regal (subsidiaries of Plaza) and Pathé Actuelle and Perfect (of Pathé) were synchronized labels, that is, they issued identical material, usually the same "take" of a record, for different prices and markets. The cheaper label tended to be geared for chain or department stores. (Perfect, for example, sold for fifty cents against Pathé Actuelle's seventy-five-cent disks.) The companies competed for a share of the same market. Although Pathé had a wider range of artists and repertory, both firms had popular music series with hundreds of dance records designed to appeal to a broad general audience. Meanwhile, among the companies for which the early Henderson band recorded regularly, Ajax was an anomaly. It was one of a handful of small, race-record series that perished with the end of the blues craze and the advent of electrical recording in 1925. Through these various outlets, most of the Henderson orchestra's records reached a larger audience than its accompaniments for blues singers, which came out mainly on race records, such as Columbia's 14000 series. The range and number of its disks show that the band competed well in the general, mainly white, market.[20]

The sheer quantity of recordings by Henderson's band, and the record labels for which it recorded, reveal that Henderson's brand of dance music was a commercially viable product. That a black band could make dozens of recordings outside the domain of "race records" marks a major achievement in the early 1920s. The early recordings of Henderson's band are usually interpreted on stylistic grounds alone and found lacking jazz interest. Seen collectively as a rare feat for a black band, however, they stand as an important legacy of the possibilities of black culture in the period.

At the "Home of Refined Dancing"

Public performances complemented recording work. In the public arena, as in the recording studio, Henderson's band stood out as a remarkable exemplar of black achievement in the early 1920s. Beginning in January 1924, Henderson's band played regularly at the Club Alabam, a pricey central Manhattan venue frequented by a mostly white clientele and a few black celebrities. The Club had just opened when Henderson began playing there. Its evening's entertainment included dinner, dancing, and a floor show. Such entertainment had become increasingly popular through 1923, and standards of performance were apparently rising in inverse relationship to the availability of alcohol during Prohibition. In this milieu, the Club Alabam stood out for its quality entertainment and exclusive clientele. Don Redman called it "the Cotton Club of that era," and other musicians have testified to its elite standing in New York's nightlife in the early 1920s.[21]

In July 1924, Henderson and his sidemen began a steady job at one of the most important ballrooms in downtown Manhattan, the Roseland Ballroom at 1658 Broadway, between Fifty-first and Fifty-second Streets. Henderson's band would maintain a regular seasonal (October to May) residence at the Roseland until the 1930–31 season, spotted by increasingly far-flung tours and other engagements in the New York area. Ballrooms such as the Roseland occupied a social middle ground between the high society hotels and restaurants and the lower-class cabarets and taxi-dance halls. But in its category, Roseland stood out. In October 1924, *Variety*'s monomial columnist Abel (Green)—who covered Henderson's and other leading dance bands closely—wrote that "The Roseland for years has been the 'class' dance place on Broadway."[22]

The Roseland provided "the elite level of jobs for black musicians." These jobs encouraged good musicianship and three- to six-minute arrangements. Single male patrons paid a cover charge for a fixed number of dances with the hired dance partners, or "hostesses." Thereafter they paid a small charge, often a nickel, per dance. (By 1930, the average charge had apparently doubled at many ballrooms, though it was barely enough for a hostess to thrive, as suggested in the Rodgers and Hart hit of that year, "Ten Cents a Dance.") In contrast, the lower-class dance venues—called "taxi-dance" halls for relying heavily on hired dance partners—required bands to play arrangements that lasted just one minute to maintain a brisk pace of commerce for the hostesses, who might collect just a penny per dance.[23]

Established in 1919, the Roseland became one of the most popular midtown spots for dancing. As was customary at most ballrooms, the Roseland featured two house orchestras, one white and the other black, each with its own stage and alternating sets. By taking the job in 1924, Henderson replaced A. J. Piron's New Orleans Orchestra as the Roseland's resident black band, while Sam Lanin and His Orchestra remained a fixture as the regular white band.

The Roseland is a key to understanding Henderson's early work. Advertised as the "Home of Refined Dancing," the Roseland was a place for respectable dances, such as the fashionable fox-trot and the traditional waltz, but not for vigorous or suggestive full-body dances like the Charleston or the Shimmy. The Roseland was a place for "wholesome entertainment." Roseland musicians had to be able to shift quickly among a variety of styles, play with precision, and keep a clear beat.[24]

For its musical variety and respectability, the Roseland made an especially attractive choice for on-location radio broadcasts. Radio station WHN, for example, frequently broadcast dance music from the Roseland, often featuring Fletcher Henderson and his Orchestra. By the end of July 1924, after Henderson's band had played at the Roseland for just a couple of weeks, a radio columnist who heard the band on WHN claimed that it "is one of the best in the field, colored or white, and dishes up a corking brand of dance music." In the context of the 1920s, when most black musicians were excluded from radio work, Henderson's regular presence on the air by mid-1924 marks another powerful, and pioneering, achievement.[25]

Venues like the Club Alabam and the Roseland Ballroom, and by extension radio station WHN, required music that combined pep and sophistication, a kind of music that could release a reserve of energy while sounding suitably urbane to the cosmopolitan clientele. Henderson's orchestra filled this need by playing arrangements of popular songs that balanced improvised spontaneity and rehearsed polish.

Before Louis Armstrong began playing in the band in the fall of 1924, Henderson already enjoyed an unusually high profile among black musicians in New York. While black musicals had enjoyed success in Broadway theaters since the turn of the century, black orchestras were just beginning to find steady work in the lucrative downtown musical scene. And it was indeed lucrative for Henderson—at least by comparison to other black bands—as the band's weekly pay in April 1925 won a headline in the *New York Age*: "From $300 to $1,200 per week in less than 2 years for orchestra." Only a few other black orchestras—those of Leroy Smith, Armand J. Piron, and Elmer Snowden (soon to be taken over by Duke Ellington)—were regularly appearing in downtown venues in the early 1920s, and none of them made that kind of money.[26]

From Tin Pan Alley and Broadway

Like the white orchestras against which it competed in the early 1920s, Henderson's band played a repertory dominated by arrangements of new songs fresh from Tin Pan Alley publishers and Broadway shows. Sometimes the band made a recording of a song before it was even published, which shows that Henderson enjoyed close proximity to the popular music business, and that publishers saw his band as a important "plug" for their latest products.

The prominence and diversity of the publishers whose new songs Henderson's band performed provides an index of the band's integration into New York's burgeoning popular music scene. The song titles collectively evoke some of the manic, trendy language of jazz-age publishing. For example, Henderson's early repertoire featured many songs by long-established Tin Pan Alley firms, such as M. Witmark and Sons ("Long Lost Mamma, Daddy Misses You," "Me Neenyah"), E. B. Marks ("Say! Say! Sadie"), T. B. Harms ("Manda," "Shake Your Feet," "Swanee River Blues"), and Leo Feist ("I'll See You in My Dreams," "Linger Awhile," "Where the Dreamy Wabash Flows," "Cold Mamas (Burn Me Up)," and "Prince of Wails"). Other prominent publishers whose songs Henderson took into the recording studios included Irving Berlin ("When You Walked Out Someone Else Walked Right In," "My Papa Doesn't Two-time No Time," "Charley My Boy," "I Can't Get the One I Want," "Driftwood," "Feelin' the Way I Do," and "Mandy, Make Up Your Mind"), Henry Waterson ("Jealous," "Jimminy Gee"), Jack Mills ("Farewell Blues," "Just Hot," "Lots O' Mamma," "Cotton Pickers Ball," "Old Black Joe Blues," "Tea Pot Dome Blues," "Words"), Waterson, Berlin, and Snyder ("Beale Street Mamma," "My Sweetie Went Away," "Don't Think You'll Be Missed"), Shapiro, Bernstein, and Co. ("Go 'Long Mule"), Ager, Yellin, and Bornstein ("Hard Hearted Hannah," "Hard-to-Get Gertie," "You Know Me, Alabam"), and Jerome Remick ("Down by the River," "The Grass Is Always Greener in the Other Fellow's Yard," "A New Kind of Man," and "Why Couldn't It Be Poor Little Me?").[27]

Witmark, Marks, Feist, and Harms had been solid presences in New York popular song publishing since the 1890s. That they adjusted to changing fashion and published peppy jazz-age songs shows the lengths to which established publishers would go to keep up with the latest trends. That Henderson recorded their songs suggests how thoroughly his band had become threaded into New York's complex popular music industry.

Henderson's extensive performing and recording of this repertory suggests something else as well. Many of the leading publishers and composers of songs Henderson performed were Jewish. If, as Jeffrey Melnick has shown, the prevailing mode of popular music production was the adaptation and dissemination of black styles by Jewish culture brokers,[28] then Henderson's recording activity is a reminder of the complex, multifaceted interaction of black and Jewish sensibilities in the 1920s. For in the case of Henderson, we have a black bandleader adapting songs by Jewish publishers and songwriters in a style suggestive of Paul Whiteman, the leading white (and *non*-Jewish) bandleader of the day. And, as already shown, black critics were praising him for doing this.

Meanwhile, Henderson's band also recorded "race" songs in instrumental arrangements: songs by black or white composers published by firms focusing on "race" music, such as Rainbow Music Corp. ("Charleston Crazy," "Chattanooga," "Red Hot Mama," "Wish I Had You [and I'm Gonna Get You] Blues"), Down South ("I Wish I Could Make You Cry," "Dicty Blues," "Do Doodle Oom," "It Won't Be Long Now," "Potomac River Blues," "Why Put the Blame on You, Little Girl?"), Clarence Williams ("Ghost of the Blues," "Gulf Coast Blues," "Sud Bustin' Blues," "West Indies Blues," "Everybody Loves My Baby"), and W. C. Handy ("The Gouge of Armour Avenue"). Henderson and his sidemen also performed a large amount of race material as accompanists to female blues singers. Such work reinforced the impression of Henderson's versatility, the bedrock of success in early 1920s New York.

Henderson's access to this current material was clearly enhanced by his threefold prominence in midtown Manhattan venues, on WHN radio, and on a variety of leading record labels. The Roseland Ballroom itself was only the most public space in the Roseland Building, which housed several sheet-music publishers in the 1920s and beyond, including the Joe Davis Company, the Triangle Music Publishing Company (Joe Davis's race subsidiary, formed in 1919), Richmond-Robbins (Robbins-Engel by 1924; and Robbins Music Corp. in 1927), and Down South Music Publishing Corporation, the race subsidiary of Jack Mills's publishing concern of which Henderson was announced in 1923 as co-owner or "business manager." Through the 1920s, Henderson's band recorded several songs by these and other publishers housed in the Roseland Building. Many other song publishers had offices nearby: new ones having just recently opened, or older ones having years earlier followed the uptown shift of Tin Pan Alley from Twenty-eighth Street to the Times Square neighborhood. For the moment, an African-American man from Cuthbert, Georgia, stood at the epicenter of American popular music. If such a position made his band seem overly "commercial" to later commentators, in the 1920s it made the band stand out as a uniquely successful black band, the pride and envy of other black musicians, and a band that had overcome barriers that had kept other bands on the periphery of mainstream entertainment.[29]

What, then, did this band sound like? To what extent do the recordings reinforce the image of popularity and success constructed here? Or, put another way, how must we adjust our hearing to the pre-Armstrong conditions in which Henderson thrived in 1923 and 1924? To answer these questions, we must shift the focus to a key figure in Henderson's early band, Don Redman.

3.

Inside the Strain
The Advent of Don Redman

WHEN THE DOUGH-FACED, pencil-mustached, baton-wielding "King of Jazz" Paul Whiteman proclaimed that "the new demand is for change and novelty" in his 1926 book, *Jazz*, he offered this rather conservative view of actual practice: "after the tune is set the instrumentation shall be changed for each half chorus." Whiteman's own arranger, Ferde Grofé, had paved the way more than a decade earlier by shifting instrumentation for every chorus of dance-band arrangements for Art Hickman in San Francisco. Grofé came east and joined Whiteman in 1919, introducing countermelodies and more timbral contrast to his charts. He helped Whiteman's orchestra become the premier dance band in New York, a position it solidified—and attempted to transcend—on February 12, 1924, when Whiteman presented his "Experiment in Modern Music," culminating in the world premiere of a piece he had commissioned for the occasion: George Gershwin's *Rhapsody in Blue*, orchestrated by Grofé.[1]

Whiteman's dictum may sound amusingly ordinary today, but 1920s listeners and dancers relished the opulent colors that arrangers for the "modern dance orchestra" applied to the period's popular songs. By 1923, however, a few arrangers had already taken another step and regularly changed instrumentation much more frequently than Whiteman suggested. It was a technique some referred to as arranging "inside the strain," and it wasn't something that just any musician could master. When Sam Wooding's orchestra succeeded Henderson's at the Club Alabam in 1924, for example, Wooding was still a novice. "At that time," he recalled, "I was only making introductions and endings. But inside the strain I wasn't doing it, you see."[2]

Don Redman, Henderson's principal arranger, *was* doing it—and he did it more regularly and creatively than any other arranger of the period. Recognized as "the first master of jazz orchestration" and the first among "the most outstanding and influential pioneer arrangers" in 1920s jazz, Redman revealed the full range of his talent in his work in Henderson's band from 1923 to 1927. Henderson could hardly have found a more apt partner than Redman, whose "no-nonsense" approach to band leadership matched Henderson's desire for strict discipline. (Henderson's infamous "lassitude," as John Hammond called it, would not begin to appear until the late 1920s.) Recent scholars have questioned Redman's primacy, since other arrangers such as Grofé had already demonstrated the techniques for which Redman regularly gets credit: separating the brass and reeds into distinct, independent sections and writing call-and-response patterns that anticipated big-band arranging—including Henderson's style—in the swing era. This chapter makes no attempt to challenge that point. It argues instead that Redman has been hailed for the wrong reasons.[3]

Coming to terms with Redman's significance means recognizing that an arranger can be as much a creative force in jazz as a composer or an improvising soloist. Like a composer, an arranger gives an original shape to a piece of music, creating unity and contrast through a variety of musical elements, including melody, harmony, rhythm, form, tempo, texture, and timbre. Like an improvising soloist, an arranger takes existing material—in Redman's case, usually a popular song or blues piece—and uses it as the framework for a fresh, new conception.

From that perspective, the Henderson band's first four years must be construed as the "Redman period," even though it encompasses Louis Armstrong's brief but influential tenure in the band. Gunther Schuller called Don Redman the "architect" of the Henderson band's distinctive style in the 1920s. And Schuller's notion that the 1920s were a decade of "restless curiosity" sums up Redman's work in particular, including: his ability to rethink a song's rhythm, melody, harmony, orchestration, and form to make it fresh; his penchant for tailoring accompaniments to suit different soloists; his fascination with instruments, both conventional ones and novelties; and, not least, his musical sense of humor. Redman's early arrangements with Henderson often aim to dazzle the listener (and challenge the dancer) with a barrage of contrasting colors and patterns.[4]

Even as he gets praised as a "pioneer," Redman's early efforts have been dismissed as "overwritten arrangement" and "baroque doodling." Coming to terms with Henderson's early band, however, calls for reassessing how the arrangements not only reflect the arranging techniques of white bands but also exhibit distinctively African-derived approaches to music making. Indeed, it is possible to hear in Redman's arrangements some tendencies in African-American music described by Olly Wilson: first, "a tendency to create a high density of musical events within a relatively short musical time frame, or to fill up all the musical space," and second, to introduce "a kaleidoscopic range of dramatically contrasting qualities of sound (timbre)"—otherwise known as the " 'heterogeneous sound tendency.' " A "density" of musical events, "kaleidoscopic" contrasts, and a "heterogeneous" ideal: Redman began to develop all of these tendencies in the period when Henderson was the "Paul Whiteman of the Race."[5]

Those points lead suggestively to the notion that Redman's work reflects another widespread practice in African-American music and culture, that of "signifying." Although often used to describe improvisatory practices, the concept applies equally well to the written or planned elements in Henderson's recordings, for they fit Henry Louis Gates, Jr.'s, description of signifying as "resemblance ... by dissemblance." Gates developed this concept to open a door to understanding African-American literature, but the concept's applications to music have been widely recognized and explored, and I believe it provides a key to going beyond the confining "Paul Whiteman of the Race" trope that has governed Henderson's reputation in the crucial early years of his bandleading career. From this new perspective,

Redman's rearrangements of the period's popular dance-band repertoire emerge as more than imitations: they are savvy, playful parodies of popular song and dance styles.[6]

The chief material Redman signified upon comprises the so-called stock arrangements of current songs that publishers issued by the thousands in the 1920s, eager to swell the tide of public dancing. In fact, with stocks in hand, we can hear in the recordings how Redman rearranged what the publishers had supplied. Long regarded as transcending the commercial marketplace in which stock arrangements were created and disseminated, Redman now emerges as a figure working creatively within that milieu. In this crowded, fast-paced world, Redman stood out as a key figure who showed that stock arrangements were not to be read straight from the music sheets from beginning to end, but rather served as raw material that could be cut and pasted in novel ways. For Redman, a piece of sheet music was not a road map but a playground or a puzzle whose parts could be altered, extended, truncated, and otherwise rearranged at will. In other words, Redman's arranging technique has its roots in the common practice of "doctoring" published arrangements; in dozens of recordings made in the year before Armstrong came to New York, Redman demonstrated a unique genius for it.

Doctoring Stocks

Stock arrangements of popular songs of the early 1920s usually had a four- to eight-bar introduction, followed by the song's verse and two or three statements of the song's refrain, also known as the "chorus." Each section featured one predominant texture and timbre—whether played by the full ensemble, a section of the band, or, more rarely, a soloist—from beginning to end. Many stocks offered a choice of instrumentation by aligning two staves on each part. An occasional duet or trio break might be inserted for color. Largely, however, instrumentation on stocks tended to change more *between* chorus statements than *within* them. Although stocks would become more intricate through the 1920s, the publishers' in-house arrangers of stocks generally aimed more for maximum accessibility than for ingenuity "inside the strain." Redman took these generic works and gave them a distinctive twist. A comparison of printed and recorded sources shows how a fledgling orchestra of the early 1920s went about the process.

As a benchmark for comparison, we can begin with a recording that reflects several changes to a stock, but that contains few changes inside the strain. The tune is "Oh! Sister, Ain't That Hot," a typical Tin Pan Alley attempt to package the new excitement of jazz in sheet-music form. The whole context shows the band's tight links to Tin Pan Alley publishing. Both "Oh! Sister" and another song on that day's recording session, "Mamma's Gonna Slow You Down," were published by the firm of Stark and Cowan in late 1923, and both were arranged by Ted Eastwood, probably one of the publisher's in-house arrangers. The stocks also reveal the publisher's address, at 234 West Forty-sixth Street, to be only a couple of blocks from the Club Alabam. The recording for the Emerson company dates from early January 1924 and thus has the added advantage of capturing the band just about the time it began playing at the Club Alabam.

The recording clearly derives several elements from the stock, including its key, much of its form, and several specific passages (fig. 3.1).

Fig. 3.1. "Oh! Sister, Ain't That Hot," stock arrangement and Henderson recording

Stock arrangement (1923)	Henderson recording (early January 1924)
Moderato	$\rfloor$ =ca. 180
key of B♭ major	key of B♭ major
Intro. (8 bars) (C minor)	Intro. (8 bars) (C minor)
Verse (16) cor./vln melody, ens.	Verse 1 (16) tpt. melody, ens.
Chorus 1 (22) cornet melody, ens. on backbeat (with optional vocal)	Chorus 1 (22) alto sax melody, brass on backbeat with piano obbligato
	Verse 2 (16) trumpet lead, ensemble
Chorus 2 (22) tbn. melody	Chorus 2 (22) clar. solo
Patter (12) ens., syncopated rhythm	Patter (12) ens., Charleston rhythm
	Chorus 3 (22) tenor sax solo
Chorus 3 (22) out-chorus: cornet/ vln. melody, clar. obbligato, ens.	Chorus 4 (22) out-chorus: growl tpt. lead, ens. obbligato
	Tag (4) saxes (composed)

For example, the band plays the stock's introduction, a version of the macabre theme frequently encountered in popular songs and silent-film accompaniments (ex. 3.1).[7]

Ex. 3.1. "Oh! Sister, Ain't That Hot," introduction from stock arrangement by Ted Eastwood (1923), piano part

In chorus 1, moreover, the Henderson band retains the backbeat accents (in other words, accents on beats two and four) in the stock's accompaniment—a feature that a jazz-oriented listener without the stock might assume to have been added by Henderson's band (ex. 3.2).

Ex. 3.2. "Oh! Sister, Ain't That Hot," chorus 1, beginning, from stock arrangement, piano part

The principal changes consist in typical doctoring techniques: instrumental substitution (as in choruses 1 and 2, where the alto saxophone and clarinet—both probably played by Redman himself—replace the stock's cornet and trombone, respectively); the addition of sections to accommodate soloists—the band's leading "hot" players, trumpeter Howard Scott (verse 2), and tenor saxophonist Coleman Hawkins (chorus 3); and rhythmic variation. Like many 1920s songs, this one includes a "Patter"—that is, a passage after the chorus designed for rapid-fire delivery of many words over a simple, repeated rhythmic figure. In this case, Redman changes the original Patter's syncopation to a Charleston rhythm, reflecting a fad ignited just a couple of months earlier. Redman also composed a brief new tag ending for saxophones.

There's another device that locates the tune in its time and place: Both the stock and the recording feature a climactic final section—known as the out-chorus—simulating improvisatory heterophony in the style of small groups of New Orleans players such as the Original Dixieland Jazz Band (first recorded in 1917) and King Oliver's Creole Jazz Band, whose early recordings had just hit New York. Stocks aim to evoke improvisation in a variety of ways, including an occasional "ad lib" cornet part, a "hot chorus" for trombone including glissando slides indicating the so-called tailgate style, or an obbligato line—the last of which appears in the clarinet part of final chorus of the "Oh! Sister" stock. Henderson's band plays in a more flexible style that reflects as much what they are listening to, as what they are reading from. As he would do on many out-choruses in Henderson's band, Howard Scott leads the way with his growling trumpet, and the rest of the band does its best to conjure the spirited playing of New Orleans musicians. Considering the stock and recording together, we get a more vivid picture of the band's early, and somewhat awkward, efforts to blend the imported excitement of New Orleans small-group jazz with the polished precision of arranged dance music.

"Beale Street Mamma" shows a more adventurous departure from a stock arrangement. The tune belongs among a plethora of "Beale Street" songs spawned by W. C. Handy's "Beale Street Blues" of 1916. Looking at a simple diagram of the stock and recorded performance (fig. 3.2) reveals that the recording preserves the stock's key and routine, but adds one chorus and modulates to A♭ major for the last two sections.

But if the band was familiar with the stock made by the formidable white bandleader-arranger Arthur Lange, it used the published music only as a

Fig. 3.2. "Beale Street Mamma"

Stock arrangement (© February 21, 1923)		Henderson recording (May 1 or 2, 1923)	
G Major	Intro. (4 bars)	G major	Intro. (4 bars)
	Verse (16)		Verse (16)
	Chorus 1 (32)		Chorus 1 (32)
	Chorus 2 (32)	A♭ major	Chorus 2 (32)
			Chorus 3 (32)

foundation for improvisation, virtuoso display, and above all, instrumental variety. Following the stock's format but ignoring its notes, each chorus features a soloist creating his own obbligato above (or between the phrases of) the given melody. In chorus 1, the alto saxophonist (possibly Redman) plays the melody and an unknown tenor saxophonist plays breaks characterized by rapid, brilliant flourishes. In chorus 2, the clarinetist (again possibly Redman) weaves a flowing blues line over the melody, whose halves are split between the trombone and trumpet. In chorus 3, a trumpeter (probably Elmer Chambers) plays a somewhat mournful solo over a backdrop of improvisatory ensemble polyphony. In sum, while Henderson's recording retains the melody, as in a stock, its arrangement exploits every opportunity to spotlight its soloists and to introduce instrumental variety. All six melodic instruments—three brass and three reeds—at some point carry important, independent lines.

An even more radical departure from a stock occurs in "He's the Hottest Man in Town," arranged by one W. C. Polla, a recurring name in early published arrangements. Here, the band not only introduces substantial alterations to the stock's form and instrumentation but also changes its mood. The stock prescribes a "Slow Blues" tempo, but the Henderson band transforms the piece into an up-tempo dance number (at more than 200 beats per minute). The recording begins with a tricky, disorienting introduction that bears no relationship to the one on the stock (ex. 3.3).

Ex. 3.3. "He's the Hottest Man in Town," intro. from Henderson recording (September 8, 1924), partial transcription

A further look at the stock, however, reveals that the introduction did not entirely spring from Redman's imagination. Polla's arrangement supplies a coda, called an "optional break" in the stock. Its last two bars, with chromatic ascent and cadence, are the source of the opening phrase of the Henderson band's introduction (ex. 3.4). Redman has lopped off the tail to create the head.

Ex. 3.4. "He's the Hottest Man in Town," last two bars of "optional break" from stock arrangement, piano part

The Henderson recording, rather than using the "optional break" supplied by Polla, plays a coda that picks up where its introduction left off by continuing the additive rhythmic pattern begun there (ex. 3.5)

Ex. 3.5. "He's the Hottest Man in Town," coda of Henderson recording

The recording alters the stock in other ways. Where Polla's arrangement supplies the piece's full thirty-two-bar chorus, Henderson's band consistently truncates the chorus to thirty bars, eliding its final cadence with the next section. The device, a hallmark of 1920s jazz and dance music, reinforces the tune's restless energy.

Most unusual of all, however, are several entirely new passages, including a new strain, several breaks, and bridge (the "B" section of the AABA form) added between choruses 2 and 3 (indented and boldfaced in fig. 3.3), resulting in a much more complicated routine than the straightforward stock version.

The new strain—with its moseying trumpet-trombone duet and tuba-banjo boom-chick accompaniment filling an irregular nineteen-bar section—seems oddly out of character with the rest of the piece. Its relaxed, countrified air contrasts sharply with the peppy syncopation that prevails in the choruses. Yet that contrast points to a key feature of Redman's emerging style. Here, two years before Whiteman would publish his call for "change and novelty," we can hear Redman taking a stock arrangement, opening it up, rearranging its parts, and creating kaleidoscopic juxtapositions inside the strain.

Fig. 3.3. "He's the Hottest Man in Town"

Stock arrangement	Henderson recording (September 8, 1924)
C major	C major
"Slow Blues"	♩ = ca. 204
Intro. (8 bars)	**Intro. ("Optional break," 5 bars)**
Verse (12)	Chorus 1 (30)
Chorus 1(32)	Verse (12)
Chorus 2 (30)	Chorus 2 (30)
"Opt[ional] Break" (6)	**Wah-Wah Brass Break (3)**
	Clar. Break (3)
	Vamp, Wah-Wah Brass (2)
	New Strain (19)
	Ens. break (4)
	Bridge (8)
	Chorus 3 (30)
	Coda (4)

The Arranger's Chorus

In the same year that Whiteman published *Jazz*, Arthur Lange issued his landmark *Arranging for the Modern Dance Orchestra*. In a chapter on "Forms and Routines," he refers to "the arranger's chorus" of a performance to describe the freedom allowed after the melody statement. (It was 1926, and it's noteworthy that Lange wrote no corresponding chapter on "the soloist's chorus.") For Redman, almost any chorus could be an "arranger's chorus."[8]

We can date Redman's arranging work for Henderson to as early as March 1923, when the band recorded a tune called "Down by the River," and the record label, unusually, included the phrase "Arr. by Don Redman." In the arrangement's middle section, Redman begins to subdivide the song's structure into four-bar segments alternating between solos (for himself and the bandleader) and ensemble polyphony. In the bridge, the pattern accelerates into a rapid-fire exchange of one-bar phrases between Redman's clarinet and the rest of the band.[9]

Two recordings from later 1923 show even more dramatically the kind of inside-the-strain subdivision with which Redman made his mark. The first reveals how fast the band picked up on the Charleston craze ignited by the black Broadway show, *Runnin' Wild*, with its hit song, "Charleston." The show opened in late October 1923, almost simultaneously with Henderson's first attempt at a related tune called "Charleston Crazy."

"Charleston Crazy" reveals as much enthusiasm for savvy arranging as New Yorkers were showing for the dance that inspired the song. In one twenty-bar passage toward the end of the recording—the arranger's chorus—the instrumentation changes in almost every measure (ex. 3.6).

Ex. 3.6. "Charleston Crazy" (November 30, 1923), beginning of twelve-bar strain following chorus 2

The passage begins with a blues chorus consisting of a quick volley between a brass duo and two solo saxophones. This pattern recurs twice (slightly varied in its second appearance to adapt to harmonic change), making a twelve-bar blues chorus. The next eight bars continue with similarly variegated instrumentation that changes in every measure: the full ensemble plays a syncopated rhythm in call and response with trumpet and bass sax breaks.

The band's recording of "I'm Gonna See You" extends the principle to even greater extremes. After the introduction and verse, the band plays twenty-three breaks in three-and-a-half choruses. The result is an arrangement built largely in two-bar chunks, an orchestral exercise in breaks (fig. 3.4).

Once again, although nearly every member of the band gets to shine as a soloist, the spotlight, in effect, remains on the arranger throughout. During 1924, the band made several more recordings in which at least one chorus had phrases shifted among the band in this way. In its sheer concentration of instrumental variety, however, "I'm Gonna See You" would not be rivaled until 1927, with kaleidoscopic arrangements of "symphonic jazz" such as "Whiteman Stomp."

Breaking down a chorus by scattering its phrases among different instruments was just one way that Redman worked inside the strain. The technique called for careful planning but did not necessarily involve written music; the players could have exchanged ideas orally. Redman developed several other methods of arranging choruses during the band's first eighteen months, most of which must have required more writing.

Soft-Shoe Stoptime

Rex Stewart once wrote that "When Smack heard Louis Armstrong, in Chicago, playing licks that emphasized the dancing of a team called Dave

Fig. 3.4. "I'm Gonna See You"

Intro.	ens. (4 bars)
Verse	ens. (12)
Chorus 1	ens. + tpt. (2 + 2)
	ens. + tbn. (2 + 2)
	ens. + muted tpt. (2 + 2)
	ens. + clar. (2 + 2)
	ens. + clar. (2 + 2)
	ens. (4)
	tpt. + tbn. (2 + 2)
	ens. (4)
Chorus 2	ens. (4)
	ens. + tpt. (2 + 2)
	ens. + tbn. (2 + 2)
	ens. + tpt. (2 + 2)
	ens. + clar. (2 + 2)
	ens. + banjo (2 + 2)
	ens. (4)
	tpt. + tbn. (2 + 2)
	ens. (4)
Chorus 3	alto sax + ens. (2 + 2)
	" " (2 + 2)
	" " (2 + 2)
	alto sax (4)
	ens. + bass sax (2 + 2)
	" " (2 + 2)
	" " (2 + 2))
	ens. (4)
Chorus 4	= Chorus 2, second half

and Tressie, this was quickly orchestrated in the Redman way. The new concept (featuring figures made by the brass that paralleled the syncopation of the dancers) was copied immediately by other bands." Indeed, dancing inspired arranging, and no technique reveals that more clearly than *soft-shoe stoptime*. In this device, we hear the melody played staccato, creating lots of gaps for instrumental fills—and for soft-shoe dancing. On record, Henderson's musicians fill the gaps with runs, chords, or a sandblock playing a shuffling pattern.[10]

The device represents another of Redman's typical variations, which preserves the melody while allowing room for the arranger's whim. Here, one section of the band plays the melody staccato, leaving plenty of room for another section or soloist to provide filler in the gaps between the melodic notes, especially where the original melody had long tones.

The device appears early in the band's recordings. In chorus 2 of Irving Berlin's "When You Walked Out Someone Else Walked Right In," the trumpets play a skeletal melody (ex. 3.7) that functions as a stoptime accompaniment to an active banjo solo by Charlie Dixon.[11]

Ex. 3.7. "When You Walked Out Someone Else Walked Right In" (mid-May 1923), chorus 2, beginning

The chorus 2 bridge of "Chicago Blues" also sets the melody in staccato brass, while a sandblock shuffles like a dancer on the beats between the melodic notes (ex. 3.8).

Ex. 3.8. "Chicago Blues" (March 25, 1924), chorus 2, bridge

No chorus like this appears on the stock arrangement by William Grant Still, Henderson's former associate at Black Swan. At the time the band made this recording of "Chicago Blues," it had been playing in revues at the Club Alabam for almost three months.[12]

Redman found a wide variety of ways to fill the gaps opened up by such soft-shoe passages. In chorus 3 of "Linger Awhile" the saxophones play the melody against a fashionably amusing "doo-wacka" trumpet riff, a popular sound effect created by the combined use of two mutes: one fixed in the horn's bell, the other (a plunger) covering and uncovering the bell on alternate beats (ex. 3.9).

Ex. 3.9. "Linger Awhile" (November 27, 1923), chorus 3, beginning

This chorus on the Henderson recording replaces the "Special Chorus" on the stock, where the saxophone choir plays the melody in a creamy legato over a "delicatissimo" brass staccato accompaniment. But the Henderson band's "doo-wacka" chorus owes nothing to the stock. The stylistic juxtaposition here is remarkable, for "Linger Awhile" stood among the year's smoothest and most popular sentimental songs, while a song called "Doo Wacka Doo"—already recorded by Paul Whiteman's band and by the California Rambers—celebrated jazz's quirky novelty. Few listeners and dancers of the early 1920s could have mistaken the parodistic, signifying gesture.[13]

The rests in a staccato-melody variation invited virtuosic display, and Redman accepted the challenge, both as a soloist and an arranger. In chorus 2 of "After the Storm" Redman fills in the large gaps in the melody (played by trumpets) with as many notes as possible, running up and down the scale in a barrage of triplets that sound like a page out of an exercise book—one that Redman might have practiced a bit more before the recording session (ex. 3.10).

Here, Redman is undoubtedly aiming to emulate the fast, fluid triplet filigree associated with white alto saxophonists Rudy Wiedoeft and Bennie Krueger.[14]

Ex. 3.10. "After the Storm" (May 1924), chorus 2, beginning

"Driftwood," on the other hand, shows Redman trying to evoke the fleetness of a soloist with a written passage for the saxophone section, probably consisting of Hawkins and himself. As in Redman's solo in "After the Storm", the passage is a bit beyond the players' ability but manages to hold together in a fairly steady tempo for a breathtaking thirty-four bars (ex. 3.11).

Ex. 3.11. "Driftwood" (May 1924), chorus 2, beginning (top lines only)

Melodic Interception

In soft-shoe stoptime passages, musicians play in rapid dialogue, but the melodic line remains in only one section or instrument. Other arrangements go a step further by actually breaking up the melodic line among two or more soloists or sections of the band, in a device that might be described as *melodic interception*. Here, Redman shifts the instrumentation in the middle of a phrase, as if tossing the tune around among the band members. Henderson's first recorded example of this device appears in an arrangement of a new song written for the *Ziegfeld Follies of 1923* called "Shake Your Feet," composed by the longtime *Follies* songwriters Dave Stamper and Gene Buck. The show opened on October 20, the song's copyright was claimed on November 8, 1923, by T. B. Harms, and Henderson's band made its first recording of the song later that month, on November 27—illustrating a typical sequence of events leading to a Henderson recording.

The recording shows how Redman deployed a major soloist in service of an arranging concept. In the arrangement's second chorus, Coleman Hawkins, on tenor saxophone, trades snippets of melody with muted trumpets, and the bass saxophone inserts quick breaks during the rests (ex. 3.12.)

Ex. 3.12. "Shake Your Feet" (late December 1923), chorus 2, beginning

The isolated trumpet "wah" adds comic spark to each phrase. The whole passage has the character of musical sleight of hand, with its sudden leaps between registers and quick shifts among instruments. Yet the melody remains in the foreground throughout. For early 1920s listeners, musicians, and critics who saw the future of jazz in arrangement, Henderson's version of "Shake Your Feet" was hardly a commercial "concession" but a way of putting theory into practice, so to speak. Meanwhile, although Paul

Whiteman's Orchestra often featured frequent shifts of instrumentation around this time, nothing in its own recording of "Shake Your Feet" a month earlier comes close to matching the variety of Redman's arrangement for Henderson. If that all sounds like "baroque doodling" to later jazz critics, well, that was the point.

In choruses where the arranger felt free to experiment, change was prized over continuity. Almost all elements of musical performance— including rhythm, phrasing, timbre, texture, articulation—were subject to variation, even sudden change. Thus, in chorus 4 of "I Wish I Could Make You Cry," just when it would appear that the trombone soloist (Teddy Nixon) who began the phrase would also finish it, Redman allows the trumpets to intercept the melody for two bars (in the staccato style familiar from many other recordings), only to have Nixon resume the phrase for its last note (ex. 3.13).

Ex. 3.13. "I Wish I Could Make You Cry" (March 1924), chorus 4

"Say! Say! Sadie" contains a similar passage (ex. 3.14). In the last eight bars of chorus 2, Nixon again carries the melody, which is interrupted by the trumpets (m. 29), then resumes the phrase (m. 30) only to relinquish its resolution to the saxophones (mm. 31–32).

Ex. 3.14. "Say! Say! Sadie" (March 1924), chorus 2, ending

Concentrated into a single measure, melodic interception becomes a "chase" break between the trumpets and trombone in "Feelin' the Way

I Do." This brief showcase for brass—played at nearly 200 beats per minute, must have demanded more rehearsal than usual; judging from the recording, it could have used even more (ex. 3.15).

Ex. 3.15. "Feelin' the Way I Do" (May 1924), chorus 2, mm. 15–16

Cymbal Punctuation

When Kaiser Marshall began to record with Henderson in fall 1923, the band acquired its first drummer and a new timbre for Redman's increasingly colorful arrangements. In fact, on recordings, Marshall's chief role lay not in his background beat on drums, which could not be successfully recorded before the microphone era launched two years later, but in various choked and open cymbal hits at the beginnings, middles, and ends of phrases. Marshall proved indispensable in Redman's constant search for variety. In the last two weeks of June 1924, Marshall made two notable recordings with Henderson, "Jimminy Gee!" and "Jealous." In the first, he (with the brass) provides punctuation and a musical punch-line, complete with a broad "wah-wah" from the brass (ex. 3.16), and, in the second, his choked cymbal crashes fragment the previously flowing line (ex. 3.17).

Ex. 3.16. "Jimminy Gee!" (June 1924), chorus 3, beginning

Ex. 3.17. "Jealous" (June 1924), chorus 2, mm. 1–8, 17–24

A recording of "Houston Blues," by black composer and publisher George Thomas, features a strain that breaks up the lilting ragtime-style melody among four sections and soloists of the band: trombone, cymbal, trumpets, and saxophones (ex. 3.18).

Ex. 3.18. "Houston Blues" (June 21, 1924), strain 3, beginning

The use of mutes, the abrupt silence of the trombone in mid-phrase (mm. 2 and 6, where the original melody would continue as shown), and the sudden shifts among the instruments add up to a parody of Thomas's piece.

Rhythmic Variation

Another kind of playful variation on the original melody involved rhythmic recasting. While leaving the tune recognizable, Redman sometimes altered its rhythm in a way that could trip up a dancer as quickly as the timbral refraction in arrangements like "Jimminy Gee!" or "Jealous."

An up-tempo dance arrangement of "Lots O' Mamma" is a case in point. Chorus 2 presents the melody in its clearest form (ex. 3.19a); chorus 4 shows its rhythmic variation (ex. 3.19b).

In chorus 4, Redman alters the original theme in two fundamental ways: he begins the tune on the downbeat, one beat earlier than in chorus 2; and he augments the rhythm from its basic syncopated pattern of dotted quarter notes (in chorus 2) to a sequence of quarter and half notes, resulting in an irregular 3 + 3 + 2 pattern of accents (in chorus 4). Textural differences highlight the contrast between the two choruses. Chorus 2 is an informal, overlapping dialogue between the trumpets and trombone; chorus 4 is a chordal setting in which all the instruments—including piano and banjo—move together in two-bar phrases separated by cymbal hits.

Ex. 3.19. "Lots O' Mamma" (January 29, 1924)

Ex. 3.19a. Chorus 2, mm. 1–4

Ex. 3.19b. Chorus 4, mm. 1–4

Chorus 4 also features an unusual disruption of the thirty-two-bar song form. Almost invariably, the arranged variations heard on Henderson's recordings occur within the conventional song forms given by the composer. In "Lots O' Mamma," however, Redman extends the first half of chorus 4 to seventeen bars, thus adding an "extra" measure at the midpoint of the tune's ABAC form, which now contains thirty-three bars (ex. 3.20).

Ex. 3.20. "Lots O' Mamma," chorus 4, mm. 15–17

Similar rhythmic tricks transform "Say! Say! Sadie" from a lyric senti-mental song into a peppy dance number. Chorus 1 presents the melody clearly and sweetly in the saxophones (ex. 3.21a). Chorus 2 combines timbral variety and rhythmic variation; Teddy Nixon's "straight" rendition of the melody is interrupted by syncopated variations (and saxophone inter-jections) in mm. 3–4 and 7–8 (ex. 3.21b). Chorus 3, in contrast, varies the parts of the melody left "straight" in the previous chorus. Here, the brass play a syncopated version of the melody in mm. 1–2 and 5–6, punctuated by a sharp cymbal jab at the end of each phrase (ex. 3.21c).

Ex. 3.21. "Say! Say! Sadie"

Ex. 3.21a. Chorus 1, mm. 1–4

Ex. 3.21b. Chorus 2, mm. 1–4

Ex. 3.21c. Chorus 3, mm. 1–4

Novelty

Train whistles, horse whinnies, baby cries, sobbing, laughs, and sneezes: 1923 marked a peak in the fad for musical novelty. Publishers issued how-to books revealing the secrets of novelty playing: Louis Panico's *The Novelty Cornetist* and Zez Confrey's *Modern Course in Novelty Piano Playing* both appeared that year. And as Mark Tucker points out, even after Paul Whiteman's much-publicized attempt to "reform" jazz with his "Experiment in Modern Music" at Aeolian Hall on February 12, 1924, "many bands continued their imitation animal noises, solos on slide whistle and goofus, and good old-fashioned hokum." Piano novelty style contains a strong streak of parody (of ragtime and player-piano music), and

Redman's novelty effects would certainly seem to extend that to the realm of the dance orchestra. Indeed, novelty's parodistic thrust forms a natural bridge to the signifying impulse.[15]

For Redman and other arrangers, songs with place names in their titles served as invitations to feature the sounds of railroad travel. Such sounds made their first modest appearance in the Henderson band's recordings in late November 1923 with "31st Street Blues," a song that became popular in the Charleston-marked show *Runnin' Wild*, which had opened on Broadway just a month earlier. Redman's introduction begins with a heraldic brass phrase that simulates the call of a train whistle (ex. 3.22).

Ex. 3.22. "31st Street Blues" (late November 1923), introduction, mm. 1–2

Similar phrases—scored in block chords with plaintive half-step dips— appear in "I'm Gonna See You," "Chicago Blues," and "That's Georgia," songs that touch on travel or far-off places.

The band's railroad specialty in this period was "Chicago Blues." Promoted as a "blues novelty number, popular with dancers and singers alike," and identified with the Henderson band, the piece offered a catalog of train effects. The band recorded "Chicago Blues" twice, the first (early February 1924) featuring an introduction that begins with bells signaling the last call to board and the gradually accelerating percussive chugging of the train engine, which in this case sounds like the real thing, not a sandblock simulation. In the first chorus, the saxophones propel the performance with a motoric riff, suggesting that the train from (or to) Chicago is moving full speed ahead (ex. 3.23).[16]

Ex. 3.23. "Chicago Blues" (early February 1924), chorus 1, beginning (saxophones)

Toward the end of chorus 2, the trombone and saxophones join together for a train-whistle phrase reminiscent of the introduction to "31st Street Blues" (ex. 3.24).

Ex. 3.24. "Chicago Blues," chorus 2, mm. 25–28

Despite some similarities with a stock arrangement by William Grant Still, the Henderson band clearly plays its own arrangement by Don Redman. A *Phonograph and Talking Machine Weekly* article mentions Redman's "special phonograph record arrangement" of "Chicago Blues."[17]

Meanwhile, in a guest appearance at Harlem's Lafayette Theatre in May 1924, the band scored a hit with its rendition of "After the Storm," complete with "electrical effects" from an unidentified instrument evoking the sound of whistling wind. On the recording, the storm dies down at the end of a lengthy introduction, and the clouds seem to part as a sweet melody emerges in the saxophones and violin. The wind wails again in the coda, but more to round off the arrangement than to suggest that the storm has returned.[18]

At about the same time, a couple of Henderson's musicians began to caricature the human voice through their instruments. The band's up-tempo, jovial rendition of "Somebody Stole My Gal" (recorded April 16, 1924) exaggerates the sentimentality of this Leo Wood hit of 1922. In chorus 2, Coleman Hawkins delivers the melody on bass saxophone like a tony ballad singer (including little turn figures and grace notes), and Redman interjects squeaky sobs between phrases. Redman himself then takes the melody, continuing to play with comic inflections. Hawkins returns to the melody for the remaining sixteen bars, with one of the trumpet players (Chambers or Scott) inserting speech-like exclamations rising to mock anger between phrases. The ironic effect of Hawkins's elephantine bass-sax tone singing the melody, combined with the quasi-vocal utterances of clarinet and trumpet, reduces the song's sentiment to crocodile tears. It's the musical equivalent of the pouting face of a sad clown. This tongue-in-cheek rendition of "Somebody Stole My Gal" was typical of the way Henderson's orchestra parodied popular songs of the day. But there were precedents. The Isham Jones orchestra's version of "Wabash Blues," for example, had been one of the best-selling records of 1921, highlighted by "sobbing" effects created by a "wah-wah" muted trumpet.[19]

Unusual instruments appear in several of the band's recordings from this period. Tolling chimes were one of the chief attractions of "Dicty Blues." In addition to "electrical effects," "After the Storm" featured single-tone interjections by a celeste. In "Mobile Blues" Redman played two breaks on a kazoo. Redman's scat singing in "My Papa Doesn't Two-Time No Time" also ranks as a novelty effect. Louis Armstrong would later transform scat into a serious vocal alternative to straight singing, but Redman's half-chorus scat solo—perhaps the first on record—places the technique in the domain of novelty, its effect chiefly arising from humor and surprise.

Late summer 1924 marked the entrance of a funny little instrument that, like the hokum on "Somebody Stole My Gal," would cast an air of parody on the conventional sentiments of popular songs. The goofus, or couesnaphone, was a wind instrument with an outcropping of keyboard and a reed for each key; it sounds like a harmonica, but with a thinner, reedier tone. Redman must have been listening closely to the competition, for his use of the goofus on recordings came less than two months after Adrian Rollini had unveiled the instrument in recordings with the Little Ramblers, a small spin-off group from the California Ramblers, a popular white orchestra. Over the next month, from late August to late September, Redman played goofus on three recordings: "You'll Never Get to Heaven With Those Eyes," "A New Kind of Man (With a New Kind of Love for Me)," and "Cold Mammas (Burn Me Up)."[20]

The band boasted yet another novelty instrument reflecting Redman's fascination with unusual sounds. In "Forsaken Blues" (recorded September 24, 1924), a Klaxon—the loud horn used on motor vehicles of the period—makes its first appearance on a Henderson recording. "Forsaken Blues" (in 32-bar popular song form, not 12-bar blues) had what a popular "blues" needed for instant success: novelty, humor, surprise, and danceability. The heavy-handed bass saxophone vamp in the introduction sets a tongue-in-cheek mood, which is sustained by the wah-wah trumpets in chorus 1. The Klaxon intrudes in the middle of the chorus, with a unique sound that seems to combine a horse's neigh and a cough.

"Forsaken Blues" features another element of early 1920s dance band novelty: quotation. For the past year, Henderson's recordings would occasionally surprise the listener with a knowing allusion to a popular song. A brief transitional passage in "Dicty Blues" makes clear reference to "Royal Garden Blues," a hit by Clarence Williams and Spencer Williams published in 1919. Toward the end of "After the Storm," Redman plays the pastoral melody from Rossini's *William Tell* on oboe, the first time this instrument appears on Henderson's recordings. In "Wait'll You See My Gal," Coleman Hawkins plays conspicuous quotations of the familiar wedding march from Wagner's *Lohengrin*.

The novelty craze also saw a rash of "doodle" tunes: "Deedle-Deedle-Dum," "Doodle-Doo-Doo," "Doo Wacka Doo," and "Doodle-Um Blues," and Henderson's own "Do Doodle Oom." As in other pieces of this ilk, Henderson's title represents a phonetic analogue to the music's predominant rhythm (ex. 3.25). The rhythm itself was widely heard around New York in the early 1920s, as in Irving Berlin's "Pack Up Your Sins and Go to the Devil," a new tune for the *Music Box Revue* of 1922.

Ex. 3.25. "Do Doodle Oom," (August 9, 1923), mm. 1–2

Whether making the sounds of trains, car horns, wind, animals, or human sobbing; alluding to other songs through quotation; or just using unusual instruments for their eccentric timbres; the band fed the popular demand for music that was surprising, funny, and above all, entertaining. In adopting these effects, the band tapped into the fashion of altering a song's original mood with an ironic twist. Novelty effects were only the most obvious examples of an attitude that viewed popular song as a sketch in black ink whose given form and harmony could be colored and animated according to a musician's whim. Driven by Don Redman's insatiable search for new sounds, the Henderson band excelled in folding novelty into dance music.

The Fox-trot Blues

Blues recordings reveal an intriguing side of the early Henderson band. By the time he began recording with his orchestra, Henderson was already well known as a pianist on race records. And through the first year with his regular band, he continued to make more recordings as an accompanist— usually with at least one of his sidemen—than as a bandleader. (He made more recordings with Bessie Smith than any other musician did.) The majority of those recordings were blues, which in the early 1920s meant anything from pieces with twelve-bar forms and melancholy lyrics to cheerful popular songs whose only connection to the "blues" was the word in their titles.

As a result, in 1923 Henderson the ubiquitous accompanist came to be seen as an emissary for the blues. Some of the blues songs Henderson played as an accompanist filtered into his band's recorded repertory. In its first few months, the band recorded "Beale Street Mamma," "Down Hearted Blues," "Gulf Coast Blues," and "Midnight Blues"—all of which were recorded around the same time by singers accompanied by Henderson.[21]

Striving to become a leading dance orchestra, Henderson's band made blues recordings with an eye toward broad commercial appeal. Performing without singers, the band tailored such numbers for America's most popular dance since 1914: the fox-trot. Like virtually every other popular instrumental record of the period, these blues records sported labels describing them variously as "Fox Trot" or "Dance Music—Fox Trot" or simply "Dance." Some were in "Blues Tempo, For Dancing," and yet others were labeled "Fox Trot Blues" or "Blues Fox Trot," apt monikers signifying commercial hybrids that would have been incomprehensible to the public just a decade earlier. After a decade of mostly independent popularity, the blues and the fox-trot now seemed natural allies.

Turning a blues song into an instrumental dance number meant quickening the tempo and constantly shifting attention to different sections of the band for variety. It also meant introducing some of the gritty quality of a southern-style, gutbucket blues performance, with strongly rhythmic accompaniments, solo interjections between melodic phrases, and instrumental effects like growls and bent notes. "Midnight Blues" (recorded for Columbia on June 11, 1923) offers a good example of how the conversion worked. Henderson was well acquainted with this Spencer Williams tune, having accompanied Ethel Waters in its first recording some three months earlier, and Hannah Sylvester—known as "Harlem's Mae West" for her buxom figure and bawdy routines—on another recording of it just a few weeks before. The tempos are telling. The band plays the tune at about 120 beats per minute, certainly faster than Sylvester (at ca. 86 beats per minute) and Bessie Smith (at a glacial ca. 74 beats per minute), who sang the tune just four days later with Henderson at the piano.[22]

A typical recording session with a blues or popular singer involved ad hoc planning but little, if any, written music. "You didn't have written music to back singers in those days," recalled Garvin Bushell. With its straightforward blues form and semi-improvised polyphony behind the singer, the band's routine on "Midnight Blues" with Hannah Sylvester could easily have been worked up in the studio and played without much rehearsal or written music. But the band's instrumental version of "Midnight Blues" reflects more planning, writing, and rehearsal. The two-bar vamp in the introduction, for example, reappears at the end of a ten-bar transition. The heavy emphasis on beats one and four in the vamp then becomes the accompanimental rhythm for solos in the two choruses following the transition. Recycled introductory material would become a Don Redman trademark.[23]

Unison duets reveal another Redman fingerprint: melodic variation written in a soloistic style, as in chorus 4 featuring Redman (on clarinet) and Chambers (on trumpet) (ex. 3.26)

Ex. 3.26. "Midnight Blues" (June 11, 1923), Redman-Chambers duet

Redman's ideal sound here—although not fully realized on the recording—seems to have been a single brass/reed timbre resulting from perfectly blended unison playing and a melodic line that had the quality of an improvised solo. In short, the passage anticipates the style popularized by Henderson with Benny Goodman a decade later.

Whereas the duets simulate an instrumental solo, chorus 3 suggests a vocal. Although the chorus's stiff rhythmic feeling and decorous tone quality stand far from the gutbucket blues, the exchange between instruments recalls the typical format of a blues vocal chorus. Here, Redman (on alto saxophone) renders the melody in the sweet style of a popular singer while Chambers plays filler between phrases. Throughout, only trumpeter Joe Smith (not a regular band member until 1925) sounds fully at home with the material, with his startlingly fluent, expansive breaks in choruses 2 and 7 and in the transition.

Another horn player looms over Henderson's sidemen: the Memphis-born cornetist Johnny Dunn, who had popularized double-timing—marked by a sudden burst of speed—on his records since 1921. Henderson's "Gulf Coast Blues" reveals Chambers playing a double-time break in Dunn's style (ex. 3.27).[24]

Ex. 3.27. "Gulf Coast Blues" (June 7, 1923), Elmer Chambers solo, mm. 7–8; "Hawaiian Blues" (August 18, 1922), Johnny Dunn's Original Jazz Hounds, Johnny Dunn solo, mm. 7–8

"Down Hearted Blues" reveals an even more obvious source for blues playing. Bessie Smith's version of this popular blues was a bona fide hit. Recorded in February, it was released in June, between the two dates on which the Henderson band recorded the piece—in mid-May and again on June 28. Bessie Smith's approach to the melody must have made a strong impression on at least two members of the band. Smith's melody contrasts markedly with the tune on the sheet music (see ex. 3.28). Although the written melody falls from the third degree, Smith stretches the tune's range and descends from the fifth, G—a prime instance of her tendency to use a "center tone." Following her lead, an unknown tenor saxophonist and Elmer Chambers also start on the fifth, use her phrases, and, in the case of Chambers, play her version nearly note for note. (All lines are transcribed in C major, the key of Smith's recording. The sheet music is in Eb; the original key of the Henderson recording is Ab.)[25]

Ex. 3.28. Melody of "Down Hearted Blues": as published by Alberta Hunter and Lovie Austin (1923); as sung by Bessie Smith (February 15, 1923); as played by Fletcher Henderson's musicians (June 28, 1923), tenor saxophone and trumpet solos (choruses 1 and 3, respectively)

Nothing resembling these saxophone and trumpet solos appears on the earlier Henderson recording of "Down Hearted Blues," made before Smith's was released.

Howard Scott draws from another a previously recorded source in his solo on "Lonesome Journey Blues" (December 1923). The only other recording of the piece was made several months earlier by its composer and his band: Thomas Morris Past Jazz Masters. Scott's solo reveals that he had listened to Morris's recording and tried to imitate it, adhering a bit rigidly to the downward tumbling motif where even Morris himself varies the melody (ex. 3.29). Four years later, Louis Armstrong would explore a similar idea in "Gully Low Blues" and "S. O. L. Blues." It appears to have been a common approach to playing blues on high brass in the 1920s.

Ex. 3.29. "Lonesome Journey Blues." Top line: Howard Scott solo with Henderson (December 1923); bottom line: Thomas Morris Past Jazz Masters (April 1923), Morris solo

Henderson's blues repertoire reveals a fascinating clash between gutbucket and glitz that captures perfectly the uneasy but exciting position of a black dance orchestra in early 1920s New York. A dance orchestra playing blues in New York had to strike a balance between the exotic and the familiar. On the one hand, Henderson's band incorporated into its arrangements sounds that evoked the earthy music associated with southern, rural black culture. On the other hand, it always cast those elements in the comfortable context of a fox-trot. As an accompanist for blues singers and as the bandleader of a rising society orchestra, Fletcher Henderson had one foot in each world, and his band's blues playing reflected that.

In that light, Henderson's original blues composition, "Dicty Blues," is perhaps the band's most revealing work in this idiom. Once again, it shows Henderson drawing on current blues trends, for it belongs to the small group of blues tunes with chimes effects appearing around this time, such as King Oliver's "Chimes Blues," Johnny Dunn's "Four O'Clock Blues," and "Midnight Blues." Henderson initially conceived it as a piano piece called

"Chime Blues," and recorded it as such in a rare solo session in early 1923. The work offers an unusual perspective on the blues. The "dicty"—or high-class—element of the piece is the four-bar chimes break that initiates the twelve-bar blues choruses.

There is something deliberately ironic—and perhaps self-effacing—in the sound of chimes within a blues by Henderson. The piece perhaps suggests a gentle mockery toward black migration—the rural rube (blues) dressing up as an urban sophisticate (chimes). If so, the mockery was rather reflexive, for in a period when Henderson was known as "one of the best informed among contemporary 'blues' specialists," he took up residence in one of Harlem's most "dicty" neighborhoods, the exclusive stretch of West 139th Street known as "Striver's Row." Writer Carl Van Vechten even referred to Henderson by name as one of the Row's "rich negroes" in *Nigger Heaven*, his popular novel of black Harlem life published in 1926.[26]

The piece also fits perfectly within the band's aesthetic of kaleidoscopic juxtaposition, although in this case Don Redman seems to have little or nothing to do with its conception or arrangement. In the first chorus of an arrangement credited to Raymond Mathews and published by Down South (the race firm nominally headed by Henderson) the four-bar chimes break segues directly into an eight-bar passage of rambunctious ensemble heterophony a la New Orleans jazz. Again we hear the Henderson band negotiating musical tensions inside the strain. Above all, the piece may also be heard as a savvy demonstration of musical versatility: an effort to gesture toward a conventional racial marker (the blues) while undercutting it with material far outside the stereotype.

Whatever the attitude behind its conception, "Dicty Blues" was a blues carefully tailored for New York tastes. The fact that it was recorded by three different companies, including the prestigious Columbia label, suggests that record company managers considered it a potential hit. By importing the "dicty" sound of chimes into a traditional African-American idiom with a southern pedigree, Henderson lightheartedly captures the unique tensions in black Manhattan in the early 1920s, where aspiring New Negroes sought to refashion traditional cultural forms.

Hot Soloists

An arranging aesthetic that depended so much on variety and contrast required a cadre of distinctive soloists. Henderson had three key figures, each with a unique sound and style: trumpeter Howard Scott, saxophonist Coleman Hawkins, and trombonist Charlie Green.

Scott, whose work with Henderson would be all but eclipsed by the arrival of Louis Armstrong, stood out as the band's first hot trumpet. His plunger-muted style—now chattering, now growling—owed a lot to Johnny Dunn, once again, the first cornetist to use a plunger on record. One of his more striking solos occurs in the first chorus of "Lots O' Mamma." Over stoptime accompaniment, his impish sound projects an almost speech-like quality (ex. 3.30).

Henderson relied on Scott to cook up a little excitement with a solo or a lively obbligato line, but the dominant solo voice in the band belonged to Coleman Hawkins. When Hawkins joined the Henderson band in early

August 1923, he was already an imposing musical figure. Garvin Bushell recalled his first encounter with Hawkins in Kansas City in 1921: "He was outstanding, ahead of anything I'd ever heard. He read everything at sight without any mistakes; his sight reading and musicianship was faultless even at that young age."[27]

Ex. 3.30. "Lots O' Mamma," Howard Scott solo (with trombone line of stoptime chords), mm. 1–4

Hawkins brought his big sound and his flair for the dramatic to the Henderson band, and the bandleader and his chief arranger made sure he was heard. His first extended solos appear on recordings of Henderson's "Dicty Blues" and "Do Doodle Oom." Hawkins's solos stand out as the expression of the strongest single voice on the records. Each of the solos features the traits of Hawkins's early style that Schuller has identified so precisely: the wide range; the clipped, slap-tongue articulation; the "harmonic" rather than "linear/melodic" choice of notes; the rhythmic "stiffness"; the "forceful attack"; and the full-bodied tone and "dynamic energy."[28]

Although recorded within two months of one another, the "Dicty Blues" solos are notably dissimilar. Even the two Vocalion takes, with nearly identical beginnings and endings, are almost entirely different in their middle eight bars. The first Vocalion solo (ex. 3.31) has a distinctively undulant contour. About every four measures Hawkins reaches a stressed high pitch, a melodic peak, balanced by regular dips down to low E♭. Hawkins connects the peaks and valleys with the bald arpeggios that characterize many of his early solos. In short, he is "running the changes"—as jazz musicians describe playing the chords unimaginatively—while showing a sense of musical drama.

Today, such a solo may seem to have the drama of a seesaw. But in 1923, a solo imparted excitement less through ingenious melodic nuance than through more overt qualities like a distinctive tone and incessant rhythmic activity, two traits that were surely the most appealing qualities of Howard Scott's style as well.

Meanwhile, Hawkins was occasionally out-of-sync harmonically with the band. A few details can serve to explain this to a listener with access to the recordings. On the downbeat of the last full measure of the Columbia solo, for example, Hawkins lands hard on the fourth degree, making for a dissonance with his accompaniment's tonic chord. In the Ajax solo, the discrepancy is more obvious and systematic. For six measures (mm. 3–8), Hawkins is two beats ahead of the band. He finally realigns himself in

m. 9 by holding onto a G for four-and-a-half beats. The most telling moments lie in the way he outlines the subdominant (over tonic harmony) beginning in the middle of m. 4, and how he returns late to the tonic (with his arrival on the E♭) in the middle of m. 7. The solo features an unusually high number of long tones (in mm. 3, 5, 6, 7, 8, and 9), almost as if Hawkins senses he has strayed and is trying to find a way to get back on track. Nevertheless, taken together, the Columbia and Ajax solos reveal that Hawkins, at nineteen, was already a commanding figure. The force and breadth of his tone more than compensated for some harmonic insecurity, which in 1923 either passed unnoticed or was not considered a bad enough transgression to spoil a take.

Ex. 3.31. "Dicty Blues" (Vocalion, August 9, 1923), Coleman Hawkins solo

At about the same time the band began playing at the Roseland Ballroom, Henderson acquired a new trombonist, Charlie Green. "Big Green," as Rex Stewart referred to him (see chap. 2), could play with a sound as broad and raucous as his behavior. Although usually celebrated as one of the first hot jazz trombone players, Green made a mark in his first few recordings with the band as a versatile player. On sweet popular song arrangements and hot dance numbers, he could play a melody as clearly and straight as Teddy Nixon, whom he replaced. On blues tunes and other slower numbers, he exhibits a roaring, gritty style. Frequently, he tears off a startling hot break that soars above most of his fellow band members. The highlight of Green's first six weeks in the band was a mammoth solo that forms the centerpiece of "The Gouge of Armour Avenue."

Over a shuffling F-minor vamp, Green constructs a heaving, monstrous rhapsody coarsened by growls and smears (ex. 3.32). Much of the solo's expressive tension arises from Green's blues-drenched blurring of C (the 5th degree) and B (the flatted 5th), which exerts a strong pull to the tonic. The force of his tone against a mute adds to the palpable strain. Although he remains within a fifth in the beginning, Green leaps to the top of his range in m. 8 and closes (m. 27) in the murky low register, ultimately encompassing an ample two-and-a-half octaves. Rhythmically, Green continually loosens himself from the tug of the beat and bar-line, anticipating the freedom that Louis Armstrong would bring to the band two months later. Indeed, the solo stands out as one of the most remarkable passages among the dozens of recordings by the pre-Armstrong Henderson band, and several other musicians would echo it into the 1930s.[29]

Ex. 3.32. "The Gouge of Armour Avenue" (July 31, 1924), Charlie Green solo

"If Fletcher was a white man"

Henderson never again made so many recordings in such a short time as he did in the eighteen-month period leading up to the arrival of Armstrong, who made his first records with Henderson on October 7, 1924. Heard collectively, they reveal that even before Armstrong came along, Henderson's band was a formidable musical force, thanks to the bandleader's ability to assemble top talent; his band members' ability to absorb the coexisting— and sometimes conflicting—currents of New York's blues, jazz, novelty, Tin Pan Alley, and Broadway worlds; and his chief arranger's creative impetus to take a wide range of musical material and give it a distinctive style. Heard in the contexts of the emerging "modern dance orchestra," of black musical professionalism, of record companies, radio, and venues, the band also stands out as a unique symbol of black achievement in the early years of the Harlem Renaissance. Henderson may have been the "Paul Whiteman of the Race," but he and his band were no mere imitators, and they held a unique, solid, and prominent professional position in 1923–24. That it could never be as prominent as that of Paul Whiteman himself, however, is poignantly suggested by Howard Scott, whose words may serve as a final caveat and somber punchline: "Paul Whiteman came himself to hear Fletcher's band, and he said if Fletcher was a white man, he would be a millionaire. That's just what he said. I heard him."[30]

4

A New Orleans Trumpeter in a New York Band

H E WAS BIG AND FAT, AND WORE HIGH TOP SHOES with hooks in them and long underwear down to his socks. When I got a load of that, I said to myself, who in the hell is this guy? It can't be Louis Armstrong. But when he got on the bandstand, it was a different story."[1] Don Redman's recollection of his first encounter with Louis Armstrong offers a vivid image of the twenty-three-year-old trumpet player. It also projects the self-image of Henderson's band in 1924, in which sartorial dash paired with polished music making to create a sophisticated aura. Armstrong's rube-like appearance clashed with the band's urbanity, and it took some time for the young trumpet player from New Orleans via Chicago to be accepted into the New York band. Storyville had met Striver's Row and found little common ground. In Armstrong's first rehearsal with Henderson, the band was playing through "an intricate, well-marked arrangement" (either a "medley of Irish waltzes" or the sentimental ballad "By the Waters of Minnetonka," depending on the source), and, as Henderson told it:

> One passage began triple fortissimo, and then it suddenly softened down on the next passage to double pianissimo. The score was properly marked "pp" to indicate the pianissimo, but when everybody else softened down, there was Louis, still blowing as hard as he could. I stopped the band, and told him—pretty sharply, I guess—that in this band we read the marks as well as the notes. I asked him if he could read the marks and he said he could. But then I asked him: "What about 'pp'?" and he answered, "Why, it means *pound plenty*!"[2]

On the surface, the story shows that Armstrong struggled with music reading, a point some historians have emphasized. Kaiser Marshall, however, recalled that Armstrong was already "a good reader" by the time he joined the band. He *did* know what "pp" meant, so his comment was not made in ignorance but in humor—as an attempt to break up the tension that Henderson created by pointing out the mistake. Nevertheless, upon his arrival in New York, Armstrong neither looked the part—nor quite played the part—of a downtown dance musician. The disparity between Armstrong and the rest of the band, at first an apparent liability, became a rich source of creative tension, ultimately pitting Redman's arranging concept against the solo improvisational approach that Armstrong presented. Redman claimed that, "Louis, his style, and his feeling, changed our whole idea about the band musically." Redman's statement sums up the standard interpretation, which involves tracing how Armstrong changed Henderson's band—but there is more to it than that.[3]

No doubt Armstrong's brief but influential tenure in Fletcher Henderson's band in the mid-1920s forms a crucial moment in the history of jazz. It started on the bandstand. Howard Scott, sitting next to Armstrong in the trumpet section, watched the reaction of listeners and dancers:

> Louis played that opening night at Roseland, and my goodness, people stopped dancing to come around and listen to him. . . . And they could hear him out on the street . . . we were told that there were some people passing by that stopped, listening to him. He was so loud. . . . The next night you couldn't get into the place. Just that quick. It had gone all around about this new trumpet player at Roseland.[4]

As the story continues, Armstrong transformed the Henderson band from a dance orchestra to a jazz band, and he began to transform jazz, as a whole, from an ensemble practice to a solo art. For critics, Armstrong saved Henderson from becoming the "wrong" kind of black band and for redirecting the band—and jazz itself—from the Whiteman (and "white") arranging paradigm to the Armstrong (and "black") improvisational paradigm. Amiri Baraka, in his seminal work of social and musical criticism, *Blues People*, argued that Armstrong's arrival in New York in late 1924 "is more than a historical event . . . it may be seen as a musical and sociocultural event of the highest significance" because Armstrong "moved jazz into another era: the ascendancy of the soloist began." Gunther Schuller's *Early Jazz*, after chapters on "Origins" and "Beginnings," continues with a full chapter on Armstrong, titled "The First Great Soloist."[5]

Like Beethoven in the history of European concert music, Armstrong created the conditions for the interpretation of jazz history, and that has affected the way Henderson's band has been heard during his tenure in New York. The Great Man narrative has taken hold: Armstrong emerges as an extraordinary artist transcending an ordinary musical context, and there is enough truth in it to allow for a consensus on the issue in jazz historiography and criticism. Everyone seems to agree: on one hand, Armstrong sounds powerful, vivid, and modern; on the other hand, the rest of Henderson's band sounds impossibly passé. Henderson's musicians, next to Armstrong, "appear painfully dated and about as hot as yesterday's dishwater." For others, Armstrong's solos "shine like a solitary star in the sky at night" and "come from a different world," and Armstrong himself "exists within his own musical universe."[6]

Yet there is a substantial amount missing from that interpretation. Who had set up the conditions for this "aural shift," as Schuller has called Armstrong's effect, but Don Redman himself, with his conception of an arrangement as a succession of contrasts? What better place to stand out than in an arranging concept that already stressed surprise, variety, and kaleidoscopic changes of color and texture?[7]

The Great Man interpretation also fails to take into account the Henderson band's reception in the black press, where arranged, not improvised, jazz appeared to be the means to attain a higher cultural standing, as shown in chapter 2. Henderson and his sidemen were praised because they quietly challenged the primitivist stereotype. They challenged it not with hot solos but with their refined image, reading ability, difficult arrangements, and prestigious jobs. If Armstrong later became the first hero of jazz history, he was clearly not a Renaissance man. Indeed, Locke's *New Negro* makes no mention of Louis Armstrong.

Finally, the Great Man approach has obscured another key point. At most, Armstrong's powerful presence accelerated a process that had already begun. Each new reed and brass player that Henderson hired since 1923 gave a new jazz voice to the band: Coleman Hawkins (August 1923), Howard Scott (November 1923), Charlie Green (July 1924), Armstrong and clarinetist Buster Bailey (October 1924), and, soon thereafter, the smooth-toned trumpeter Joe Smith (April 1925). These additions had a cumulative effect: by mid-1925 musicians who could play "hot" dominated the brass and reed sections. Behind them stood a rhythm section (Henderson, Dixon, Marshall, and Escudero) that had crystallized into a unified group after more than a year of active public performing and recording. No wonder the whole ensemble brought a new sense of drive to its expert reading of arrangements.

An added stimulus came from outside the band. Changes in songwriting and publication play a significant, though underestimated, role in stoking how bands played. By 1923 the Melrose Brothers Music Co. in Chicago, for example, had begun to inspire jazz-based songwriting, with pieces by such jazz musicians as Ferdinand "Jelly Roll" Morton. The publishing equivalent of "race records," Melrose billed itself as "the House that Blues Built" with the "World's Greatest Collection of Blues-Stomps and Rags." It launched a "syncopation series" in 1923, and two of its publications served as the basis for the most frequently mentioned Henderson record-ings made during the Armstrong year: "Copenhagen" and "Sugar Foot Stomp." Meanwhile, the Gershwin musical *Lady Be Good!*, which opened in New York barely two months after Armstrong's arrival, drove a nail in the coffin of operetta and moved Broadway toward more rhythmic, jazz-inflected scores. About the same time, in the November 12, 1924, edition of *Variety*, columnist Abel Green noted that "the current disk recording vogue in dance numbers is for the 'hot' order." Henderson, whom Allen suggests made "a conscious effort to maintain good relations with the music publishers," stayed abreast of these trends in songwriting and sheet-music publication. Something had changed in those domains, and the Great Man theory alone cannot explain it.[8]

Links between style and repertory explain something else about Henderson's "Armstrong year." What may seem like an unwonted variety in performing styles is better understood as a consistent approach to repertory. The band's style depended on the piece. Armstrong's solos "cause the listener to make an aural shift," as Schuller has written, partly because Armstrong made no such adaptation. Hired as the band's chief hot soloist, he approached every piece as raw material for hot improvisation.[9]

Tuning our ears to the 1920s, then, we hear Armstrong not as a "solitary star" in the night sky but as a strong streak of color in a crazy quilt. That is the only way to hear the band's rendition of a new popular song called "Words," for example. The arrangement, recorded on October 30, 1924, pits symphonic gestures against hot jazz in the spirit of Paul Whiteman's "Experiment in Modern Music" earlier that year. Introductions, interludes, and endings invited the most elaborate symphonic effects. For example, the arrangement opens with a heraldic fanfare worthy of a concert overture—or is it a parody of such a piece? Modulating interludes further cast a formal air on the whole score. The brief but dramatic coda intercepts the melody and accents a device that Redman used frequently in 1924–25: secondary rag, a rhythmic effect that superimposes a repeated three-beat pattern over a four-beat meter, so that the pattern begins on a different beat in each reiteration (ex. 4.1).

Ex. 4.1. "Words" (October 30, 1924), ending

The "Words" arrangement reveals its contradictions most clearly in its trumpet solos. Howard Scott's style stays faithful to the arrangement's classical resonance, with its clean, precise articulation, downbeat emphasis, and crisp dotted rhythms. In contrast, Armstrong charges into the scene like a bull in a china shop, with a strikingly different style of tonguing, articulation, and rhythmic conception soon familiar as "swing." In later years, as Armstrong scholar Brian Harker has pointed out, Scott's style of playing would be dismissed as "ricky-tick," a kind of "stylistic obtuseness" unworthy of Armstrong. Heard from a 1920s perspective, however, the contrast between Scott and Armstrong reveals a cultural fault line in the band. On one hand, the band understandably continued to strive for the kind of musical legitimacy prized in its Renaissance milieu; on the other hand, it struggled to embrace the new exciting sounds emerging from Armstrong's horn.[10]

Contrasts of a different sort emerge in "Go 'Long Mule," from Armstrong's first recording session with Henderson. The piece dramatizes the "stylistic tug-of-war" among the band members and the material. Committed to the Great Man narrative (which made strategic sense in the early years of jazz scholarship), Gunther Schuller implies that the tug-of-war is unintentional, an inevitable outcome of a disparity between Armstrong's advanced improvisational style and the band's backward sensibility. Actually, the backwardness resides entirely in the song itself, which harks back to minstrelsy, with dialect lyrics (omitted by Henderson's band), simple harmony, and small-range melody. The archaic style invites a generous helping of parodistic novelty: animal imitations, a solo on a saxophone mouthpiece, and a "doo-wacka" brass trio. These "deliberately banal figures" frame Armstrong's solo and make it "wholly out of keeping with the comic tone of the rest of the piece."[11]

Indeed, Redman plays up the contrast by giving Armstrong a spare accompaniment, setting a precedent for the entire Armstrong year. That accompaniment had a name: "western" style. Trumpeter Louis Metcalf recalled that "the controversy about the two different styles of playing, Eastern and Western, came to a head when Louis Armstrong joined Fletcher Henderson." Rex Stewart describes "western style" in his memoir *Boy Meets Horn*, as "a heavy accented back beat on the second and fourth bars. When you soloed, it was called 'taking a Boston.'" He also emphasizes that, "about 1923," very few New York musicians soloed in this manner because it had only just begun to come east through Oliver and Armstrong. Although Stewart does not explain why the name of an eastern city denoted a solo backed by a "western" style accompaniment, the essence of his description—an accented backbeat—sums up the kind of support Armstrong enjoyed as Henderson's chief hot soloist. We can hear that kind of accompaniment behind a few solos in the band's pre-Armstrong period, but once Armstrong came on board, it was reserved almost exclusively for him. In "Go 'Long Mule," the "western" style accompaniment helps Armstrong stand apart from the rest of the band.[12]

More than that, however, the band streamlines the song's already simple harmonic foundation further to stress Armstrong's difference. The modified harmony comes from a language Armstrong knew well: the last eight bars of the twelve-bar blues (see fig. 4.1).

Fig. 4.1. "Go 'Long Mule," showing modified harmony under Armstrong's solo

Original harmony:	[: Ab	Ab	Eb	Eb	Ab7–Eb	Ab7–Eb	Bb7	Eb :]
Modified harmony:	[: as above			Bb		Bb		Eb	Eb :]

With another soloist, the western style accompaniment and altered chords might have created little distinction from the surrounding musical context, but here they frame a spectacular solo—an early instance of the new coherence Armstrong brought to solo improvisation.[13] In other words, beyond the considerable surface appeal of his sheer power and range, Armstrong also built solos that make melodic sense, that "tell a story," to use a common metaphor for jazz improvisation after Armstrong. Armstrong's solo can be said to tell a story because it features the elements that all storytellers need: statement, contrast, development, climax, and return (ex. 4.2).

Ex. 4.2. "Go 'Long Mule" (October 7, 1924), Armstrong solo and original melody

To carry the metaphor further, Armstrong uses two basic melodic figures, or "characters," in his story: a syncopated figure (emphasizing upbeats) and an unsyncopated figure (emphasizing downbeats). The figures tend to appear in pairs that form larger phrases: the syncopated figure in even-numbered measures (for example, the pickup and mm. 4, 6, 12), and the unsyncopated figure in odd-numbered measures (for example, mm. 1, 3, 5, 9). By pairing them in this way, Armstrong creates a dialogic effect that usually demands at least two players; that is, he creates call-and-response. The climax appears just before the midpoint in the two-bar arpeggiated break of measures 7–8, with its peak on a high G. The climactic break features another crucial pitch: D♭ (m. 8). With that pitch, Armstrong creates a strong harmonic thrust toward the second half of the solo. In musical terms, he tonicizes the subdominant, so that musical material that repeats in the original song now sounds like a logical continuation of the story, rather than a rehash. The two figures, in various guises, continue their call-and-response dialogue to the denouement in the last five measures, where the syncopated figure takes over for two consecutive bars (mm. 12–13), creating unprecedented tension before the final resolution in the solo's last note, which brings the listener full circle back to the note (E♭) with which Armstrong began. Given two consecutive eight-bar refrains, Armstrong effectively constructs a continuous sixteen-bar statement dramatized by dialogue between two contrasting musical figures. He has told a short story in music. "He was backin' up everything I had been trying to tell," said Louis Metcalf, "only *he* made them understand."[14]

Don Redman understood. In "Go 'Long Mule," we catch a glimpse of how he began to cope with Armstrong's impact. The whole arrangement derives from a heavily doctored stock (fig. 4.2).

Redman restructures the piece by (1) omitting its vamp, (2) using the verse as a bridge, to create a thirty-two bar AABA song form in the arrangement's first section, (3) making sixteen-bar strains by repeating the eight-bar chorus, (4) emphasizing color changes and novelty, including breaks, and, as we've seen, (5) streamlining the harmony for Armstrong's solo. In short, Redman's changes emphasize both contrast and continuity. They also create an effect that will become a Redman trademark: formal symmetry. The hot solos of Charlie Green and Louis Armstrong stand like two pillars framing the arrangement's novelty centerpiece, the C-minor trio (labeled C in the diagram). There, in contrast to the uneventful stock, the regular pulse shifts to stoptime and the soloists (first a clarinet then a bass saxophone) volley two-bar phrases with the brass section. In sum, Redman's tendencies toward variety, contrast, novelty, and parody remain in tact, but he also reveals an

Fig. 4.2. "Go 'Long Mule"

Stock (Mornay D. Helm)	Henderson recording
(key of E♭ / C minor)	(key of E♭ / C minor)
Moderato	♩ = ca. 224
Introduction and vamp (6 bars)	Introduction (4 bars)
B (Verse) (8)	A saxes (16)
A (Chorus) (8)	B ens. (8)
Vamp (2)	A ens. (8)
C (Trio)[:8:]	B ens. (8)
B(8)	A tbn. solo (Green) with "western style"
A(8)	accomp. (16), tpt. break (1)
	C clar. and brass, stoptime (8)
	C bass sax and brass, stoptime (8)
	B ens. (8)
	A' tpt. solo (Armstrong) with "western style"
	accomp. (14), mouthpiece break (2)
	A sax mouthpiece/clar. melody (16)
	A' muted tpts. (16)
	A clars. (16)
	A ens. (16 + 1)

interest in unifying them. Armstrong's presence actually serves to enhance Redman's goals.

The clarinets that play "Go 'Long Mule"'s penultimate strain point to another change in the band. As Redman worked to channel Armstrong into his arranging concept, a new clarinetist with both improvising experience and reading skills also started redirecting Redman's arranging focus and helping to push the band toward a more jazz-oriented ensemble style. William "Buster" Bailey, a Memphis native whose first exposure to New Orleans jazz came in 1917, brought a polished technique nurtured under Chicago Symphony clarinetist Franz Schoepp—the same "strict German disciplinarian" who taught Jimmy Noone and Benny Goodman in the early 1920s. Armstrong himself had lobbied for Bailey: the two had played together in King Oliver's Creole Jazz Band in Chicago. But after unsuccessful bids for two other musicians (Vance Dixon and Milt Senior), Henderson acquired Bailey and the band had its first capable hot clarinetist. Now when the band needed a clarinet solo, Bailey's fluent cascades of notes, wide range, and full though sometimes shrill tone stood far above Redman's clarinet hokum and relieved Hawkins of a soloing duty he had not relished. Bailey's solos bring a graceful ease and blues feeling to the band's reed playing (ex. 4.3).

Ex. 4.3. "Money Blues" (May 19, 1925), Buster Bailey solo

Bailey's experience in New Orleans small-group improvisation also enabled him to assume one of the roles that Howard Scott had filled in the previous year—playing a free-ranging obbligato over the ensemble during out-choruses.

One further contribution eclipses all others in its novelty appeal and therefore the attention it has received from historians: Bailey's arrival gave the band a third reed and thus sparked Redman's development of the clarinet trio as another arranging trademark. At first, Redman and Hawkins had not wanted anyone new; they had already worked out so much intricate material for their two-man reed section. Soon, however, Redman realized what an asset he had and exploited it. Although Redman had already used clarinets as an alternative reed section, Bailey's presence spurred him to use them more regularly. In fact, in the Armstrong year, half of Henderson's recordings feature the clarinet trio.

Now with Bailey, who doubled on alto saxophone, the band's saxophone section—the "string section" of any "jazz orchestra," according to Paul

Whiteman—also became a fully independent entity able to play complete triads. The group soon developed an ability to sustain the drive and swing of a jazz performance while keeping the united, polished phrasing it had already demonstrated. Any account of changes in Redman's arranging style after Armstrong came along must also include Bailey's impact on the reed section.

"Copenhagen" gives us a vivid image of all of the forces driving the Henderson band's rapidly changing style. With its inclusion on the Smithsonian's *Big Band Jazz* anthology and a detailed discussion by Schuller in *Early Jazz*, "Copenhagen" has taken on canonical status in jazz history. But perhaps it has won that status for the wrong reasons. "Copenhagen," in Schuller's view, forges a key link between Armstrong's solo aesthetic and Redman's arranging style and represents Redman's "brilliant realization" of a bridge between the competing claims of New Orleans and New York jazz. To clinch the case for "Copenhagen" as a crucial moment in the evolution of jazz, Schuller pushes several dozen other Henderson recordings into evolutionary oblivion. "[An understanding of] how exceptional 'Copenhagen' was can be gained from the fact that all other late 1924 and early 1925 Henderson recordings . . . seldom rose above the level of stock arrangements."[15]

By now it should come as no surprise that Henderson's "Copenhagen" also drew heavily from a stock arrangement. Redman's "brilliant realization" amounts to creative stock doctoring with inside-the-strain juxtapositions and an Armstrong solo intended to stand out from the surrounding musical landscape. And, thanks to the availability of an alternate take (a second recording of the same arrangement on the same day), we can hear clearly that by the time they entered the recording studio, Fletcher Henderson's musicians—including Armstrong—played "Copenhagen" almost as if each note were etched in stone, or at least written in score. Although improvisatory in spirit, the lively, loose-limbed jazz classic "Copenhagen" features virtually no improvisation.

How can we account for that apparent anomaly, when the spirit and definition of jazz seem so dependent on improvisation? One answer lies in the hegemony of a bebop aesthetic emphasizing improvisation and swing rhythm in a way that has eclipsed all the messy contradictions inherent in the musics labeled "jazz" in the 1920s. Another answer lies in the particular circumstances leading to "Copenhagen"'s arrival on Henderson's bandstand in late 1924. Unlike the Tin Pan Alley repertoire the band continued to play, "Copenhagen" had roots in the more raucous, freewheeling midwest jazz scene: specifically, in a performance by the Charlie Davis Orchestra in Indianapolis; in a recording inspired by that performance by the Wolverines Orchestra made in Richmond, Indiana, for Gennett Records; and in a stock arrangement based on the recording and published in Chicago by the Melrose Brothers Music Company.

So "Copenhagen" had a hot jazz pedigree before Redman and Armstrong got their hands on it, and the Melrose Brothers advertised the fact on the stock's cover page:

> this arrangement is RED HOT as written. Play what you see and the horns will start smoking. Take it from us as publishers of the "World's Greatest Collection of Blues-Stomps and Rags"—COPENHAGEN is red hot and then some!

The page also highlights a link to the Wolverines' recording, revealing a tight business connection between the publisher and the fledgling Gennett label, where many early jazz musicians had already made some of their first recordings:

> A study of the recording made by the Wolverine Orchestra (Gennett Record No. 5453) will give a clear idea of the many effects obtainable that cannot be indicated in black and white.

A habitual stock doctor, Redman could not allow the Henderson band simply to play "Copenhagen" as Melrose published it, no matter how "red hot" it appeared to be "as written." Figure 4.3 shows how much of the structure and solos of the Wolverines's recording found their way into the Melrose stock arrangement, and how Redman then rearranged the stock for Henderson's band within a month of its publication.

How can we know that Redman used the stock and not the Wolverines recording as his model, and why does it matter? Schuller's focus on recordings leads him to the conclusion that Redman's arrangement "reveals some parallels" to the Wolverines version. Indeed it does, but Schuller's analysis, like much early jazz criticism, omits the mediation of published music in the process of transmission and therefore underestimates the importance Henderson placed on reading music. We can see and hear that in two particularly revealing passages identified in the diagram as the first "B" strain and

Fig. 4.3. "Copenhagen"

Wolverines	Stock	Henderson
May 6, 1924	©October 1, 1924	October 30, 1924
A(16) ens.	A(16) ens.	C(16) brass (4)
		ens. (4)
		clars. (4)
		ens. (4)
B(12) clar. solo	B(12) clar. solo	[:B12:] clars.
B(12) tenor sax solo	B(12) tenor sax solo	B(12) tpt. solo
A(16) ens.	A(16) ens.	A(16) ens.
D(16) cor. solo (8)	D(16) cor. solo	D(16) tpt. trio
ens. (8)		
C(16) brass/reeds (4)	C(16) brass/reeds (4)	C(16) clars. (4)
ens. (4)	ens. (4)	brass (4)
brass/reeds (4)	brass/reeds (4)	saxes (4)
ens. (4)	ens. (4)	brass (4)
[:E12:] tuba (4)	[:E12:] bass (4)	[:E12:] tbn. (4)
ens. (8)	ens. (8)	ens. (8)
D(16) ens.	F(16) ens.	F(16) clar./brass
C(10) ens.	C(10) ens.	C(7) brass/reeds (4)
		ens. (3)
		Coda (14) brass (4) [A]
		clars. (4) [C]
		ens. (2) [A/C]
		ens. (4) [C]

the "F" strain. The "F" strain, a syncopated full-ensemble passage did not appear in the Wolverines version. It only appears in the stock (ex. 4.4) and in other recordings based on it such as Henderson's.

Ex. 4.4. "Copenhagen" (October 30, 1924), "F" strain

Even more telling is the first "B" strain (ex. 4.5). Here, the Wolverines feature a clarinet solo in E♭, and the stock arrangement alters it slightly and transposes it to B♭. From there, Redman takes the stock's version of the clarinet solo and harmonizes it in block voicing for his clarinet trio: Bailey, Hawkins, and himself. Clearly, Redman has adapted the printed version, not the earlier recorded version. Significantly, the trio gets a western style accompaniment, with just a light backbeat tick from Marshall, as if he were supporting a hot solo.

Ex. 4.5. "Copenhagen." Top line: clarinet solo by Jimmy Hartwell on Wolverines recording (May 6, 1924); middle line: clarinet solo from stock arrangement; bottom line: clarinet trio on Henderson recording (October 30, 1924)

To make room for Armstrong, Redman transfers the stock's tenor saxophone solo (the other "B" section) to him. What did the proud Coleman Hawkins, Henderson's tenor star, think of that? We'll never know, but it was a reasonable choice. The "B" section is a twelve-bar blues, and despite his exhibition on "Dicty Blues" a year earlier, Hawkins was not a fluent blues interpreter. Armstrong was, and the results are powerful. Armstrong once again delivers an authoritative solo with an audible "storyline" (ex. 4.6).

Ex. 4.6. "Copenhagen," Armstrong solo on matrix 13929, with numbers showing where the alternate take (matrix 13928) differs

① Note is B♭"
② Rhythm is 𝅘𝅥 𝅘𝅥𝅮𝅘𝅥𝅮 𝅘𝅥 𝅘𝅥
⑩ Note is D♭"

Like a singer, Armstrong parses this blues into three four-bar phrases. And, as in a blues vocal, the first two phrases begin similarly, with a five-note figure (cf. the pickup and m. 1, and mm. 4–5), and the last phrase begins with a climactic contrast (mm. 8–9). Armstrong further shapes his solo into a coherent, story-like statement by creating three types of figures in each phrase: a two-part call-and-response pattern followed by a brief tag. Each figure lasts two measures or less and typically straddles the barline. The final phrase provides a final summing up, encompassing the solo's entire almost two-octave range. The whole thing sounds improvised, but by the time he recorded it, at least, Armstrong had set the solo as firmly as if he had written it down. The alternate take reveals that Armstrong made only three slight changes in pitch or rhythm to his original effort (see footnotes 1, 2, and 3 in ex. 4.6). When Armstrong played the solo in public, it struck listeners as new and unusual. Louis Metcalf recalled a midnight show at Harlem's Apollo Theater featuring Armstrong with Henderson's band. "The first number they played was 'Copenhagen.' And Louis' solo was *so* good. But different, and the audience didn't know about how much to applaud."[16]

Part of the reason Armstrong sounded "different" was the contrasting sound coming from the horn of the man who replaced Howard Scott in April 1925: Joe Smith. Joe was the youngest of three trumpet-playing Smith brothers—including Russell and Luke—from Ripley, Ohio, all of whom played in Henderson's band. Born in 1902 (and thus a year younger than Armstrong), he had initially joined Henderson briefly on tour with Ethel Waters and the Black Swan Troubadours in February 1922. Back in New York a few months later, he played in dance and theater orchestras and with blues singers such as Mamie Smith (no relation) before rejoining Henderson in 1925. Joe Smith's place in the band had probably been cleared by Fletcher's wife Leora, who seems to have been particularly involved with the fortunes of the trumpet section and has been generally underestimated as a force in Henderson's career. In her recollections published in Shapiro and Hentoff's *Hear Me Talkin' to Ya*, Leora gives particular attention to her memories of Joe, whom she called "Toots" and knew "before he could even play trumpet." She reserved special praise for Joe's "big soft beautiful tone." Joe seems to have served as a kind of surrogate younger brother for Leora. Before marrying Henderson, after all, she had been the wife of Joe's eldest brother, Russell, who would replace Armstrong in late 1925 and serve as Henderson's lead trumpet player well into the 1930s. Coleman Hawkins, who also had classical training, also appreciated Joe, "a very sensitive player" with a "very pretty tone." Unlike Armstrong, Smith "played quiet," as Hawkins put it. Louis Metcalf summed up the difference this way: "Louis represented the Western style of jazz, while Joe Smith was the Eastern." Even at the end of 1925, just before Armstrong's return to Chicago, *Variety* reported "a considerable discussion among colored musicians as to who ranks the highest in the east as cornetists. It is claimed by many that the best two are Joe Smith and Louis Armstrong." Bessie Smith (no relation) sang with both, but she preferred Joe's modest clarity to Armstrong's boldness. "Bessie Smith was just crazy about his playing," recalled Leora. Henderson himself called Joe Smith "the most soulful trumpeter I ever knew."[17]

No wonder, then, that soon after he joined Henderson, Joe Smith earned some prominent solo spots, most notably in a new tune called "What-Cha-Call-'Em Blues." Here again, the band plays an adapted stock, this time by Elmer Schoebel, a "key figure" in 1920s jazz. A white pianist, composer, and arranger, Schoebel was a talented and versatile musician who collaborated as songwriter on tunes that became early jazz standards (such as "Farewell Blues," "Bugle Call Rag," and "Nobody's Sweetheart") and had led the Chicago-based New Orleans Rhythm Kings in a manner similar to the way Henderson and Redman ran their own band: with discipline and an effort to balance crisp arrangements and improvised solos.[18]

Predictably, Redman's adaptation of the stock features an entirely new introduction featuring call-and-response between saxophones and brass, a passage played with startling combination of ensemble precision and relaxation rarely heard from the band before now. The saxophones' bluesy, fading glissando break in mm. 7–8 stands out as a perfectly unified effect (see ex. 4.7), echoing a similar break the clarinet trio had featured in "Copenhagen."

Ex. 4.7. "What-Cha-Call-'Em Blues" (May 29, 1925), introduction

Smith then enters with a syncopated, Armstrong-like pickup, but his solo's bell-like clarity immediately sets him apart from the band's star. The solo sets the mood of relaxed energy that pervades the entire recording. Yet Smith is not improvising here, nor would he have been expected to in the first chorus, where arranging convention calls for unadorned melody. Smith paraphrases the melody, embellishing here and there with syncopations and neighbor notes but largely respecting the pitches and overall contour as printed in the stock (ex. 4.8).

Ex. 4.8. "What-Cha-Call-'Em Blues." Top line: trumpet solo in second chorus of stock arrangement (Elmer Schoebel, 1925). Bottom line: Joe Smith solo on Henderson recording.

The recording's most remarkable quality lies not in solos, however, but in the way the entire ensemble imparts a loose-limbed improvisatory quality to written music. The performance did not even require an Armstrong solo. But like "Copenhagen," "What-Cha-Call-'Em Blues" had come to Henderson's band with jazz credentials; and this time it did not come from Chicago but from much closer to Henderson's home base at the Roseland Ballroom. Indeed, the piece was published by Triangle Music Publishing Company, housed inside the Roseland Building itself. To get this piece, Henderson didn't even have to leave the building.

"Sugar Foot Stomp" came from an even more proximate source: Armstrong. Originally titled "Dipper Mouth Blues," it had been written by him and King Oliver in 1923 and recorded twice by Oliver's band. Don Redman's story of the tune's transmission is well known among jazz musicians and historians. It has the attraction of offering a direct link between New Orleans and New York jazz without mediation by the commercial publishing industry in which most of Henderson's repertoire was steeped:

> [Armstrong] showed a little book of manuscripts, some melodies that he and the famous King Oliver had written in Chicago.... He asked me, "Just pick out one you may like and make an arrangement for Fletcher's orchestra." So I did and the one I picked out was "Sugar Foot Stomp."[19]

The piece would become a keystone in the swing era repertoire, with recordings by Benny Goodman (in Henderson's revision of Redman's 1925 arrangement), Artie Shaw, Glenn Miller, and Chick Webb, among others. Beginning with Armstrong in Henderson's band, a tradition developed in which trumpet players imitated or paraphrased King Oliver's famous solo on "Dipper Mouth Blues." In Redman's words, "['Sugar Foot Stomp'] was the record that made Fletcher Henderson nationally known." It ranked among the best-selling records of late 1925. Henderson himself later referred to it as his favorite recording among the hundreds he had made as a bandleader.[20]

Gunther Schuller, however, would have none of it. "The whole association with Oliver's 'Dipper Mouth Blues,' the fact that Armstrong is supposed to have brought the music with him from Chicago, is the kind of 'legendary' material jazz writers have frequently pounced upon in lieu of criteria based on musical analysis." Cutting through the crust of legend, Schuller went back to the source and pronounced Henderson's recording of it to be of "very mixed quality." Schuller holds that "Redman is responsible for the negative elements.... The shrill and badly played clarinet-trio choruses and the later sustained 'symphonic' sections are out of place next to the solos or semi-improvised passages." The passages certainly stand out to any listener who knows Oliver's original "Dipper Mouth Blues," where ensemble polyphony is the textural norm, even in Oliver's famous "solo," around which the clarinet and trombone weave independent lines. Perhaps we can hear the "problem" passages differently, however, with ears more finely tuned to Redman's tendencies in the early 1920s. Indeed, in light of the willful variety in his pre-Armstrong arrangements, the anomaly of the clarinet trio and the "sustained 'symphonic' sections" seem precisely to the point: the more contrast they provided, the better they fulfilled Redman's aims. The "mixed quality" of the arrangement is more aptly heard as deliberately mixed styles.[21]

A closer look at those "sustained 'symphonic' sections" gives a clue to what Redman was up to. The first of them directly follows the vaudevillian vocal break, "oh play that thing!" borrowed from Oliver's version. In the Oliver recording, the break flows directly into a boisterous New Orleans-style out-chorus, all musicians blowing independent lines in harmonious counterpoint. In the Henderson recording, however, the break leads to the enriched blues chords that Schuller calls "symphonic." Another scholar has argued that, far from "symphonic," the sustained chords actually serve to imitate "old-time gospel music" as played on a "country harmonium." (There might be something to that: Fred Longshaw had played such an instrument to accompany Bessie Smith and Armstrong in their famous

recording of "St. Louis Blues" just four months earlier.) Whether Redman
was tapping an "old-time gospel" or a "symphonic" sound here may be
debatable. But one thing is clear: Redman intends a sharp, even comic,
contrast between the semi-improvised passages (a la Oliver) and the
sustained-chord passages.[22]

The same can be said for the clarinet trio. The passage may be, as
Schuller states, "shrill and badly played" (the early recordings reveal many
instances where the musicians could not play—or did not have time to perfect—the material Redman gave them). But the artistic goal behind the passage remains a familiar one from Redman's other efforts: startling variety.
The passage stands out in a number of ways: timbre (as a clarinet trio
between brass statements), harmony (as the only nonblues section in an otherwise straightforward twelve-bar blues piece), and length (as the only sixteen-bar strain). In its good-natured aimlessness and harmonic simplicity,
the passage recalls the brass duet in "He's the Hottest Man in Town" and the
muted "doo-wacka" brass trio in "Go 'Long Mule," both of which were
tongue-in-cheek additions to stock arrangements. Moreover, like the chimes
in "Dicty Blues," the clarinet trio functions as a novelty effect that helps distance Redman's revision from the piece's southern blues folk roots.

Other signs that Redman was playfully signifying on Oliver's version lie
in the framing passages: the introduction and the brief tag ending. Oliver
had begun his version with a dramatic arpeggiated diminished chord: a
tense harmonic effect resolved just before the first chorus. Redman retains
the diminished-chord phrase but then introduces a new harmonic twist. In
mm. 3 and 4, instead of arriving emphatically on the dominant (F) as in
"Dipper Mouth Blues," the band plays a series of descending parallel chords
in the "wrong" key, C minor, as follows: Cmin / B♭ / A♭ / G. Finally, the alto
saxophone steps down to the dominant at the last possible moment (the last
beat of m. 4), and the tonic arrives "on time" at the downbeat of the first
chorus (ex. 4.9). The effect is a harmonic sleight-of-hand, delaying and
obscuring the tonic key (B♭).

Ex. 4.9. "Sugar Foot Stomp" (May 29, 1925), introduction

The tag ending also features a surprise. Throughout the arrangement, the
band plays many more breaks than Oliver had featured, adding to the score's
textural and timbral variety. Many of them are linked by a common
rhythmic figure derived from the "oh-play-that-thing" vocal break. The tag
ending for saxophones uses the same figure (ex. 4.10), which actually begins
in the twelfth bar of the final chorus, as if it were just another break based
on the same rhythm.

Ex. 4.10. "Sugar Foot Stomp," coda

It could have acted as the final cadence, too, for it is a root position tonic chord. But Redman's ending, extending the pattern two more bars and dropping the root a half-step for each reiteration, recalls the deceptive descending chord effect from the introduction. The piece ends indecisively, on a seventh chord, a cliffhanger. Ending a performance on a tonic-seventh chord was common in the 1920s, but voicing the chord with the seventh on the bottom was much more unusual in 1925. To the very last note, Redman's "Sugar Foot Stomp" transforms the stylistically consistent "Dipper Mouth Blues" into a colorful prism of New York jazz.

For all its clever spin on Oliver's version, Henderson's recording preserves a key feature of the original: the three-chorus showcase for the trumpet soloist. Armstrong plays Oliver's solo nearly note for note, departing from his mentor's approach less in pitch than in tone quality. In contrast to Oliver's quasi-vocal, plunger-softened wah-wah effects, Armstrong's tone slices through the band, stands far above its accompaniment, whereas Oliver's—still rooted in New Orleans collectivity—is merely the most prominent thread in a polyphonic knit. Once again, the accompaniment helps to foreground Armstrong's solo with a strong western-style backbeat from Kaiser Marshall's cymbal. On top of that, another accompanimental layer appears in the form of riffs in the saxophones: short, repeated humming figures that provide both harmonic and rhythmic support. In Armstrong's first chorus, in particular, we hear the kind of texture that would become formulaic a decade later: a soloist soaring over a charged network of riffs played by the opposite section of the band (in this case, a brass soloist accompanied by reed riffs), grounded on a solid rhythmic groove. After setting the groove and riffs, the accompaniment then proceeds through a variety of irregular stoptime patterns, playfully interacting with the solo in a way that anticipates Redman's last arrangements before Armstrong left.

The whole process—including the central placement and textures of Armstrong's solo passage—resembled the Redman stock-doctoring touch. Yet in this case, Redman did not work from a stock. In fact, the usual process was reversed. Instead of adapting published music, Redman's arrangement itself got adapted and published by none other than the Melrose Brothers. The copyright card for "Sugar Foot Stomp" at the Library of Congress gives joint credit for the Melrose arrangement to Redman and Elmer Schoebel, but only Schoebel's name appears on the stock. The card also shows the first copyright claim date as August 15, 1925, eleven weeks after Henderson's band recorded the piece for Columbia. Schoebel's stock actually conflates ideas from Henderson's and Oliver's recordings. (In fig. 4.4, letters A–F denote changes in instrumentation, harmony, or texture, even though all but one chorus is in twelve-bar blues form.)

"Sugar Foot Stomp," recorded often and also published as a stock, became a mainstay of the jazz repertory, and Redman's arrangement became the model on which other bands based their versions into the 1940s. Even King Oliver, with his ten-piece band, the Dixie Syncopators, recorded the piece under the new title. But "Sugar Foot Stomp" did not eclipse its source. Many bands continued to make records of "Dipper Mouth Blues," in obvious attempts to recreate the excitement of its first recording by the Creole Jazz Band. In the 1930s, Henderson's band would

Fig. 4.4. From "Dipper Mouth Blues" to "Sugar Foot Stomp"

"Dipper Mouth Blues" King Oliver's Creole Jazz Band (April 6 and June 23, 1923) ♩ = ca. 180	"Sugar Foot Stomp" pub. arrangement by Elmer Schoebel [and Don Redman]	"Sugar Foot Stomp" Fletcher Henderson and His Orchestra ♩ = ca. 200
Introduction (4) ⟶	Introduction (4)	Introduction (4)
A (12) Ensemble	A (12) Saxophones ⟵	A (12) Alto sax
A (12) Ensemble	A (12) Brass ⟵	A (12) Brass
B (12) Clarinet	E (12) Reed trio ⟵	F (16) Clarinet trio
B (12) Clarinet	D (12) Trombone ⟵	D (12) Trombone
A (12) Ensemble	C (12) Trumpet ⟵	C (12) Trumpet
C (12) Cornet ⟶	C (12) Trumpet ⟵	C (12) Trumpet
C (12) Cornet ⟶	C (12) Trumpet ⟵	C (12) Trumpet
C (12) Cornet ⟶	A' (12) Ensemble	E (12) Ensemble
A' (12) Ensemble ⟶	Coda (2) Ensemble	A (12) Ensemble
Coda (2) Ensemble ⟶		E (12) Ensemble
		A (12) Ensemble
		Coda (2) Saxophones

The arrows point from the source of materials published in the stock. In the case of the cornet/trumpet solo, arrows stem from both sides because, although Armstrong played Oliver's solo, the stock is lifted from Henderson's record. Yet in some cases, Schoebel bypassed "Sugar Foot Stomp" in favor of "Dipper Mouth Blues." In the introduction, he replaced Redman's deceptive C-minor twist with Oliver's straight-forward move to the dominant. Schoebel also omitted Redman's whole-note "symphonic" (or gospelized harmonium) brass choir strain and the sixteen-bar clarinet trio. But elements of these two strains coalesce in the stock's third strain: a reed trio composed over the enriched blues progression Redman used in the "symphonic" chorus (labeled [E] in the diagram). The stock also borrows the final chorus and coda of Oliver's version. Henderson's final chorus restates the opening chorus in full ensemble; Oliver's changes it. In "Dipper Mouth Blues" Armstrong (as lead trumpet player) plays a line different from that of the opening choruses, while Honoré Dutrey restates his trombone line. The stock reflects this alteration, preserving Armstrong's new line and Dutrey's old one for the final chorus. Neither line, however, can be heard in Henderson's recording. The stock's debt to Redman is further revealed in its separation of the saxophones and brass in the first two choruses. Clinching the case that Schoebel worked from Henderson's recording, the stock includes a literal transcription of Charlie Green's solo.

revisit "Sugar Foot Stomp" several times, taking a fleeter tempo but preserving the substance of the popular 1925 version to a remarkable degree. The piece, in Henderson's adaptation of Redman's revision, would also become a standard in Benny Goodman's repertoire from 1935 onward.[23]

Given the legendary and canonical aura surrounding "Copenhagen" and "Sugar Foot Stomp," it may be easy to agree with Schuller that Henderson's recordings in the period directly after "Sugar Foot Stomp" "do not represent any significant steps forward." In many ways, in fact, "T.N.T." matches "Copenhagen," recorded almost exactly a year earlier. Both pieces are instrumentals with multiple sixteen-bar strains. Both were composed by white jazz bandleaders. Both arrangements subdivide the strains into smaller segments of instrumentation and, moreover, alternate almost seamlessly between composed and improvisatory passages. Both begin immediately with the first strain, foregoing the complex introductions and interludes heard in many of the band's recordings of 1924–25. "T.N.T." does display a sophisticated design, yet all of the sudden shifts and startling variety of orchestration and rhythmic underpinning, not to mention the frequent interactions between soloists, never inhibit the surging flow of the band's performance. Finally, "T.N.T." also reveals a symmetrical design, another feature that Redman had already brought to his arrangements. And its composer-arranger, Elmer Schoebel, was already a familiar figure in Henderson's book of "hot" dance tunes.

Yet "T.N.T." exhibits two qualities that Redman had not yet explored: (1) subtle changes to the main melody that may be aptly termed "motivic variation" and (2) the integration of Armstrong's solo inside the strain. "T.N.T." thus reveals a new direction that Redman might have explored further had Armstrong remained in Henderson's band. It reveals that even as Redman strove to integrate Armstrong, he retained his interest in sophisticated, even symphonic, arranging devices.

"T. N.T." was an apt vehicle for Henderson's band. Like "Copenhagen" and "Sugar Foot Stomp," it is an instrumental number written by a jazz musician—in this case, Elmer Schoebel. Instead of the conventional verse-chorus form of a Tin Pan Alley song, "T.N.T." contains three sixteen-bar strains, deployed in a modified ragtime structure and, like ragtime, distinguished more by rhythmic vitality and harmonic character than by melody. The title carried a clever double meaning: TNT forms the abbreviation of a chemical compound used for explosives—a recent coinage in 1925. The Library of Congress copyright card also reveals another meaning, one not given on the published arrangement, but which accounts for the title's punctuation: "the nifty tune."

The title's resonance becomes clear in the first strain, which opens with a series of tense, surging full-ensemble block chords and cymbal crashes. No imitative novelty device, this beginning makes a powerful musical effect when played by the confident, well-rehearsed ensemble that the Henderson orchestra proves to be on this record. "T.N.T." fits the Henderson band in another way. The second strain of Schoebel's stock arrangement features a call-and-response passage, a device that would soon become associated with the band, and with Henderson's arranging style in the 1930s (ex. 4.11). (Redman replaced saxophones with clarinets.)

Ex. 4.11. "T.N.T." Stock arrangement (1925), strain 2, beginning (edited)

Was the stock based on Don Redman's recorded arrangement? As we've seen, "Copenhagen" and "Sugar Foot Stomp" reflect a trend in publishing stock arrangements based on recordings (and, in the case of "Copenhagen," advertising the fact). Indeed, Jack Mills, the publisher of "T.N.T.," did not claim copyright for the piece until three weeks after the Henderson band's recording, a much shorter period than the eleven-week lapse between the "Sugar Foot Stomp" recording and stock. Moreover, while the copyright card for "Sugar Foot Stomp" gives Redman co-arranger credit with Schoebel, Redman's name does not appear on the "T.N.T" entry (nor on the published arrangement).

For another thing, the call-and-response strain must have been conceived orchestrally. Why else would an experienced composer like Schoebel write nearly identical, consecutive two-bar phrases (mm. 1–4 in ex. 4.11) unless he meant them to be played by different sections of a band? In other words, Schoebel wrote the piece with its orchestration already in mind. Although it may not have been published until after Henderson's recording, the stock still could have served as Redman's source for the arrangement. The other piece on this October 21 recording session, "Carolina Stomp," was also issued in a stock arrangement by Schoebel. Perhaps Schoebel instigated the recording session: the Henderson band made the first recording of both pieces.

If Schoebel wanted Henderson to be the first to record "T.N.T.," he got all he could have hoped for. The recorded arrangement is a tour de force of mid-1920s jazz arranging and ensemble performance. The recording includes a total of ten choruses divided among three strains, but with each chorus featuring new instrumental combinations or rhythmic variations that distinguish it from the others.

The motivic variations on the first strain ([A] in fig. 4.5) are particularly ingenious, and they represent Redman's extensions of traits dating back to 1923: constant rhythmic and melodic change of the main idea and several strategically placed cymbal shots by Kaiser Marshall. In its six appearances—distributed almost symmetrically throughout the recording—the first strain has four varieties of orchestration and four different rhythmic guises (ex. 4.12).

Ex. 4.12. "T.N.T." (October 21, 1925), variations on strain 1 theme, beginning

The instrumentation used for these variations are: Ensemble (first and last choruses and A''), Ensemble with Armstrong (trumpet solo trading four-bar phrases: A''), Ensemble with Green (trombone solo trading four-bar phrases: A''), and Smith (trumpet solo leading ensemble: A'''). No combination of instrumentation and rhythmic pattern recurs, thus Redman achieves the most variety with a minimum of actual variations (fig. 4.5)

Fig. 4.5. "T.N.T."

Stock (C major)	Henderson recording (C major)
[:A(16):] ens.	A(16) ens.
B(16) brass and saxes	A' (16) ens. and tpt. solo (Armstrong)
B(16) saxes and brass	B(16) clars. and brass
[:A'' (16):] ens.	B(16) tpt. solo (Armstrong) and saxes
C(16) a saxes and ens.	A'' (16) ens.
a " " "	C(16) a saxes and ens.
b clar. (or A. sax) solo	a " " "
a saxes and ens.	b tenor sax solo (Hawkins)
A'' (16) ens.	a saxes and ens.
Coda(2) ens.	A' (16) ens. and tbn. solo (Green)
	C(16) clar. trio
	A''' (16) tpt. (Smith) and ens.
	A''' (16) ens.
	Coda(2) ens.

The diagram shows two instances where Redman brings Armstrong together with other parts of the band inside the strain: the second and fourth strains. Redman had shown signs of seeking greater integration of Armstrong with the rest of the ensemble. "Sugar Foot Stomp," for example, features an extremely active, constantly changing accompaniment under Armstrong's three-chorus solo. In "T.N.T." and "Carolina Stomp," Redman goes a step further by creating a dialogue between Armstrong and other members of the band. "Carolina Stomp" contains a sixteen-bar strain that pits the low brass against Armstrong; each eight-bar segment begins with Green and Escudero playing in octaves and continues with Armstrong's solo (ex. 4.13).

Ex. 4.13. "Carolina Stomp" (October 21, 1925), Armstrong with low brass

"T.N.T." contains a more elaborate interaction between Armstrong and other members of the band. As in "Carolina Stomp," Armstrong has two solo choruses, and each alternates between a group of players and himself. In a variation on the second strain call-and-response passage, Armstrong engages in a dialogue with the saxophones, who play elaborate, soloistic responses to his ringing calls (ex. 4.14).

Ex. 4.14. "T.N.T.," Armstrong and saxophones (top line only)

Shifts in the rhythm section's underlying beat enhance the crispness of this interaction. Under Armstrong, the rhythm section taps the beat; under the saxophones it lays out, giving the lead line the quality of a break.

The "hot" dialogues in "Carolina Stomp" and "T.N.T." suggest that Redman had new confidence in the band's ensemble playing. Armstrong's solos no longer had to be granted an independent chorus; they could be included among the contrasting elements inside the strain. Exploited since the band's earliest recordings, the principle of strain subdivision remained. Now, however, the ensemble playing was charged with the vibrancy of hot jazz.

As Redman had said, Armstrong "changed our whole idea about the band musically." Recordings such as "Copenhagen," "Sugar Foot Stomp," and "T.N.T." chart a qualitative change in the band's playing. In a word, the style sounds more "horizontal," more linear, more driving; whereas, in the pre-Armstrong recordings, the style is comparatively "vertical," more choppy, less continuous and flowing. Yet Redman's fundamental conception of arranging had not changed. The foundation of that conception lay in taking existing tunes and arrangements and "doctoring" them to create unique charts custom-designed for the strengths of the Henderson band. And that uniqueness lay in deploying stylistic variety and inside-the-strain juxtapositions of timbres, textures, rhythms, and solo personalities. Armstrong may have helped change *how* the band played, but he did not necessarily change *what* it played. "T.N.T." and "Carolina Stomp," recorded at Armstrong's last session with the band on October 21, 1925, preserve the tendencies Redman had shown from his earliest arrangements, and Armstrong's startling power and musical storytelling, while showing the band a new conception of the jazz solo, also served as a tool in Redman's colorful arsenal of sound.

By the fall of 1925, then, the musical synergy in Henderson's band had reached unprecedented intensity. Henderson continued to hold court for dancers at the Roseland, reaching thousands of other listeners through its radio wire, and recording for a variety of record labels both with his full orchestra and with selected members of the band as accompanists for blues singers. And there were also continuous bookings in the summer between seasons at the Roseland, large crowds in venues up and down the East Coast, and consistently hyperbolic press coverage. By his own account, Armstrong enjoyed himself and fit in musically and socially. "I had 'Wedged' in there just that much," Armstrong wrote later, capturing rather well the new way that Redman had learned to integrate Armstrong inside the strain. He later referred to the band members as "those fine boys who treated me just swell."[24]

Why, then, in November 1925, some thirteen months after arriving in New York, did Armstrong leave Henderson and return to Chicago? Several reasons have been offered. Armstrong's biographers tend to emphasize reasons for dissatisfaction. James Lincoln Collier finds much "in the situation ... that made Armstrong feel uncomfortable." Laurence Bergreen cites Armstrong's "all-too-brief solos" and "mounting dissatisfaction" with Henderson's band. And Gary Giddins states, "The stopper was still on.... The full radiance of Louis's music and personality was simmering, waiting for release."[25]

Armstrong, admittedly, provided some fuel for that perspective. Much later, he reflected that "Fletcher didn't dig me like Joe Oliver. He had a million dollar talent in his band and he never thought to let me sing." It's almost true: the only Armstrong vocal among his records with Henderson consists of a brief tag ending in "Everybody Loves My Baby." Yet the singing issue appears to be a red herring, since Armstrong noted elsewhere that Oliver didn't let him sing either, but he does not suggest that as a reason he left Oliver's band to go to Henderson. Armstrong also indicates that discipline started to break down and the "cats" got "careless with the music."[26] Yet all together, Armstrong's published memories of the band leave an at least ambivalent legacy, and they are actually more glowing than bitter.

Other, nonmusical, reasons also account for Armstrong's departure. Among them are that he was homesick for Chicago, where he had a cadre of fellow musicians from New Orleans; that he missed his wife, the pianist Lil Hardin Armstrong ("He used to write to his wife every day," recalled Kaiser Marshall); and that she was pressing her husband to ratchet up his career and become a bandleader with star billing and a salary to match. Lil coupled a more classically oriented musicianship and a stronger entrepreneurial streak than her husband. She had joined Louis in New York soon after his arrival there but then returned to Chicago. There, the "bands were always changing," she said. "So I went to the Dreamland and I said: 'I want to put a band in, I want to bring my husband back from New York, and I want him to be featured, I want $75 a week for him, and I want his name out there in front....' I had him make a sign—'Louis Armstrong, the World's Greatest Trumpet Player.'" Having arranged that, she continued to urge Louis to return home, but he resisted. As she recalled, she then issued an ultimatum—"if you're not here by this date, then don't come at all"—and Armstrong relented. But even Lil conceded that Louis "kind of liked playing with Fletcher. He wasn't anxious to be a star." Armstrong appears to have seen the situation as less a career choice than a cut-and-dried personal matter. As he later wrote, "I had to choose between—My Wife + Fletcher's Band. After all—I chose'd being with my wife."27

The night before Armstrong left for Chicago, Henderson threw a farewell party at Small's Paradise in Harlem. Thanks to Thomas Brothers's publication of selected writings that reveal Armstrong's unedited, unvarnished voice, we can now read the story of that party as written by its guest of honor, complete with Armstrong's inimitably playful syntax, punctuation, and capitalization style as performed on his second favorite instrument, the typewriter:

> All the boys in the Band hated to see me leave—And I hated like hell to leave them too.... We all had a wonderful time. We had a Special reserved Table—And the Place was packed + Jammed. And after Fletcher made his 'Speech and I made my little 'Speech—most of my 'Speech' was Thanks to Fletcher for the wonders he had done for me—etc. Then the whole Band sat in and played several fine arrangements for the Folks—Another Thrilling moment for me.—After we finished playing we went back to our table and started drinking some more 'liquor.—I gotten so 'Drunk until Buster Bailey and I decided to go home. And just as I went to tell Fletcher Henderson Goodbye as I was leaving New York for Chicago the next morning, I said—"Fletcher 'Thanks for being so kind to me." And—er—wer—er—wer—And before I knew it—I had "Vomit" ("*Puked*") directly into Fletchers' "*Bosom*." All over his Nice Clean 'Tuxedo Shirt. 'Oh—I'd gotten so sick all of a sudden—I was afraid Fletcher would get sore at me, but all he said—"Aw—that's allright 'Dip' " (my nick name at that time [short for "Dipper Mouth"]). Fletcher told Buster Bailey to take me home and put me to 'bed, so Buster did. The next morning—'my 'Headache and all—Boarded the Train for Chicago.28

Armstrong's exit, it appears, was even more unceremonious than his entrance thirteen months earlier. Had Armstrong stayed in New York, it is hard to know how he, Don Redman, and Henderson's band might have developed differently. Those final recordings of "T.N.T." and "Carolina Stomp" suggest that perhaps Redman's arranging might have explored more new territory. But soon, Armstrong was back in Chicago, playing in the band Lil had organized at the Dreamland, becoming "the Talk of Chicago," and making records as leader of the Hot Five, a group that included Lil and his old New Orleans friends clarinetist Johnny Dodds, trombonist Edward "Kid" Ory, and banjo player Johnny St. Cyr. Judging by the now separate paths of Armstrong and Henderson's band over the next two years, Armstrong's gain from returning to familiar people and places was greater than Henderson's loss. For, as Allen has noted, after Henderson's New Orleans trumpeter left town, his New York band began climbing "to greater heights."29

5.

A Paradox of the Race?

FROM ONE POINT OF VIEW, Armstrong's departure left his former colleagues—and all other aspiring solo improvisers—with the "problem" of how to develop a personal style out of Armstrong's powerful model of what a jazz solo could be. From this perspective, Henderson's post-Armstrong band has tended to be seen as a group of musicians struggling to make the paradigm shift, but sometimes failing the aesthetic challenge because of severe commercial demands that led to lapses in taste and integrity. Many of Henderson's musicians were indeed trying to absorb Armstrong's ideas, and they had to do it "on the job" during a period of intense demand for their music, but how they did it comprises only part of the story of Henderson after Armstrong. That perspective fails to take into account the multiple musical currents that Henderson's band was both absorbing and defining, and, in particular, the increasing power of the Paul Whiteman paradigm, which cannot be dismissed as merely a transient commercial alternative. By 1926 the Whiteman approach encompassed a whole mode of performance, in what has been called a "revue-derived variety entertainment format." Whiteman defined the project broadly as the development of "Modern American Music," which included self-conscious fusions starting to be known as "symphonic jazz."[1]

For many, such efforts constituted not just the wave of the future for jazz but the only kind of jazz there was. This was a point on which white commentators intersected with the New Negro press and intelligentsia—such as Dave Peyton and J. A. Rogers—noted in chapter 2. Arthur Lange's *Arranging for the Modern Dance Orchestra*, serialized in sections through 1925, was published in 1926, as was Paul Whiteman's autobiographical *Jazz*. In the same year, the first book-length effort to define the nature and scope of jazz appeared in Henry O. Osgood's *So This Is Jazz*. Osgood's book developed one part of the agenda advanced by the maverick cultural critic Gilbert Seldes, whose 1924 book *The Seven Lively Arts* bundled jazz with comic strips, vaudeville, musical theater, and film in an effort to bring serious attention to popular, indigenous American art forms. For Osgood, as for Seldes, jazz's present and future lay chiefly in arranged, written-down, stylized dance music, and its leading exponents were white: Paul Whiteman and his arranger Ferde Grofé; other orchestra leaders such as Vincent Lopez, Ben Bernie, and Isham Jones; composers George Gershwin and Irving Berlin; plus novelty piano wizard Zez Confrey and clarinet hokum specialist Ted

Lewis. Not for Osgood were the "improvisation and irresponsibility" of small combos with musicians "jolting up and down and writhing about in simulated ecstasy, in the manner of Negroes at a Southern camp-meeting afflicted with religious frenzy." Osgood did not become a "happy convert" to the music until he heard a band of "eight gentlemen," each playing "a definite part that some clever musician had written for him in preparing the score." There was, Osgood noted, "no careless improvising" in this band. For Osgood, apparently, improvisation, with its clear links to ecstatic African-American worship styles, was by definition "irresponsible" and "careless." Writing while the Armstrong Effect still resonated in the New York music world, Osgood had not fathomed the disciplined coherence in Armstrong's solos that became a touchstone for later jazz musicians and historians.[2]

It would be easy to dismiss Osgood's book as irrelevant to jazz, since it makes no reference to the musicians—such as Armstrong, Jelly Roll Morton, King Oliver, Bessie Smith, Henderson, and Ellington—now commonly identified as the great jazz innovators of the 1920s. And it would be easy to condemn Osgood's book as racist, since, with the exception of W. C. Handy (whose landmark *Blues: An Anthology* also appeared in 1926), all of the musicians it celebrates are white, and also because he devalues the role of ecstatic music-making and improvisation—key elements of traditional African-American musical practice. Indeed, although it never invokes an explicitly moral dimension, Osgood's linkage of improvisation, race, and disorder echoes similar fears about ragtime's corrupting influence two decades earlier—not to mention reactions to rock and rap in the decades to come. Yet if Osgood's perspective now seems aesthetically and socially narrow, on a practical level he was right about one thing: working musicians had to be able to read musical notation. "If you didn't read by 1927 or 1928, you got left out," recalled trombonist Clyde Bernhardt. "No place for you in a good-quality band." In this context, Henderson's band continued to compel attention for its unique combination of expert reading and hot improvisation.[3]

The musical tensions that Henderson's band was trying to balance, then, reflect a larger clash of values: between black folkways and the White-manesque—and New Negro—agenda that called for a refinement and stylization of those folkways. As exciting as his music was, Armstrong intoned a threat to white modernist and black assimilationist values; he presented a potentially regressive force, as if he was too "raw"—too "black"—to "advance the race," or to advance jazz, or modern music, for that matter. That is the *social* reason that his solos needed the musical framing of Redman's intricate scoring, and that it took a while for the band, collectively, to absorb Armstrong's impact. Individually, some band members, such as Coleman Hawkins, quickly took up the challenge because of the irresistible musical appeal of Armstrong's model. Individually, Henderson's sidemen could make their own peace with the Armstrong Effect as long as the arrangements gave at least a semblance of framing and containing the solos.

The result could be heard as another manifestation of "double consciousness," the phrase coined by W. E. B. DuBois in his classic 1903 study, *The Souls of Black Folk*, to describe "this sense of always looking at one's self through the eyes of others ... [so that] One ever feels his twoness,—an

American, a Negro; two souls, two thoughts, two unreconciled strivings; two warring ideals in one dark body." DuBois claimed that "The history of the American Negro is the history of this strife." But every generation, and every individual within each generation, manifests its double consciousness differently, according to particular conditions of time, place, and culture. Henderson's double consciousness in the later 1920s might be described as a unique negotiation between Armstrong and Whiteman, between orality and written expression. The question remains, does that negotiation reflect DuBois's "unreconciled strivings"? Or can it be viewed as a more deliberate strategy, a deft balancing act, a set of apparent contradictions with an underlying consistency?[4]

The questions come to a head from 1926 onward, marking a watershed for the direction of the various musics dubbed "jazz" and for Henderson's band, which found itself in the vanguard of musical change and at a new pinnacle of popularity and prestige.

In an influential book built on a powerfully linear conception of the jazz tradition, the French jazz critic André Hodeir identified 1926–27 as a "transitional period" between the "oldtime" New Orleans style of collective improvisation and the "pre-classical" style of big-band swing. He claims Ellington, "and to a lesser extent" Henderson and Redman, as the transition's key figures, responsible for "the replacement of spontaneous collective music by a worked-out orchestral language."[5]

Henderson's work in the years around 1926 suggests that Hodeir's evolutionary scenario needs some adjustment. A change was in the air, but the "transitional" style of 1926–27 is not so much a matter of big-band swing "replacing" small-band collective improvisation as of large-orchestra dance music absorbing some of the New Orleans style, especially the impact of Armstrong, and becoming more Armstrong-inflected—or, as later jazz commentators might simply put it, more jazz-inflected. Before Armstrong, the band attached a hot out-chorus to most arrangements like so much appliqué, an exciting effect that proved a dance orchestra's versatility. After Armstrong, we can hear Armstrong's rhythmic conception—his "swing"—pervade the entire band in a deeper way. In other words, Henderson's approach combined two coexisting streams, one flowing from New Orleans and the other from New York.

The Revised Original Dixieland Jazz Band

Henderson's recordings reflect these competing and intersecting currents, nowhere more clearly in the band's intensive effort to revise "old" pieces that had made an impact before 1923, that is, before Henderson formed his own band. Here, Henderson turns decisively away from the current Tin Pan Alley and Broadway repertoire that had formed its foundation through 1925 and taps into older material with a ready-made jazz pedigree: "Panama" (published 1911), "The St. Louis Blues"(1914), "The Wang Wang Blues" (1921), as well as four pieces composed and recorded by members of the Original Dixieland Jazz Band (ODJB): "Sensation" (1917), "Livery Stable Blues" (1917), "Clarinet Marmalade" (1918), and "Fidgety Feet"(1919).

The predominance of ODJB material obscures the Whitemanesque roots of the project. After all, Whiteman had opened his famous Aeolian Hall concert of February 1924 with "Livery Stable Blues" to illustrate the primitive sources of jazz in "true form," so that the ultimate refinement of jazz presented at the end of the program—in the form of Gershwin's *Rhapsody in Blue*—might be thrown more powerfully into relief. In his effort to raise jazz's social status, Whiteman first had to define it as music with a history.

Henderson's increasing adoption of old tunes reflects that phenomenon—a strong sense that jazz not only had a past, but that it had crossed over into a new era. Indeed, rather than presenting these tunes in anything like their original form, Henderson's band adapted and updated them, following Redman's penchant for doctoring preexisting musical material. In just one obvious respect do the band's revisions honor their models: speed. Except for the two true "blues" pieces ("Wang Wang" was a blues tune in name only), these recordings stand out by sporting faster tempos than the band had ever played on record. "Panama," "Clarinet Marmalade," "Fidgety Feet," "Sensation," and "The Wang Wang Blues" all clock in at over 240 beats per minute. Speed was fundamental to this repertoire; it was certainly one of the attractions of the ODJB, which burst onto the New York jazz scene in 1917 with ferocious energy. The Henderson band recaptured some of the original spirit of the pieces; with twice as many musicians, its visceral impact exceeds that of the band that created them.

In other ways, Henderson's recordings pour new wine into old bottles. Compared to the ODJB's unrelenting polyphony, Redman's arrangements sound colorful and varied. Even when the band was not actually "reviving" such older numbers—some had received several recordings between the ODJB and the Henderson versions—it was unmistakably playing fresh interpretations.

For example, in "Clarinet Marmalade" (recorded December 8, 1926), the band offered listeners a new encounter with this already familiar piece, transforming it from an ensemble number into a vehicle for soloists. Three earlier recordings of the tune—by the ODJB (1918), James Reese Europe's 369th Infantry Band (1919), and the New Orleans Rhythm Kings (1923)—had featured the whole ensemble, including only a few solo breaks and closely following the piece as it appeared in published (sheet music) form. In those recordings "Clarinet Marmalade"'s ragtime roots remain clear.

Henderson's version told another story. It began with a new, off-tonic introduction (in D minor, rather than the F-major one played by other bands), followed by a series of solos over riff accompaniments. The arrangement also includes two new ensemble riff-choruses that Redman liked enough to reuse in later recordings (one in "Stockholm Stomp;" the other—the out-chorus—in "Sensation"). After the Henderson recording, "Clarinet Marmalade" became a big-band standard, with a dozen recordings in the period 1927–29, and many more in the 1930s and 1940s. Most of them featured a string of solos and ensemble riffs. As a result, "Clarinet Marmalade" represents one of several older pieces, such as "King Porter Stomp" and "Chinatown, My Chinatown" in the years to come, that Henderson's band virtually reinvented, in effect showing other bands how to make them sound new.[6]

The band also made of "Fidgety Feet" an exuberant parade of soloists: Bailey, Hawkins, Joe Smith, Jimmy Harrison, and Tommy Ladnier. Arranging nuances along the way reveals the care with which Redman rethought the piece. He doubled the length of the introduction, interspersing Marshall's cymbal work and a torrid trombone break by Harrison between the original ensemble phrases. In the second strain, the original theme, with its on-the-beat block chords, becomes a stoptime accompaniment for solos by Hawkins and Bailey. The firm chords anchor Bailey's flowing line of eighth notes, which peaks at the solo's midpoint with a high G whole-note (ex. 5.1).

Ex. 5.1. "Fidgety Feet" (March 19, 1927), Bailey solo and stoptime accompaniment

In the last chorus—a new section probably added by Redman, but possibly based on the original "trio"—a hair-raising, full-ensemble, whole-note wail launches Ladnier's solo (ex. 5.2).

Ex. 5.2. "Fidgety Feet," beginning of last chorus

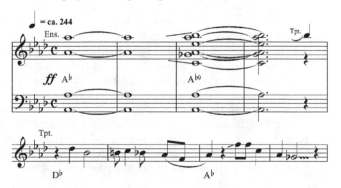

The recording closes, appropriately, with several bars of rambunctious free counterpoint evoking the New Orleans style.

The band plays with less abandon on "Sensation"—another ODJB tune recorded the same day as "Fidgety Feet"—as it harks back a few years to the principle of surprise, variety, and contrast. The arrangement includes plenty of solos, but it also imposes several devices that were becoming clichés in 1920s dance music, including full-bodied organ-like chords in the introduction and a fancy interlude of the kind the band had played in several 1924–25 recordings. "Fidgety Feet" allowed the soloists to stretch out; "Sensation" interrupts them with ensemble breaks. These interruptions, however, arise out of the original piece. A comparison of Henderson's recording with the ODJB version reveals how the Henderson band takes the space between the ensemble's staccato chords and replaces the ODJB's simple trombone fillip with hot breaks. Likewise, in the trio Redman preserves the ensemble chords and fills the two bars between them with breaks by Hawkins and Ladnier. The meeting of New Orleans and New York jazz styles produced a smoother blend in "Fidgety Feet" than it did in "Sensation," where the seams are meant to show.

Among the older pieces in Henderson's repertory, "The Wang Wang Blues" came closest to a kind of historical revival. The piece was composed by Whiteman sidemen Henry Busse (cornet), Buster Johnson (trombone), and Gus Mueller (clarinet). Although it became popular following Whiteman's 1920 recording, the piece lay dormant in the recorded jazz repertory for five years, until King Oliver and his Dixie Syncopators made "The New Wang Wang Blues" in Chicago in 1926. As with the ODJB pieces, Henderson led the first New York band to record the piece after a hiatus of several years.[7]

The Henderson recording actually deserves the "new" billing more than Oliver's version does. Oliver (at ca. 180 beats per minute) preserves the moderate tempo of Whiteman's version (at ca. 168); Henderson once again exceeds 240 beats per minute. Oliver's band, like Whiteman's, stays close to the melody and includes no hot solos. Henderson's band uses the chorus's melody as a background for solo improvisations—as in this effort by Ladnier, whose syncopated double leap (m. 2) and terminal vibrato on held notes (mm. 2, 5, 6, 10, 14) reveals Armstrong's influence (ex. 5.3).

While allowing room for the band's instrumental solo stars, Redman takes the spotlight himself with a half-chorus of scat vocalizing. He also makes his presence felt in the ingenious augmentation of the song's "patter" theme, using the familiar accents of secondary rag. By augmenting the quarter notes to dotted half notes—a quasi-symphonic variation device—Redman expands an eight-bar phrase into a fourteen-bar section that serves as a coda (ex. 5.4).

In adapting repertory from the late 1910s and early 1920s, the Henderson band excelled at blistering tempos. Schuller argues that in playing the ODJB repertory, "the band tried hard, and the records sold well, but the material was wrong and the efforts sounded forced."[8] Heard in the context of earlier recordings of the same pieces, however, many of the

Henderson versions of older repertory, by the ODJB and others, sound like fresh and inspired efforts to blend conflicting currents in the shifting New York jazz scene. Curiously among this older repertory, the slower-paced "Wabash Blues," "Livery Stable Blues," and "St. Louis Blues" sound almost perfunctory—suggesting an ongoing ambivalence about the blues. To understand Henderson's relation to the blues more clearly, we need to turn to pieces by Henderson himself.

Ex. 5.3. "The Wang Wang Blues" (March 23, 1927), chorus 1, Ladnier solo and saxophone melody

Ex. 5.4. "Wang Wang Blues," original patter theme and coda in Henderson recording

Henderson's Blues

Although Henderson continued to accompany Bessie Smith and other singers throughout the 1920s, the blues craze had faded by mid-decade. That he continued to play blues accompaniments might seem rather remarkable. An urban, Striver's-Row sensibility typically either held the blues at arm's length through stylization or ignored it entirely as an irrelevant legacy of the rural South—a phenomenon that stands at the foundation of Amiri Baraka's classic critique of the New Negro. Accordingly, the blues—that is, the twelve-bar blues with its arsenal of expressive growls, slides, and thumping bass—have a shrinking role in Henderson's repertory. Yet Henderson continued to explore the idiom through a striking series of original compositions that extend the "Dicty Blues" impulse of 1923—those instrumental blues featuring harmonic, formal, and orchestral enhancements that reflect a New York stylization of the raw, earthy southern style. Unlike a stock arrangement acquired from a publisher, these blues pieces represent a type of number known as a "special," a piece written for a specific band and tailored to its strengths; the band's fame and distinction rested increasingly on such material.

"Hot Mustard" (1926) offers a clear example of a blues "special." It has four distinctive strains, three modulations, and an orchestration that changes not only in two- and four-measure units but often in every measure (see fig. 5.1). The slow tempo signals a blues mood, and the band transcends the piece's complexity with an amiably loose-jointed ensemble performance. The descending-chord passage that opens the first twelve-bar blues strain recalls "Dicty Blues" in particular, although its harmony—straying as far as an A♭ seventh chord in m. 3—is richer than that of the 1923 piece (ex. 5.5).

Ex. 5.5. "Hot Mustard" and "Dicty Blues"

Ex. 5.5a. "Hot Mustard," strain 1, beginning

Ex. 5.5b. "Dicty Blues," strain 1, piano part

Additional details further stylize the approach. For example, the arrangement adds variety by suspending the rhythm section to create a break-like effect, a device that appears in many of his recordings around this time. The piece's texture is chock full of such rhythmic "holes," especially in the second and third strains. The piece ends away from the home key, on the minor subdominant.

To balance all this variety and surprise, the arrangement has an overall design marked by roundedness and symmetry, with the return of the initial (A) strain in its original key and orchestration at the end. (In fig. 5.1, the two twelve-bar strains differ in harmony, melody, and orchestration, and are thus labeled A and B, although both are recognizable variations on the blues.) It remains unclear who did the arrangement. It seems likely at this point that Henderson was still following the procedure by which "Dicty

Blues" came to life: as a piano piece by Henderson that was orchestrated by someone else, in this case possibly by Redman. The form suggests an ongoing effort to fuse folkways and classical technique into a kind of mini-symphonic blues that shares some of the spirit of the slow middle movement of Gershwin's new *Concerto in F,* which received its world premiere in New York just a year earlier.

A later piece called "'D' Natural Blues" (1928) shows Henderson's ongoing interest in elaborate blues. The piece includes three different versions of the twelve-bar blues, including chromatic chord substitutions and secondary dominants, all in the context of D major. The title itself may be a pun on the music's blend of sophistication and earthiness. On one hand, the key of D major was rare for dance bands, forcing brass and reeds alike into unusual tonal regions and thus calling for sophisticated score-reading ability. On the other hand, the title implicitly conjures stereotyped black dialect still familiar from minstrel and coon songs, shifting the title's meaning to the opposite of artifice and sophistication, as if it were "De *natural* blues."

Fig. 5.1. "Hot Mustard"

F major:	A(12)	tpt. solo (4)
		tenor sax solo (4)
		ens. (4)
	B(12)	clar. (1) + tuba break (1), four times
		tpt. solo (4)
C major:	C(8)	clar. (1) + ens. (1)
		tpt. (1) + ens. (1)
		tpt. solo (2) + saxes (2)
	Transition(4)	Brass break (2) + saxes (2)
G minor:	D(16)	saxes (3) + tpt. break (1)
		tpt. (2) + tpt. solo (2)
		tpt. solo (4)
		clar. (4)
	Transition(6)	clar. (1) + brass (1), twice, + tpt. solo (2)
F major:	A'(12)	ens. (4)
		tpt. solo (8)
	A''(12)	piano solo
	A(10)	tpt. solo (4)
		tenor sax solo (4)
		ens. (2)
	Tag(4)	brass (1) + saxes (1) + brass (1) + ens. (1)

The piece also reveals Henderson's continuing association with Paul Whiteman, for the arrangement came from a key figure on Whiteman's staff: Bill Challis. Through a two-year collaboration with cornetist Bix Beiderbecke in the bands of Jean Goldkette and Whiteman, Challis had proven adept at weaving hot solos into dance arrangements, composing attractive ensemble variations on a melody, and including solo-like passages for the reeds and brass, sometimes in the style of Beiderbecke himself. These abilities meshed well with the Henderson band's orientation.

" 'D' Natural Blues," however, omits space for improvised solos. In fact, the whole recording radiates the poised quality of a performance read from a score. Even Bobby Stark's trumpet solo in the second chorus, underscored by the kind of strong cymbal backbeat that usually spurs hot improvisation, keeps the melody intact. But hot jazz is not the main goal of " 'D' Natural Blues." Instead, the piece reinforces Henderson's emerging blues project: to "elevate" the gutbucket style into the symphonic jazz realm.

Blues conventions, however, serve as points of reference. The slow tempo and the gritty, grunting tuba lend the whole performance a lowdown character. The middle section evokes the conventional interaction of a blues singer and instrumentalist. Clarinets carry the melody, broadly sliding between pitches, while the trombone interjects lazy filler between their phrases. The literal repetition of this chorus, however, reminds a listener that the whole exchange proceeds from composed parts.

Another "symphonic" feature of the arrangement is its overall design, in this case an orchestrated crescendo calculated to peak in the final chorus (fig. 5.2).

The arrangement builds intensity chorus by chorus. The last three choruses, whose "melody" has the beat-marking simplicity of a riff, forms an exercise in additive orchestration. The recording culminates in a chorus of single-note outbursts from the three wind sections while Kaiser Marshall's animated cymbal work provides continuity. Like so many other recordings of the 1920s, " 'D' Natural Blues" offers the period charm of a captivating experiment.

Fig. 5.2. "'D' Natural Blues"

Intro.	
Chorus 1	ens.
Chorus 2	tpt. solo
Chorus 3	clar. trio with tbn.
Chorus 4	as above
Chorus 5	clar. trio, syncopated variation
Chorus 6	brass, cymbal
Chorus 7	ens., cymbal
Chorus 8	ens., with high brass, low brass, clar., and cymbal playing independently
Coda	

Yet "'D' Natural Blues" survived the 1920s and, at a faster tempo, became a musical calling card for the band. Horace Henderson recalled a battle with the Casa Loma Orchestra, probably in the early 1930s, when Henderson called out his "special" arrangements, and the crowd "ran across the floor ... and man they started swinging ... to things like " 'D' Natural Blues."' In 1936 Henderson dubbed the tune "Grand Terrace Rhythm"—after the Chicago's Grand Terrace Café, where the band had an extended run—and made another record under the new title. Henderson's sidemen relished the piece. Two decades later, at the Second Great South Bay Jazz Festival on Long Island in 1958, Rex Stewart led "The Fletcher Henderson Alumni" in a set that included just two titles from the 1920s: "What-Cha-Call-'Em Blues" and " 'D' Natural Blues."9

Even as the symphonic jazz vogue faded in the late 1920s, Henderson continued to write in his "dicty blues" idiom. The modestly titled "Just Blues" (1931), however, presents a much more straightforward approach, and, lacking credit to the contrary, and given Henderson's increasing involvement in arranging in the early 1930s, it seems likely that he did the orchestrating himself. The title is apt. "Just Blues" comprises a series of seven twelve-bar blues choruses ending with a brief tag. The tempo is typically slow (about 116 beats per minute), and there are no modulations. The key remains in A♭, reinforcing the title's suggestion of simplicity. Even the first section, which sounds like an elaborate introduction, actually turns out to be the first chorus, that is, it is "just blues."

Yet while the piece's overall structure merits the title, the contents do not, because in this piece Henderson does a truly remarkable thing for the period: he separates the brass into three distinct units of trumpets, trombones, and tuba. From the perspective of scoring, the first chorus is the most compelling section of the piece (ex. 5.6).

Ex. 5.6. "Just Blues" (April 10, 1931), beginning

The band presents a sequence of five distinct figures in turn: a piano tremolo, a two-bar trumpet motif on an A♭ chord, a two-note saxophone cry, a short syncopated figure in the trombones, and a single grunt from the tuba. Thus, not only are the brass instruments treated separately, the piano and tuba are freed from their conventional rhythm-section roles and play distinctive figures in an interlocking sequence of textural and timbral effects. (Only the guitar performs the usual role of a blues rhythm section, strumming every beat.)

The rest of the piece consists of a sequence of solo and ensemble choruses with the full rhythm section grinding out chords on every beat—the conventional commercialized blues accompaniment of the twenties. The whole performance sounds immaculately well rehearsed. Unlike "Hot Mustard" and " 'D' Natural Blues," the piece incorporates a variety of hot solos, by Hawkins, trombonist Benny Morton, and trumpeter Bobby Stark, whose rapid-fire obbligato playing animates much of the recording. Toward the end, the full band forges a kind of riffing symphonic-blues out-chorus where, once again, the saxophones, trumpets, and trombones present layers of distinct material.

Variety columnist Abel Green, a close and opinionated observer of Henderson's band since early 1924, dubbed Henderson "a paradox for one of his race" in a brief article entitled "Fletcher Henderson's 'Blues,' " published in January 1927.

> The whites do their darndest to simulate the native negro 'blues' and suceed [*sic*] indifferently with but occasional exceptions. Henderson on the other hands [*sic*] 'cleans up' his music with the result he delivers a white man's blues style that is not at all faithful, coming as it does from a crack negro aggregation. Henderson is a scholar and of the advanced type of negro. His erudite discussions while pounding the piano are refreshingly fetching, and most impressive. The contrast of jazz and erudition is what makes for the effect, but on the indigo music delivery Henderson reflects the Caucasian compromises very plainly.

Green's commentary represents a crude prototype of a theme that resonates through later jazz criticism, which we've already seen applied to Henderson's early band. Finding Henderson unfit for his stereotyped association of race and style, Green finds fault not with the stereotype but with the musician. With the notion of Henderson's "Caucasian compromises," Green's assessment also reinforces an image of DuBoisian "unreconciled strivings." In Green's account, we get a picture of Henderson as a black musician struggling vainly with his double consciousness. At the same time, Green's perspective differs notably from Henry O. Osgood's, for Green recognizes the validity and distinctiveness of African-American musicality in its own right—something that Osgood, Whiteman, Lange, and the New Negro intelligentsia tend to view as raw material for a more refined, stylized approach.

The qualities that disappoint Green merit praise from Dave Peyton, the *Defender* columnist and dean of Chicago's black professional music scene. In February 1926, for example, Peyton heard Henderson's band and was "astonished at the artistic rendition" of nineteenth-century chestnuts such as

"Song at Twilight" ["Love's Old Sweet Song"], "Swanee River" ["Old Folks at Home"], and "Old Black Joe" in "symphonic arrangement." A week earlier, Peyton had reported that Henderson and his band played both "soft, sweet and perfect" and " 'hot,' too," although he hastened to add, in a way that Osgood might have, that Henderson's "hot" style was "not the sloppy New Orleans hokum, but real peppy blue syncopation." Peyton relished Henderson's ability to draw appreciative crowds both on the South Side for chiefly black audiences and downtown, in the Loop, for whites. He was particularly hopeful, after Henderson's appearance at the Congress Hotel, that Henderson would "redeem us in the Loop"—meaning that Henderson would more responsibly and elegantly represent The Race than local black bands and their "rotten blues songs," as Peyton called them. Where Green hears compromise, Peyton hears versatility.[10]

In a climate where music was so explicitly racialized, no wonder Henderson strove to foil easy generalizations. "Henderson's blues" thus represent another savvy effort to challenge the stereotypes, a delicate and knowing balance between sleek arrangement and gutty improvisation, between creative control and collaboration, between "southern" musical tradition and "northern" reinterpretation. It anticipates the kind of effort that Scott DeVeaux identifies in the emerging bebop generation: "to incorporate elements of what the white world respected as musical knowledge and literacy *into* the cultural practices that fueled the stereotype. A form of swing that was both earthy and erudite ... *that* was a goal worth reaching for." That perspective grants Henderson more authority over his musical course, and indeed, ample evidence exists to support it.[11]

While maintaining his home base downtown at the Roseland, Henderson's ballroom work now ranged across a remarkable array of venues. From 1927 on, for example, the band became a perennial favorite at college proms and fraternity parties, especially at elite northeastern schools such as Yale, Princeton, Cornell, Dartmouth, Brown, and Amherst, but also as far afield as the University of Kansas. A sampling of eyewitness accounts suggests the breadth of Henderson's appeal. At Kansas, at the "Senior Cakewalk," a student reporter observed "something in the jungle beat of Fletcher Henderson's rhythm that did things to our supposedly civilized university students." At Yale, the *Defender* reported that Henderson continued to cast a longstanding spell, as "Students and their 'girls' crowd the bandstand with Henderson." Far from evoking the primitivist strain that caught the Kansas reporter's ear, however, the *Defender* assumed its familiar uplift-the-race style and proposed that Henderson's Ivy League appeal might have something to do with the "scholarly and gentlemanly background and intellect of the suave, tasteful Atlanta University alumnus, the son of two of the educational pioneers in the Colored race." Contemporary press reports reveal more about the writer's perspective than about Henderson's music, but together they suggest that Henderson's band had not only mastered but even expanded the difficult art of connecting with a wide range of dancers and listeners. For further examples of how Henderson's band tailored its music for contrasting purposes, we turn now to three of its most remarkable specials of the late 1920s, the first for dancing, and the other two for listening. They reveal that the aesthetic opposition of Armstrong and Whiteman is to some extent grounded in a practical contrast in venues and functions.[12]

Stampede at the Savoy

The first is an original piece recorded during a period when Henderson performed at the Savoy Ballroom, where he became a regular and popular guest in the late 1920s. The Savoy opened in 1926 with a pricing scale that enticed audiences from a wide social spectrum, black and white. The management conceived it as a respectable, "safe" haven for Dionysian music and dancing, and that balance sustained large crowds of local Harlemites, downtowners, and out-of-towners. It became not just a hub of Harlem nightlife but a laboratory for virtuosic, athletic dancing that produced the Lindy Hop. Savoy events conjured a unique frenzy in which musicians and dancers fed off one another's energy. "It was always inspiring to have people dancing in front of you," said trombonist Dicky Wells, who recalled that the Savoy even had a "sprung floor" that was "built to vibrate." Wells even suggests that dancers—especially women—played an active role in shaping a band's style and repertoire. "We wouldn't have played that music the way we did if we hadn't got the spirit of things from watching those girls dance.... Lots of times the dancers more or less dictated what the bands played.... There was more soul when jazz and dancing went together."[13]

The Savoy's grand opening on March 12, 1926, featured the two house bands—the Charleston Bearcats and Fess Williams's Royal Flush Orchestra—plus "Fletcher Henderson ('Himself') and his Roseland Orchestra," as an advertisement put it. (The phrase indicates the extent of Henderson's popularity: by 1926, several bands appeared under Henderson's name or sponsorship, sometimes performing without the bandleader "himself.") An estimated four thousand people attended the opening, and such figures became typical in the months and years to come. Henderson's band returned twice more to the Savoy in the spring of 1926 to perform opposite the house bands, including a May 11 appearance by "overwhelmingly popular demand."[14]

Although we lack accounts of what and how Henderson played at the Savoy that spring, there is no doubt that one item in the band's book there was another "special" credited to Henderson himself: "The Stampede." Henderson recorded it on May 14, 1926, just three days after the band's third Savoy appearance in two months. Don Redman is widely assumed to have arranged Henderson's piece, but jazz writers tend to praise it for qualities rarely ascribed to Redman—namely, that the arranger largely stays out of the way of the soloists. There are, however, several telltale Redman trademarks. In the introduction, for example, the arranger creates a terraced, orchestrated crescendo—with an insistent rhythmic figure volleyed among parts of the band—spilling over into a clamorous improvisatory trumpet solo (fig. 5.3). With its quick shifts and solo-ensemble alternation, the passage evokes not just Redman in general, but also what might be called his "Armstrong Style," in particular, as heard in "T.N.T." and "Carolina Stomp," where Armstrong had been integrated inside the strain. That perspective gains credibility from recognizing the passage's trumpet soloist, Rex Stewart, and the "western style" backbeat behind him. He had been hired, Stewart recalled, "to play like Louis, which meant play above the band." "Stampede" gives a clear example of Stewart doing his job.[15]

Fig. 5.3. "The Stampede"

Intro. (16)

   piano + saxes + tpt. + ens. (4)

   Stewart solo (4)

   piano + saxes + tpt. + ens. (4)

   Stewart solo (4)

A(32) ens.

A(32) Hawkins solo

Transition saxes (2) + ens. (2)

B(32) Smith solo (piano break)

Transition ens. (2)

B(32) clar. trio (Stewart break)

A(24) Stewart solo (12) + ens. break (4) + ens. (8)

Coda ens. [= last 8 bars of B strain]

Instead of continuing the pattern of solo-ensemble exchange, however, the arrangement proceeds to focus on one or the other. In fact, now the ensemble and sectional music serves mainly as a frame and scaffold for the solos, by Coleman Hawkins, Joe Smith, and Stewart again. The arrangement's loosely symmetrical design helps project the individuality of each soloist, as do the custom-designed riffs: brass accents behind Hawkins, saxophone humming behind Smith. Smart breaks punctuate the solos, here and there topped off with Marshall's patented cymbal shots. The solo sequence gives way to the clarinet trio (another sign of Redman's hand), which launches a wailing theme that Henderson will revisit several years later in a composition called "Can You Take It?" Stewart's final solo barges in with breathless urgency to announce the final strain, then relents finally for a brief reprise of the opening ensemble theme and a brisk tag ending.

If Armstrong's influence resounds in the "brass hyperboles" of Stewart and Smith, it also leaves a profound mark on Hawkins. Hawkins's "Stampede" solo, one of his most celebrated efforts from the 1920s, offers an opportunity to take stock of the dramatic change that had taken place in his style in the time—fewer than three years—since his first recorded solo in "Dicty Blues" (ex. 5.7).[16]

In "The Stampede," Hawkins now deploys a legato fluency in place of the heavy, slap-tongued staccato articulation of his "Dicty Blues" style. Moreover, a relaxed rhythmic variety now takes the place of the jerky, breathless syncopations and flurries of eighth notes Hawkins tended to rely on in 1923–24. In the first four bars, for example, Hawkins takes a cue from Armstrong's openings, with a syncopated phrase leading to the familiar three-note figure (mm. 1–2). The next phrase answers the opening statement, picking up its pitches (A♭ and C) and using them to set off a spiraling broken chord in eighth notes. Rhythmic variety also comes in mm. 13–14, where Hawkins plays a run of even eighth notes, momentarily suspending

Ex. 5.7. "The Stampede" (May 14, 1926), Hawkins solo

the conventional "swung" eighths common to jazz solos. Other Armstrong-like effects spring up confidently, like the syncopated double-leap in m. 10, and the rising, chromatic, downbeat triplet in m. 11. Beyond these details, Williams notes an Armstrong-like "developing pattern of melody," perhaps referring to the literal return of the opening syncopated figure in m. 24 (at the end of a long, unbroken stretch of solo), and the development of a melodic figure beginning on C♭ (mm. 16, 18, 21, 22) that adds resonance to the same pitch, spelled B♮, in the syncopated figure itself. Even the surprising, low Ab "honk" in m. 22 can be heard as an octave-wide exaggeration of the leap to Ab in m. 8. In "The Stampede" we can hear Hawkins telling a story, working on the musical "coherence" that made Armstrong's solos unique. At the age of twenty-one, fueled by his encounter with Armstrong, Coleman Hawkins had made impressive strides toward achieving an original solo voice.[17]

Hawkins's dramatic solo may have been one reason that "The Stampede" was taken up by many other bands. A simplified version of the solo appears in a stock arrangement published in September 1926, but no other solos are included. Other saxophonists echoed Hawkins's "Stampede" phrases, and even Roy Eldridge learned the solo on trumpet and got his first job after playing it for an audition—provocative confirmation of the solo's links to another trumpeter's style.[18]

Meanwhile, the stock's publication launched a veritable stampede of recordings by various bands over the next five months, though not all of them followed the stock. One of the bands that did was the Charleston Bearcats, the Savoy house band also known as the Savoy Bearcats on record labels. Taking a faster tempo than Henderson's, the Bearcats' recording (October 11, 1926) includes saxophone and trumpet solos that try to copy not only Hawkins's solo but also Stewart's—revealing that the Bearcats probably both saw the stock and heard the record. That the Bearcats took such an interest in Henderson's "Stampede" offers further justification for believing that Henderson played it—and perhaps conceived it—especially for the Savoy Ballroom in its opening weeks. Certainly the interior sequence of solos lends itself to the kind of spontaneous expansion that tends to happen when musicians sense a rise in the crowd signaling a desire to extend the dance—a phenomenon that, to judge from the remarks of Dicky Wells and others, was common at the Savoy.[19]

"The Stampede" gives us a musical snapshot of how Henderson and his sidemen channel Armstrong's legacy in a piece well-designed for a Harlem dance venue. It also gives us a glimpse of the future. The basic procedure outlined in "The Stampede" becomes a template for Henderson's band in the late 1920s and early 1930s—a streamlined solo-riff style rising up as an alternative to Redman's intricate early work.

Whiteman Stomp

Far from disappearing, however, the band's richly textured mosaics grew more complex. Two specials from early 1927—"Rocky Mountain Blues" and "Whiteman Stomp"—illustrate an intensive exploration of symphonic jazz, intricately orchestrated pieces placing the burden much more on well-rehearsed ensemble performance than on improvised solos.

Despite its title, "Rocky Mountain Blues" (recorded January 21, 1927) had no links to the mood, style, or structure of a blues (and bears no relation to the identically titled piece that Duke Ellington recorded in 1930). The title simply hides what the piece really is: a paradox of old structure and progressive content. The form, in fact, is a throwback: an old da-capo march structure with nineteenth-century roots that even John Philip Sousa had largely abandoned by the early 1890s, including five sixteen-bar strains, several brief interludes, a modulation to the subdominant for the trio (or "C") strain, and a return to the opening strain (da capo, "from the top") to

A suave portrait of Henderson used as a publicity photo in the late 1930s. *The Stanley Dance and Helen Oakley Dance Archives, Yale University Music Library.*

The Henderson family, ca. 1909. Front: Fletcher Sr., Horace, Ozie; back: Irma, Fletcher Jr. (then named James). *Fletcher Henderson Papers, the Amistad Research Center at Tulane University*.

Fletcher, Irma, and Horace Henderson, ca. 1915. *Frank Driggs Collection.*

The Atlanta University Class of 1920. Left to right: Clayton Yates, Albert Edwards, Marcia Brown, Herbert Thompson, Herbert Greenwood, Horace Hodges, Charles Elder, Ralph Jefferson, Fletcher Henderson, Nolden White, Margaret Moore, George Hodges, Clayton Cornell. In the class yearbook, it was Charles "Snap" Elder who wrote the "prophecy" claiming future comparisons between Henderson and Sergei Rachmaninoff. Family photos also show Henderson and Margaret Moore together informally on the university campus. *Fletcher Henderson Papers, the Amistad Research Center at Tulane University.*

Fletcher Sr. and Jr. at home, New York, ca. 1923. *Frank Driggs Collection.*

Probably Henderson's first professional portrait alone, signed "To Mamma + Papa," early 1920s. *Duncan Schiedt Collection.*

"He was a strict leader," recalled Howard Scott. "Every night you had to … stand inspection." Fletcher Henderson and His Orchestra, New York, probably summer 1924, soon after opening at the Roseland Ballroom. Left to right: Charlie Dixon, banjo; Howard Scott, trumpet; Fletcher Henderson, piano; Elmer Chambers, trumpet; Charlie Green, trombone; Don Redman, reeds; Kaiser Marshall, drums; Ralph Escudero, tuba; Coleman Hawkins, reeds. *The Stanley Dance and Helen Oakley Dance Archives, Yale University Music Library.*

"The 'class' dance place on Broadway." The Roseland Ballroom, at 1658 Broadway, between West 51st and 52nd Streets. *Duncan Schiedt Collection.*

Roseland interior, ca. 1926, featuring two bandstands on the right, each with a banner featuring the bandleader's name: Harvey Marburger and Fletcher Henderson. *Duncan Schiedt Collection.*

"The next night you couldn't get into the place," said Howard Scott. "Just that quick it had gone all around about this new trumpet player at Roseland." Fletcher Henderson and His Orchestra with Louis Armstrong, late 1924. Left to right: Howard Scott, trumpet; Coleman Hawkins, reeds; Louis Armstrong, trumpet; Charlie Dixon, banjo; Fletcher Henderson, piano; Kaiser Marshall, drums; Buster Bailey, reeds; Elmer Chambers, trumpet; Charlie Green, trombone; Ralph Escudero, tuba; Don Redman, reeds. *Frank Driggs Collection.*

Fletcher Henderson and His Orchestra, 1927, soon after Don Redman's departure. Left to right: Henderson; Charlie Dixon, banjo; Jimmy Harrison, trombone; Don Pasquall, alto saxophone; Benny Morton, trombone; Buster Bailey, clarinet, alto saxophone; June Cole, tuba; Coleman Hawkins, tenor saxophone; Kaiser Marshall, drums; Tommy Ladnier, trumpet; Joe Smith, trumpet; Russell Smith, trumpet. *Frank Driggs Collection.*

Don Redman, the key figure in Henderson's early band, in a relaxed pose that belies his intricate scores. *Duncan Schiedt Collection.*

Louis Armstrong stayed with Henderson only thirteen months, but his sound and style continued to resonate in the band's soloists and in Henderson's arrangements for Benny Goodman. *Duncan Schiedt Collection.*

Leora Henderson performed many crucial roles for her husband: booker, straw boss, copyist, talent scout, auditioner, and substitute trumpet player. *Duncan Schiedt Collection*.

Benny Carter said that joining Henderson's band was "a great, great thing for me," and his elegant arrangements helped shape the "Henderson" style. *Duncan Schiedt Collection.*

Horace Henderson both idolized and competed with his older brother; he wrote many great arrangements for his band and some for Benny Goodman as well. *Duncan Schiedt Collection*.

Henderson in the driver's seat of his beloved Packard, Atlantic City, 1929, with participants in Vincent Youmans's *Great Day*, including an unidentified man, Harold Arlen, Bobby Stark, Lois Deppe, Will Marion Cook, and Rex Stewart. *Frank Driggs Collection*.

The hub of Harlem entertainment: The Lafayette Theatre, Tree of Hope, and Connie's Inn on Seventh Avenue near 131st Street in the late 1920s. *Frank Driggs Collection.*

Inside the exclusive Connie's Inn, Henderson's home base in the early Depression years. *Frank Driggs Collection.*

By 1932, Henderson had become "easygoing" and the band had become a loosely run collective of all-star musicians. Fletcher Henderson and His Orchestra, Atlantic City boardwalk, July 1932. Seated: Edgar Sampson, alto saxophone, violin; Sandy Williams, trombone; J.C. Higginbotham, trombone; Fletcher Henderson, piano; Russell Smith, trumpet; Walter Johnson, drums. Standing: John Kirby, bass; Coleman Hawkins, tenor saxophone; Russell Procope, clarinet, alto saxophone; Rex Stewart, trumpet; Bobby Stark, trumpet; Clarence Holiday, guitar. *Frank Driggs Collection.*

Building the Kingdom of Swing: Benny Goodman and His Orchestra, with Helen Ward, during a *Let's Dance* broadcast, 1935. *Duncan Schiedt Collection.*

The King of Swing: Benny Goodman in the film *Hollywood Hotel*, 1936. *Duncan Schiedt Collection.*

Goodman's success helped re-ignite Henderson's bandleading career: the "Grand Terrace" band of 1936, another all-star group. Left to right: Chu Berry, tenor saxophone; Joe Thomas, trumpet; Horace Henderson, piano; Sid Catlett, drums; Fletcher Henderson, piano; Dick Vance, trumpet; Teddy Lewis, vocal; Buster Bailey, clarinet; Ed Cuffee, trombone; Elmer Williams, tenor saxophone; Roy Eldridge, trumpet; Israel Crosby, bass; Fernando Arbello, trombone; Bob Lessey, guitar; Don Pasquall, alto saxophone. *Frank Driggs Collection.*

Advertisement for the "New Grand Terrace," July 1937, emphasizing cool air and hot music and attributing the hit "Christopher Columbus" to Fletcher Henderson alone. *Frank Driggs Collection.*

Helen Ward, Benny Goodman, and John Hammond with Fletcher Henderson, about two months before Henderson's death. "Nobody could have done more than John and Benny," recalled Leora Henderson. *Duncan Schiedt Collection.*

round off the arrangement. The content has all the hallmarks of what by now was widely known as Redman-Henderson style in its darting style of orchestration, made up of a tightly woven collage of one-, two-, four-, and six-bar units—including *seventeen* two-bar breaks. Adding to the festive color is Kaiser Marshall's arsenal of percussive effects, from familiar choked cymbal hits to the more unusual sounds of a woodblock, a slapstick, and a "hiss," produced by some kind of noisemaker (novelty sounds still held appeal in 1927).

From the off-tonic whole-tone introduction to the final, rather inconclusively chattering woodblock break that ends the recording, every section of the arrangement brims with well-played ideas. Schuller has noted "Redman's prophetic ensemble background" in the third strain—a six-voice reed/brass harmonization that anticipates big-band writing of a decade later. In addition, the band once again invokes the break texture (with the rhythm section dropping out) for points of structural contrast inside the strain, not only for conventional end-of-strain solo flourishes. (Boxes highlight these break passages in fig. 5.4.) The penultimate strain (E), for example, alternates

Fig. 5.4. "Rocky Mountain Blues"

B♭:   Intro(2) ens.

      A(16) ens. (2) + ⬚piano break (2)⬚ + ens. (4) twice

      Transition(4) ⬚brass⬚

      B(16) saxes w/brass riff (6) + ⬚brass break (2)⬚ + saxes (8)

      Transition(4) ⬚cymbal and tpts.⬚

E♭:   C(16) [:tpt. solo over reed/brass harmony (6):]

            1st ending breaks: tpts. (1) + clars. (1)

            2nd ending break: tpt. break (2)

      C(16) [:tbn./piano/celeste over clars. riff (6):]

            1st ending break: clars. (2)

            2nd ending break: tpts. (2)

      C(16) tuba/piano lead over brass and saxes (6) + piano break (2) +

            brass (6) + tenor sax break (2)

      D(16) [:brass/tenor sax dialogue (6):]

            1st ending: "hiss" break (2)

            2nd ending: slapstick break (2)

      D(16) [:Saxes/tpt. dialogue (6):]

            1st ending: tpts. break (2)

            2nd ending: cymbal break (2)

      E(16) ⬚saxes (4)⬚ + tbn. (4) + ⬚saxes (4)⬚ + tbn. (2) + tpts. (2)

      Transition(2) saxes and tbn.

B♭:   A(16) ens. (2) + ⬚piano break (2)⬚ + ens. (4), twice

      Coda(4) brass and woodblock

between four-bar saxophone-section phrases without rhythmic backing and trombone solo phrases with the rhythm section. The brass play their long-tone transition between the first and second strains with a sleek hairpin crescendo and diminuendo.[20]

Despite the constantly changing texture, the band drives forward with controlled urgency. The sectional playing is consistently unified, even in several highly exposed end-of-phrase breaks—like this one by the clarinets (ex. 5.8).

Ex. 5.8. "Rocky Mountain Blues" (January 21, 1927), strain 3, clarinet trio break

The rapid-fire dialogue between the brass and Coleman Hawkins in the fourth strain (D) provides another good example of how the musicians maintain momentum through the thicket of scoring (ex. 5.9).

At a tempo of well over 220 beats a minute, the recording evokes the feeling of trying to focus on nearby images from a high-speed train. Every phrase, break, cymbal shot, and trombone blat is perfectly timed in a feat of circus-like exuberance and disciplined precision. "Rocky Mountain Blues," unlike "Stampede," keeps a tight leash on solo improvisation; the performance remains uninhibited and controlled, a mix of uptown and downtown. It would seem, at least, that Forrest S. Chilton, publisher of the stock arrangement, believed the piece would hold broad appeal. The stock's title page announces that the music inside appears "as Played on Columbia Records by FLETCHER HENDERSON AND HIS ORCHESTRA." The stock, however, whose credits read "arranged by Don Redmond [sic]" and "edited by Ken Macomber," does not deliver as advertised. Macomber's "edition" omits many of the breaks and much of the dialogue between sections and soloists (including Marshall's sparkling cymbal work) that marked the colorful original. As with "The Stampede," the stock publisher knew that no band could match what Henderson had played on record.

If "Rocky Mountain Blues" shows Henderson's symphonic leanings, "Whiteman Stomp" stands as an apotheosis of symphonic jazz. Recorded on May 11, 1927, some three months before Redman left the band for good, it also seems to mark the end of an era. In 1927 it was recognized as new territory for Henderson's band, something far from the kind of hot jazz material expected from most black bands. "After a lot of top level discussion," writes Rex Stewart, "it was decided that Henderson would record something musical and beautiful ... for this momentous break with tradition in recording, we set out to prove something, and that is what we did. It was on this date that Don Redman's 'Whiteman Stomp' was produced." Stewart's comment about "this momentous break with tradition" refers not so much to musical innovation per se as to a "break" between musical style and racial stereotype. Nothing about "Whiteman Stomp"—not least its title—suggests its origins in a black band. (Is that why the difficult terrain of "Rocky Mountain" needed to be dubbed a "Blues"—that succinct signi-

Ex. 5.9. "Rocky Mountain Blues," strain 4, Hawkins and brass (top line only)

fier of blackness in the 1920s?) Not that Henderson's recording remained a secret. "The biggest thing Fletcher ever did was 'Whiteman Stomp,'" recalled Russell Smith; "all the bands wanted that one.[21]

As Stewart suggested, the appeal of "Whiteman Stomp" does not lie in its hot solos. The recording does include brief saxophone, trombone, and piano solos, but they sound almost like interludes between the ensemble passages, which are clearly the focus of the arrangement. Now Redman intensifies a familiar technique. Written variation had long been a trade-

mark of his arranging style. As we've seen, after the statement of melody
in the first chorus, each later chorus—when not an improvised solo—
usually drew from Redman a new rhythmic or orchestrational twist. But
in previous arrangements, the written variation of an AABA chorus
remained the same in each of the three "A" phrases. The basis of variation
changed between choruses. In "Whiteman Stomp," however, variation
occurs within each chorus, so that *every* "A" phrase heard after the first
chorus's melody statement is unique. The process resembles the technique
of motivic development in a symphonic score and results in a more fluid
conception—one that Henderson would later use selectively in his arrangements for Benny Goodman. As a result of this new approach, Redman
introduces five variants of the main phrase in just one-and-a-half choruses,
including chromatic and whole-tone harmonic enrichments as well as
rhythmic alterations (ex. 5.10).

Ex. 5.10. "Whiteman Stomp" (May 11, 1927), original melody and subsequent variations

In the last variation, we hear the phrase augmented to five bars, thus
producing another familiar Redman trademark—the "extra" bar. Other
typical traits of Redman's arranging appear, such as subdividing eight-bar
phrases into two halves, one for the ensemble or a section of the band, and
the other for a soloist. In the second strain, a dialogue is created by one-bar
alternations. Another effect with a precedent lies in the third strain. Here the
orchestrational subdivision occurs within the measure, resulting in a quick,
obviously well-rehearsed exchange between the brass and reeds, similar to
an effect heard as far back as the 1924 recording of "Driftwood" (ex. 5.11).

Ex. 5.11. "Whiteman Stomp," strain 3, beginning

Yet another familiar technique includes the break-like suspension of the rhythm section as a structural device creating variety, heard in at least one variation of each of the piece's three strains. The arrangement also includes a "pyramid" effect, a stack of four notes played one-at-a-time by the tuba, trombones, saxophones, and trumpets. Altogether, "Whiteman Stomp" reveals a store of devices packed tightly together in an arrangement of dizzying variety—so dizzying that in the end it is possible to detect a strong dose of parody in the whole conception. The very title was a joke: for all of Whiteman orchestra's considerable achievements, the last thing that could be said of it was that it was the kind of hard-charging, rhythmically aggressive ensemble known at the time as a "stomp" band. That a co-composer credit goes to Fats Waller supports the notion. Waller, who even appears as guest pianist on the "Whiteman Stomp" recording, had an almost compulsive urge to signify on a style or a piece.

Perhaps the parody was lost on the piece's namesake. Paul Whiteman himself recorded the piece on August 11, 1927, and his band performs the arrangement almost exactly as the Henderson band had played it three months earlier, but at a slightly faster tempo. Even Whiteman's soloists followed the Henderson version, virtually note-for-note. That Whiteman adopted the same arrangement as the Henderson band's shows two things. First, it reveals that "Whiteman Stomp" was entirely—or almost entirely—scored, solos and all; in this, as well as in its motivic development and its harmonic and orchestrational sophistication, the piece was both a bona fide symphonic jazz composition and a parody of the whole style. It also suggests a role reversal. Now, the orchestra whose success had provided a model for Henderson's band just four years earlier was following the lead of its protégé—as if Paul Whiteman had become the Fletcher Henderson of his race.

6

Beyond the Ballroom

I F THE INTRICATE SCORING of pieces such as "Rocky Mountain Blues" and "Whiteman Stomp" places them in a different stylistic world than streamlined arrangements such as "The Stampede," the explanation lies not just in aesthetic matters but in practical ones: Henderson's symphonic jazz repertoire was not for dancers but for listeners. Whiteman himself regularly played such works in concert halls, but most bands—black and white—tended to cultivate listeners in another venue: the theater. In the later 1920s and early 1930s, Henderson played in many theaters—the Harlem Opera House, and the Lafayette, Lincoln, Alhambra, and Public Theaters in New York; the Howard Theater in Washington, DC; and the Pearl Theater in Philadelphia, among others. And Henderson's work in these venues covered the spectrum of popular genres, from vaudeville to revues to musical comedies. Henderson's band was better for dances than for theaters, and indeed Henderson had mixed success in this realm, including a notorious failure that briefly dissolved the band.

A band could still play a varied repertoire in the theater. After all, theatrical performance included a great deal of dancing, and bands could even include a few hot solos in their accompaniments and features. But theater work did not encourage a band to stretch out a number indefinitely in response to the crowd, as at the Savoy. In Bushell's words, the theater required a bandleader to "be more particular in choosing a program ... A smart bandleader would change things for a theater gig: he would cut down the time, use spectacular stuff." "Rocky Mountain Blues" and "Whiteman Stomp" count among the most "spectacular stuff" that Henderson ever recorded, and although no report exists to confirm it, those pieces—and other "symphonic" repertoire in Henderson's book—would have been well-suited for performance in a theater.[1]

For black bands, theater work increased in the 1920s, in part, because Noble Sissle and Eubie Blake's *Shuffle Along* (1921) had sparked a resurgence of interest in all-black shows. In the fall of 1928, for example, the band played for a revue called *Jazz Fantasy* at Harlem's Lafayette Theatre. Dancers, singers, comedians, and chorus girls appeared "and through it all Henderson's master musicians wove a spell of wonderful music—dance music, jazz music, classical airs!" Later that year, Henderson's band substituted for Allie Ross's orchestra in the pit for the *Blackbirds of 1928*, with songs by Jimmy McHugh and Dorothy Fields. In 1932, the band played one-week stints in revues called *Big House Blues* (at the Lafayette Theatre) and *Harlem Highsteppers* (at the Public Theater in lower Manhattan), where most of the band routinely showed up late and ultimately lost the job. All of these engagements reveal Henderson to be well connected, if sometimes indifferent, to the thriving black musical theater scene.[2]

Such experiences help create a context for the band's most infamous brush with the theater: Vincent Youmans's Broadway-bound *Great Day* in 1929. Many theater jobs allowed a band to play its own book; a Broadway show did not. Youmans conceived the show as a grand mixed-race pageant of the South, tapping a vein that had been so successful for Jerome Kern and Oscar Hammerstein II's *Show Boat*, which by summer 1929 had just closed after a spectacular run of 572 performances. The musical would include a substantial cast, announced as 150 performers in the *Pittsburgh Courier*, which along with other black newspapers covered the show's preparation because it involved a large cadre of African-American talent, including vaudeville headliners (Flournoy) Miller and (Aubrey) Lyles and a chorus of some forty "jubilee singers." The chorus was to be directed by Will Marion Cook, by now a legendary composer and arranger prominent in musical theater for three decades. The pit orchestra was intended to feature equally illustrious black musicians: Duke Ellington and his orchestra. But after a conflict between Youmans and Ellington's agent, Irving Mills, Ellington had to be replaced, and the solution appeared to be Henderson's band. Playing in the pit orchestra of what promised to be a major production by a leading Broadway composer even enticed Louis Armstrong to move back east to participate.[3]

Within a month, however, things fell apart. Youmans hired several white musicians to augment the orchestra and eliminated six members of Henderson's band. Henderson, still in position as the orchestra leader, apparently had difficulty coordinating the expanded ensemble. The *New York Age* claimed that there was "no race conductor on the horizon capable of conducting this large show," and soon Henderson himself got fired, and his remaining sidemen either quit or also got fired. (Armstrong quit too, but he nevertheless found his way to Broadway by way of Harlem's Connie's Inn. There, he starred in Fats Waller's revue, *Hot Chocolates*, the platform from which he would help make Waller and Andy Razaf's "Ain't Misbehavin' " a popular song.) Although the experience was almost entirely negative for Henderson, it did lead to an unusual publication: his composition called "Water Boy Serenade (A Pianistic Spiritual)," brought out by Youmans's publishing house and possibly intended for *Great Day*, but not used. With its chromatic harmony and accented syncopations in a black spiritual context, the piece reveals obvious links to the stylized vocal arrangements recently published by James Weldon Johnson and J. Rosamond Johnson in their two *Books of American Negro Spirituals* (1925–26), part of the renaissancist impulse to preserve black oral tradition in written forms.

At first glance, there may seem to be nothing remarkable about the *Great Day* incident. Bands got hired and fired all the time; it was a rough business. But the experience amounted to an embarrassing failure for Henderson. Covered closely by the black press, the behind-the-scenes maneuvering publicly transformed the show from a model of racial integration into another case study in racial inequity. Moreover, Henderson was hurt by lack of agency. Mills had fought for Ellington; but Henderson had no one to back him up. So when six of his sidemen got fired, Henderson continued on the job with half his band, augmented by several white substitutes. His action—and more importantly, his inaction—lost him credibility with his sidemen, a pattern that would haunt him for the rest of his career. *Great Day* itself went on to Broadway for a paltry run of thirty-six performances. The band, temporarily dissolved, would not make another record for well over a year. Soon, however, Henderson was able to pull together an ensemble of new and old sidemen and embark on a promising new venture. Oddly enough, in the early years of the Depression, two years of instability would resolve for Henderson into a brief period of stability and prosperity at a Harlem nightclub called Connie's Inn. In the meantime, Henderson's prestige grew from an increasingly demanding schedule on the road.

Speed Men

By the late 1920s, the band's reputation had spread far from its New York hub thanks to radio and records. Rex Stewart reported, "we went further and further afield on our summer tours." Walter C. Allen's itinerary of the band's "known playing engagements" for the period from July 1927 to September 1930 confirms Stewart's memory of the tours. It lists appearances by the band in more different venues and in a wider geographical range—possibly extending as far as Tulsa, Oklahoma—than any earlier period.[4]

Life on the road was grinding and even dangerous, but Henderson's band sustained an aggressive touring schedule from 1926 until the band dissolved in late 1934. The roads were generally uneven, or at least unpredictable. "[T]he highways were bad in those days," recalled trombonist Sandy Williams, who joined Henderson's band in January 1932. "You might have to make a detour, get stuck in muddy roads, or make a stop at one of those dinky gas stations." And traveling posed a greater risk of racial incidents, ranging from mild annoyances to "ugly" comments or worse. In at least one instance (in Pennsylvania), Henderson requested and received a police escort out of town. At another time, Rex Stewart recalled that Leora, acting as straw boss when Fletcher was committed to appear elsewhere, was forced to wait on the bus while the proprietor of a "nice, clean looking place" argued with his wife about whether light-skinned Leora should use the "white" or "colored" facilities. Leora finally resolved the dilemma by declaring herself "a Negro ... and proud of it." Out of self-defense, "In those days, everybody would have his own gun," Williams explained. "You could buy a gun as easy as a pack of cigarettes." Dicky Wells claimed that "the cats started to carry firearms" around the time "when the Charleston first came out" (1923–24), after hearing about a drummer who got castrated and killed in Florida.[5]

In spite of all the struggles and threats, Henderson and his men greeted the prospect of tours like kids out of school for summer vacation. The musicians enjoyed traveling, and they lived life on the road with reckless abandon. "All the restraint broke down when we had to leave to go on tour," noted Stewart. As its prestige grew, the band became a closed, masculine, and hierarchical social system with a clear "pecking order" and a penchant for organized vice. Stewart recalled the band as "crazy with gambling fever." J. C. Higginbotham, who joined the band in late 1931, said that "[e]verybody in the band drank. If you didn't drink you weren't a member of that band." Higginbotham would later rue his image as a hard-drinking hell-raiser because it attracted what he called "liberal" whites who liked to "prove" their tolerance by "getting drunk with us or asking us to share a stick of marijuana with them ... but we soon learn that they rarely want normal, 'respectable' relationships with us."[6]

Alcohol intake was ameliorated by plenty of food. In Stewart's memorable phrase, "Smack's band was the eatingest band I've ever known," with macho competitions between band members, especially Jimmy Harrison and Coleman Hawkins. "A typical meal after work," Stewart recalled, "would consist of half a dozen eggs, a triple order of ham or bacon, a toasted loaf of bread, plus fried potatoes, jelly, coffee, pie, and perhaps a meat sandwich—just to keep the sweet taste of the pie out of his mouth, as Jimmy used to explain." Harrison overindulged his passion for ice cream during a stint in Harrisburg, Pennsylvania, in 1930 and landed in the hospital with an exacerbated ulcer. He died the following year. Despite the hazards, the rest of the band tried to keep up, and Stewart, as a result, gained twenty-five pounds in one summer. Dicky Wells recalled similar eating contests between Redman, Carter, and Hawkins. For many band members, prodigious appetites extended to the opposite sex, and, as Wells wryly put it, "If you own a boarding house, you have to be on the ball to prevent your family being larger after the band leaves." Henderson himself enjoyed playing pool and gradually developed his reputation as a ladies man, but he generally remained aloof from the informal social club that his band had become. Higginbotham noted that Henderson drank, but only after a performance; and clarinetist Russell Procope described Henderson as not much of a "mixer." But one thing that Henderson did indulge was his love of fast cars.[7]

At a time when many bands rode in buses, guaranteeing that everyone arrived in the right place at the same time, Henderson and his sidemen often took automobiles. The practice was remarkable enough to merit comment from Duke Ellington, who noted that the Henderson band took "cars, instead of buses." In the 1920s, car buying had risen to an all-time high, and a boom in road construction in New York City itself enhanced the appeal of the power and beauty of automobiles. In the 1920s "modern New York ... with its skyscrapers, tunnels, bridges, and adjacent speedways, was under noisy and, it seemed, perpetual construction." That headlong, "noisy" rush into modernity suited the hard, fast lifestyle of Henderson and his sidemen.[8]

Cars opened up personal opportunities that a bus could not, including the chance to drive fast and to "linger" in the previous town, as trombonist Benny Morton suggests:

in the early years [probably around 1926–27] there were four regular car owners: Fletcher, Russell Smith, Joe Smith, and Kaiser Marshall. Don Redman sometimes had a car. Coleman Hawkins came along later with his, and he was a speed man. But Fletcher was the fastest driver, and he belonged on the Indianapolis Speedway! Because he was the fastest, he would linger longer in a town, and anything might happen. He would start late, and he might have the key players in his car, so those who got there earlier couldn't get started. Maybe he was speeding and a cop took him back twenty miles to a judge, and he came in an hour or so late … then Fletcher would walk in like nothing had happened.[9]

To Henderson and his sidemen, cars signified freedom and success. "Fletcher was car crazy," recalled Wells. Every year, Henderson himself bought a new Packard, a visual symbol of elite status. Band members took great pride in lining up their cars outside the Rhythm Club at 132nd Street and Seventh Avenue—a hub of the Harlem entertainment scene—before a road trip and having "a real second line of spectators" gather around the assembled band. The thrill of the ride easily matched the spectacle of lining up before the trip. "Smack's guys used to drive fast," said Wells. Stewart concurred: "Those were the days of running up and down those bad roads at 75 and 80 miles an hour," he wrote, " … hung over on whatever we had had to drink the night before." Sandy Williams remembered exceeding one hundred miles an hour in Hawkins's car. Even Henderson's serious accident in 1928 did not subdue their obsession with speed.[10]

Sometimes they had no choice. One night the band finished a performance in Louisville, and Henderson realized he did not know where to go for the next job. So the musicians made a caravan back to New York. When they arrived at Henderson's home on West 139th Street, Leora met them at the door and asked why they had returned: they were due in Lexington—seven hundred miles back the other way—the next day. There was no question of skipping the date. "So," wrote Stewart, "we gassed up immediately, stopped by the bootlegger's and got some whiskey, and hit the road."[11]

"A Victim of the Times"

Aside from its vivid picture of a freewheeling lifestyle on the road, Stewart's anecdote evokes a larger issue affecting Henderson's band—and all others—by the late 1920s: agency. "Our tours preceded the days of booking agents," he wrote. The role of securing these free-lance engagements fell to Fletcher and Leora, "a large-framed, imposing figure of a woman who had a thorough knowledge of the music business." After marrying Henderson (on Christmas Day, 1924), she became the band's "de facto booking agent," arranging summer tours and setting other dates not claimed by the Roseland contract. As we've seen, Leora had a stronger command of the band's schedule than her husband did, and the couple had no professional manager who could have arranged the band's schedule. Later, in the early 1930s, Leora also acted as the band's straw boss and road manager, going on the road in a bus with the musicians during a period when Fletcher was double-booked and had to appear elsewhere. Such ad hoc arrangements increasingly revealed Henderson's band to be as professionally backward as it was musically advanced.[12]

Despite the band's prestige, Leora and Fletcher simply lacked the connections—and the complexions—to find the most lucrative jobs when professional band managers began to enter the scene in the late 1920s. Thomas J. Hennessey has identified the years 1929–35 as the transitional period when white managers created and consolidated the business practices that dominated the swing era. Agents had become the business's "gatekeepers." Duke Ellington's success highlighted Henderson's deficiency in this area. From 1927 on, Ellington had the white publisher and music entrepreneur Irving Mills on his side. Rex Stewart sums up Henderson's predicament, in contrast to Ellington's good fortune, in the late 1920s:

> Henderson might have maintained his advantageous position but the cards were stacked against him. This was mainly due to his own temperament which was basically not competitive enough even to seek out a manager like Ellington's, who had the connections to all of the important outlets for work. The good engagements were concentrated in the white theaters and the big white clubs. Since Henderson was never able to get a manager with effective ties to the scene where the real money was, he became a victim of the times.[13]

Managers and agents began getting into the act just as Henderson felt more competition from other bands, black and white. In the late 1920s, many large black orchestras began to make recordings that rivaled Henderson's. Ellington's orchestra, now in residence at the Cotton Club, had hit stride with its distinctive style (in such pieces as "East St. Louis Toodle-Oo," "Black and Tan Fantasy," and "The Mooche") and was turning out more recordings than ever. McKinney's Cotton Pickers, the Missourians, and bands led by Charlie Johnson, Bennie Moten, and Luis Russell all began competing for a share of the market that Henderson's band had played a large role in creating. The multifaceted Clarence Williams, always attuned to the latest musical trends, also formed a large orchestra in the late 1920s. Moreover, all but Russell and Williams were recording extensively on the prestigious (and sonically beautiful) Victor label. Meanwhile, Paul Whiteman, who shifted his allegiance from Victor to Columbia between 1928 and 1930, had begun to focus his band upon a greater jazz orientation, with the crucial addition in 1927 of two key jazzmen from Jean Goldkette's band: arranger Bill Challis and cornetist Bix Beiderbecke. Goldkette himself continued to manage one of the period's hotter white bands, which also recorded for Victor.

Henderson's inability to shift with the rise of agency, then, forms the larger context for viewing two events that many accounts of the Henderson band point to as reasons for a temporary decline in its quality in the late 1920s: Don Redman's departure in July 1927 and Henderson's car accident in late August 1928, and his supposed subsequent lack of ambition and discipline. These claims have some merit but tend to be overexaggerated.

The main reason usually given for the band's apparent decline is the departure of Don Redman. During the band's summer tour in the Midwest, Redman parted ways with Henderson in Detroit and joined McKinney's Cotton Pickers, a band he helped transform into a leading dance and jazz ensemble of the late 1920s and early 1930s. (The band's racialized name reflects the same impulse for plantation exotica that charged some of Duke Ellington's Cotton Club shows.) Henderson was able to replace the vacancy in the reed section with Jerome "Don" Pasquall, whose operatic nickname, after Donizetti's *Don Pasquale*, tagged his classical training. Pasquall had ideal qualifications for the job: he had played in Doc Cook's orchestra (considered by Rex Stewart "the Chicago counterpart of Fletcher

Henderson") before attending New England Conservatory and, apparently, graduating from there in late June of 1927.[14]

Replacing Redman the reedman was one thing, but filling Redman's shoes with a new arranger was a different matter, a problem that has led historians toward overstatement. It appeared that "Henderson never completely filled the enormous gap left by Redman's departure," and Schuller states that "as architect of the band's style he [Redman] was virtually irreplaceable." Coleman Hawkins also suggested that the band had become rudderless without Redman. Apparently referring to the late 1920s and early 1930s, Hawkins noted that Henderson began "exchanging arrangements with other bands," such as Jean Goldkette, the Casa Loma Orchestra—"all the big-time bands"—and, as a result, Henderson's band was "beginning to sound too much like other bands." As we'll see, Redman's departure did indeed incite Henderson to seek out other arrangers, but it also spurred Henderson to begin to take on more arranging himself.[15]

Henderson's serious car accident in late August 1928 is widely assumed to have exacerbated the decline in leadership and discipline. Henderson's wife, Leora, claimed that after the accident near Frankfort, Kentucky, in which Henderson supposedly suffered a head injury, he became "careless" and indifferent to maintaining a high level of precision in the band. Yet according to Theresa Henderson Burroughs, Henderson's niece, "the story about the head injury sustained in Frankfort, Kentucky, and his subsequent lack of interest and motivation is totally false." Fletcher injured only his collarbone. He received treatment from a local doctor and, because no hospitals in the area would admit blacks, recuperated "for a few days" at the home of Burroughs's mother (Horace Henderson's wife) in nearby Winchester. While she could not explain why Leora would have spoken of a head injury, Mrs. Burroughs said that relations between Fletcher and his wife were strained, that the couple had been separated at the time of the accident, and that Fletcher was involved with another woman. Nevertheless, the couple stayed in contact and Fletcher sent Leora $75 a week during their separation. Given Leora's crucial role in the band's business affairs, it seems likely that the couple's separation by 1928 further affected Henderson's ability to secure engagements.[16]

Henderson's injuries, then, may have been overestimated, but many observers have still noted an apparent loss of focus. Success had apparently brought with it a relaxation of discipline, though no loss of musical verve. In public, "Fletcher's band had some of the worst starts you ever heard in your life," Hawkins recalled. "We'd be starting off—half the band would be looking for the music. . . . That used to happen regularly. . . . But when it got down to the core of the music—I mean, when it's supposed to be sounding good, everybody was together and everybody was playing like mad." The live performances were "sloppy," but, to Hawkins, the recordings were worse. "The majority of [other bands] sound one hundred percent better on record than they do in person. . . . Fletcher's band was just the opposite. The records sound terrible, sound like cats and dogs fighting."[17]

Players and listeners alike have often noted the disparity between the band's public performances and recordings in the 1927–34 period—Hodeir's so-called transitional period. Rex Stewart stated that "people who didn't hear the Henderson band in person are misled by listening to the records." John Hammond published an article making the same point: "Don't let yourself be impressed by the records of Fletcher Henderson," he wrote in September 1934, "because they don't do him justice." White jazz critic Wilder Hobson heard the Henderson band perform in public in 1927 and 1928, and his memory of the experience inspired poetic encomiums. Few of the band's recordings, he noted, "give anything like the golden, seething spirit of a Fletcher Henderson occasion." Although Hobson offers the usual criticism of Redman's "fussy and fancy" arrangements, he writes that "in the relaxation of the dance hall they came off with much more ease and swing."

> Furthermore, with no time limit as in recording, Henderson could let his soloists stretch out for several choruses, building up to those fiery full-band improvisations which had an ecstatic freedom such as I have heard from no other jazz orchestra. In action before a dancing crowd (not to mention the cluster of standing addicts) Henderson offered not the elegance of Duke Ellington, not the incredible buoyancy of the early Basie, but a dionysiac heat.[18]

In Hobson's view, recordings fail to capture both the quality and length of the Henderson band's live performances in the late 1920s.

Streamlined Stocks

A few recordings, however, give at least a glimpse of that "dionysiac heat," especially when heard in the context of other contemporary sources, in print and on record. These show the post-Redman band in action, revealing new twists on an old approach—the thorough renovation of stock arrangements. Now, however, instead of chopping up the material into quickly shifting phrases and colors, the music receives a streamlined treatment comparable to "The Stampede."

"Hop Off" has been celebrated as one of Henderson's best recordings of the late 1920s. For Schuller and Williams, the solos, which are said to illustrate "how far the soloists had gone in absorbing Armstrong," hold the primary appeal. The arrangement, on the other hand, is "not quite so well balanced." Yet when observed from other perspectives, the arrangement seems every bit as impressive as the solos it incorporates. Considered together, the stock arrangement and two recordings, from October (for Paramount) and November 1927 (for Columbia), throw into relief the dramatic revision that the later recording represents.[19]

There is some question whether the first "Hop Off" recording, in October 1927, was Henderson's, since it was made under the pseudonym "Louisiana Stompers." At least a few Henderson sidemen played in this band. Buster Bailey's fluid style, tinged with a little shrillness in the upper register, marks the clarinet solo. More telling are the trombone (Harrison) and bass saxophone (Hawkins) stoptime breaks; they provide glimpses of passages that reappear more vividly—especially in the case of Hawkins, who transfers to tenor sax—on the more famous recording of a month later (ex. 6.1).[20]

Ex. 6.1. "Hop Off" (1927), trombone and saxophone breaks

Despite the presence of at least three of the same soloists on both versions of "Hop Off," it is still possible that the "Louisiana Stompers" recording was made by a pick-up band led by Clarence Williams, the composer of the piece. Several Clarence Williams recording sessions in late 1927 and early 1928 included both Buster Bailey and Coleman Hawkins.

The record label itself supports claims for either band. This "Hop Off" and its reverse side, "Rough House Blues," appeared on Paramount's 12000 "race" series. Although Henderson's nonvocal recordings almost always came out on general series, there is precedent: Henderson's band did make two sides for Paramount's race series in the spring of 1927. Meanwhile, Clarence Williams also recorded for Paramount's race series in January, July, and October, the last date including Bailey and Hawkins as sidemen.

Whether the band that first recorded "Hop Off" performed under Henderson's or Williams's leadership, it delivered the piece essentially as it appears in the stock arrangement, published by Williams's own company in 1927. The performance follows the format and orchestration of the stock,

Fig. 6.1. "Hop Off," Louisiana Stompers, October 1927

Ab:	Intro(4)	brass
	Vamp(4)	bass sax
	A(32)	ens.
	B(16)	brass (8) + saxes (8)
	C(16)	saxes (8) + brass (8)
	A(8)	ens.
	Trans(4)	ens.
Db:	D(16)	clar. solo
	D(16)	tpt. solo
	Trans(4)	ens.
	D(16)	ens., with tbn. break
	D(16)	ens., with bass sax break
	A(16)	ens.

adding two choruses of the last strain for the clarinet and trumpet solos, a transition, and the two solo breaks in the ensuing ensemble choruses (fig. 6.1).[21]

Henderson's Columbia recording the next month (November 4, 1927) kept this overall design, with only slight alterations, but fills it with many new ideas, and changes entirely the character of the piece. Far from the jovial, relaxed bounce of the earlier recording, the Columbia version transforms "Hop Off" into a searing, aggressive stomp—without significantly increasing the tempo. The Columbia version replaces the original introduction—and its rigidly martial secondary rag rhythm—with an explosive solo by Tommy Ladnier over sustained ensemble chords (ex. 6.2).

Ex. 6.2. "Hop Off"

Ex. 6.2a. Stock arrangement, introduction, as played on Louisiana Stompers recording (ca. October 1927)

Ex. 6.2b. Ladnier solo on Henderson recording, introduction (November 4, 1927)

The first strain of the Columbia recording completes a process of transformation that had begun modestly in the Paramount version. Example 6.3 shows the first four bars of melody in the stock. In the Paramount recording, the saxophones divide the melody's whole notes (in mm. 1 and 3) into three quarter notes and a rest, while a trumpet and trombone weave obbligato lines around it.

Ex. 6.3. "Hop Off," beginning of strain 1, stock arrangement, piano part

In the Columbia recording, the three quarter notes become a stoptime accompaniment to Tommy Ladnier's hot breaks, which grow increasingly spectacular (ex. 6.4).

Ex. 6.4. "Hop Off," Ladnier solo, first strain, mm. 1–4, 9–12

Only in the third appearance of this phrase (the "A" part of an AABA chorus) does the band play the original melody (as shown in ex. 6.3), dramatizing it with hairpin crescendos on the whole notes. When the phrase (shown as A[8] in fig. 6.1) returns again after the third strain, Coleman Hawkins bursts in a bar early with a powerful solo that erases all signs of the original melody (ex. 6.5).

Ex. 6.5. "Hop Off," Coleman Hawkins solo

The Columbia "Hop Off" seethes with tidal power and inevitability. The ensemble playing combines polish and drive, from the theme statement in the second half of the first strain, through the surging saxophone-section passage in the second strain, to the final, improvisatory ensemble choruses and coda, topped off by Buster Bailey's wailing clarinet. And the two ensemble out-choruses build on the intensity that flows out of a series of hot solos—by Harrison, Bailey, Ladnier, and Smith. Who holds responsibility for structuring such an accumulation of musical energy? Redman usually gets credit as the arranger, but, since he no longer played in the band, on what basis is that credit earned? Most likely, "Hop Off" resulted from the band's collective reworking of the stock arrangement. Its solution lay chiefly in letting the star soloists take the spotlight.[22]

"Hop Off" represents what we might call the "liquidation" of a stock arrangement. Instead of introducing complications inside the strain,

Redman style, the band simplifies the piece, emphasizing horizontal flow and continuity instead of surprise and textured contrast. This is precisely what the band does even more vividly in the piece that became closely associated with it in this period and beyond: "King Porter Stomp."

Composed by Jelly Roll Morton in the peak decade of ragtime, "King Porter Stomp" ranks among the oldest pieces in Henderson's repertoire, yet, in the band's revision, it became one of the most influential arrangements in the swing era. Henderson had first recorded the piece in 1925, when Armstrong was in the band, but the recording was never released. Soon thereafter, the piece seems to have dropped out of the dance-band repertoire. When Henderson's band revisited the piece in 1928, it became the main conduit through which "King Porter Stomp" passed from the jazz age to the swing era. Henderson made three different recordings of the piece: the revised version recorded in 1928, the so-called "New King Porter Stomp" of 1932, and another revised version of 1933. In these recordings we hear his band transform the piece from a stock to a head arrangement, that is, an arrangement developed through discussion and demonstration with little or no written music. In the process, "King Porter Stomp" changed from a multi-strain rag-based piece to a streamlined "jamming" piece for improvising soloists, a shift graphically revealed in figure 6.2.

The 1928 recording occupies a pivot point in the piece's biography; it can be heard in at least two contrasting ways. Retrospectively, it marks the earliest documented stage of Henderson's transformation of the piece. So it

Fig. 6.2. Form Outlines of "King Porter Stomp" Recordings, 1923–35

Morton (1923)	I(4)	A A B B X Cx Cx Cx' T
Melrose stock (1924)	I(4)	A A B B X C Cx Cx' T
Morton (1924)	I(4)	A A B B X C Cx Cx' T
Lanin (1925)	I(4)	A B B X C C C Cx Cx' T
Creath (1925)	I(4)	A A B B X C C Cx Cx Cx' T
Morton (1926)	I(4)	A B B X C Cx Cx Cx' T
Henderson (1928)	I(8)	A B X C C C C Cx' Cx' T
Henderson (1932-33)	I(8)	A X C C C C C C Cx Cx' T
Goodman (1935)	I(8)	A X C C C C C Cx Cx' T

I = Introduction
A = first strain
B = second strain
X = interlude
C = Trio
Cx = Stomp 1
Cx' = Stomp 2
T = Tag ending

stands as a rough early version of the arrangement that evolved in the early 1930s to become a national hit for Benny Goodman in 1935 and a big-band standard thereafter. As I've written elsewhere, listening to Henderson's recordings of 1928–33 "from a classicized perspective on musical composition is like hearing a sketch develop into a finished score."

Yet the "sketch" analogy, however apt in retrospect, obscures the arrangement's basis in aural, not written, music-making, and the exciting, even radical nature of Henderson's revision. So it takes some effort to hear the arrangement from the contrasting perspective of the 1920s. The band announces its distinctive approach from the opening bars, with a new eight-bar introduction featuring a fiery trumpet solo by Bobby Stark that resonated into the swing era and beyond (ex. 6.6).

Ex. 6.6. "King Porter Stomp," introduction. Top line: Bobby Stark solo (March 14, 1928). Bottom line: solo on 1936 published arrangement by Fletcher Henderson.

The solo's tone, figuration, and structure further suggest Louis Armstrong as a kind of "missing link" in the piece's evolution. Armstrong's trademarks permeate the solo, including the syncopated leaps of a fourth at the opening, characteristic of Armstrong's solos with Henderson three years earlier, and the big, blaring tone throughout. The whole eight-bar unit parses clearly into a pair of parallel four-bar phrases, with the rhythm of mm. 5–6 nearly identical to that of mm. 1–2. That reveals a new sense of the importance of linking and relating phrases of a solo, of the coherence that Armstrong had brought to the jazz solo since his early days with Henderson.

The overall form of the arrangement throws greater emphasis on the trio and stomp than ever before, beginning a pattern that would extend into the swing era. Henderson's band omits the repeats of the first and second strains, setting another trend that would become standardized in the 1930s. The first trio hews close to Morton's original melody; subsequent choruses of the trio are used for solos backed by riffs. The stomp, on the other hand, becomes the place for the whole band to shine. In the 1928 recording, the band runs through the stomp just once, but that chorus would become the most famous of all: the call-and-response chorus that Schuller has termed "the single most influential ensemble idea in the entire swing era" (ex. 6.7).[23]

Ex. 6.7. "King Porter Stomp," beginning of final strain (1928) (from Fred Sturm, *Changes Over Time*, 63)

While many ideas anticipate standard swing arranging practice, the rhythm section marks this as a 1920s recording. Two instruments in particular signify the recording's twenties vintage: the tuba, mostly plugging alternate beats (one and three), and the banjo, strumming a steady four-beat pattern. Close listening also reveals a haze of ride cymbal and high hat work, including a cymbal hit after the final cadence—a trademark of Henderson's drummer, "Kaiser" Marshall, since 1923. The whole recording lopes along at around 180 beats per minute, approximately the same tempo as Henderson's former competitor, Sam Lanin, had taken it in 1925. Rhythmically, the 1928 version looks not forward but backward.

When Henderson recorded the piece again on December 9, 1932, it was issued under a revised title: the "New King Porter Stomp." This "King Porter" is "new" in many respects. The band quickened the tempo to 210 beats per minute. The string bass (played by John Kirby) and guitar (Freddy White) impart a lightness and forward momentum far from the comparatively heavy, "vertical" tread of the 1920s tuba-banjo combination. Formally, the new version makes a decisive shift toward the trio and stomp: the band omits the rag-like second strain entirely, adds two solo choruses to the trio, and creates a new stomp strain acting as an intensive build-up to the final call-and-response shout chorus, which now features saxophones in place of the outmoded clarinet trio. Howard Spring has convincingly argued that the differences between Henderson's first and second "King Porter" recordings may partly be explained by the development of the Lindy Hop in the late 1920s and early 1930s—another instance of music-and-dance symbiosis.

Despite fundamental changes, however, it remains a "head" arrangement whose basic structure, procession of solos, riff foundation, and climactic antiphony remain intact from 1928. With the second strain's omission and the trio and stomp's expansion, the first strain now sounds like an extension of the introduction: an introduction to a series of solos over a riff foundation. That foundation, poured in 1928, now solidifies in Henderson's 1932 and 1933 recordings. Under Stark's first-trio solo, the saxophones play a syncopated variation on Morton's original trio melody, which had been in the foreground in Henderson's 1928 recording. Coleman Hawkins's solo appears over a four-note syncopated brass riff. The first chorus of J. C. Higginbotham's trombone solo is accompanied by a falling-thirds figure in the saxophones that had its origins under Jimmy Harrison's trombone solo in 1928.

By 1933 the riff foundation has become more pronounced. Now, the recording balance shifts so that the solos interact with the riffs rather than soaring above them. The band retains the basic structure from 1932 while changing some of its contents. Henry "Red" Allen's trumpet solo fills the two-chorus slot, previously taken by J. C. Higginbotham, preceding the ensemble out-choruses. Morton's original trio melody, suggested in the saxophones' variation of it under Stark's solo, comes to the fore in a clarinet in the next trio strain A transcription and analysis of the 1933 recording by Dave Jones and James Dapogny allow for a closer look at it, revealing several things. First, they notate and discuss the exceptional solos of Coleman Hawkins and Red Allen. Both soloists demonstrate an uncanny ability to "float against the rhythm," to create and sustain "motivic coherence" apart from the original melody, and, in general, they reveal "improvisers thinking compositionally." All of this suggests the ongoing impact of Armstrong. Second, they reveal "many small disagreements among members of the band about what notes and rhythms to play and how to play them," reinforcing the notion that even five years after his band's first issued recording of the piece, Henderson's "King Porter Stomp" remained unnotated, a "head" arrangement "made collectively by the band members and played from memory."[24]

By then, public performance practice had departed from recording practice, which had to fit the arrangement into the three to three-and-a-half minute limit of a 78 rpm record. "King Porter Stomp" provides yet another example. According to Sandy Williams, who would soon be playing the piece with Bobby Stark in Chick Webb's band, on Christmas night at the Apollo Theater, "I counted the choruses I played on 'King Porter Stomp'— twenty-three. Bobby Stark and I could play as many choruses as we felt like on that, so long as each chorus was a little more exciting. That was *our* tune." The piece also became an exhibition for the whole ensemble. In public, the call-and-response chorus developed a visual analog. Rex Stewart recalled that, in a battle of bands with McKinney's Cotton Pickers in Detroit, Horace Henderson's Collegians, led by Benny Carter, played "King Porter Stomp" "bobbing in rhythm on the two out-choruses ... the combination of motion, screaming brass and pulsating saxophones tore up the Graystone Ballroom. The crowd roared, whistled and demanded more, more, more. So we had to repeat the out-choruses four times!" Accounts like Williams's and Stewart's are reminders that part of "King Porter"'s appeal came from things that were never captured on a printed page, a sound recording, or any other media.[25]

In retrospect, it appears that "Hop Off" shaped the band's approach to "King Porter Stomp." Indeed, the two recordings are so similar in approach that "King Porter Stomp" sounds like an attempt to revisit the musical method of the earlier piece. Both pieces have old-fashioned multistrain forms, and their arrangements use the final strain as the basis for a series of solos culminating in a climactic ensemble passage. Coincidentally, both tunes also have identical key schemes. Both begin in A♭, then modulate, in a dramatic four-bar transition, to D♭ for the final strain. Their arrangements also begin in the same way—with a blaring hot trumpet solo that replaces the introductory melody of the stock. The approach to the final strain choruses also link "Hop Off" and "King Porter Stomp." Both alternate between brass and reed solos accompanied by riffs or chords played by the opposite section of the band.

"King Porter Stomp" was the oldest in the repertory of old jazz pieces that the Henderson band played. It originated as one of Jelly Roll Morton's piano solos, before 1911, then began its second life as a band arrangement in late 1924. In response to the publication of the stock, several bands recorded the piece in early 1925. Although Henderson's version of February 1925 was never issued, recordings by Lanin's Red Heads (February 1925) and Charles Creath's Jazz-O-Maniacs (March 1925) follow the stock arrangement.

Between 1925 and 1928, the year Henderson revived it, "King Porter Stomp" received only one recording, Morton's own solo piano performance in 1926. There exists a tantalizing hint about how Henderson may have come to decide to re-record the piece in 1928. The four sides made in the Columbia studio just a day before Henderson recorded "King Porter Stomp" featured Morton at the piano. Perhaps Henderson received the piece, or the suggestion to play it, from the composer himself. Morton did not hesitate to take credit. According to Horace Henderson, "He [Morton] and Fletcher were great friends. . . . Fletcher won quite a few battles of music with 'King Porter Stomp.' And Jelly Roll Morton knew this, and he used to go and say, 'I made Fletcher Henderson.' And Fletcher used to laugh at all these things and say, 'You did,' you know. He wouldn't argue."[26] These circumstances further support the notion that the 1928 "King Porter Stomp" is a "head" arrangement, worked out on the spot by the band's lead musicians. According to Allen, the arrangement stems from Hawkins's ideas, while trombonist Sandy Williams credited material in the arrangement to Charlie Dixon.[27] There is no contradiction in these claims; the arrangement that came to be known as Henderson's "King Porter Stomp" was doubtless a collaborative effort. It was an effort that established a pattern for developing head arrangements of popular songs in the early 1930s, and one well suited to a band on the move, beyond the Roseland Ballroom.

7

Connie's Inn Orchestra

I N THE FALL OF 1930, Henderson's fortunes took an upward turn after a long hiatus from recording and the bitter experience of *Great Day*. His band returned to the recording studio for the first time in almost seventeen months, and it began a new job at a prestigious venue. For much of 1929 and 1930, the band had lived a precarious but joyfully reckless existence on the road, driving prized automobiles and reaping the widespread popularity that radio performances and recordings had sown. Back in New York, however, they had to be more professional and reliable, seeking the financial security and stability that a long run in a coveted venue could bring. With the end of the long tenure at the Roseland (where from now on Henderson would appear mainly as a guest), Henderson naturally sought a comparable situation: he found it in Harlem.

Now the band had a new home base, and the labels of several records advertised the fact by calling it the "Connie's Inn Orchestra." Opened in 1923 by the brothers Connie and George Immerman, Connie's Inn was a basement venue in a central location. At Seventh Avenue and 131st Street, it added luster to an already hallowed ground occupied by the Lafayette Theatre (next door) and the fabled Tree of Hope, an old elm thought to give good luck to those who rubbed its bark (or met an agent or booker there)— especially performers looking for work in this entertainment-rich area. Musicians who worked there remembered the neighborhood vividly. Clarinetist Russell Procope, who would join Henderson in March 1931, described it as a place where "almost every doorway you'd pass you'd hear some music coming out." The white clarinetist Mezz Mezzrow recalled with particular relish the whole area along "Seventh Avenue, going north from 131st Street," including the "dicty Connie's Inn."[1]

Nightclubs represent yet another distinct type of venue for Henderson's work in the 1920s and 1930s. Unlike theaters and ballrooms, most nightclubs offered intimate spaces where customers sat at tables, drank, and sometimes ate while watching a professional floor show. In those ways, Connie's Inn must have reminded Henderson of his band's first job at the Club Alabam. Meanwhile, like the nearby Cotton Club, where Duke Ellington would soon end his long run, it offered all-black entertainment to a mostly white crowd from about 10 P.M. until 3 A.M. Although next door to the famed Lafayette Theatre, "Connie's Inn was in a different bracket entirely," said Procope, who played at both venues. By the early 1930s, the populist Lafayette staged mostly variety and vaudeville for large crowds of black Harlemites, known to be vocal in expressing their critique of the talent. The exclusive Connie's Inn, charging a steep cover of fifteen dollars, offered a more intimate atmosphere in a smaller space, and "[m]ost of the people came from downtown," Procope said. Blacks were generally not admitted unless they were light-skinned enough to pass—or else they were entertainers or waiters.[2]

Celebrities enhanced the venue's aura. "I remember seeing Clara Bow and Harry Richman. They were big stars ... and they came up there in an aluminum-bodied Rolls Royce," recalled Procope. Thinking back on it nearly a half century later, he marveled at how Connie's Inn offered an oasis of plenty in the early Depression years. By early 1931, unemployment was much more severe in Harlem than in other parts of the city. "Well, no Depression for the movie people," Procope noted, and "there were some bands that just kept rolling, like Fletcher Henderson." Procope also fondly recalled how "in those days nobody was afraid to go anywhere. You'd see the people from downtown with high silk hats and the ladies in diamonds and furs and things, and just strolling down the street, you know, three or four o'clock in the morning." The night before joining Henderson, Procope had been playing in Chick Webb's band at the Roseland Ballroom—the cream of the downtown jobs. But at Connie's Inn "I almost doubled my salary.... Connie's Inn was one of the top nightclubs." Vaudevillian Jimmy Durante thought Connie's Inn was the "swankiest" Harlem nightclub. He might have been right from an observer's standpoint, but musicians saw it differently. Guitarist Lawrence Lucie, who joined Henderson a few years later, recalled simply that the Cotton Club was "the Number One job," and Connie's Inn was "Number Two."[3]

The Connie's Inn job offered not only a choice location, better pay, and a more elite clientele than most venues, it also presented live broadcasts on network radio. Henderson had gotten radio exposure through the 1920s over local station WGN from the Roseland, of course, but network broadcasts on the Columbia Broadcasting System's WABC from Connie's Inn held out the promise of making Henderson a national presence on the airwaves. The black press observed that Henderson's was the "only colored band" featured on WABC. Such radio appearances sparked recording activity, so that in 1931 Henderson's band released far more recordings than it had in the whole three-year period of 1928–30. Now, with regular recording sessions complementing the Connie's Inn gig and its radio wire, Henderson had a "good deal," as Allen writes, "especially at a time when the entertainment business was dropping to its low ebb." Allen goes on to claim the Connie's Inn Orchestra as "a great one ... one of Fletcher's best."[4]

Other jazz historians assessing the Connie's Inn Orchestra through its recorded legacy have been considerably less enthusiastic. Gunther Schuller has argued that Henderson's band had "some severe artistic lapses" in the early 1930s, revealed in "desperate maneuvers" to transform Tin Pan Alley songs into jazz. Similarly, John Chilton notes that Henderson's band appears to "backtrack" during this time, "producing dull recordings of the indifferent commercial songs of the day." As a result, by 1931, Henderson "had failed to consolidate the position he had gained as the foremost black bandleader of the era." At least some of the blame, Chilton continues, may be placed on recording executives, "who were quite aware that a record packed with improvisation (no matter how brilliant) was unlikely to achieve high sales figures." The critical response to Henderson's Connie's Inn legacy echoes the prevailing interpretation of Henderson's pre-Armstrong band of 1923–24. On one hand, the band enjoyed a high-prestige job and widespread admiration. On the other hand, it fails to make consistent progress toward the swing era, as revealed in its recordings, and thus comes up short in the assessment of later commentators.[5]

Again, resolving the conflicting views begins with looking at the venue, not the recording studio, and seeing the extent to which recordings manifest one by-product of the band's professional activity, not its chief focus. Like the Club Alabam and the Roseland, Connie's Inn required a versatile band with the stylistic dexterity to shift quickly among numbers in a disparate repertory. Russell Procope recalled that the band played "tangos, waltzes, foxtrots, college songs, current hits, excerpts from the classics in dance tempos, just about everything," and for Procope, that kind of versatility marked success. Benny Carter, who was "traded" for Procope in March 1931, concurred. "I don't recall any 'desperation' while I was in the band," Carter explained. "I felt it was always at a high musical level—just look at the personnel! . . . We played a wide variety of material, as I think all bands tried to, because that's what people wanted to hear . . . the band was doing quite well and seemed to be working regularly."[6]

In the early 1930s, then, the job—rather than a desperate need for one—led Henderson's band to make records of current pop tunes among many other kinds of pieces. Recordings of Tin Pan Alley fare that sound like "severe artistic lapses" or "backtracking," then, simply reflect part of the varied repertory demanded by the job. In fact, the recorded legacy is less lamentable for mixed artistic success than for its highly selective view of the band's repertory and style. Among the records there are no tangos, no waltzes, no college songs, no dance arrangements of the classics. Together, the records comprise a detail from a broad canvas that we will never see.

That phenomenon is a reminder of something several black musicians have pointed out about the period from the mid-1920s to at least the mid-1930s. It was the "pop" material, not hot jazz, that record producers often discouraged (or forbade) black bands from recording because it neutralized their exotic, racial appeal. In the mid-1920s, Elmer Snowden's early band played soft, muted music instead of "growling stuff," but Victor did not issue it on record because "our music wasn't the kind of *Negro* music they wanted" (emphasis original). Rex Stewart, one of several Henderson sidemen who had been associated with Snowden in the 1920s, noted that "there was an unwritten custom among record people that no negro orchestra should be allowed to record anything that wasn't blues or hot stuff." Bandleader Andy Kirk had a similar experience in the early 1930s. "All the time we were making race records we were playing our pop tunes, romantic ballads, and waltzes for the dancing public. . . . But the people who controlled the output and distribution for Brunswick and Vocalion never gave a thought to that side of our band. . . . It was all part of the racial setup and climate of the times." Such observations, considered along with Henderson's activity in the period, reveal the ongoing resonance of musical renaissancism, where black musicians prized versatility—not just the ability to improvise hot jazz—as the ultimate mark of mastery because it challenged stereotypes that the white-controlled music industry had reified.[7]

Coming and Going

The Connie's Inn Orchestra was indeed a versatile and varied group of musicians. They could also be volatile, freewheeling, and proud. And they were "gentlemen," which Benny Carter has noted too often gets forgotten amid the lingering stereotypes of early jazz musicians, Henderson's sidemen in particular.[8]

The *Great Day* fiasco of 1929 at first appeared to cause a complete breakdown, but the band's accumulated prestige and talent acted as centripetal forces that drew many musicians back to the fold. Meanwhile, however, other bandleaders tried to lure Henderson's musicians away with attractive offers; Chick Webb, in particular, continually raided Henderson for new talent. For the next five years, then, Henderson's band would continue to operate on a revolving-door policy, with several musicians coming in, staying a few months or a year or two, and going out (see fig. 7.1). Although musicians became increasingly frustrated with Henderson's inability to "take care of business," as Procope referred to it, they came and went mainly because that was common practice in the band business of the late 1920s and early 1930s. Work came "fast and furious," Procope said, because, in his view, "the business was good at that time. You could leave one job and go on another job or just freelance around with different people." The most notable instance occurred in March 1931, when Henderson and Webb pulled off "The Big Trade," as Procope called it: Benny Carter and Jimmy Harrison (to Webb's band at Roseland) in exchange for Procope and Benny Morton (to Henderson's band at Connie's Inn). The swap was remarkable enough to be reported in the press. In a Columbia recording session soon thereafter, Horace Henderson marked the event with a new piece called "Comin' and Going."[9]

Several musicians who had been with Henderson in the late 1920s were back by the time Henderson opened at Connie's Inn in late November 1930, or else they had never left. The trumpet section remained intact. Russell Smith, a Henderson stalwart and one of the finest black lead trumpet players of the era, remained in first chair. Rex Stewart and Bobby Stark took the hot solos. Stewart, as we've seen, had been hired to "play like Louis." In the early 1930s, Stewart may also be heard imitating the solos and styles of others, including King Oliver and the white cornet star Bix Beiderbecke, whom he admired. Stewart carried a "dignified" air, recalled his fellow Washingtonian Duke Ellington (with whom Stewart later played, from 1934 to 1945). Ellington praised Stewart as an "extremely versatile" and "exciting player" who harbored "intellectual ambitions."[10]

Bobby Stark, if less ambitious and less versatile, was perhaps the more original improviser. A key figure in the illustrious Hendersonian trumpet lineage that connects Louis Armstrong in the 1920s to Henry "Red" Allen and Roy Eldridge in the 1930s, Stark was a daring, "bravura" soloist known for taking spectacular chances and sometimes missing notes along the way. His adventurous, reckless behavior off the bandstand seemed to mirror his seat-of-the-pants approach to soloing. A heavy drinker (with trombonist Sandy Williams he would form part of a dynamic duo known as "Mr. Bar and Mr. Grill"), he was chronically late, and for his supreme combination of irresponsibility and talent, he got "fired and hired at least twice a season," according to Stewart. Stark remained with Henderson almost continuously

Fig. 7.1. Coming and Going: Henderson's Personnel, 1930–34 (brief substitutions not included)

	1930	1931	1932	1933	1934
Trumpets	Smith				
	Stewart			Allen	
	Stark				Thomas___Randolph
Trombones	Harrison___Morton_Higginbotham			Wells	Johnson
	Jones		Williams		Jones
Reeds	Boone	Sampson		Jefferson	
	Carter	Procope			
	Hawkins				Young___Webster
				Bailey	
Piano	Hendersons				
Guitar	Holiday			White_Holiday___Addison	Lucie
Bass	Kirby				James
Drums	Johnson				

for more than five years (beginning late 1927), finally getting fired for good after setting off firecrackers with Sandy Williams during a dance in Pelham, New York, on July 4, 1933.[11]

Unlike the steadfast trumpets, the trombone section was in flux. Until his death in July 1931 Jimmy Harrison continued as the section's leading soloist and an occasional singer, emerging as one of the most influential improvisers of the era; after appearing in a few more remarkable recordings, he went with Benny Carter to Chick Webb's band in "The Big Trade." Benny Morton, who acknowledged Harrison's influence, summed up his importance in what might have been as apt epitaph: "Jimmy had soul and drive, and everybody was crazy about him. He had the warmth of a good Baptist preacher, and he made other people happy. And it all came out in his music."[12]

Harrison was paired with Claude Jones, who had joined Henderson to play in the *Great Day* pit orchestra in May 1929, remained until the end of 1931, and returned sporadically thereafter. Born in Boley, Oklahoma, Jones had spent several years under the disciplined leadership of William McKinney, beginning in 1921 or 1922 and continuing through the band's legendary period of the late 1920s as McKinney's Cotton Pickers with Don Redman. In his early years he showed the influence of white trombonist Miff Mole, but:

> by the time he was with Henderson he had a big, velvety tone and a refined sense of melody; his solos were propulsive and inventive, and, unlike most of his contemporaries, he frequently employed the upper register of the instrument. He could handle changes of pace in a deft manner ... and his use of upward rips became something of a trademark.[13]

Such qualities stand out in his "Sugar Foot Stomp" solo. As a product of McKinney's band, Jones was also a crack reader. He can be heard playing straight melody and refined section work in Henderson's Connie's Inn band recordings.

The Connie's Inn reed section fluctuated with the trombones. It began with Hawkins, Carter, and Harvey Boone, all of whom had been with Henderson in the late 1920s. Hawkins remained the undisputed star. Even with Stark, Harrison, and others playing spectacular improvised solos, Hawkins stood out. With some residual frustration, Rex Stewart recalled that "[y]ou could play a solo that was created with every ounce of your ability and no one on the bandstand would even bother to listen. Yet the minute Coleman Hawkins started playing, all the guys would start nodding their heads in approval." To keep his increasingly impatient star happy, Henderson soon began to resort to giving Hawkins special billing during tours.[14]

By March the reed section began to change. Benny Carter went to Chick Webb in the trade for Russell Procope, who would remain with Henderson until the band dissolved in late 1934. In June, Boone would be replaced by the multifaceted Edgar Sampson. A few words on these figures are in order.

Harvey Boone appears to have been hired mainly to play lead and featured little or no solo work. He had attended a New Haven music school in the early 1920s.[15] Like several of Henderson's reedmen (Carter, Redman, Sampson), he had played with Duke Ellington briefly in that band's pre-

Cotton Club days. He was among many Henderson sidemen whom Carter described as a "gentlemen."

Edgar Sampson played reeds and violin, and later became better known as a composer and arranger. His bluesy violin playing may be heard on a few Henderson recordings in 1931, including "House of David Blues." He had come up through several key bands of the 1920s, including the band of the refined and savvy Billy Fowler and the gritty Charlie Johnson band. His quiet gentleness earned him the nickname "the Lamb," but he would be heard loud and clear later in the 1930s through his two compositions played by Chick Webb and popularized by Benny Goodman: "Stompin' at the Savoy" and "Don't Be That Way."

Russell Procope was another key figure for his dependability and comparative longevity in the band, staying more than three and a half years. And, besides Stewart, no other musician in Henderson's Connie's Inn band left a more vivid account of the period. He played professionally in at least ten different bands in the six years leading up to his tenure with Henderson. That was the longest period he spent with any band until landing his final long-term job in 1946 with Duke Ellington, with whom he stayed until Ellington's death in 1974. Procope cut an impressive profile similar to those of Henderson's early 1920s musicians, and thanks to his valuable oral history, we have more detailed information on his career than on almost any other Henderson sideman of the early 1930s.[16]

Born in New York City, Procope had grown up in a black middle-class family that, like Henderson's family, took classical music seriously—in itself and as a symbol of respectability. He remembered listening to everything from opera singers (Alma Gluck, Luisa Tetrazzini, and Ernestine Schumann-Heink) to early jazz and blues musicians such as Ted Lewis, the Original Dixieland Jazz Band, and Mamie Smith on "an old Victrola." He also recalled his father, a violinist, and his mother, a pianist, playing at home popular classics such as the "Poet and Peasant." These musical experiences at home instilled a taste for musical diversity and versatility that clearly shaped his attitudes as a professional musician and his memories of jobs. He would later admire Henderson in particular for the unusual range of his repertoire at the Roseland and at Connie's Inn. He called Henderson "more advanced" than other bandleaders because "at Roseland you have to play all types of music, not only jazz."

Thanks to his father's model of diligence ("he studied and studied and played at home") and guidance, he began his musical studies on the violin, and "I took to it" and "loved it." Like many talented young black musicians in early 1920s New York (including Bobby Stark), he then took up studies with Eugene Mikell (which he pronounced like "Michael"), the former associate of James Reese Europe, and played in the 369th Cadet Band. He also played violin in the high school orchestra, which won first prize among comparable groups in New York. His life took a turn when he became fascinated with reed instruments, taking up the clarinet then alto saxophone, both of which were purchased by his mother over the objections of his "old school" father, Procope recalled.

Procope remembers hearing Louis Armstrong in Henderson's band as a life-changing experience. Saving up $1.10 to go to the Roseland, Procope "stood there with my mouth open all night. I didn't move away from the front of the bandstand.... And I think right then I decided what I was going to do with my life." His musical education continued on two fronts: playing stock arrangements in dance bands, beginning in 1926 with his first professional job; and listening to jazz on records, especially the ones of Armstrong in Henderson's band. "I started playing these Louis Armstrong records," he said, "and in about six months the whole damned neighborhood was playing Louis Armstrong and Fletcher Henderson's records." Procope went through several bands in the 1920s, ultimately playing with some major bands and bandleaders, including Jelly Roll Morton (at the Rose Danceland dancing school), McKinney's Cotton Pickers, Benny Carter, and Chick Webb. Not a star like many of Henderson's sidemen, Procope was nevertheless a key figure in the band, a solid section player, and dependable soloist. Duke Ellington, with whom he played for nearly thirty years, wrote a characteristic tribute, calling him "a master of the old New Orleans style" and "a man of dignity and gentility, of clean and gentlemanly appearance. What is more, he became a conscientious, all-around musician, one always to be depended upon."[17]

While the trombones and reeds were in flux, the Connie's Inn rhythm section formed a solid anchor. Much of Henderson's musical power in the early 1930s came from talent and consistency in this group. Henderson himself continued to play piano, now in alternation with his brother Horace. Clarence Holiday continued on guitar, earning the nickname "Lib Lab" (or perhaps "Lib Blab") for his tendency to talk a lot in the presence of young women, whom he eagerly sought and courted. Holiday, too, had played in the band of Billy Fowler in the mid-1920s before joining Henderson in 1928. He left Henderson in the summer of 1933, about the time his daughter, Billie, was just beginning to make a name for herself in Harlem nightclubs. Lawrence Lucie, who channeled Holiday's influence while playing for Henderson in 1934, admired Holiday for his "way of accenting the backbeat a little," which "set up a terrific swing."[18]

A couple of other musicians joined Henderson's rhythm section for the first time in the transitional year of 1929–30 and stayed through the Connie's Inn engagement and into 1934. They were the key figures at Connie's Inn and beyond: Walter Johnson and John Kirby.

Walter Johnson, born in New York City, became one of the leading drummers of the early swing era while in Henderson's band from mid-1929 to late 1934 (with one or two brief breaks in 1930)—the most extended presence in the band than anyone but Hawkins, Russell Smith, and Henderson himself. He had begun working professionally by the age of twenty, moving through dance bands led by Freddie Johnson, Bobby Brown, Elmer Snowden, and Billy Fowler, the saxophonist-bandleader through whose band some half a dozen musicians—including Benny Morton, Jimmy Harrison, Tommy Ladnier, Benny Carter, and Clarence Holiday—passed on their way to become Henderson's sidemen. Johnson joined Henderson in June 1929 and became, in Gunther Schuller's words, "the real leader of the Henderson band." Johnson's drumming has inspired unusually vivid commentary from historians as well as musicians who played with him. T. Dennis Brown has emphasized how Johnson's "simple, metrically accurate, legato hi-hat accompaniments ... bridged the gap between the choke-cymbal style of the 1920s and the swing style of the 1930s." Henderson, however, seems to have had a hard time adjusting to Johnson's new style—or something about his behavior—for he fired Johnson in the spring of 1930, rehiring Kaiser

Marshall briefly, only to rehire Johnson for more money soon thereafter. Johnson's drumming seems to have "sonically enveloped the band," in Schuller's words, especially through his use of cymbals, to create, like only a handful of his contemporaries, a "more linear conception of playing jazz drums." Words such as "flow" and "line" described Johnson's playing, capturing the uncanny "horizontal" momentum and drive a drummer can create beyond the simple ability to mark beats. All of these qualities are clearly heard on Henderson's recording of "Business in F" from late 1931. Lawrence Lucie, who would join Johnson in Henderson's band in 1934, said: "They used to call Walter 'Stick and Brush'..... He used brushes a lot on the cymbal, and he was a great cymbal player, a smooth cymbal player," comparable to Count Basie's great drummer Jo Jones, Lucie noted, in his light yet intense time-keeping.[19]

John Kirby formed the other half of Henderson's unique rhythm combination. Born in Baltimore, he was orphaned as a young boy. The first musical instrument he learned was trombone. After moving to New York about 1925, his trombone was stolen, and he briefly worked at odd jobs, including a stint as a Pullman train porter, to earn money to buy a new instrument. With the money, he now turned his sights on a tuba, a fundamental feature of a typical dance-band rhythm section in the 1920s. While playing in a band called Bill Brown and His Brownies in 1928–30, he began learning the string bass under the auspices of two the instrument's leading exponents: Wellman Braud, a key Ellington sideman, and Pops Foster, a New Orleans native and veteran musician who had played a major role in sparking the wholesale shift from tuba to string bass in the late 1920s New York jazz, thanks to his impact in Luis Russell's band. When Kirby walked into his first rehearsal with Henderson's band, his rube-like ways inspired derision in the band. With exaggerated precision, Stewart called Kirby "nine-tenths Caucasian," and Kirby learned to affect an ignorant white country-boy routine that got the band out a tight situation when it was low on gasoline while touring through Virginia.[20]

In Henderson's Connie's Inn period, Kirby alternated between tuba and string bass, sometimes on the same recording session. His string bass at the time was made from aluminum, which gives off a powerful resonance in recordings such as Henderson's "Chinatown, My Chinatown." By 1933, he had switched from aluminum to a more conventional wooden instrument and rarely played tuba. Kirby also imparted a powerfully linear feeling to Henderson's performances, which are especially vivid when he plays the more modern four-beat style of the early 1930s, which he could blow on the tuba as well as he could pluck on the bass. Kirby would stay with Henderson from April 1930 to March 1934, almost as long as Johnson did. With Kirby and Johnson together for four solid years, Henderson had "one of the finest rhythm teams of the thirties."[21]

Although the Connie's Inn Orchestra had never existed as such before, most of the musicians knew each other, and many had worked together. In the "fast and furious" business described by Procope—and with the Harlem neighborhood around Connie's Inn already established as a favorite gathering place for musicians—most of Henderson's sidemen had crossed paths before and felt entirely at home playing music together in an elite Harlem nightclub and in a variety of Manhattan recording studios.

Although recording activity thus presents selective slices of Henderson's work that year, the records nevertheless tell an important dimension of the story. Even within the narrower range of recorded repertory, variety is still the keynote: instrumentals and vocals mix in almost equal proportion, and the band plays old Tin Pan Alley tunes ("My Gal Sal," "Chinatown, My Chinatown"), early jazz standards ("Tiger Rag," "Clarinet Marmalade," "Milenberg Joys"), recent popular songs ("Star Dust," "Somebody Loves Me"), recent jazz pieces from white composers and arrangers ("Singin' the Blues," "Business in F"), Horace Henderson originals ("Hot and Anxious," "Comin' and Going"), Fletcher Henderson's "Just Blues," and a few distinctive numbers by one Nat Leslie, whose "Radio Rhythm" stands out as one of the band's most remarkable recordings of the early 1930s. It was also in this period that the band revisited—and transformed—its biggest hit from the 1920s, "Sugar Foot Stomp," making fully four new recordings of the piece in 1931 alone. Meanwhile, the band veered between "sweet and hot," to quote the title of a Harold Arlen/Jack Yellen song that the band recorded in 1931. In several numbers, the band accompanied popular vocalists in lighthearted love songs and a variety of racialized material, reflecting the exaggerated racial difference on which Connie and George Immerman's enterprise depended. These records mark a qualitative change in Henderson's recording career.

The New Jazz Singing: Fox-trots with Vocal Refrain

In the Connie's Inn year, Henderson made eighteen records that featured a vocal refrain—about 40 percent of Henderson's total in the period. That marks a striking shift in emphasis from the previous decade. Throughout the 1920s, Henderson had played vocal accompaniments, mostly for vaudeville blues singers such as Bessie Smith, and often with small pickup groups of sidemen from his current band. The record labels gave the singer top billing. That work, spawned by the blues craze, featured few instrumental passages and formed a distinct sideline to his public appearances and recordings with the full band under his name. The early 1930s, however, placed emphasis on the newer "vocal refrain" format, which usually featured just a single vocal chorus framed by at least two instrumental choruses. The record labels give top billing to the band, usually do not name the singer, and call the numbers "fox trot . . . with vocal refrain."

Jazz historians have found in these vocal recordings signs of Henderson's struggle and desperation in the early Depression years. But a closer look at the music and its context reveals little sign of hardship. Indeed, the amount, variety, and quality of these records during the Connie's Inn year suggest the opposite: they add to the impression of a thriving, versatile band that kept current with the latest trends in jazz-oriented dance music. Collectively, these recordings resonate with a revealing, sometimes attractive, period flavor, which can only be heard if the recordings are framed within developments in popular singing during the period.

The years 1929–32 witnessed an expansion and diversification of male popular singing, thanks especially to two young vocalists who came to prominence during that time: Louis Armstrong and Bing Crosby. Armstrong, known throughout most of the 1920s as a trumpet player first and a scat singer second, began to be known as an interpreter of lyrics from 1929 onward. He launched this new phase of his career with his hit record of "Ain't Misbehavin'," a song that Armstrong featured in *Hot Chocolates*, a revue that had originated at Connie's Inn and gone on to Broadway. Meanwhile, Crosby was becoming another influential figure in popular singing, beginning in 1926 as part of a group called the Rhythm Boys, the vocal attachment of Paul Whiteman's orchestra, then as a full-fledged soloist. By 1931 he had emerged as a national star, singing with what Will Friedwald has called a "warm B-flat baritone with a little hair on it, the perfect balance between conversational and purely musical singing." Amid the new styles represented by Armstrong and Crosby, soft, intimate male crooners also continued to thrive, including Gene Austin and Rudy Vallee. At the same time, a brand of peppy, vaudevillian vocalism flourished, though few strove to match the manic belting of Al Jolson, whose style was on the wane.[22]

Henderson's singers work within this vocal terrain. Some came from inside the band. Most notable among them was Jimmy Harrison, who delivers a witty, flexible rendition of "Somebody Loves Me," backed by a harmonizing trio. Harrison also sings a vocal refrain on the band's recording of the Arlen/Yellen tune "Sweet and Hot," a new show tune that embraced popular music's fundamental dichotomy through a comparison with feminine allure. Harrison's delivery mixed speech and singing in a resonant baritone, and his drawling, sometimes stuttering, but perfectly timed delivery grew from his imitations of the legendary vaudevillian Bert Williams.

Henderson's records also featured Dick Robertson, a popular white tenor who appeared regularly on radio and records with a variety of dance orchestras from 1927 on. Robertson's increasing popularity may be gauged by his appearance in January 1931—six months before singing with Henderson—on records bearing the label "Dick Robertson and his Orchestra," a group that included jazz-oriented musicians such as the Dorsey brothers and guitarist Eddie Lang. Robertson sings a variety of material on a four-song session with Henderson in July 1931. These sides feature consistently bright, peppy, loose-limbed performances. They include ample space for hot solos, a rollicking rhythm section founded on John Kirby's two-beat tuba, and a device that was all the rage in the vocal-refrain format: an active instrumental obbligato line in counterpoint with the singer's melody. Robertson's material ranges from slightly risqué courtship confections, such as "My Sweet Tooth Says I Wanna (But My Wisdom Tooth Says No)," to a back-to-Dixie number called "Malinda's Wedding Day," describing an idyllic celebration in the Old South, complete with stereotyped pet names for African Americans that had been in circulation for at least a century ("Old black Joe and Mammy Clo with Sambo by the ear"). Under the circumstances, it may seem remarkable that the band's performances sound so relaxed and spirited, but "plantation" songs and scenes had been common currency at the Cotton Club while Ellington was there from 1927 to 1931 and would continue to form a staple of Tin Pan Alley repertoire.

Henderson also recorded with George Bias, known as the "colored Gene Austin" for his light, intimate style comparable to the era's leading white crooner. Although his advertised link to Gene Austin suggested his appeal, his work with Henderson stands far from typical crooner material. Instead, it features two explicitly racialized songs of a kind that had proved remarkably persistent since the heyday of minstrelsy. One is a pseudo-revival number called "Moan, You Moaners," which exoticizes the emotional intensity of Pentecostal worship. The other, "Roll On, Mississippi, Roll On," is another back-to-Dixie song with a familiar nostalgia for an idealized South. Allusions to other songs reinforce the mood, from Foster ("Swanee folks I adore") to Hammerstein ("Come on, you ol' man river, come on"). The recording launches and docks the song with a steamboat whistle that harks back to railroad effects popular in 1923–24. The whole arrangement clearly derives from a stock, yet the performance sounds flexible and spirited (see fig. 7.2).

Fig. 7.2. "Roll On, Mississippi, Roll On"

Stock arrangement (Frank Skinner) (Shapiro, Bernstein & Co., 1931)			Connie's Inn Orchestra (Victor, April 29, 1931)		
Fast Fox-Trot			$\downarrow$ = ca. 268		
G major modulating to E♭ major and A♭ major			G major modulating to E♭ major and back to G		
Intro(8) steamboat whistle, with saxes and tbn. (4) + ens. rising chromatic line(4)			same		
A(40)	Vocal with saxes doubling melody, vn. obbligato, and brass interjections		A(40)	a	ens. melody
				b	"
				a	saxes melody muted tpt. obbligato
				c	"
				a'	"
A(40)	repeat		A(40)	vocal, with saxes doubling melody, muted tpt. obbligato	
B(24)	brass lead, with ens. playing punctuating chords on beats 2 and 4		same		
A(40)	a	clar. solo	A(40)	a	alto sax solo
	b	"		b	"
	a	"		a	tbn. solo
	c	ens.		c	ens.
	a'	"		a'	saxes (add tpt.)
X(4)	modulating transition based on two-bar figure from final cadence previous chorus		same		
A(22)	a	ens., with tbn. obbligato	A(24)	a	same
	c	saxes with brass answers		c	saxes with tbn. slides
	a	ens. (truncated to 6 bars)		a	same
Tag (4)	steamboat whistle effect as in intro		same		

In addition to featuring popular songs and stock arrangements, the Connie's Inn run marks a crucial period when Henderson tapped a variety of arrangers, black and white, for "special" material, arrangements not only custom-made for his band but recorded by few others or none at all. In bringing focus to such material, historians and critics have understandably emphasized Henderson's all-star sidemen as the foundation of his success, but their solos must be heard within the context of the arranging styles and arrangers with whom Henderson worked during this period. They too became a key force in shaping Henderson's later work.

"Fletcher used all sorts of arrangers" at Connie's Inn, recalled Procope. Yet it is also precisely this period when Henderson himself took over some arranging chores. For his part, Benny Carter had no recollection of Henderson's arranging activity when he was in the band in 1930 and early 1931. "I don't recall him ever working on an arrangement or modifying one at a rehearsal," although Carter acknowledges that "I was never that close to Fletcher and had very little contact with him off the bandstand." Before Carter left, clearly, Henderson did not rely only on himself to create his band's book. After the "Big Trade," however, he does seem to have exerted more creative control. Horace Henderson, who played in his brother's band intermittently in the early 1930s, recalled that Fletcher "would write skeleton things . . . and he would explain where to jump, and 'I want to insert this, but I didn't have time to do this,' and so on, because he was always busy." But Horace also recalled Fletcher as "pretty thorough at rehearsals." Horace's remarks suggest that Henderson's early arranging activity comprised ad hoc efforts that combined elements of written and head arrangements, so that rehearsing amounted to an extension of arranging.[23]

That, then, forms the key point in understanding the Connie's Inn period's role in shaping big-band jazz. What Schuller has termed "Hendersonese"—the basic style of Goodman's arrangements from 1935 onward, and by extension the standardized style of the swing era—began to coalesce in the early 1930s from such informal activity plus the specials of a variety of arrangers, including John Nesbitt and Benny Carter, then Bill Challis, Nat Leslie, Archie Bleyer, Horace Henderson, and Fletcher Henderson himself.

"A spectacular, out-of-this-world swinger" (John Nesbitt)

When Henderson took his band back into the Columbia recording studio on October 3, 1930, the band played works by Nesbitt and Carter, two of the leading black arrangers of the period. In the mid-1920s, John Nesbitt had joined William McKinney's band (which became McKinney's Cotton Pickers) as a trumpet player and played a large role in developing that band's book of hot specials. Don Redman joined that effort when he left Henderson and became a member of McKinney's band in 1927. In the early 1930s, Nesbitt "made arrangements for Henderson like mad," according to Horace Henderson, but only one known Nesbitt chart got onto disk: "Chinatown, My Chinatown." Rex Stewart, who played it, describes the arrangement as "a spectacular, out-of-this-world swinger" that brought out the best Henderson's band had to offer. "[W]e tore into that music with such a vengeance that, wherever we played, dancers screamed for more," he recalled. The band, he added, "could hardly wait to get back to New York to record this blockbuster."[24]

The introduction breaks out like a cavalry charge, with a fiercely galloping groove topped off by brass and reed shouts. John Kirby enters with the first chorus, slapping down a track of beats, four to the bar, and thereby presenting a kind of rhythmic foundation that will become the swing-era norm in the years to come. The band surges through six choruses at a giddy tempo of about 280 beats per minute.

Hearing the recording leaves a listener astonished by Stewart's assessment of it. "When the long-awaited record date finally took place," he recalled, "by some strange quirk of fate *Chinatown* proved to be merely a second-rate performance." It's hard to know what Stewart is talking about. A look into the band's activities at the time, however, provides a clue to his disappointment. Henderson would not begin at Connie's Inn for another eight weeks. But in the two weeks leading up to the "Chinatown" recording session on October 3, Henderson's orchestra had been playing regularly at the Savoy Ballroom. Perhaps, in Stewart's memory, a studio performance of "Chinatown" could never rival the vital energy of playing it for the Savoy dancers. And this may be another reminder of how the band's recorded legacy may fall short of re-creating the experience of performances in a public arena, where dancers choreographed the music, and where, undoubtedly, the band would have extended its performance (especially the solo sequence) for several minutes beyond the three-minute length of its 78-rpm record.[25]

If records did not reflect the arrangement's true quality, other hot bands nevertheless found in the tune worthy material for recording because of Nesbitt's arrangement. Horace Henderson credits Nesbitt as "the one that brought that old tune back." A glance at the discographical record supports Horace's claim. In fact, this 1911 ethnic novelty from the songwriting team of William Jerome and Jean Schwartz received many recordings by jazz bands after Henderson's—but very few before. Discographer Brian Rust also suggests a gap in the song's appeal: "Chinatown" received no jazz recordings until 1928, even by Rust's broad, inclusive notion of jazz. Yet from Henderson's recording in October 1930 to the end of the decade, "Chinatown" was recorded a total of twenty-one times by seventeen different jazz groups (more often than not without its stereotyped lyrics), making it one of the decade's most widely recorded standards.[26]

Since then, "Chinatown, My Chinatown" has become the focal point of an intriguing controversy. Schuller claims that John Nesbitt exerted some influence on Gene Gifford, the chief arranger for the period's leading hot white band, the Casa Loma Orchestra. In particular, Schuller has explored several substantial similarities between Nesbitt's "Chinatown" arrangement and Gene Gifford's early swing classic "Casa Loma Stomp," recorded by the Casa Loma Orchestra two months later (and by Henderson in 1932). Richard Sudhalter challenges Schuller's claims that Gifford absorbed Nesbitt's influence, but without addressing Schuller's case in point, the "Chinatown"/"Casa Loma Stomp" comparison to which he devotes three pages. Without resolving the issue, we might pause to consider it emblematic of the difficulty of assigning creative priority in early jazz, and of how competing claims may be amplified by a racial resonance. For in this period, ideas were freely exchanged—and stolen—between and within the races, even while the business itself remained strictly segregated.[27]

The Advent of Benny Carter

When Benny Carter joined Henderson for recording sessions in 1928 he could claim four years of experience as a professional musician. He had gained this experience in bands that several other musicians had passed through on their way to Henderson—bands led by June Clark (with whom

Jimmy Harrison and Bobby Stark had also played), Billy Paige (Don Redman, Joe Smith, Rex Stewart), Horace Henderson (Rex Stewart), Billy Fowler (Jimmy Harrison, Tommy Ladnier, Benny Morton, Rex Stewart), and Charlie Johnson (Jimmy Harrison). These experiences helped make Carter a natural addition to Henderson's orchestra. He had played in taxi-dance halls, an informal rookie league for future jazz musicians; and he had had plenty of opportunities to improvise in Harlem, especially with Charlie Johnson's band, and to play more staid, arranged music on Broadway under Billy Fowler, whose band he remembered as playing "popular music, mostly bland stock arrangements, with a ten- to twelve-piece orchestra." Charlie Johnson also gave Carter the chance to hear his own arrangements, two of which appeared on disk in January 1928.[28]

Carter's truly distinctive work with Henderson—the recordings on which his style and sensibility pervades the entire arrangement—begins to appear before the Connie's Inn year, on three sides made in the band's last two Columbia sessions in the 1920s: "Come On, Baby!" and "Easy Money" (December 12, 1928), and "The Wang Wang Blues" (May 16, 1929). Carter's writing resonates in Henderson's later arrangements for Goodman, so it's worth exploring in some detail.

"Easy Money" is drenched in the sultry elegance of Carter's writing for saxophones. If "Stark's brief but spectacular trumpet solo" and "Kaiser Marshall's smart, inventive cymbal work" stand out as the most immediately exciting features of the performance, Carter's accompanimental backgrounds and his writing for saxophones do more than anything to shape the arrangement's mood and continuity. A different accompaniment backs each of the four soloists. A simple boom-chick tuba/banjo pattern prods Buster Bailey; placid brass long tones support Charlie Green; and saxophone and brass riffs stroke the active solo lines of Stark and Hawkins. The saxophones, topped by Carter's sweet-toned alto, rise here and there in gentle waves. In the last chorus, they emerge to play the melody with a rich, full choir of sound (ex. 7.1). The melody gradually rises to a bursting trill at its peak in m. 4, then slowly ebbs. Set off against this smooth flow of block voicing, the brass play between-the-beats staccato notes paced by June Cole's firm tuba notes on beats one and three. The whole performance proceeds at an unusually relaxed, flowing tempo.[29]

Recorded on the same day, "Come On, Baby!" reveals Carter's arranging as an extension of his solo style. Comparing the "Easy Money" saxophone choir and the "Come On, Baby!" solo (ex. 7.2), one sees the importance of ornament, especially trills, in both approaches.

Ex. 7.1. "Easy Money" (December 12, 1928), last chorus, saxophone choir

Ex. 7.2. "Come On, Baby!" (December 12, 1928), chorus 2, mm. 8–16, Benny Carter solo

The trills in both passages often occur at the peaks of phrases, in mm. 4, 12, and 15 of "Easy Money" and in m. 9 (attempted) and 11 in "Come On, Baby!"

Carter's arranged variation in "Come On, Baby!" shows soloistic qualities as well (ex. 7.3), with its angular, darting melodic line, its ghosted notes (mm. 4 and 16), its minor-third dips (mm. 8 and 11), and perhaps, too, in its Armstrong-like tendency to favor a stabilizing three-note figure (or slight variant of it) at the beginning of each four-bar phrase (mm. 1, 5, 9, and 13).

Ex. 7.3. "Come On, Baby!" chorus 3, trumpet line of arranged variation with saxophones

The band's last recording of the 1920s indicates the breadth of Carter's arranging talent: "The Wang Wang Blues." Henderson's 1927 version of this piece represented a new departure from the established conventions of playing the tune since Whiteman's orchestra recorded it in 1920 (see chap. 5, ex. 5.3). For the first time, the original melody formed the backdrop for a series of hot solos. Carter's arrangement departs even more dramatically from the original tune. Carter signals the uniqueness of his arrangement in the introduction, which opens with parallel tritones—in a spiky palindromic rhythm—resolving to octaves in m. 5 (ex. 7.4).

Ex. 7.4. "The Wang Wang Blues" (May 16, 1929), introduction

In the course of the performance Carter exhibits four composed para-phrases of the melody, the first, second, and last of which showing at least some relation to the original melody (ex. 7.5)

Ex. 7.5. "The Wang Wang Blues," melody, and Benny Carter's ensemble variations (top line only)

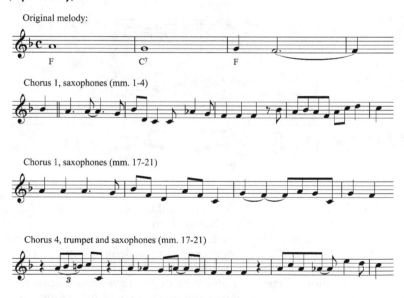

Unlike the variations in ex. 7.5, the third chorus, for saxophones, makes no allusion to the original melody (see ex. 7.6).

Ex. 7.6. "The Wang Wang Blues," chorus 3, beginning, saxophones variation (two of three lines shown)

Unlike most variations in dance arrangements of the 1920s, then, Carter's third chorus variation on "Wang Wang Blues" is not a melodic paraphrase so much as a new melody over the original harmony. This new melody, moreover, reveals again Carter's characteristically solo-styled lines, angular and animated with plenty of triplet figures, like his "Come On, Baby!" solo.

Carter left the band in 1929 and came back the following year. He continued to make charts for Henderson in the early 1930s, including "Somebody Loves Me," "Keep a Song in Your Soul," "My Pretty Girl," and "Sweet and Hot," all recorded in late 1930 and early 1931. Among the many arrangers Henderson commissioned and collaborated with in the period, Carter stands out as a key figure in the transition from the Roseland band that featured Redman's work and the later Henderson band in which the leader gradually took over more of the work. At this point—unlike Benny Goodman, who would sometimes be very specific about what he wanted from Fletcher as an arranger—Fletcher himself left repertoire and musical decisions to his arrangers. Carter could not recall Henderson giving any guidelines for an arrangement. "He would give me the title or some sheet music but he left it up to me to arrange it as I wanted to. Occasionally I would just write an arrangement on something I wanted to do and just bring it in."[30]

From a distance, we can hear these arrangements—and their recorded performances—straddling the two decades. If Nesbitt's "Chinatown" represents the state of the arranger's art in 1930, then Carter's look both backward and forward from there, combining some now-dated practices of 1920s arranging and performance, and advanced elements that anticipate swing band arranging of the mid-1930s.

The second chorus of "Somebody Loves Me" presents a particularly clear example, with the three Henderson saxophones (Carter, Hawkins, and Harvey Boone) playing supple arabesques that culminate in Carter's patented bursting trills at the end of the sixteen-bar passage.

"Keep a Song in Your Soul" features a solo-style saxophone writing (in chorus 2) along with several other features. Myriad textures and timbres resulted from Carter's effort to combine the sections and soloists in every conceivable grouping. More than that, textural and timbral shifts inside the strain—even within the phrase—create further variety while revealing an underlying concern for balance and unity.

The arrangement of "Keep a Song in Your Soul" also bears scrutiny for its rhythmic conception. Although the rhythm section features John Kirby playing the increasingly passé tuba instead of string bass, Kirby often plays on all four beats of the measure and avoids the two-beat bounce typical of the 1920s. Above that explicit four-beat feel, Carter writes several passages featuring extended syncopation, creating a tug-of-war effect between the melody and accompaniment. Here Schuller finds in Carter's melodic variations "the final key to the 'Henderson style' . . . and the solution for making a section swing: . . . syncopation." More specifically, what Carter explores in this arrangement is a device that Henderson would use with great ingenuity and variety in his work for Benny Goodman to the point where it became a hallmark of his style and, by extension, of the swing era: the *chain* of syncopation, an uninterrupted sequence of offbeat notes (ex. 7.7).[31]

Ex. 7.7. "Keep a Song in Your Soul" (December 2, 1930), syncopated variation of melody (from Schuller, *EJ*, 274)

Carter's departure in "The Big Trade" of March 1931 left Henderson without a key figure in the band. Procope modestly claimed that in trading him for Carter, Webb got the better deal. Certainly, the recorded legacy suggests that Henderson now had to draw on a much larger pool of arrangers. One arranger he seems to have relied on more frequently was Bill Challis.

Revisiting Bix and Tram (Bill Challis)

"When Henderson began playing at Connie's Inn," Challis recalled, "I was living in Greenwich, Connecticut. . . . when I'd go back home . . . I'd stop in at Connie's Inn. Fletcher and I became good friends. I wrote a lot for that band. They paid me well."[32] Challis and Henderson went back several years. Challis had arranged Henderson's own "'D' Natural Blues" in 1928 and received credit for a 1931 arrangement of the old Tin Pan Alley waltz "My Gal Sal," transformed into a fox-trot. After Carter's departure, Challis now contributed two charts clearly based on transcriptions of recordings by the Frankie Trumbauer Orchestra made on the same date, February 4, 1927, and which appeared back-to-back on the same OKeh record: "Singin' the Blues" and "Clarinet Marmalade."

"Singin' the Blues" has received the most attention, as it stands out as an anomaly of the period: a performance that aims to re-create the style, structure, and solos of another band's arrangement—in other words, a performance in the spirit of a jazz repertory band of a half-century later. Figure 7.3 outlines the three related versions of "Singin' the Blues": Trumbauer's February 1927 recording with a seven-piece band including Bix Beiderbecke, Bill Challis's 1928 arrangement for an orchestra at least twice the size of Trumbauer's, and Henderson's April 1931 recordings with a twelve-piece orchestra.

Henderson's recordings follow Challis's special arrangement for Whiteman in many respects, most notably in the setting of Frankie Trumbauer's first-chorus saxophone solo in block voicing for three saxophones, and in

Fig. 7.3. "Singin' the Blues"

Frankie Trumbauer and His Orchestra	Bill Challis arr. for Whiteman	Connie's Inn Orchestra
(February 4, 1927)	(1928?)	(April 10 and 29, 1931)
(♩ = ca. 136)	("slow tempo")	(♩ = ca. 150 and ca. 128)
E♭ major E♭ major	E♭ major	
I(4) sax, tpt.	I(4) 2 clars., tpt., vib.	I(4) saxes
A(32) c-mel. sax solo (gtr., piano)	A(32) 3 saxes	A(32) 3(?)saxes
A(32) cor. solo (gtr., piano)	A(32) tpt. solo (sax long tones)	A(32) tpt. solo
	A' (32) 4 tbns.	
A(32) a ens.	A' (32) a saxes (brass)	A(32) a ens.
b clar. solo	b clar. solo ("improvise")	b clar. solo (= 1927 solo)
a ens., tpt lead	a brass sync. (clar. cont's imp.)	a ens.
c ens. with guitar bk.	c ens. with clar. bk.	c ens. with piano bk.

presenting Bix Beiderbecke's cornet solo in the second chorus. Both solos were becoming legendary. Lester Young reportedly carried around a copy of the Trumbauer recording in his horn case, and once told an interviewer, "Ever hear him [Trumbauer] play 'Singin' the Blues'? That tricked me right there, that's where I went." "Everybody memorized that solo," recalled Budd Johnson. "Frankie Trumbauer was the baddest cat around." In playing a harmonized version of Trumbauer's solo, Henderson's lead alto player (Procope or Boone) even adopted the sweet, sensuous tone of the model.[33]

In many ways beyond that, the Henderson version, recorded twice in April 1931, goes directly back to the original recording, not to Challis's arrangement. For example, Henderson omits the third chorus for trombones to preserve the three-chorus structure of Trumbauer's recorded version. In addition, Henderson's solo clarinetist, probably Procope, plays Jimmy Dorsey's 1927 recorded solo, note-for-note. Moreover, Henderson's band, instead of playing the syncopated brass arrangement that Challis wrote in the last sixteen bars, steers a course somewhere between Challis's and Trumbauer's versions, with an early 1930s dance band's adaptation of a New Orleans-style out chorus, featuring trumpets in the lead (three trumpets here instead of Beiderbecke's single lead). In other ways, Henderson's version goes its own way, as in the saxophone chords that accompany Stewart's Beiderbecke imitation.

Stewart's presentation of Beiderbecke's solo has been a source of much commentary among historians of early jazz, since he plays nearly note-for-note what Beiderbecke played in 1927, and thus provides a particularly clear early instance of a black musician paying musical tribute to a white musician. Sudhalter, in his unique position as historian and trumpeter, claims that Stewart plays the solo "in the inflections and accents of his own style." Indeed, there's no mistaking the Armstrong-inspired Stewart for Beiderbecke, but here Stewart also imposes restraint to emulate what Hoagy Carmichael called Bix's mallet-on-chimes tone. Stewart himself commented on his solo in a 1967 interview, claiming that his own taste fell in line with the record company's directions: "Admiring Bix as I did, it was not difficult for me to attempt to copy his memorable solo on 'Singin' the Blues,' especially since the phonograph company for which Fletcher recorded the number wanted my solos as close to the original as possible."[34]

Although Henderson's version follows the form and solos, and attempts to simulate its tone quality, it does not quite capture the lacy lightness of its model. The opening chorus for three reeds is a case in point. Trumbauer's famous 1927 "solo" really should be heard as a duet: Eddie Lang's guitar weaves a delicate counterpoint against Trumbauer's melody; whereas in the Henderson version the three saxophones have a more conventional rhythm section accompaniment that cannot match the quality of crystalline chamber music of Trumbauer and Lang.

Typically, records were released about two to three months after the recording date. Bix Beiderbecke died on August 6, 1931, soon after Henderson's homage would have begun appearing in stores. The record became an apt, if accidental, memorial.

The tendency to single out Henderson's remarkable emulation of "Singin' the Blues" has obscured the other Challis arrangement that Henderson's band recorded a month earlier, on March 19, 1931—in the first recording session after "the Big Trade." The recording history of "Clarinet Marmalade" was now more than a decade old, and the piece had already developed the kind of complex identity of a standard—instantly recognizable but ever changing. It had begun in 1918, with the Original Dixieland Jazz Band, as a small-combo ensemble piece with strong links to the march tradition. (The following year, James Reese Europe's band played it, preserving the ensemble emphasis.) In 1926, Henderson's first recording of the tune had transformed it into a vehicle for hot soloists and ensemble riffs, including a new introduction and the streamlining omission of several transitional passages. In a burst of recordings that Henderson's band seems to have inspired for many pieces (e.g., "Sugar Foot Stomp," "King Porter Stomp"), several white bands adopted the piece in 1927–29, following Henderson's model to some extent, including groups led by Phil Napolean, Berlyn Baylor, Ted Lewis, Lud Gluskin, and Bill Carlsen, and most notably, by Frankie Trumbauer. As figure 7.4 shows, Trumbauer, like Henderson, used the piece's second strain as the basis for a sequence of solos but also introduces a new ensemble variation on the second strain's tune. Unlike Henderson, however, Trumbauer's band retains the tune's original introduction and reiterates the four- and twelve-bar transitional passages, which Henderson had minimized in 1926.

Once again using a Challis arrangement ostensibly based on a Trumbauer recording, Henderson's March 1931 recording follows the format of the piece played by Trumbauer, not the innovative revision recorded by his own band in 1926. Henderson's 1931 recording returns to the tune's original introduction, and follows almost exactly the same pattern of "B" strains, transitions, and solos that appeared in Trumbauer's version. Moreover, Henderson's "new" version omits the riffs it had played in 1926 and includes an ensemble variation that Trumbauer's band had introduced as the second "B" strain in its 1927 recording.

Fig. 7.4. "Clarinet Marmalade"

Henderson (December 1926)	Trumbauer (February 1927)	Henderson (March 1931)
($\downarrow$ = ca. 240–50)	($\downarrow$ = ca. 250–60)	($\downarrow$ = ca. 230–40)
F major	F major	F major
Intro(8) new, D minor	Intro(8) original	Intro(8) original
A(32) tpt. solo	A(32) ens., cor. lead	A(32) ens., tpt. lead
X(4) ens.	X(4) ens.	X(4) ens.
B(16) clar. melody	B(16) tbn. solo	B(16) tbn. solo
B(16) tpts. riff	B(16) piano solo	
	X(12) ens.	X(12) ens.
B(16) clar. solo	B(16) ens. variation, cor. lead	(12) ens. variation, tpt. lead
B(16) tpt. solo	X(4) ens.	X(4) ens.
B(16) tenor sax solo	B(16) C-melody sax solo (Trumbauer)	B(16) tenor sax solo (Hawkins)
X(12) ens., with high clar.	B(16) cor. solo (Beiderbecke)	B(16) tpt. solo
B(16) clar. solo	X(12) ens.	X(12) ens.
B(16) ens. riff chorus (breaks by clar. and tenor sax)	B(16) clar. solo	B(16) clar. solo
	B(16) ens. (breaks by cor. and tenor sax)	B(16) ens. (b. sax break)
	B(16) ens.	B(16) ens.

In sum, "Clarinet Marmalade" documents a more complex symbiotic relationship between the Henderson and Trumbauer bands than does "Singin' the Blues." Trumbauer's 1927 recording clearly reflects the impact of Henderson's 1926 revision, but Henderson's 1931 recording even more clearly follows the model of Trumbauer. Once again, Bill Challis served as the medium. Henderson's 1931 "Challis version" strips away many of the novel features of its 1926 "Redman version." It replaced Redman's D-minor opening with the original introduction, lifted an entire twenty-bar passage from Trumbauer's recording, and omitted the riff accompaniments to the solos. The result is a simplified, less imaginative version of the piece.

Why did Henderson opt for Challis's arrangement rather than the more adventurous Redman version his own band had played in 1926? The question is especially intriguing because Henderson did return to his mid-1920s "Sugar Foot Stomp" in the same year. Perhaps Redman had taken his own version along with him to McKinney's Cotton Pickers. Perhaps it was more difficult and less readily performable by the early 1930s Henderson band. Perhaps it sounded old-fashioned, too "twenties," for Henderson and his sidemen. Yet although it remade the piece, the 1926 recording had few traces of the cleverness and novelty that mark much of Redman's work for Henderson. Probably, Challis had made his arrangement of "Clarinet Marmalade" much earlier, perhaps while working for Trumbauer in 1927, and his sporadic work with Henderson over the ensuing four years had led Henderson to develop a closer professional relationship with Challis than with Redman. For Redman—still with McKinney's Cotton Pickers and soon to form a band under his own name—now stood in direct competition with Henderson. Yet Henderson had many other sources to draw from, including one of the more elusive figures of the early 1930s.

Nat Leslie, Irving Mills, and "Radio Rhythm"

Evidence strongly suggests that the music entrepreneur Irving Mills also entered the picture with arrangements for Henderson. Although Henderson did not have a contractual relationship with Mills as his agent until 1934, the discographical record suggests that Henderson and Mills had at least a temporary association in 1931. That association is revealed as one similar to many others Henderson cultivated with music businessmen since his band's early days in 1923–24: a mutually beneficial agreement in which Henderson performed new and recent pieces by a particular publisher. By the early 1930s, Mills had become the preeminent plug-organizer in jazz. In some cases, the repertoire choices resulted more from a relationship between a record company and publisher, such as the Melrose/Gennett connection in the 1920s, in which Gennett recorded many new Melrose publications and advertised the fact. In this case, however, Henderson recorded Mills pieces in 1931 on at least two distinct labels, including Crown and Brunswick. Among them, Hoagy Carmichael's "Star Dust" (for Crown) would become the best known. Others are the Schoebel/Meyers/Mills tune "The House of David Blues," and "Blues in My Heart," by Benny Carter with a co-credit to Mills. But the Mills-linked composer whose work got the most attention from Henderson's band in the period was Nat Leslie.

Leslie remains an elusive figure.[35] At least two prominent figures named Leslie were active in American musical entertainment in the 1920s and 1930s—songwriter Edgar Leslie and producer Lew Leslie—but citations of their work include no mention of Nat as a relative. Circumstantial evidence strongly suggests that he served on Mills's staff in the early 1930s, although Benny Carter, also on Mills's staff at the time, had no memory of him. Three pieces that Henderson recorded in the summer of 1931 are credited to Leslie and Mills: "Low Down on the Bayou," "Radio Rhythm," and "Blue Rhythm." (Leslie almost certainly deserves sole credit for music, as Mills was well known for adding his name to a song to cut in on its royalties.) All three pieces were also recorded by a black band under Mills's management that was variously known as the Blue Rhythm Boys, the Blue Ribbon Boys, Mills Blue Rhythm Band, and King Carter and His Royal Orchestra. (The last, among Mills's series of "royal" orchestras, was named after Benny Carter, but lacked its namesake.) Henderson's and Mills's bands made recordings of the pieces within a period of three months in 1931, and Rust documents no other recordings. Thus the brief but concentrated recording activity of Leslie's pieces bears all the signs of being Mills-instigated "plugs."

If facts about Nat Leslie's career remain elusive, we can nevertheless say more about his music. The three Leslie pieces share several tendencies. Clearly conceived as jazz instrumental numbers, they all feature a riff-based, rhythmic conception of melody; cast in song or strain forms, they make frequent gestures toward the blues and exhibit formal irregularities; and they show a predilection for the minor mode, unusual in jazz and popular music. In their evocative moodiness, they suggest the influence of the so-called jungle style that Duke Ellington developed during his Cotton Club stint, which had ended just a few months earlier in February 1931. The knowledge of Leslie's link to Mills reinforces a sense that his music was partly inspired by Mills's flagship band.

Henderson's recording of "Radio Rhythm" (July 17, 1931) is an exceptional performance of a unique piece. The arrangement recalls the restlessness of 1920s orchestration, but the performance brims with the fiery energy of an early swing band. Like many Redman arrangements of the 1920s, the piece is mostly built from two- and four-bar motifs and melodic fragments tossed among several soloists and sections of the band. Only alto saxophonist Russell Procope is allowed to stretch out, with a full-chorus solo after the theme statement. From there, the arrangement proceeds in cut-and-paste style.

"Radio Rhythm" sparkles with refreshing weirdness, again more in the spirit of the experimental 1920s than of the swing era. The introduction sets the tone with a menacing mood rare for big-band jazz—a churning, insistently repeated saxophone triplet figure, the primal beat of the tom-tom, the minor mode, and the sustained-tone growl trombone break that swells into the first chorus.

Meanwhile, the piece's harmonic and melodic basis could hardly be simpler. Harmonically, it is strung together from oscillations between chord pairs with strong gravitational attraction: C#dim7 and D minor, Edim7 and F, D minor and Eb9, and A7 and D minor. Melodically, Leslie built the piece on a basic two-bar motif first stated by saxes and trumpets, and punctuated by a growling trombone exclamation.

The exclamation undergoes a metamorphosis. In the first section of the first chorus it appears in the trombone as a stinging tritone dissonance— G# against a D minor chord—rearing its head in two different registers (See ex. 7.8).

Ex. 7.8. "Radio Rhythm" (July 31, 1931), chorus 1, beginning (transcribed by Frank Davis)

In the last section of the same chorus, the note, also coarsened by a growl, appears in a plunger-muted trumpet part. Before the first chorus ends, this one-note interjection has expanded into two accented high notes, quickly articulated by an unmuted trumpet. The first chorus's rise in heat and tension owes much to the way this little interjecting figure gets transformed as it appears in three registers, each higher than the preceding one.

"Radio Rhythm" also features a formal anomaly. Although the main chorus comprises a conventional thirty-two bars, it has an atypical ABA structure with two twelve-bar phrases (A) framing an eight-bar bridge (B). The A sections combine to offer fully twelve statements of the syncopated main motif. In another twenties-style gesture, the ensemble forces the key up a half step to E♭ minor for an extended coda, which ends off of the tonic, on an A♭ major triad, a tritone away from the original key.

The soloists contribute their share of surprises. Procope's solo, for example, does not end so much as it dissolves at the bottom of a modal cascade of notes. A trumpeter (either Stark or Stewart) fills the last bridge with a long, tense chromatic ascent to high D. All of this might produce an amusingly offbeat novelty in an ordinary dance orchestra, but Henderson's band makes it a seething hot number propelled by menacing growls and a brisk tempo.

"Business in F" (Archie Bleyer)

Archie Bleyer is another key figure in Henderson's legion of arrangers. And of all the recordings that anticipate the next phase of Henderson's career, Bleyer's "Business in F" stands out. The reason may be that the arranger knew the band well: Rex Stewart recalled Bleyer among several arrangers who "haunt[ed] the Roseland to learn from the master."[36]

The music has all the earmarks of a hot Hendersonian number. Recorded during the band's last recording session of 1931 (October 16), "Business in F" is a riff-based swinger in popular-song form. The format features a streamlined succession of five choruses based on the familiar AABA form that had begun to predominate in Tin Pan Alley since around 1925. Eschewing the obligatory introduction, it jumps right into the first chorus. And the title means business: the piece begins and ends in F major, avoiding the easy excitement of sudden and sometimes distant modulations, effects that typified the arrangements Henderson's band had played in the 1920s, and for which Henderson himself would become famous in his charts for Benny Goodman. Moreover, the harmonic scheme of the principal (A) section of the piece could hardly be simpler, featuring an eight-bar chord progression that moves from tonic to subdominant to dominant to tonic—having the quality of a modified blues progression. Hawkins is the featured soloist and Johnson's drumming makes an electrifying effect, but "Business in F" is largely an ensemble piece bursting with riffs.

Archie Bleyer now appears to be an obscure figure in American popular music and jazz of the early 1930s. But Bleyer's name was a "household word wherever musicians gather." Horace Henderson called him simply "the great Archie Bleyer." Bleyer made his impact not just from the quality of his work but also from its sheer quantity, including several hundred stock arrangements. Benny Carter mentioned Bleyer among several arrangers whose stocks Carter used as "valuable technical reference works." For his part, Bleyer acknowledged the influence of black musicians and arrangers, whom all musicians, black and white, witnessed at work in Harlem. "Every professional musician admired and was greatly influenced by the blacks, and they for the most part were what we called jazz musicians. As a white musician developed, he incorporated more and more of the black idiom into his arranging and playing."[37]

Just Blues? (Horace Henderson)

While playing songs and stocks and using arrangements by Challis, Leslie, and Bleyer, Henderson began drawing from closer to home: from his brother. Horace contributed two pieces that recall Fletcher's quasi-symphonic blues forays of the 1920s: "Hot and Anxious" and "Comin' and Going," both recorded for Columbia on March 19, 1931, under the band's short-lived and covertly racialized pseudonym, the Baltimore Bell Hops. That Horace would aim to emulate his brother in his early compositions should come as no surprise. Although the two brothers would have their differences, Horace's admiration for Fletcher emerges clearly in an interview from the 1970s, in which Horace talked about taking notes on the Roseland bandstand as his brother talked. "I had nothing but admiration for him. And I thought he was God," recalled Horace. Responding to a published statement that Horace was "resentful" of Fletcher, Horace insisted that "I idolized that man ... because he had done too much to help me in college."[38]

Unlike Fletcher, however, Horace plays with the blues structure, disrupting expectation with extensions and truncations of the twelve-bar form, as Duke Ellington would do in his double-sided 1937 record, "Diminuendo and Crescendo in Blue." In "Comin' and Going," for example, the last three sections comprise ten-bar-blues choruses so that each section dovetails into the next. (The last two bars of blues harmony employ the same chord as the first two bars and thus can be easily elided with them.) As I've suggested, the title almost certainly reflects the sudden change of personnel after "the Big Trade," but the title may have musical resonance as well, since the new chorus is "comin'" at the same time as the previous chorus is "going."

In "Hot and Anxious," Horace writes consecutive blues choruses of fourteen, thirteen, and twelve bars. Yet Horace's method here consists of creating the impression of a nonsectional blues where textures and colors shift without consistently calling attention to the formal seams. Two sections in the middle, however, are rather markedly distinguished from the surrounding material: the second and third blues choruses, of thirteen and twelve bars respectively. Both are based on two-bar riffs. The first features a riff derived from a trumpet phrase played by Wingy Manone in a 1930 recording called "Tar Paper Stomp." The riff itself comprises a triadic figure in a secondary-rag rhythm that would have sounded contemporary in 1924 or even earlier (ex. 7.9). Yet it traversed the decade of the 1930s to become the single most recognizable figure in big-band music during the early years of World War II—as the principal theme of Joe Garland's "In the Mood," as adapted and recorded by Glenn Miller's orchestra in 1939.

Ex. 7.9. "Hot and Anxious" (March 19, 1931), riff

The fourth strain, comprising an anomalous eighteen bars, features a subtly alternating emphasis on reeds and brass. The piece continues with two unexpected blues solos—a clarinet solo by Coleman Hawkins, and a rare guitar solo by Clarence Holiday. The piece closes with an ensemble chorus that leads to a fade-out ending based on the two-bar riff from the introduction.

In contrast to "Hot and Anxious," "Comin' and Going" does not begin as a blues, but rather with two unusual strains, and it becomes almost a showcase for trombonist Benny Morton, who had returned to the band in "the Big Trade." The first is a sixteen-bar strain featuring a powerful, smeary solo by Morton clearly derived from Charlie Green's "Gouge of Armour Avenue" solo from 1924. Indeed, with its minor mode, its moody trombone solo, and the low hum of saxophone chords, the first strain has some of the earmarks of Ellington's "jungle style." On top of that, Henderson borrows a prominent riff from Ellington and Miley's 1929 "Doin' the Voom Voom" and uses it as a recurring vamp (ex. 7. 10).

Ex. 7.10. "Comin' and Going" (March 19, 1931), riff

Before and after the vamp's reappearance Horace distributes ideas among the band in a series of abrupt early-twenties-style shifts from solo trumpet to saxes, then to a brief alto saxophone solo by Procope. Thereafter the piece becomes all blues, with riff-backed solos by Morton (twelve bars) and Stark (ten bars). The third blues chorus (also ten bars) begins with another sequence of quick-shifting orchestration—from piano to brass to saxes and back to piano—followed by another brief solo by Morton. In the final chorus, Horace himself takes a four-bar solo and the ensemble continues with a sultry chromatic figure that segues directly into a coda for saxophones, who repeat the figure as they taper off into a quiet cadence. Again, as in "Hot and Anxious," unusual shifts of timbre and texture obscure formal seams and the piece closes in a "fade out" ending based on a repeated riff.

Less than a month later, Fletcher himself contributed his own "Just Blues." Yet of all the blues Henderson's band developed in 1931, the one to which it devoted the most attention was not a new composition, but a revised version of an arrangement of its greatest hit from the twenties: "Sugar Foot Stomp."

"Sugar Foot Stomp" Revisited

In one five-month span, Henderson recorded "Sugar Foot Stomp" on four separate dates, each for a different record company. If anything suggests that

Henderson resorted to "desperate maneuvers" during the early 1930s, it is not the "pop tunes" in its repertory, but the continual reiteration of this proven jazz standard. But then again, it might be more accurate to say that the record companies were desperate, not Henderson himself. For what better way to ensure record sales than to feature a name band performing a new version of its greatest hit?

The recordings demonstrate a remarkable continuity between the 1925 and 1931 versions, testifying to the popularity and import of the piece. Similarities among the four 1931 recordings suggest that the arrangement was possibly written down, not developed aurally as a head arrangement. If the 1930–31 period launched Henderson's serious efforts at arranging, "Sugar Foot Stomp" appears to mark a key early moment. Perhaps Henderson's chief contribution lay less in new ideas than in simply writing down the arrangement at this point (something he certainly did for Goodman a few years later).

That Columbia brought out a new "Sugar Foot Stomp" in 1931 suggests the stylistic change in big-band music that had occurred since Henderson first recorded the piece for Columbia six years earlier. The piece had to be updated to sell records. Thus, the new versions iron out the quirky 1920s features of the earlier arrangement. For example, rather than the harmonically deceptive 1925 introduction, with its move toward C minor, the 1931 versions restore the straightforward move to the dominant featured on King Oliver's 1923 recordings of "Dipper Mouth Blues." Meanwhile, although Henderson retains the enriched blues strain (the "E" section), that strain no longer acts as a staid foil to the boisterous quasi-improvisatory passages. Now the strain's alternative harmonic palette simply acts as a backdrop for solos.

The most immediately notable difference between the 1925 and 1931 versions of "Sugar Foot Stomp," however, are the latter's faster tempo (see ch. 4, ex. 4.9 and ex. 4.10). The 1925 version itself had represented an acceleration over the original Oliver version. But now, typically playing it at over 240 beats per minute, Henderson transforms the piece into a big-band flag-waver.

The faster tempos allow the band to fit four more blues choruses into the piece than it had in 1925. As a result Henderson and his sidemen clear more solo space for themselves. In fact, all of the added choruses are used for solos, not for additional arranged passages, another example of the streamlining impulse behind Henderson's dance-driven, post-Redman approach. The final chorus, echoing "King Porter Stomp," in particular, highlights a call-and-response exchange between the saxes and brass. The saxes play the main melody and the brass punctuate it with a syncopated two-note shout figure. With this passage for separated sections in call and response replacing the earlier out chorus, "Sugar Foot Stomp" leaves behind key elements of its New Orleanian roots and jazz-age reinterpretation and enters the swing era.

Yet some of those roots remain: the introductory cascading diminished chord introduction, the "oh-play-that-thing" vocal break, the clarinet trio, the three-chorus Oliver solo, which Rex Stewart plays almost note-for-note on the Columbia and Victor versions, complete with the humming saxophone riff and stoptime passages that Henderson had used in 1925. Such features had become fixtures.

Most sources credit Henderson himself with the 1931 arrangement—as a "Henderson" arrangement "patterned after" Don Redman's 1925 version. But like so many other notable Henderson recordings, especially "King Porter Stomp," which the band also developed over several years, this one was a team effort, a collaboration through time to which several creative agents made layers of contribution: Oliver, Armstrong, Redman, Elmer Schoebel, the other soloists, and Henderson himself. The 1931 "Sugar Foot Stomp" is then best described as a head arrangement that had settled into some kind of fixed form, possibly written down. That it was recorded four times in the spring and summer of 1931, in an expanded form allowing for more improvised solos, shows that hot jazz was still good for business. Far from discouraging hot music, record companies apparently found in "Sugar Foot Stomp" the single best selling point for Henderson's band.

The brief Connie's Inn period stands as a professional peak in Henderson's bandleading career. For less than ten months, the band had one of the top jobs of its kind in New York, for part of that time running parallel with Duke Ellington's band at the Cotton Club. The elite status of Connie's Inn, its high pay, its national reach over radio, and the increased recording work it created, helped to solidify the band's premier status.

The Connie's Inn recordings suggest that the creative impetus came from a mix of external and internal forces. Like Henderson's Club Alabam and Roseland bands of the 1920s, the Connie's Inn Orchestra played a varied repertoire only partially captured on record. Moving to a Harlem venue did not substantially alter the audience-centered values of public performance, where variety remained the bedrock of success. Yet surveying the recorded legacy of this brief period shows that what later became known as "Henderson style" was in the process of coalescing from the work of a wide range of creative arrangers and composers: the driving intensity of John Nesbitt's "Chinatown," the syncopated variations and elegant saxophone writing of Benny Carter, the Bill Challis-channeled legacy of the Beiderbecke/Trumbauer collaboration, the refined blues of Horace Henderson and Fletcher himself, the revised New Orleans jazz of Redman's "Sugar Foot Stomp" arrangement, and the riff-based constructions of Nat Leslie and Archie Bleyer.

Battling

After the Connie's Inn job ended in September 1931, the band continued to find a steady stream of high-profile appearances, including a return to the Roseland Ballroom and performances in Philadelphia, Washington, DC, and Pittsburgh, where its arrival was "the biggest and most outstanding dance attraction this city has ever witnessed." Radio had paved the way. Riding on its East Coast successes, the band continued west, playing a series of dates in a variety of venues—including hotels, a college prom, and a naval armory—in Cleveland, Columbus, St. Louis, Kansas City, Toledo, Detroit, Des Moines, Omaha, Chicago, and Champaign, Illinois, logging some six thousand miles and returning east "highly elated."[39]

It may have been on this tour that Henderson faced off against an up-and-coming white band in a great battle. By mid-1931 the Casa Loma Orchestra, led by saxophonist Glen Gray, had emerged as a popular dance band that played hot and cultivated a youthful audience—a model for Benny Goodman four years later. One night at Detroit's renowned Graystone Ballroom, charged by the competition with the country's leading black band, the Casa Loma offered a stiff challenge to Henderson's supremacy. Horace's account of the event amounts to the anatomy of a band battle, and shows how his brother's apparent passivity and "easygoing" nature could help him wage musical war. The Graystone's vast dance floor featured two bandstands, with the Casa Loma on one side, and the Henderson band on the other. The Casa Loma started off and "play[ed] like mad ... swinging the whole crowd [of] four or five thousand people." Henderson, however, held his guns. "Fletcher started calling ... those stocks, simple things ... And man, he was building up something. The guys in the band knew they weren't the best arrangements, [but] he did this ... for two sets." By the second set, the crowd, which typically moved back and forth between the bands, stayed with the Casa Loma band. "Okay," Horace continued, "the Casa Loma band played the third set, played like madmen." Meanwhile, Fletcher's sidemen were growing angry at their leader's apparent reluctance to compete. "They had their heads down," Horace recalled, "and Rex Stewart was so mad, just fuming." But then Fletcher did the unexpected. He started calling out "special" arrangements, the kind of charts that his sidemen all knew would excite the crowd. "And the people ... ran across the floor ... and man they started swinging." Glen Gray "was played out," Horace said, but "Fletcher went on from there all night long, and when Glen Gray got back to start again, the people didn't move. They stayed there with Fletcher's band." Horace concluded that Fletcher "was great at that ... and he won many a battle like that."[40]

Traveling six thousand miles would not have conjured feelings of "elation" in most people of the period. But J. C. Higginbotham, with Henderson by late 1931, explained that Henderson's band had "nothing but plain fun." The bandleader himself may not have always condoned it but he allowed it to happen. Henderson would "let you do like you want," said Higginbotham. It was a far cry from the Club Alabam and early Roseland days when Henderson was the strict leader checking for shaven faces and shined shoes. Band members continued to be chronically late for jobs. Hard experience taught Henderson some tricks, which had mixed results. "If Fletcher wanted you to start playing at nine o'clock, he'll tell you about 7:30 or 8."[41] Once the men showed up for a gig, they were not always there in spirit. In this, the Henderson band was hardly unusual, but it set a prominent example, and for their recklessness, the musicians would pay in money and work as the Depression settled in and managers increasingly controlled and disciplined the band business. As a result, by 1932, Henderson found himself engaged in a larger battle that he would ultimately lose.

8

Playing in the Mud

O N FRIDAY, DECEMBER 9, 1932, Henderson's orchestra had a remarkable
recording session for Columbia Records. For over a year, the band had
worked one-nighters and week-long engagements in theaters and ballrooms in Washington, Philadelphia, New York, and New England, but it no
longer had a home base like Roseland or Connie's Inn. And it had not made
a single record since March. The record business was at a low ebb, and
Columbia was bankrupt. Yet the young jazz promoter John Hammond, just
six days shy of twenty-two, had brokered an agreement between Henderson
and Columbia to produce a standard four-tune recording session lasting
three hours, beginning at 10 A.M. At the appointed time, however, only "two
musicians were in the studio," Hammond recalled. More than two hours
later, at 12:15 P.M., "John Kirby showed up with his bass, followed shortly
by the rest of the band. We cut three sides in less than forty-five minutes."
Yet, remarkably, "the session was one of the most satisfying I have ever had
anything to do with," Hammond claimed more than four decades later. The
Columbia session may stand as a microcosm of the fortunes, repertoire, and
style of Henderson's orchestra in the period between Connie's Inn and the
band's dissolution in late 1934. It was this period when John Hammond
walked into Henderson's life and tried to steer him toward a more visible and
influential role in big-band jazz, leading ultimately to Henderson's collaboration with Benny Goodman.[1]

Enter John Hammond

A year earlier, on December 15, 1931, Hammond had celebrated his twenty-
first birthday by moving out of the "marble halls" of his family's East
Ninety-first Street mansion and into a "modest apartment" in Greenwich
Village. An heir to the Vanderbilt family fortune, Hammond had dropped
out of Yale University in his sophomore year, drawn to New York's thriving
jazz scene. He had already become an American correspondent for the
British music journals *The Gramophone* and *Melody Maker*, where he
departed from the work of his predecessor by writing about jazz musicians
who were black. The same year, he had made his first foray into record
producing. Boundless energy and a strong current of reformist zeal, inher-
ited from his mother, fueled Hammond's effort's on behalf of black jazz
musicians. "I suppose I could best be described as a social dissident," wrote

Hammond. "To bring recognition to the Negro's supremacy in jazz was the most effective and constructive form of social protest I could think of."[2]

As a white New Yorker eager to stretch beyond what he saw as the confines of his privileged Upper East Side background, Hammond had explored Harlem's nightlife by the late 1920s, but 1931 marks the beginning of his public advocacy for its musicians. As David W. Stowe has pointed out, an "aura of noblesse oblige" suffused that advocacy, and Hammond himself admitted to "playing Pygmalion" in his effort to win respect for jazz in mainstream American culture. Fletcher Henderson's band became his most cherished project. "Fletcher Henderson was one of my earliest enthusiasms," Hammond later wrote in his autobiography, and his was "the greatest band in the country."[3]

With cash, connections, and unshakeable confidence, Hammond began finding work for Henderson's band in the increasingly spartan economic climate of 1932. In April, he arranged for an extended engagement at the Public Theater in downtown Manhattan. In December, he organized the Columbia session that produced what would become two of Henderson's most prized jazz recordings: "Honeysuckle Rose" and "King Porter Stomp." It appeared that Henderson had found just what he needed in the unstable period after the post-Connie's Inn tour. Hammond could do for Henderson what Irving Mills had been doing for Ellington: acting as a powerful white agent who opened doors to prestige and financial stability. The old business paradigm in which Fletcher and Leora patched together tours with a flurry of letters, telegrams, and phone calls had become inefficient in a milieu where more bands competed in a smaller pool of jobs and money. Therefore, Hammond—a rich white man with a passion for jazz—might have appeared as a dream come true in the darkest years of the Depression.

The trouble was that Henderson and his proud sidemen did not particularly relish the role of being Hammond's pet project. The "problem with Fletcher" first manifested itself at the outset of the Public Theater gig. "[N]ever were there more than one or two of the band members in the pit on time," Hammond recalled. "There were something like 60 violations of the show schedule during the week's 28 shows." The job might have lasted much longer, but by the end of the week, Henderson's band had been replaced by Luis Russell's Orchestra, whose every musician showed up on time.[4]

Hammond's accounts of the Public Theater job and Columbia recording session address a pair of recurring themes: the band acts irresponsibly, then makes "superb" music under difficult conditions. At the Public Theater, Hammond wrote, "the men were incapable of making time.... But the music was nothing less than superb." At the Columbia session, despite their "casual behavior" (or perhaps to "make amends" for it), the musicians once again produced "superb" music, resulting in "one of the most satisfying" recording sessions in his illustrious career.[5]

Another theme arises in Hammond's reflections on Henderson: that the disparity between indifferent professional behavior and passionate music making may be explained by systemic racism beyond individual control. His description of the Public Theater experience leads to the observation that "Fletcher was letting me down and hurting himself as well.... In part I believe it was the discouragement Negroes felt as economic victims of the times, and perhaps it was also a small and self-defeating exercise of independence." Elsewhere he notes that "Fletcher had a lassitude born of years of exploitation, so that when opportunities came to help himself he was unprepared to take advantage of them."[6]

Russell Procope put it more bluntly, citing a single reason for the band's behavior: "just because they disliked John Hammond." Hammond "was very disliked by the men in Fletcher's band," Procope insisted, suggesting Hammond's famously patriarchal, domineering style. The band members were "very outspoken, very independent," he said. "You know, they weren't just lackey dogs." In the gap between Hammond's and Procope's accounts, we are left to imagine how the talented, prestigious, and nationally known black musicians in Henderson's band, struggling to find work, must have reacted to the zealous efforts of a twenty-one-year-old trust-fund kid from the Upper East Side.[7]

Musicians developed a variety of nicknames for him, including "the Big Bringdown." Hammond was not oblivious to these attitudes. For example, although Hammond "always liked" Coleman Hawkins, the respect was not mutual. "I don't think he dug me particularly," Hammond recalled. And, more generally, Hammond conceded that "[o]ften my help and sponsorship were suspect." That suspicion could not stop Hammond's one-man juggernaut of talent scouting, record producing, and music promoting in a career that stretched from Billie Holiday to Bruce Springsteen.[8]

Bankruptcy Blues

Hammond's experiences with Henderson were not unique, lending weight to his view that the band's passive resistance to his advocacy went beyond individual personality to more systemic problems at the crossroads of race and commerce. From 1932 to 1934, indeed, the band's fortunes were mixed, partly due to circumstances beyond Henderson's control, and partly due to the band's increasingly casual approach to securing and keeping employment. On one hand, Henderson continued to get bookings and attract legions of fans. A "throng" greeted him at Atlantic City's Garden Pier Danceland (with its three hundred dance hostesses) in July 1932, for example. An unprecedented crowd of forty-six hundred attended a "breakfast dance" featuring the bands of Henderson, Cab Calloway, and Chick Webb, at the Savoy Ballroom. There, Henderson's fall 1932 engagement had been "extended indefinitely" because of the band's "great" popularity, as reported in the *New York Amsterdam News*. The band earned another extended run and regular radio exposure at the Empire Ballroom, a large, new ballroom in midtown Manhattan, at Forty-Eighth and Broadway, not far from the Roseland. That job began in late February 1933 and drew thousands on Saturday nights. For the first time since the Connie's Inn job, the band enjoyed stability and prominence in a choice Manhattan venue, but the job lasted only until early June.[9]

Within a year, in February 1934, another potentially stabilizing situation arose when Henderson signed a contract to perform under the auspices of Irving Mills. Already prominent for sponsorship of the Ellington and Calloway bands, Mills's agency offered the hope of more bookings, greater prestige, and financial stability. The *New York Age*, for one, hoped the association would lead to Henderson's "Phoenix-like rise from his ashes." Expectations for dramatic change in Henderson's fortunes had a solid foundation. Thomas J. Hennessey has emphasized Irving Mills's fundamental importance to the spread and nationalization of big-band jazz by virtue of his development and standardization of management practices. "Mills turned band management in to a full-time business" and "provided a model of success" for others, writes Hennessey. The model's goal was national impact created by the combined force of recordings, radio, publicity, and tours. None of these was new to the dance-band business, and Henderson himself stood among the few bandleaders to enjoy sustained success in all of these areas. But Mills brought new energy, more time, and a systematic effort to combine the elements on behalf of several black bands under his auspices. Mills created this "structured career pattern" for Ellington and copied it for Cab Calloway. By 1934 Ellington enjoyed a national profile thanks to recordings for Victor, the leading record company; regular appearances on the CBS radio network from the Cotton Club; a publicity barrage in print and electronic media, including a film appearance; and performances not only around the United States but in Europe, where Ellington made a successful tour in 1933.[10]

For Henderson's band, Mills's agency did produce several immediate benefits, including a recording session for Victor, a tour of the Midwest, and, above all, an escalation in the quantity and quality of press coverage of the band (a Mills trademark). Under Mills's management, Henderson played venues as disparate as the Lafayette Theatre and the Yale University junior prom. Yet due to conflicts of interest that naturally arise when an agent represents multiple clients, Mills could also hinder the very groups he had committed himself to represent. Plans for Henderson's band to visit London dissolved when Mills sent Cab Calloway's band instead. A promising run at the Cotton Club fell through when Mills placed his Blue Rhythm Band there. The *New York Amsterdam News* ominously noted that "[t]hings are going badly for Fletcher Henderson." The band then returned to the road for a series of one-nighters. The agency of Mills, so beneficial to Ellington and Calloway, his flagship bands, was clearly a mixed blessing for Henderson, and it lasted only five months out of a reported two-year contract.[11]

The kind of temporary stability conjured by Hammond and Mills only masked a rather precarious situation. Despite unwavering popularity among fans and prestige among musicians, Henderson's financial problems became severe in 1932–34. Walter Allen cites a variety of contemporary sources attesting to Henderson's debts in 1933, including an article in the *New York Age* needling Henderson to write a song called "Bankruptcy Blues," and pointedly noting his financial debt to fellow bandleader and former sideman Benny Carter.

All of this seems to have taken a toll on the band's performances. The same article that heralded Henderson's "bankruptcy blues" also noted that the band "seems to be wavering in its standards." And late in 1933, when Henderson returned for another stint at the Roseland, the same reporter claimed that "Fletcher and the boys do not seem to have struck their full stride." But other reports testify that Henderson's band was as hot as ever. Hammond, an unwavering advocate, claimed that the band "has seldom been better" than its appearance at the Savoy in December 1933, and that the "crowd of Harlemites surged around the band and gaped in amazement."[12]

Sometimes the band's struggles brought the leader and sidemen into conflict. Hammond reported a time in 1933 when "Smack had been having trouble with some of the prima donnas in his band." It got so bad, he continued, that Henderson "was toying with the idea of firing his whole orchestra" and starting "a brand new band." The trouble went both ways. Sidemen reported that Henderson regularly missed payments to them. The musicians stuck with the band nevertheless, because no other could match its quality and collective spirit. As Walter Johnson put it, "[t]he band was so good I would've played with them for nothing at that time." Trombonist Dicky Wells agreed: "That was the kind of spirit the cats had. They weren't always worrying about money. In Fletcher's band, once you started playing, once you hit the first note of those good arrangements, all that was forgotten. It was something the music would do for you."[13]

Anatomy of a Head

By the early 1930s, Henderson's band had gradually become a loosely run collective. Henderson was now, in Hammond's words, "the most disorganized bandleader there ever was," and the person who seemed least bothered by it was Henderson himself. "Easygoing" is the mantra of musicians recalling Henderson's leadership style in the 1930s. Hammond called him "too phlegmatic for his own good." Tardiness had become endemic. Instead of a reprimand, or worse, a musician who arrived late for a job might step right in with a solo then get an approving nod from the bandleader for his effort. Fletcher became "part of the whole thing," Lawrence Lucie noted, "not like a leader, but like one of the band." Although it annoyed some of the musicians, for Lucie that formed part of Henderson's appeal: "Henderson was great as a leader," claimed Lucie, because he simply "enjoyed seeing the band play."[14]

The comments point to a paradox. What Hammond called Henderson's "lassitude" seems to have brought out the fire in his sidemen. "They would seem as if they would play harder," recalled Horace, because Henderson did not reprimand them. Hammond, recalling the nearly catastrophic Columbia session, noted that "[p]erhaps to make amends for their casual behavior, the musicians really put out in the short time available to us." In general, Hammond believed that because Henderson "gave his soloists more freedom than any bandleader has ever done . . . he got the best."[15]

The band's collective spirit extended to rehearsals and arrangements. Musically, this was the time when Henderson emerges as the band's chief arranger. Yet the exact nature of Henderson's involvement remains unclear, because "arranging" at this point must be understood not as just writing things down, as he would do for Goodman, but in directing rehearsals in which the band members collaborated on arrangements. A glimpse of Henderson's method may be assembled from evocative testimony from Coleman Hawkins, from brother Horace, and from Dicky Wells. Hawkins left a vivid account in which claimed that "the majority" of the band's arrangements were "what we call 'heads.' "

> We just made 'em up . . . right at rehearsal. We'd have a rehearsal; brass would be over there doing something, saxophones over here. Finish up, we'd have ourselves another piece.

Horace was more specific about Fletcher's role. Fletcher would conduct rehearsals of a new chart by explaining its basic structure, including cuts and segues, while admitting he did not have time to write it all down. Horace recalled that because the band "knew his style," Henderson could simply "write skeleton things," "explain where to jump," and describe unwritten insertions.[16]

Dicky Wells called it "playing in the mud." One of the many coming-and-going stars who passed through Henderson's band, Wells joined Henderson for a spell in 1933, later becoming a mainstay in Count Basie's orchestra.

> That's jazz. If you get too clean, too precise, you don't swing sometimes, and the fun goes out of the music. Like Fletcher's arrangements—they'd make you feel bright inside. You were having fun just riding along. You could almost compare it to a lot of kids playing in the mud, having a big time. When the mother calls one to wash his hands, he gets clean, but he has to stand and just look while the others are having a ball. He's too clean, and he can't go back. Same way when you clean up on that horn and the arrangements are too clean: You get on another level. You're looking down on the guys, but they're all having a good, free-going time.[17]

There have been glimpses of this kind of thing before 1932—in "King Porter Stomp," "Hop Off," and the 1931 "Sugar Foot Stomp." But as Rex Stewart noted, "Fletcher had to struggle with himself to start arranging," mainly because he had always been able to rely on talented colleagues like Redman and Carter. It appears, then, that Henderson-directed head arrangements became a more frequent practice in 1932–34, as the bandleader was forced to rely more on himself for his band's arrangements.[18]

Fats Waller's "Honeysuckle Rose," recorded at the Columbia session organized by Hammond in December 1932, shows the practice in its simplest and most common form. The recorded arrangement consists of five choruses of a standard thirty-two-bar AABA song structure. Chorus 1 presents the melody, harmonized in brass, close to the way Waller published it three years earlier. Choruses 2–4 comprise a series of improvised solos over riff accompaniments. Chorus 5 then features a new variation on the tune, a climactic ensemble riff.

The format can be heard as both an extension of arranging conventions of the 1920s and as an anticipation of Henderson's approach to arranging for Goodman three years later. Conforming to 1920s techniques, the arrangement sets the melody of a current popular song, then introduces variations, culminating in what amounts to an "arranger's chorus" featuring the whole ensemble. Unlike a typical 1920s arrangement, however, this arrangement demands little or no written music. Indeed, it calls for little preliminary planning beyond agreeing on the tune and working out the riffs. (Harmonizing in thirds and sixths hardly needed rehearsal: Louis Armstrong and King Oliver had done it in their famous duet breaks in the early 1920s.) The order and number of solos, as well as the beginning of the final riff chorus, could be indicated by eye contact during the performance. The arrangement omits the song's verse, and includes no introduction, transitions, modulations, or tag ending. Clever contrast and subdivision inside the strain give way to a smooth, streamlined succession of choruses, each focusing on a single musical idea. Chorus 1 sounds perfunctory, the obligatory melody rendition (recalling Whiteman's claim that arrangements could develop new ideas and timbres only "after the tune is set"). The band's true colors emerge in the subsequent choruses. As chorus 1 ends, J. C. Higginbotham takes off with a fiery, bellowing solo in chorus 2. Hawkins follows in chorus 3 with an athletic, ornate exploration that ranges freely over the band's beat and simple harmonic foundation. Stark ignites chorus 4 with a rip and a series of blaring Armstrong-like phrases. Henderson heralds the final chorus with ringing piano octaves that summon the saxes and muted brass for the climactic riff.

Like Waller's melody, that riff has an artful, repetitive simplicity (ex. 8.1).

Ex. 8.1. "Honeysuckle Rose" (December 9, 1932). Top line: original melody. Bottom line: Henderson riff.

Waller's melody states a jaunty one-bar figure ("Ev'ry honeybee") nine times over the thirty-two bar chorus; the Henderson band's swinging two-bar riff appears twelve times. The riff, built on two notes of Waller's tune (the notes that appear on the capitalized syllables in "ev'ry HON-ey-BEE"), has strong rhythmic interest with a swinging little oscillation between two notes and a syncopated leap up to the higher note and back down. Moreover, the riff's central pitch, Bb, sounds at home in all three principal chords of the phrase: Eb minor (where it's the fifth degree), Ab major (where it's the ninth), and Db major (where it's the sixth). Thus it also meets another criterion for a good, repeatable riff by fitting snugly over the song's changing harmony.[19]

With the sequence of interior solo choruses framed by ensemble melody and riff choruses, the band has thus created a straightforward musical process that could be extended indefinitely when played in public, where the musicians did not have to observe the three-minute norm of the 78 rpm record. In short, "Honeysuckle Rose" has all the ingredients of what pianist Teddy Wilson once described as "the good head arrangements . . . that you could play for about ten minutes and get the dancers going."[20]

Over the next twenty months (until the band broke up in 1934), Henderson's band would revisit the "Honeysuckle Rose" format again and again, with varying degrees of planning and written music involved. The ingredients include many, if not consistently all, of the following:

1. A thirty-two-bar AABA popular-song structure based on an existing song or a new piece modeled on such a song.
2. Five or six choruses of that structure, in three distinct parts: (a) a first chorus stating the melody, (b) an expandable series of interior choruses featuring improvised solos over sectional riffs, and (c) one (and sometimes two) "out" choruses featuring the whole ensemble playing a new riff, sometimes presented in call-and-response style.
3. A fast tempo of well over 200 beats per minute (usually in the 220–290 range). As Russell Procope put it, "People used to dance fast in those days," and "in the ballrooms, they were used to playing fast."[21]
4. A chord structure featuring a prominent harmonic "loop," such as the one in Gershwin's "I Got Rhythm," which, after its premiere on Broadway in 1930, began to become a jazz standard and source of contrafacts—new melodies based on another tune's harmony—in the 1932–34 period. "Rhythm changes" (or just "rhythm")—as the Gershwin chords would later become known among jazz musicians—features a recycling I–ii–V–I pattern, sometimes varied by chord substitutions.

Such loops are a recurring feature of the Henderson style in 1932–34, but they have not gotten nearly as much attention as riffs. "I Got Rhythm" was by no means the only or even the earliest tune in Henderson's repertoire to feature such a loop. Example 8.2 shows several variants of it (all transcribed in C major for comparison). "Honeysuckle Rose"—with a chord structure perhaps more like an oscillation than a loop—alternates between ii and V before resolving to the tonic (I) in its fifth measure. "Nagasaki" and "Happy As the Day Is Long," also recorded by Henderson in this period, begin with an identical, repeated harmonic loop before moving to other chords. "Yeah Man!" later revised and recorded as "Hotter than 'Ell," is a "rhythm" tune that also features a passing diminished chord in a recycling progression. Horace Henderson's original "Big John Special" has a chord progression with a strong familial resemblance, as does "Rug Cutter's Swing," a partial "rhythm" tune. The band's most famous number from the period, "King Porter Stomp," has a two-bar harmonic loop in its "trio" and "stomp" sections that resembles some of the others with its passing diminished chord, but stands out as unique by beginning not on the tonic, the "home" chord, but on the subdominant. In Henderson's "King Porter Stomp" recordings of 1932 and 1933, as we've seen, the trio section gets more emphasis than ever before, as it becomes the basis for an even longer sequence of solos than the band had played on its 1928 recording. "King Porter Stomp" also stands out from this group for being structured as a multistrain piece dating from the ragtime era; all the other harmonic-loop tunes in Henderson's recorded repertoire of the period were recent popular songs with the AABA chorus structure. All of these loops share a built-in harmonic momentum that gives an improviser not just support but push. Moreover, they provide an harmonic analog to riffs: both almost always occur in two-measure cycles.

With so many arrangements sharing these basic traits, no wonder members of Henderson's band could show up late, step right in with a solo,

Ex. 8.2. Harmonic loops in Henderson's repertory, 1932–34

a. Honeysuckle Rose

b. Nagasaki, Happy As the Day is Long

c. Yeah Man/ Hotter Than 'ell/ Big John Special

d. Rug Cutter's Swing

e. King Porter Stomp

f. Queer Notions

and ignite crowds of listeners and dancers night after night. If one soloist was absent, another could fill his slot and the audience might never realize it. Such arrangements were ideal for a band on the run. Although many were collaborative efforts, with principal credit attaching to another band member such as Horace Henderson, Coleman Hawkins, or Benny Carter, or an outside arranger such as Will Hudson or Russ Morgan, it is apt to refer to them all as helping to create a "Henderson style," because the musicians shared a common goal. As Horace said, Fletcher could conduct rehearsals with minimal written music because the band knew "his style." Dicky Wells noted, "The guys in the band used to bring in arrangements, and they seemed to know just what Fletcher wanted." So, as casually collaborative as the music making may have seemed, it did have a center of gravity, and that was Henderson himself.[22]

"Hotter than 'Ell"

Before discussing selected recordings, it bears repeating the limitations of the recorded legacy as documentation of the sound, format, and style of Henderson's arrangements. Once again, the recorded legacy gives only a partial, and mixed, picture of the results. Hawkins brought out this point as he continued to describe the band's head arrangements:

> We'd play this piece like mad. Come to work next night. We'd play it: *wonderful*. Maybe about two or three days later we'd go down to the studio to record it: *horrible*. Never would it come out right.... I don't know what it was about that band. I've never understood it. Why that band could not record ... in person it was the stomping, pushingest band I ever heard. Couldn't do the record the same way; I wonder why?[23]

Dicky Wells begins to answer Hawkins's questions when he notes that recorded arrangements were not only poorer, but shorter. "When you hear some of Fletcher's old records, there may be just one jammed chorus," he notes, "but on the job there'd be a lot more. They called it 'stretching it out.'"[24]

Another answer to Hawkins's question lies again in dancing. As Dicky Wells put it, "There was more soul when jazz and dancing went together." The comments of Wells and Hawkins go far to suggest that hearing Henderson's records reveal only half—perhaps less than half—of the whole milieu in which the music and musicians thrived.

Nevertheless, the records survive, and several arrangements that Henderson's band recorded twice have much to reveal about how the band developed heads over time. A particularly vivid example is "Yeah Man!," later revised and recorded as "Hotter than 'Ell."

Composed by veteran songwriters Noble Sissle and J. Russell Robinson, "Yeah Man!" likely got its name from a Harlem speakeasy on Seventh Avenue. The tune stands as one of the earliest recorded contrafacts of Gershwin's "I Got Rhythm." Henderson first recorded "Yeah Man!" on August 18, 1933, becoming the third band, and the first black band, to do so. Thirteen months later, in September 1934, Henderson recorded a nearly identical arrangement as "Hotter than 'Ell," now billed as his own composition. Interviewed two years later, however, Fletcher gave all the credit—as both arranger and composer—to his brother.[25]

If the multiplicity of attributions suggests a head arrangement, the recorded performances reinforce that impression. "Yeah Man!" begins with a four-bar introduction built from a simple, repeated two-bar vamp that sets a groove and a blistering tempo of about 270 beats per minute. The whole arrangement stands on a riff foundation. The riffs serve several functions: as melody (chorus 1), accompaniment (choruses 2–4, and the bridge of choruses 5–6), and call-and-response figures (choruses 5–6).

"Yeah Man!" and "Hotter than 'Ell" are clearly the same piece (fig. 8.1). The harmony, riff accompaniments, melodies, call-and-response figures, and the order of solos remain the same. But there are also substantial differences between the two, and they consist in more than a mere title. The two versions suggest the difference between a newly developed head arrangement

Fig. 8.1 From "Yeah Man!" to "Hotter than 'Ell"

Yeah Man! (Sissle, Robinson)	Hotter than 'Ell (Fletcher Henderson)
(August 18, 1933)	(September 25, 1934)
Vocalion	Decca
arr. Horace Henderson	arr. Horace Henderson
♩ = ca. 268 < 276	♩ = ca. 284
G major	G major
Intro(4) repeated 2-bar vamp for rhythm, saxes	Intro(8) wailing brass and saxes C & R (from chorus 5)
Chorus 1 ens. riff	add tbn. stinger on pickups
Chorus 2 Procope clar. solo (brass riff)	reeds play mm. 1–4; Bailey clar. solo
Chorus 3 Stark tpt. solo (saxes riff)	Allen tpt. solo
Chorus 4 Hawkins tenor sax solo (brass riff)	Webster tenor sax solo
Chorus 5 A wailing brass and saxes C & R	
A " "	
B Allen tpt. solo (saxes)	B brass unison melody (saxes long tones)
A ens. C & R	
Chorus 6 A shouting brass and scurrying saxes C & R	
A " " "	
B Hawkins tenor sax solo (saxes)	B Webster (tbns.)
A ensemble	

and a revision developed over months of rehearsal and performance. The key difference lies in the increased use and precision of the ensemble in the latter version.

The band signals the difference at the outset. "Yeah Man!" had featured a simple, repeated two-bar vamp in the introduction, "Hotter than 'Ell" features a wailing call and response between brass and saxes, based on chorus 5 of "Yeah Man!" (ex. 8.3).

In chorus 1, where "Yeah Man!" had an ensemble riff, "Hotter than 'Ell" adds a trombone "stinger" that acts to ignite each phrase (ex. 8.4), a device that had been used to great effect in pieces for Henderson by two of Irving Mills's staff composer-arrangers: Nat Leslie's "Radio Rhythm" and, at a lower intensity, Will Hudson's "Hocus Pocus."

In chorus 2, where "Yeah Man!" featured a full-chorus clarinet solo, "Hotter than 'Ell" begins with four bars for the saxophones, out of which the solo clarinet emerges (see fig. 8.1). And in the bridge of chorus 5 in "Hotter than 'Ell," the entire trumpet section plays a broad, Armstrong-like melody in place of the improvised trumpet solo that appeared in "Yeah Man!" That new bridge apparently grew out of a Red Allen solo that Horace liked enough to score for the entire brass section. If the immediate source was Red Allen, the line's high-register breadth and power suggest the abiding presence of Louis Armstrong[26] (ex. 8.5).

Ex. 8.3. "Hotter than 'Ell" (September 25, 1934), introduction (transcribed by T. Unseth)

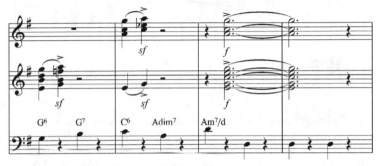

Ex. 8.4. "Hotter than 'Ell," chorus 1, beginning (transcribed by T. Unseth)

Ex. 8.5. "Hotter than 'Ell," chorus 5, bridge (transcribed by T. Unseth)

In the final chorus, "Hotter than 'Ell" preserves the call-and-response pattern of "Yeah Man!" with syncopated shouting brass answered by scurrying saxophones (ex. 8.6).

Ex. 8.6. "Hotter than 'Ell," chorus 6, beginning (transcribed by T. Unseth)

Although "Hotter than 'Ell" features the same riffs as "Yeah Man!" the later recording shows greater precision and confidence in the band's performance of them. "Yeah Man!" has all the raw excitement of a classic head; "Hotter than 'Ell" represents a more integrated ensemble revealing more rehearsal, revision, and, probably, more music writing.

From heads and head-like arrangements we move to a Henderson composition called "Can You Take It?", which introduces some variants to the basic format. The piece deserves attention for several reasons. It stands out as one of the few pieces both composed and arranged by Henderson in the early 1930s, yet it has been overshadowed by its better-known counterparts from 1934, "Down South Camp Meeting" and "Wrappin' It Up." It reveals some of Henderson's musical preoccupations of the period, foreshadows elements of the two later compositions, and also shows Henderson working out ideas that he would revisit in two arrangements he wrote for Benny Goodman in 1935. Dicky Wells cited "Can You Take It?" among the scores from the period showing Henderson at his best.[27]

The entire piece is in the key of A major, a remarkably "sharp" key that posed special challenges for the trumpets and reeds. Henderson was legendary for writing in sharp keys. His "'D' Natural Blues" announced the fact in its title. "Can You Take It?" goes one sharp better, and the title may well be more than a rhetorical question for Henderson's trumpets and reeds. Many musicians have commented on Henderson's keys; Horace mentioned Fletcher's "weird keys." Ben Webster, who would fill Coleman Hawkins's chair in the band by summer 1934, admitted to being "scared" to take the job, because "[t]he band played in every key imaginable." Trumpeter Jonah Jones claimed that "you had to see around corners" to play one of Henderson's arrangements. According to Dicky Wells, Fletcher told him that he preferred sharp keys because "it meant less notes and the band would swing more." There was more to it than that. Henderson's penchant for difficult keys—"oriental keys," as some musicians called them—served as another marker for his band's prestige and talent, and as a means of showing up the competition.[28]

While the key is unusual, the overall structure reflects standard practice: a brief introduction, a melody chorus, a series of interior solo choruses, and a final chorus featuring variations on the melody, plus a brief tag ending. Henderson scores the introduction and entire first chorus for clarinets, revealing a new preoccupation with Don Redman's trademark device that he would revisit in his own compositions as well as his arrangements for Goodman. The main melody, based on a thirty-two bar AABA form, features a series of wailing leaps that hark back to Henderson's "Stampede" from seven years earlier. The leaps, tracing a perfect fifth, also suggest another familiar source, confirmed by the underlying harmony, which is more intricate and lacks the "loop" common to many heads. That harmony consists of a descending chromatic chord progression that takes the music from the relative minor to the major tonic in eight bars. In other words, it's a contrafact of Irving Berlin's "Blue Skies," which Henderson would arrange for Goodman two years later.

The solo sequence presents Hawkins, Sandy Williams, and Hilton Jefferson, each accompanied by sustained chords or riffs from the contrasting section (brass for Hawkins and Jefferson; saxophones, punctuated by brass shouts, for Williams). Instead of improvising on the main tune, however, Williams and Jefferson take their solos on the blues. That suggests that perhaps only Hawkins—well known for his virtuosic command in all keys—had mastered the chromatic chord changes in A major, or that Henderson was pointing a unique spotlight on his star, or most likely, both. The interior blues choruses also suggest the means by which the piece would have been easily expandable during a dance or other public performance—all of Henderson's sidemen could readily solo on the blues. The final chorus—an arranger's chorus—alternates between ensemble variations and brief solos by Red Allen and Henderson himself. The last phrase, which Henderson elides with the tag ending, most clearly points the way to his later work with Goodman. Here, the ensemble plays a nifty soloistic variation on the main melody and then segues directly into a tag ending that Henderson would use again in his 1935 arrangement for Goodman of "Between the Devil and the Deep Blue Sea."

"Can You Take It?", although structured like many other arrangements in Henderson's repertoire, stands apart from the standard "head" arrangement with its difficult key and chromatic, "Blue Skies"-based chord progression, upon which only Hawkins dared answer the title's question with a solo on record.

Hawkins himself composed a piece called "Queer Notions" that also introduces a novel twist on the familiar format. Some jazz writers have noted the self-consciously "modernistic" element of the piece: the parallel augmented chords, which, when harmonized by the full ensemble, create whole-tone clusters, and thereby neutralize the gravitational pull of the tonal center (E♭). Yet the tune's harmonic novelty appears in a recognizable context. Like the other head-arrangement-type pieces "Queer Notions" is an AABA tune featuring a two-bar riff melody over a cyclic two-bar harmonic loop (ex. 8.7).

From that perspective, Hawkins's piece fit squarely within the practices Henderson's band had been developing in its head arrangements of other pieces.

Ex. 8.7. "Queer Notions" (August 18, 1933), chorus 1, beginning (transcribed by Mark Tucker)

Featuring Coleman Hawkins and Henry "Red" Allen

One of the band's "Queer Notions" recordings occurred during a unique recording session in September 1933 that deserves some special attention. Record labels of the early 1930s featured the names of bandleaders, singers, and songwriters, but as a rule they did not include the names of sidemen, even prominent ones. In 1932, however, advertisements for a few of Henderson's one-nighters on the road began to bill Coleman Hawkins as a star attraction, including one in the *Boston Post* heralding the appearance of "Cole Hawkins—World's Greatest Tenor Saxophonist." The following year a couple of Henderson's record labels include the phrase "featuring Coleman Hawkins" and "featuring Henry 'Red' Allen." In these records the soloist earns the musical spotlight for an unusually extended period.[29]

The first and most remarkable example appears on Henderson's recording of a popular song called "It's the Talk of the Town"—"featuring Coleman Hawkins." In a period when playing "hot" meant playing fast, and playing fast became the standard ballroom style, slow tempos were reserved almost exclusively for the blues, which were now decisively out of fashion. And racial stereotypes in the music business tended to reward black bands for not venturing beyond the bounds of "race" records—the repository for jazz and blues-oriented material readily identifiable with black culture. In that context, "Talk of the Town" stands out as an utter anomaly and a break from race material: a romantic ballad taken at under 100 beats per minute. As Chilton points out, Hawkins had already begun showing an interest in ballad playing as an occasional sideman in 1929–30, his solo on "If I Could Be with You One Hour Tonight" being a "prototype." Then, around 1931–32, Hawkins told Russell Procope that the real test of a great jazz player was the ability to play slow, and he offered to show Procope how to do it. The band's recording of "House of David Blues" exhibits his emerging ballad style. But through most of the 1930s—and beyond his time in Henderson's band—"Talk of the Town" was the tune that became Hawkins's case in point for improvising on a ballad, and, in fact, it was one of Hawkins's favorites and, in retrospect, a glimpse of the style he would bring to his famous "Body and Soul" recording of 1939.[30]

The recorded performance is so slow that the band manages to play only two full choruses, framed by a brief introduction and a coda. But the arrangement still shows vestiges of the style and structure of the "head" format. After a languorous, mournful clarinet solo in the introduction, the trumpets and saxophones alternate four-bar phrases of the melody, in a series of passages too slow to be heard as call and response. The first chorus ends with a remarkably controlled, rising glissando from Red Allen's trumpet. Hawkins then plays an elaborate, searching solo on the higher side of his vast range. With its broad, imposing tone and tender phrasing, the improvisation has the spirit of a gentle bear. Extending nearly one-and-a-half minutes, the solo leaves no time for an ensemble out-chorus, but Henderson manages to include a ten-bar coda in a new key for a syncopated ensemble variation of the original melody—a glimpse of what was probably conceived as a full chorus. Comprising only seventy-eight bars, the recording still extends to the limits of a 78 rpm record at three minutes and thirty-one seconds, making it one of the longest recordings Henderson ever made. Two weeks later in a recording session of Henderson's band under the leadership of Horace, Hawkins had an even longer featured solo on another romantic ballad, "I've Got to Sing a Torch Song."

Chilton suggests that Henderson was beginning to worry about losing his star and thus attempted to keep him in the fold by appealing to his ego with special billing. Henderson apparently had ample justification for worry. In addition to sidelining as a soloist or leader in a variety of non-Henderson recording sessions, Hawkins began to be incited—and perhaps distracted—by competition with rival tenor Chu Berry. By 1933, moreover, Hawkins's personal life had been disrupted by separation from his wife, leading him to spend much more time away from his apartment and to drinking—although his habits had no detrimental effect on his playing or on his stature among other musicians. Hawkins began to epitomize the Henderson band's lack of professionalism and discipline. J. C. Higginbotham recalled that "Nobody made time, nobody," but Hawkins stood out even in this company: "Coleman Hawkins was a great one on that one."[31]

Despite the unprecedented billing he enjoyed as a sideman, within six months Hawkins was gone for good; he made his last recordings with Henderson on March 6, 1934. Having performed as Henderson's sideman for eleven years, Hawkins had outlasted every other band member besides its leader. No wonder, then, that Henderson not only sought to fill Hawkins's chair, he also sought a musician with Hawkins's massive, penetrating sound, a sound that, as Harry Carney of Ellington's band recalled, could "cut the Ellington band all by itself." Henderson's first choice for Hawkins's replacement, Lester Young, could hardly have been further from Hawkins's sound and style. In contrast to Hawkins's penchant for harmonic complexity, Young preferred to simplify; in contrast to Hawkins's ripe, full-bodied tone, Young's was light and lithe. Henderson and the band recognized the "problem" immediately, and to Leora went the task of coaching Young to sound more like his predecessor in the band. "I was rooming at the Henderson's house," Young recalled, "and Leora Henderson would wake me early in the morning and play Hawkins's records for me so I could play like he did. I wanted to play my own way, but I just listened. I didn't want to hurt her feelings." Meanwhile, "the whole band was buzzing on me because I had taken Hawk's place." Thus, both insulted and overwhelmed by expectations to sound like someone else, Young left Henderson after just three or four months and never made a record with the band. Ultimately, he would land on his feet as a featured star in the band of Count Basie.[32]

Hawkins's departure may have been a "severe blow" to Henderson, as Schuller claims, but I believe the impact of Hawkins's loss has been overestimated. For one thing, Henderson had a decade of experience in replacing excellent musicians and continuing to flourish. On alto, he already had Hilton Jefferson, so he had a strong saxophone soloist. Moreover, while soloists were essential to Henderson's style, much of its distinctive identity depended on ensemble vitality, for solos tended to fill the interior choruses of its arrangements. Dicky Wells, for one, claimed that solos have been overestimated—that true fans knew the arrangements better than the soloists: "The audiences were real hip. They went for the overall musical picture without picking too much on the individual, although they might like you as a soloist." At any rate, by the time of the band's next recording session, on September 11, 1934, Henderson had found an outstanding Hawkins surrogate: the twenty-five-year old tenor man from Kansas City named Ben Webster. "[E]verybody agreed that Ben Webster had the big sound," recalled Procope—"a tone which Coleman had." On the dozen remaining sides from 1934, Webster would become a regular soloist in the band. While Young went with Basie, Webster developed his own style and became a mainstay in the Ellington band.[33]

Another musician came to Henderson with a big sound: Henry "Red" Allen. After Henderson had run him through an audition in difficult keys, Allen joined the band in June 1933. A twenty-five-old New Orleans native, Allen had learned trumpet in his father's brass band and imitated Louis Armstrong, who was seven years Allen's senior. Following Armstrong's path, Allen would go north to join King Oliver's band in 1927 and also play in Fate Marable's riverboat orchestra. In that band, Allen was "discovered" by representatives of Victor, who heard in Allen's powerful tone, fluent improvisations, and vast vocabulary of timbral effects a viable competitor to Armstrong, who at the time was recording for OKeh. From 1929 to 1932 Allen became a featured soloist in Luis Russell's band, where he developed an affinity with J. C. Higginbotham. Thus, upon joining Henderson in the summer of 1933, Allen was already used to the spotlight and quickly became one of the band's solo stars. In one of the most evocative tributes, written soon after Allen's death in 1967, Whitney Balliett wrote that Allen, with Henderson, became "a one-man avant-garde." Allen also had a memorably long, broad face, which in later years, was seasoned with what Balliett called a "bassett melancholy."[34]

In the same recording session as "Queer Notions" and "It's the Talk of the Town," Henderson's band also played "Nagasaki," a number featuring "Vocal and Trumpet by Henry Allen, Jr.," as the record label put it. The Harry Warren/Mort Dixon song "Nagasaki," published in 1928, could be called "hot chinoiserie"—a late 1920s incarnation of the oriental fox-trot theme from the teens and early 1920s, and stemming back to the Chinese song fad accelerated by "Chinatown, My Chinatown." It's also a close cousin of the McHugh/Fields song of the same year, "Diga Diga Doo." Both are rhythm songs that celebrate vice and sensuality in a distant, exoticized realm: "back in Nagasaki where the fellows chew tobaccy and the women wicky-wacky-woo." A year later, by September 1934, the song had become "the National anthem of Harlem," which Henderson's band played to satisfy a crowd at the Harlem Opera House.[35]

The first chorus arrangement takes the same approach as "Talk of the Town"—saxes and brass trade four-bar phrases of the melody, now at a much faster clip. Horace takes the first solo, an animated romp whose unexpected rhythmic and textural shifts suggest jazz piano innovator Earl Hines. The next three choruses are all Red Allen—an uninterrupted solo sequence of a length no other Henderson sideman had ever enjoyed on record. Allen's singing, like so many occasional black-band singers in the early 1930s, has several hallmarks of Armstrong's vocal style, widely circulating since Armstrong's performance of "Ain't Misbehavin' " on record and in public in mid-1929: the rhythmic elasticity, repeated notes, and lyric-slurring that meant to create more excitement than literal understanding. Horace plays a bridge to the final chorus, which alternates between solo and section work, and culminates in a final passage of ensemble shouts. "Nagasaki" has all the features of a typical Henderson band "head" of the period; the difference, in this case, is that the expandable sequence of interior solos throws the spotlight on a single performer.

Decca Records: September 1934

In a final spurt of recordings before its breakup, Henderson's band made twelve for Decca Records in September 1934. Among them are some of the best-known records Henderson ever made, including his own compositions "Down South Camp Meeting" and "Wrappin' It Up." Taken together and understood in historical context, the Decca records reveal a previously unexplored linkage of race and commerce to material that has emerged as seminal big-band jazz.

Decca was a British company, but in August 1934 it branched out into the United States, a move spearheaded by the record producer Jack Kapp. Kapp aimed to outflank his leading competitors, Victor, Columbia, and Brunswick, with a two-pronged strategy: record the most prominent musicians and issue their records at the lowest prices the market would bear. Kapp quickly signed Bing Crosby to head the roster of stars and priced the records at thirty-five cents a piece, dramatically undercutting the industry's standard seventy-five-cent price. Kapp's efforts helped the record industry recover from a five-year slump.[36]

While enhancing Decca's luster with white celebrities such as Crosby, Kapp also began aggressively developing its "race" catalog with black musicians playing hot jazz. In late August Art Tatum began recording piano solos for Decca, and he stayed on the company's roster for many years. By the end of September 1934—within a month of establishing Decca's beachhead in the states—Kapp had recorded the bands of Jimmie Lunceford, Chick Webb, Earl Hines, Claude Hopkins, and Fletcher Henderson. Lunceford and Webb would record regularly and exclusively for Decca over the next four years as the company continued to add major black talent to its roster, including the Kansas City–based bands of Andy Kirk and Count Basie. Louis Armstrong would begin recording for Decca upon his return from Europe in late 1935. Lionel Hampton and Louis Jordan would also join the fold. All together, Kapp's American Decca years produced some of the finest black jazz of the swing era.

Kapp has been reviled as an unethical businessman who exploited black talent. He has also been recognized as one of the "most innovative and successful record men" of the Depression era. As Will Friedwald put it, Kapp "is possibly the most controversial figure in all of popular music. He is revered in as many histories of the record business as he is vilified in histories of jazz." Jazz history has cast him, at best, as an impediment to the music's development. Cultural historian William Howland Kenney, who offers the deepest and most sympathetic portrait of Kapp, pairs him with John Hammond as record producers of the 1930s who "in different ways, seemed to have their fingers on the public pulse"—Kapp, as a kind of populist with an understanding of how to allay Depression-era anxiety by defining a mainstream American popular vocal music, and Hammond, as a man who strove to harness recording technology as a means of merging progressive social and artistic impulses in jazz recordings by black bands. Yet Decca's recordings of black bands in the fall of 1934 prove that Kapp also acted, unwittingly or not, as a catalyst for jazz, and the Smithsonian *Big-Band Jazz* anthology's inclusion of seven Decca records by four different black bands in the fall of 1934 alone testifies that even a half-century after they were made, the records met the jazz criteria of two leading jazz historians—Gunther Schuller and Martin Williams—who selected the anthology's records.[37]

What Kapp wanted from black bands, above all, was that they sound black. The recollection of Andy Kirk reveals that poignantly. When Andy Kirk wanted to "crack the race barrier in recordings" by playing a ballad, Kapp asked him, " 'Why do you want to do what the white boys are doing?' Right there I saw his commercial motives," Kirk wrote. "It was for the race market only." Kapp grudgingly allowed Kirk to record his ballad, "Until the Real Thing Comes Along," and it became Kirk's best-selling record. Generally, however, Kapp discouraged Kirk and other black musicians from recording anything but jazz and blues-oriented material. "He had the race thing on his mind," wrote Kirk.[38]

Even the titles of Henderson's Decca sides advertise the "race thing." The title of Henderson's "Down South Camp Meeting" resonated with northern stereotypes about black Pentecostal worship and harkened back to the turn-of-the-century cakewalk hit, "At a Georgia Campmeeting." "Memphis Blues" came from W. C. Handy's well-known blues catalog at a time when the blues remained nearly synonymous with race records. Two other songs had racial resonance through the shows for which they were written: the Arlen/Koehler song "Happy as the Day Is Long" had recently appeared in the *Cotton Club Parade*, and "Liza" had been sung as a minstrel number in the Ziegfeld production of Gershwin's *Show Girl*. The title of Horace Henderson's "Big John Special" paid homage to a beloved Harlem restaurant owner. "Hotter than 'Ell," "Tidal Wave," "Wild Party," and "Rug Cutter's Swing" more generally evoked a release from inhibition associated with Harlem's nightlife. "Limehouse Blues" and "Shanghai Shuffle" reinforce the exotic jazz-Chinese connection that had developed since those songs had been hits a decade earlier.[39]

"Shanghai Shuffle" offers unique insight into the fundamental differences between Don Redman's and Fletcher Henderson's arranging styles, and more generally between arranging aesthetics in 1924 and 1934. Redman's "Shanghai Shuffle" of 1924 was a tour de force of stock doctoring, featuring a variegated sequence of solo and ensemble passages, with unpredictable colors and rhythms, and the arsenal of musical chinoiserie so popular in the heyday of the oriental foxtrot—including tom-tom beats, gong hits, and parallel fifths. Henderson's arrangement streamlines the piece, presenting a driving introduction that omits all of the pseudo-Chinese effects, followed by a single statement of the verse, and the now-customary five-chorus sequence with arranged ensemble passages framing a sequence of solos. Chorus 2 features a deftly played exchange of melodic snippets between the brass and reeds that both typifies Henderson's call-and-response patterning while recalling Redman's early-1920s device of melodic interception. The final chorus features a more straight-ahead call-and-response chorus in which the brass and saxes exchange shouting riffs. So much distinguishes the two arrangements, recorded a decade apart, that their one point of exact similarity seems remarkable: both clock in at about 228 beats per minute. The early version, however, brims with the manic peppiness of 1920s novelty dance music, while the later version rolls along in the driving but relaxed manner of a 1930s swinger. "Fletcher had a way of writing so that the notes just seemed to float along casually," wrote Dicky Wells. "There was something he seemed to have inside there." "Shanghai Shuffle" served as a case in point for Wells.[40]

The Decca sides comprise an unusually unified collection, stylistically. Schuller heard in them a "marvelously light, finger-snapping swing," but the arrangements do not sustain his attention. He hears the "flawless ensemble passages" of the Decca sides as an "aural facade" that foreshadows the decline of vital artistry of swing, which "atrophied not long after reaching its zenith, starved from a lack of stylistic and structural nourishment." Indeed, the chief appeal of the 1932–34 Henderson band for Schuller lies in a few key individuals: Walter Johnson, Red Allen, and Coleman Hawkins. No scholar has surpassed Schuller in analyzing the contribution to Henderson's band of these musicians.[41]

Yet the arrangements create the musical conditions in which the soloists thrive, especially considering the band's penchant for collective musical creation. Heard together and in the context of the band's repertoire and working methods in the early 1930s, the Decca sides show that the playing-in-the-mud quality that Dicky Wells so vividly described, and some elements of the "head" format, had gotten distilled and perfected.

Some of the arrangements came from outside the band, yet even they sound all of a piece with the internally developed charts. "Wild Party" has the markings of a head arrangement, this time built on the chords of another recent Broadway hit, Kern and Hammerstein's "Ol' Man River," a tune Henderson's band had recorded under Horace's direction a year earlier. But the tune is by Will Hudson and was "reportedly arranged" by Russ Morgan. Both Hudson and Morgan were white arrangers from the Mills stable. In the Mills-organized Victor session in March 1934, Henderson had played two numbers by Hudson: "Hocus Pocus" and "Tidal Wave." Perhaps best known as the composer of the 1930s standard "Moonglow" (with lyricist Eddie DeLange), Hudson wrote big-band swing in a taut, clear, riff-based style that could simply be called Hendersonian. As Stanley Dance wrote, he "had an ear for uptown riffs," although he probably heard such riffs first in Detroit, where he grew up and worked with McKinney's Cotton Pickers and Cab Calloway, who in turn helped Hudson get a job working for his agent, Irving Mills.[42]

In "Wild Party," as in "Yeah Man!"/"Hotter Than 'Ell," riffs again appear as melodies, accompaniments, and as call-and-response figures. The band states the riff-based theme in the first chorus, interior choruses present solos, and the final section climaxes in a series of calls-and-responses. Key and tempo shifts enhance the impact of the final shout choruses. In these final sections, the band plays only the first half of the tune, and plays it three times, each at a higher key than the preceding one. Beginning in F, the key shifts to G, then again up to A♭. Meanwhile, the whole performance, driven by Henderson's powerhouse rhythm section, has been accelerating noticeably, from 248 to 264 beats per minute. Adding to the overall climactic effect is the appearance of clarinetist Buster Bailey, who returned in 1934 and played animated obbligatos during the out choruses. Through the last two half-choruses, Bailey's clarinet obbligato grows louder, providing a kind of sprinkling effect over the passage. All together, the call-and-response riffs, the ratcheting stepwise modulations, the accelerating tempo, and the high-range clarinet obbligato create a climactic effect that must have been irresistible on the dance floor.

"Rug Cutter's Swing," by Horace Henderson, is a partial "I Got Rhythm" contrafact built on a riff at first stated by the muted trumpet. Again, three internal choruses feature mostly solos, including an ensemble/trombone call-and-response in chorus 3, in which the ensemble's "call" is based on its introduction. The final chorus features a melodic variation reminiscent of Rodgers and Hart's 1926 hit "The Blue Room."

"Limehouse Blues" begins with a hard-driving pulsating introduction. The first chorus gives a straightforward presentation of the melody, with saxes in the A sections, and the brass taking the lead for the B and C sections. Red Allen takes the first solo, over driving saxophone riffs. Buster Bailey takes the next solo, with brass long tones and riffs. The ensemble then trades eights with the trombone, with the ensemble playing long, blaring crescendo-ing tones into the solo phrases. In the next chorus, the ensemble again plays call-and-response with a tenor saxophone soloist: Webster. The next chorus features a series of riff-based call-and-response phrases: brass shouts answered by scurrying saxophone phrases. Throughout the rhythm section sounds light, integrated, and forward moving.

"Big John Special" is another Horace Henderson piece among many in the early 1930s that Fletcher's band played. Several remarkable things are worth noting: The main theme features a trademark of early 1930s that Henderson would standardize in his arrangements for Goodman: a chain of syncopations. The piece also has a light, understated swing, a suave inter-action of Red Allen's trumpet solo and the saxophone riffs that accompany it, a lithe alto solo by Hilton Jefferson, and a sequence of call-and-response figures in the final chorus. In the middle of the arrangement there appears an ornate, solo-like passage for the full saxophone section. The title pays homage to a generous Harlem restaurant owner, about whom Dicky Wells said: "Everybody loved Big John. His nickname was Meatball. If you had a buck, okay; if you didn't, okay.[43]

"Happy as the Day Is Long" begins with an introduction that alludes to another "happy" song: "I Want to Be Happy." That kind of referential intro-duction would be revisited by Henderson in his arrangements for Goodman. After the melody chorus the arrangement shifts into Carter territory with a second chorus that features a virtuosic saxophone soli variation on the melody. Throughout, the give and take between soloists and sectional phrases is light, easy, and effortless.

"Down South Camp Meeting" and "Wrappin' It Up," both from the next-to-last Decca session, represent Henderson's masterworks for big band. They stand out as swing compositions as such—works conceived for big band. Unlike the adapted popular songs that formed the backbone of Henderson's 1932–34 repertoire, and Goodman's repertoire thereafter, they are Henderson originals for band, with melodies and rhythms better suited to instruments than voices. Moreover, they are notably slower than many of the head arrangements, both taken at about 208 beats per minute. Finally, both recordings rely less on improvising soloists than most of the band's other arrangements. "Down South Camp Meeting" includes only one full-chorus solo, by Red Allen, among its six main sections. In short, the two Henderson pieces seem more tailored for the 78-rpm record than the head arrangements and thus foreshadow Henderson's work for Goodman that would begin three months later.

The version of "Down South Camp Meeting" that Henderson's band recorded in 1934 presents the piece as it would be played by Goodman for years. All the traits for which Henderson's style would become well known are here: passages that set the band's sections in dialogue with one another, carefully worked out background figures designed to interact with the soloist or section, chains of syncopation in which the offbeat notes tug and push against the solid regular pulse, and a quality of understated, relaxed swing—powerfully present but hard to describe—that suffuses the whole. The final strain deserves special mention for bringing together several Hendersonian features that came to the fore in 1932–34: the looping harmonic progression, which Schuller and Williams hear as a "cousin" of "King Porter Stomp," the use of clarinets as a timbral alternative to saxophones, and the call-and-response dialogue between reeds and brass.[44]

While "Down South Camp Meeting" represents Henderson's use of the multistrain form derived from marches and ragtime, "Wrappin' It Up" embodies the thirty-two-bar ABAC popular-song form. The forms produce contrasting effects. "Down South Camp Meeting" has a progressive form, in the sense that it proceeds from one section to the next, modulates to a new key for each new section, and never recapitulates one section after introducing another. "Wrappin' It Up" is cyclical, presenting a single thirty-two-bar theme with three variations. The saxophones state the theme, punctuated by pointed brass interjections. The first two "variations" are solo choruses featuring Hilton Jefferson on alto saxophone and Red Allen on trumpet. The contrast between the soloists is remarkable enough to appear as a calculated compositional choice. Jefferson's elegant lyricism stands in marked opposition to Allen's blaring, bluesy exuberance. Surrounded by a bevy of stars with more aggressive improvisational styles, Jefferson comes off as understated, but he was widely appreciated by musicians. Procope praised his beautiful tone. Leora, always attracted to musicians with strong fundamental skills and smooth tone, singled out Jefferson with particular relish in her memories of Fletcher's band. "He was so good," she recalled. "I don't know why people don't appreciate him—one of the finest saxophone players I ever heard."[45]

The final chorus presents Henderson's own orchestrated variation of the theme—another arranger's chorus, this one by the composer himself. The melody contains more rhythmic than melodic interest, and its darting, syncopated line is conceived for instruments, not voices. In fact many phrases of the melody bear a striking resemblance to figures that Louis Armstrong played in his solos with Henderson a decade earlier. These figures, along with the blues inflections laced throughout the melody, are almost entirely composed, and even during the solos, the underscoring interacts with the soloists and often rises up to take the lead, only to recede into the background and allow the soloist to continue. The soloists obviously thrive on the foundation Henderson provides. Although both "Down South Camp Meeting" and "Wrappin' It Up" would become swing-era standards, the approach of "Wrappin' It Up," with its statement and variations on a song form, looks ahead to later 1930s conventions more than the more old-fashioned multistrain structure of "Down South Camp Meeting."

Late 1934 marks a turning point in Henderson's career. Musically, his band was in top form, as the dozen Decca sides from September attest. Several other black bands recruited and recorded by Jack Kapp in September made many more Decca records in the years to come; so it seems likely that Henderson's band would have had a comparable opportunity for regular recording on an established prestigious label as the recording business came out of its early Depression-era slump. Meanwhile, by many accounts, public performances exceeded the quality and excitement of the recordings. Listeners and dancers had ample chance to verify Hammond's assertion that Henderson's records "do not do him justice": the band worked continuously. In the late summer and fall of 1934, in addition to appearing at the Roseland Ballroom, the band toured widely—including stints in Montreal, Philadelphia, Pittsburgh, and Cleveland. Then, in early November, the band took up residence for several days at the Graystone Ballroom in Detroit, the scene of many great battles. The job "drew good business," according to Walter C. Allen, but the band did not get paid. This was the last straw, and the band quit en masse. The sidemen had to borrow money for bus fare back to New York, where many of them found a musical haven with Benny Carter. Fletcher Henderson was a bandleader without a band.[46]

Returning to New York, Henderson soon formed a pickup band for work in New York and New England. For a while, he stood in direct competition with his brother Horace, who had taken many of Fletcher's sidemen and arrangements and begun a job at the Apollo Theatre, down the street from the Harlem Opera House, where Fletcher himself was hired to lead a band. Facing another professional crisis, Henderson, with Leora's help, "did the unbelievable thing of having a book ready for us in three days and we opened at the Harlem Opera House on schedule for a week stand," Louis Metcalf recalled. Henderson fans, intrigued by the fraternal rivalry, went back and forth between venues. "This interest drew a great crowd for us," Metcalf recalled. On December 1, the New York Age reported that "Fletcher Henderson's band this week is 'hot.'" As it happened, however, Fletcher's future lay not in Harlem, but in midtown Manhattan, where, on the same day, a new radio program went on the air and would require his services not as a bandleader but as an arranger. For it was just around this time when John Hammond, once again making things happen for Henderson, introduced him to Benny Goodman.[47]

9

Building the Kingdom of Swing

If anyone were to ask what was the biggest thing that has
ever happened to me, landing a place on that show was it.

—Benny Goodman, talking about his spot
on the radio show *Let's Dance.*

As HENDERSON FACED HIS BAND'S DISINTEGRATION in Detroit, Benny
Goodman was a fledgling bandleader preparing to embark on a new
network radio venture. At twenty-five, Goodman already had a dozen
years of professional work behind him: he had joined the Chicago musicians'
union at thirteen by lying about his age. At sixteen, he had won a job as sideman for fellow-Chicagoan Ben Pollack, the diminutive but fiery white jazz
drummer whose California-based band became an incubator for several
white jazz musicians, including Glenn Miller, Harry James, and Jack Teagar-
den. Goodman left Pollack in 1929 and became a freelance musician in New
York with the key qualification for the work: versatility. He played in the pit
orchestra of the Gershwin musicals *Strike Up the Band* and *Girl Crazy.* He
played in radio ensembles for programs such as "The Rudy Vallee Show." He
even appeared in a film short in these early years of talking pictures. And,
thanks to an influential contact at Columbia, he made many records.[1]

He also got his first taste of bandleading, having developed an impa-
tience for the sideman's role. John Hammond heard one of Goodman's
bands in 1933 and was not impressed, dismissing it in print as "another
smooth and soporific dance combination." Yet Hammond recognized
Goodman's talent and aimed to tap his jazz potential by organizing a racially
mixed group and encouraging more improvisation on recordings for British
Columbia. Guarding his fragile professional position, Goodman balked on
both counts. Working with black musicians and improvising were risky
ventures for a white musician in the shrinking record business of the early
Depression years; Hammond claimed that Goodman even told him, "If it
gets around that I recorded with colored guys, I won't get another job in this
town." (Hammond initially protested but conceded that "he was right.") So
Goodman planned to stick with an all-white band and stock arrangements,
a prospect that nevertheless "horrified" Hammond. Surprisingly, once in
the studio, Goodman loosened up the arrangements and opened the way for
improvisation. Musically, it was, as Goodman's biographer Ross Firestone

points out, a turning point in his career and cemented the relationship of Goodman and Hammond.[2]

At the same time, perhaps because it had little to lose, the record industry began to relax its policy on segregated bands. Goodman began recording with black musicians, including Coleman Hawkins, pianist Teddy Wilson, and singers Bessie Smith, Ethel Waters, and the seventeen-year-old Billie Holiday in her first recording session. It was Hammond, Goodman avowed, "who really put me back in touch" with the hot style developed by black musicians. With Hammond, Goodman also visited Harlem nightclubs to hear the bands of Fletcher Henderson and others. No record of Goodman and Henderson's first meeting survives, although Hammond probably made it happen around this time. Given Goodman's later prominence as "King of Swing," it is worth noting that in musical and professional terms, a vast gulf existed in 1933 between Goodman and Henderson, who had been leading his band continuously for a decade and accrued enormous prestige, if not financial reward. Later accounts suggest that Goodman saw Henderson as a father figure.[3]

Prohibition's repeal in late 1933 changed the landscape of Manhattan's nightlife, and several new venues opened. One of them, Billy Rose's Music Hall, needed a band, so Goodman gathered a new one and got a job there in June 1934. Gilded by the name of a major impresario, the place seated a thousand people and featured variety entertainment. Goodman recalled the Music Hall job as "some sort of a pinnacle to me," but, behind Rose's back, the venue's mobster owners abruptly fired the band in October for reasons having nothing to do with musical quality. It was "probably the toughest blow I ever received," Goodman recalled. Before the blow came, however, Goodman had already sown the seeds of his next job. A radio contractor named Josef Bonime had visited the Music Hall on Goodman's invitation. Goodman had worked for Bonime as a freelance, and he knew that Bonime was scouting bands for a new project for the NBC radio network: a three-hour dance-music program to air weekly across the country. It was called *Let's Dance*.[4]

As a network radio program sponsored by the National Biscuit Company to promote its new Ritz cracker, *Let's Dance* soon stood among the music industry's most coveted means of disseminating its products. Network radio was less than a decade old, and commercial sponsorship had only recently taken hold as its chief promotional style, a phenomenon validated by the federal Communications Act of 1934. Broadcasting live music on radio was not new, of course. Listeners had heard Henderson himself playing the Roseland on WHN New York as early as 1924, and radio stations carried many other bands and singers in on-location broadcasts, or "sustaining programs," from hotels, ballrooms, and nightclubs through the 1920s. Such programs certainly expanded a musician's audience in a way that had been impossible before the advent of radio in 1920. But commercially sponsored network programs guaranteed a broad national audience on a regular basis. These were the choice jobs, bringing unprecedented prestige and remuneration.[5]

Having polled listeners and discovered that they prized dance music above all, NBC aimed to create a virtual ballroom where all listeners heard the same music, as in a real ballroom, but danced in their homes. It became the ideal format for listening and dancing to music during the Depression:

the radio audience could listen and dance for several hours every week without buying a single record or paying a cover charge. Several features enhanced the ballroom ambience. The program aired every Saturday night from a newly built studio with a capacity of a thousand spectators. (As a live broadcast from NBC's Studio 8H, *Let's Dance* could be called the original *Saturday Night Live*.) The large crowds and familiar sounds of applause created the aura of an on-location broadcast. The program connected with the listening audience even more directly through an emcee who announced the tunes and dedicated selected numbers to listeners around the country. On a May 4, 1935, broadcast, for example, the emcee introduced Gershwin's "I Got Rhythm" "for the *Let's Dance* party of Mr. and Mrs. Frank Callahan of Philadelphia." Meanwhile, studio dancers captured the attention of the live audience. The word "dancers" on surviving original parts, usually notated at the end of the first chorus, indicates the precise moment when professional dancers appeared. Even the singers danced. Helen Ward, Goodman's principal female vocalist "used to pair up [with tenor Ray Hendricks] and perform for the *Let's Dance* studio audience between our song stints," she recalled.[6]

The program's format not only encouraged but required Goodman to play jazz-oriented music. Three bands played a series of thirty-minute sets in alternation, beginning with Kel Murray and His Orchestra playing sweet dance music, continuing with Xavier Cugat's orchestra playing Latin music, and ending with Goodman's band playing hot music. NBC's contract with Goodman included an allowance to commission eight new arrangements per week at $37.50 each for the show's thirteen-week run (reduced to four per week when the show was renewed for its second, and last, thirteen weeks). For a fledgling band with a small book, "this was what we needed more than anything else," Goodman recalled, and it proved to be "the most valuable thing about the program."[7]

Arrangements came from many sources, especially from experienced white arrangers such as George Bassman, composer of the band's theme song "Let's Dance"; Gordon Jenkins, composer of the band's sign-off theme, "Goodbye"; Deane Kincaide, whom Goodman singled out as "an outstanding musician among white arrangers"; and the prolific Spud Murphy, who was known to make as many as four arrangements per week. Goodman also used charts from black arrangers Jimmy Mundy, from Earl Hines's band, and Edgar Sampson, the former Henderson sideman who arranged for Chick Webb. All of these arrangers expanded Goodman's repertoire and assured his appeal on the radio in the first weeks of *Let's Dance*. After the show began, however, Goodman realized that new arrangements were not enough; his band needed a distinctive sound. And that distinctive sound, he was advised, should come from a major black jazz arranger with fewer commitments to another band. An obvious first choice was Benny Carter, who had written for Goodman's Music Hall band, and whom Goodman singled out for writing a "swell arrangement" for one of that band's records. Carter's career, however, was in transition. He disbanded his own orchestra in February 1935 and joined up with the Willie Lewis orchestra, on the verge of departing for an extended visit to France.[8]

"But about the most important thing that happened then," Goodman noted in his 1939 autobiography *The Kingdom of Swing*, was that "Fletcher Henderson was around town." Henderson was mainly trying to keep a band together, despite gaps between jobs and frequently changing personnel. He was usually, but not always, "around town." The band played one-nighters in New England in February and May and found occasional work at the Apollo Theatre and Roseland Ballroom in New York, but nothing steady. During this period, Henderson apparently heard the teenaged Ella Fitzgerald sing at the Apollo, but, despite a promise to contact her, never followed up. ("I guess I didn't make too much of an impression," Fitzgerald reportedly said.) Meanwhile, 1935 marked the first year since he came to New York that Henderson made no records. Henderson's bandleading career was at a low ebb.[9]

Before the story of the Goodman-Henderson collaboration begins to take on a quality of destiny, we might reflect on the roads not taken. With Henderson trying to lead a band in New York, why didn't he get the *Let's Dance* job? A network radio job exerted the kind of centripetal force that could have allowed Henderson to attract and hold the best sidemen, as surely his advocate John Hammond understood. Moreover, Henderson's band was well known on the airwaves, having proven successful in broadcasts from the Roseland and Connie's Inn for years. All things being equal, Henderson should have been a prime candidate to play hot music on *Let's Dance*. But all things were *not* equal. A regular, sponsored network show stood on an entirely different level of the music business than on-location broadcasts. In that context, no black band could entertain the possibility of having a commercially sponsored network radio program. In the logic of institutional racism of the era, a black band on such a program would signify the denial of white talent. And even the aggressive advocacy of a white agent like Hammond, who had stronger ties to records than to radio anyway, could not conquer that pervasive thinking. There were other reasons that Henderson's band might not have been ideal for the job, of course. The band's proud disdain for white patronage, even when advantageous, and its resistance to a highly structured professional life would likely have resurfaced in this context.

If the band could not come from Harlem, then, at least the arrangements could. So with Hammond's encouragement, Goodman's generous allowance, and Henderson's long experience in hot dance music, Henderson stood in a prime position to become the key arranger for *Let's Dance*. Of the three, however, Henderson apparently harbored the most doubts about the situation. For Henderson, arranging had been organically linked to bandleading. Up to now, his modus operandi for arranging typically involved collaboration with a specific group of musicians who assumed some responsibility for coming up with riffs and harmonies, not to mention playing hot solos. Arranging, for Henderson, arose from dialogue and communal exchange. It involved a combination of oral directions, cues, and sketchy notations that coalesced only in rehearsal. To an outsider, the arranging process might have seemed casual and haphazard, but, as explained earlier, his sidemen attest that Henderson brought precision to the work. Now, however, he was being asked to arrange for a band that he would not lead or perform with (at least not yet) and that featured much less improvising. These conditions—along with his reflexive resistance to highly structured, white-controlled milieu—undoubtedly intensified Henderson's well-known diffidence. No wonder, then, that although Goodman and others saw Henderson as an ideal arranger, Henderson "had to be convinced of it himself."[10]

In fact, Henderson adapted quite rapidly to the *Let's Dance* format and flourished in his new line of work. But we need to take stock of what Henderson was being asked to do for Goodman and remember its specific context: the thirty-minute radio set. Henderson's reputation as a jazz arranger rests chiefly on arrangements with roots in his own band—especially a handful of up-tempo, hard-driving instrumental numbers by jazz musicians, such as "King Porter Stomp" (Morton), "Sugar Foot Stomp" (Oliver and Armstrong), and "Wrappin' It Up" (Henderson). In swing-era parlance, the fast jazz instrumentals, sometimes called "flag-wavers" or "killer-dillers," or what Goodman himself simply called Henderson's "big arrangements," occupied a small but special part of a radio program: the climactic closer. The rest of the program, which Goodman referred to tellingly as "the *regular* sequence of numbers" (emphasis added), featured more melodious popular songs from Tin Pan Alley publishers, who saw Goodman's new job as a major opportunity to plug their latest products. "It was then," Goodman writes in his autobiography, "that we made one of the most important discoveries of all—that Fletcher Henderson, in addition to writing the big arrangements ... could also do a wonderful job on melodic tunes such as 'Can't We Be Friends,' 'Sleepy Time Down South,' 'Blue Skies,' 'I Can't Give You Anything But Love' and above all 'Sometimes I'm Happy.' ... These were the things, with their wonderful easy style and great background figures, that really set the style of the band." Henderson flourished because the job required him to write music based on the kind of repertoire his first band had played: popular songs. Goodman continued, "Without Fletcher I probably would have had a pretty good band, but it would have been something quite different from what it eventually turned out to be."[11]

Once Goodman realized the value of Henderson's style, he wanted more of the same and he wanted it fast. In fact, Henderson wrote so many arrangements, and his approach became so influential, that Gunther Schuller has lamented that the style quickly became commercialized and "ground into a formula." Yet the key players did not hear it that way. John Hammond, for one, recognized Henderson's popular-song arrangements as marking a crucial moment when jazz preserved its integrity in the face of commercial corruption. Henderson's work was significant, he claimed, because, for "the first time," it broke "the stranglehold music publishers had on the performance of popular songs." Goodman likewise heard Henderson's work as innovative. "Fletcher's ideas were far ahead of anybody else's," he claimed. Because they represented "something that very few musicians could do," Goodman referred to Henderson's arrangements as art.[12]

Perhaps the issue of whether Henderson's work represents "formula" or "art" may be resolved by seeing the arrangements in a tradition of other forms, such as the Shakespearean sonnet or the blues, where artistry lies in the flexible manipulation of highly conventionalized idiomatic features. Henderson worked comfortably within a set of stylistic conventions but continually found ways to refresh those conventions. For Henderson, moreover, such conventions coalesced around the particular requirements of *Let's Dance*. If the swing era represents "the only time when jazz was completely in phase with the social environment," then Henderson's arrangements for Goodman form the perfect lens through which to understand that merger of social and musical impulses.[13]

How can a musical arrangement be "in phase" with its social context? First of all, as Goodman pointed out, "melodic tunes"—that is, popular songs, not blues or jazz numbers—comprised the foundation of the band's repertoire. Thanks to Goodman's new position on network radio, Tin Pan Alley publishers saw him as a prime target for their aggressive plugging tactics. Early in the *Let's Dance* run, lead vocalist Helen Ward worked with Goodman to pick out the potential hits. Together, they "would sift through the current pop tune advance copies thrust at us at every chance by the music publishers' song-pluggers" and "guess which ones of these might turn out to be future public favorites." Luckily, as Ward noted, "Benny had a fantastic feel for good tunes."[14] Goodman would then assign a tune to an arranger. Working from the professional copy of sheet music that publishers typically provided for prospective performers, Goodman's chosen arranger would then tailor the song for the band, aiming for a length of approximately three minutes. That length developed nearly liturgical significance for Goodman in his work on radio, where a typical half-hour set could include eight such numbers (almost always framed by brief renditions of the theme song "Let's Dance" and the sign-off "Goodbye"), and on record, where the 78-rpm record could fit little more than three minutes per side. Dancers, Goodman observed, also came to expect each number to last about three minutes. More than that, in Goodman's view, usually revealed musical "over-indulgence." "[W]e were thinking of a dancing audience," Goodman said. "When people were dancing, you couldn't play one piece for ten minutes." Goodman must have been thinking particularly of white dancers, for his comment stands in stark contrast to Henderson's own experience playing head arrangements that could be extended indefinitely for dances in Harlem. Teddy Wilson also discovered that head arrangements were best for dancers because a band could extend them for "ten minutes"—the same length that signaled "over-indulgence" to Goodman.[15]

Within that framework, Henderson developed a standard but flexible format ideally suited for Goodman's position as the hot band on *Let's Dance.* Omitting the song's verse, a key element of an arrangement's variety in the 1920s, Henderson conceived the arrangement as a sequence of variations on the song's refrain, or chorus. The model was streamlined head arrangements of popular songs such as "Honeysuckle Rose." The chart would begin with a brief introduction. It would proceed directly to the first chorus featuring a swung version of melody close to its original, published form. It would continue with at least two more choruses, one featuring improvising soloists accompanied by ensemble riffs and one more featuring a written variation on the tune, a swing-era survival of what Arthur Lange had called the "arranger's chorus" in 1920s dance music. Hammond recognized the approach as the key to breaking the publishers' "stranglehold" on performing style. After the "first chorus emphasizing the tune," he wrote, the approach "after that allowed the band to take off with background figures for jazz soloists and last choruses in which the Goodman style, rather than the tune, prevailed." For Hammond this approach was starkly anticommercial. He notes that the arrangements reflect "the liberties Goodman was allowed on *Let's Dance.*" Whereas Cugat and Murray played the show's first two sets "in straight, commercial fashion," Goodman came on last and "could play his own way." The arrangements, in effect, took the listener step-by-step from the original tune to the "Goodman style"—in short, from Tin Pan Alley to jazz. Yet it is worth noting that Hammond's use of the word "commercial" is paradoxical, since commercial sponsorship formed the very foundation of a network show such as *Let's Dance*. The term "commercial" is a loaded one in jazz writing. Probably Hammond is using it in the same way that Goodman claimed agent Willard Alexander used it: to distinguish "musical" bands from "commercial" ones. Moreover, whatever variations Henderson might play on the original melody, his arrangements reflect a musical consensus among musicians, audiences, and their mediators that the tune should be audible and identifiable. If, as Ross Russell has argued, Henderson's work represents a "war" against the "horrible products of the tunesmiths," they also represent the opposite: an agreement on the value of the melody, chords, and structure of those "products."[16]

Goodman himself emphasized several other features of Henderson's arrangements that he claims gave his band a distinctive style. Each arrangement featured a cohesive plan in which the solos and "background figures" were integrated, one chorus flowed naturally into the next, and the written passages were "in the same style that a soloist would use if he were improvising." Goodman also highlights the importance of key changes and the sequence of solos so that the arrangement "works up to a climax." Above all, he notes how Henderson's arrangements "hung together and sounded unified." In short, the Henderson style that set the standard for 1930s swing arranging represented a contrast to the Redman style that marked the 1920s: flow and cohesion had replaced variety and contrast.[17]

On top of that, Henderson established several devices that, though practiced by other arrangers, have become so closely associated with him that Gunther Schuller termed them "Hendersonese": harmonizing sections in close three- or four-part harmony known as "block voicing"; dividing brass and reed sections into discrete units that played off of one another; using riffs—short, repeated melodic figures with strong rhythmic profile—in melodic and accompanimental roles; and scoring call-and-response passages for climactic moments.[18]

Another device stands out as a way in which Henderson both "swings" the original melody and makes an arrangement sound unified: the *chain of syncopation*. A chain of syncopation is a rhythmic effect in which several consecutive pitches are played between the beats. Henderson's arrangements feature two types of chains, one based on quarter notes that could be called the *short-link chain* (ex. 9.1a) and another based on longer note values, the *long-link chain* (ex. 9.1b).

Ex. 9.1. Hendersonian chains of syncopation

Ex. 9.1a. Short-link chain

Ex. 9.1b. Long-link chain

In both, the rhythm tugs and pushes against the beat to build musical tension that can only be resolved when the rhythm finally lands on the beat. The rhythm forms a key means by which swing goes beyond ragtime, which features constant syncopation but rarely in such "chains." In ragtime, syncopated patterns typically occur within the measure, but rarely extend beyond the measure. Moreover, ragtime does not swing. Thus when Goodman's band performs chains of syncopation, the effect gets pronounced by the uneven accents of swing rhythm, where the offbeat pitches are played shorter than on-the-beat pitches. As a result the pitches in a Hendersonian chain of syncopation produce a crisp, bright effect when played in a swing style. The device dates back at least to 1930, when it appeared in Benny Carter's arrangement of "Keep a Song in Your Soul." Thus, although Henderson himself does not appear to have originated the idea in swing arranging, his band had been its incubator. Now, as Goodman's arranger, Henderson uses it regularly as a means of creating musical unity.

Two of Henderson's early arrangements for Goodman deploy the chain of syncopation effect as a unifying device, producing the "hung together" quality that Goodman prized: "Blue Skies" and "Between the Devil and the Deep Blue Sea." Irving Berlin had composed "Blue Skies" in late 1926. The song was introduced to the public as an interpolation in a Rodgers and Hart show called *Betsy*, starring vaudeville veteran Belle Baker. The show flopped, but the song had staying power. Berlin published it in early 1927, and later that year it found its way into another show, the landmark "talking picture" *The Jazz Singer*, starring Al Jolson. Thanks to the film's success, Jolson became closely identified with the song throughout the world. By the time Goodman played Henderson's arrangement of "Blue Skies" on *Let's Dance* on January 26, 1935, then, the song was well known and nearly a decade old, but it was by no means a staple in the jazz or swing repertoire. Goodman's performance of Henderson's arrangement launched the tune's life as a jazz standard.

Goodman's June 25, 1935, recording captures the arrangement soon after the *Let's Dance* run ended. It begins with a dissonant full-band blast and brass fanfare figures, far afield from Berlin's original tune. Playing it on a radio broadcast in September 1938, Goodman stopped the band during the introduction and asked Henderson, "Wait a minute. Hold on. . . . Where did that introduction come from? What's that got to do with 'Blue Skies'?" Since at least the early 1920s, arrangers typically launched a chart with a unique introduction: it staked a claim for a band's distinctive approach to a song. Here, however, Henderson had an expressive goal, one that both perplexed and amused Goodman. In an obviously scripted exchange, Henderson exclaims, "Well, Benny, I'm surprised at you. . . . That's the storm [before the] blue skies from now on." Goodman relished the explanation so much that he repeated it almost fifty years later, during a concert in October 1985 in which he had the band play the introduction twice, just as he had done in the 1938 broadcast.[19]

This kind of pictorial, or programmatic, introduction became a trademark for Henderson, and to it he brought a subtle, allusive wit. Sometimes the wit comes out in a reference to another song, as in the quotation of Mendelssohn's famous wedding music for *A Midsummer Night's Dream* in the introduction to "Minnie the Moocher's Wedding Day" and in the two-bar quotation of "I Got Rhythm" in the opening bars of "Get Rhythm in Your Feet," a quotation later extended in chains of syncopation. On the other hand, Henderson's arrangement of "Lost My Rhythm" includes no quotation but begins with a densely syncopated pattern that aptly obscures the beat. Such gestures have precedents in the arsenal of effects that Don Redman developed a decade earlier. Henderson's allusive and pictorial introduction to "Blue Skies," then, forms part of the ongoing legacy of the novelty impulse in early 1920s dance band music.

After the "stormy" introduction, the arrangement settles in and explores "Mr. Berlin's idea," as Henderson called the tune in that 1938 broadcast. The arrangement features four choruses, meaning that Henderson must find a way to maintain musical interest while stating Berlin's principal melody—the "A" phrase of the song's AABA form—twelve times. In many arrangements, Henderson simply repeats each "A" phrase within a chorus. "Blue Skies," however, presents a case of internal variations—melodic changes within as well as among choruses. No wonder it was one of Goodman's favorites. The written passages have a soloistic quality; the background figures are carefully integrated into the melodic and harmonic fabric; one chorus flows naturally into the next; the arrangement develops a carefully calibrated climax; and the whole thing hangs together and sounds unified. "Blue Skies" stands out as particularly effective for the way Henderson gradually effaces "Mr. Berlin's idea" with his own swinging variations, reserving a melodic surprise for the climactic final phrase.

The first chorus features three variations on Berlin's main melody (the "A" phrase). In the first eight measures, Henderson arranges the melody for brass and reeds in thick block voicing with lots of open "air" (rests) where Berlin's original had long tones (see ex. 9.2). He further spikes his new version with plenty of syncopation and blue notes (such as F♮ in m. 2; A♭ in m. 3; and C♮ in m. 5). Meanwhile, Henderson enriches the song's "vertical" dimension by adding sixths and sevenths to Berlin's triadic harmony. The phrase illustrates a perfect balance of Tin Pan Alley and swing, keeping "Berlin's idea" recognizable and transforming it with Hendersonian trademarks.

Then Henderson begins to depart further from the source. He launches the second eight with a new triplet figure, followed by two-note slurs with offbeat accents (ex. 9.3). It culminates in a few long-link chains of syncopation—a rhythmic device that grows more prominent throughout the arrangement.

In the final eight bars, the saxophones alone take the lead in a suave, blues-inflected, and newly syncopated version of the original melody (ex. 9.4). Henderson punctuates the melody with a trombone "stinger" (m. 31) heralding the next chorus. This effect, which becomes a familiar device in Henderson's popular song arrangements for Goodman, has its roots in pieces played by Henderson's own band, such as "Radio Rhythm" and "Hotter than 'Ell."[20]

In the second chorus, Henderson further complicates the texture. Omitting the trombones, he now separates the reeds and brass for the first time, building an elegant call-and-response pattern between the melody in the muted trumpets and a smooth countermelody in the saxes (ex. 9.5).

Ex. 9.2. "Blue Skies" (1935), chorus 1, mm. 1–8. MSS 53, The Benny Goodman Papers in the Irving S. Gilmore Music Library of Yale University.

Ex. 9.3. "Blue Skies," chorus 1, mm. 9–16. MSS 53, The Benny Goodman Papers in the Irving S. Gilmore Music Library of Yale University.

Ex. 9.4. "Blue Skies," chorus 1, mm. 25–32. MSS 53, The Benny Goodman Papers in the Irving S. Gilmore Music Library of Yale University.

Ex. 9.5. "Blue Skies," chorus 2, mm. 1–7. MSS 53, The Benny Goodman Papers in the Irving S. Gilmore Music Library of Yale University.

Halfway through chorus 2, the arrangement makes room for improvised solos. The tenor sax (Art Rollini) takes the bridge and final eight, going his own way from Berlin's melody, supported by long tones and syncopated banter from his section mates. Trumpeter Bunny Berigan begins the third chorus with a solo over chattering saxophone riffs. The full ensemble returns for the second half of the chorus in new dialogue for brass and saxes, featuring a cooperative exchange of melodic phrases. The final eight of chorus 3 grows insistently louder with prominent chains of syncopation (ex. 9.6).

Chorus 4 forms Henderson's master stroke of climactic integration, soloist and ensemble, original melody and swing variation. Flowing directly out of the preceding ensemble passage, Goodman takes a brief solo over sustained saxophone chords that establishes another call-and-response dialogue with the full ensemble, extending the chain-of-syncopation device

Ex. 9.6. "Blue Skies," chorus 3, mm. 25–28. MSS 53, The Benny Goodman Papers in the Irving S. Gilmore Music Library of Yale University.

over a longer, and louder, sequence. The pattern repeats, and Berlin's original "A" melody has completely dissolved in Henderson's textural and figural changes and Goodman's improvisation. In the final eight bars, however, Henderson introduces a surprising and climactic twist: as the saxophones and trumpets play a spiky countermelody, Henderson brings in the trombones to blast the principal melody exactly as Berlin wrote it, for the first time (ex. 9.7).

Ex. 9.7. "Blue Skies," beginning of last phrase. MSS 53, The Benny Goodman Papers in the Irving S. Gilmore Music Library of Yale University.

The style served Goodman well in his position as point man for the music industry's paradigm shift. It represents a particularly fine example of Henderson's principal work for Goodman, this is, arranging popular songs, more than half of which comprise the thirty-two-bar AABA song form. Whatever variations Henderson might play on the melody, the arrangement preserves the integrity of the original song. In this way, Henderson's arrangements appear less oppositional, and more consensual, than John Hammond claimed. The consensus lies in finding an elegant musical balance between Tin Pan Alley and swing.

Goodman named "Blue Skies" among the melodic tunes on which he believed Henderson had done such a wonderful job. Even among dozens of Henderson arrangements that Goodman played repeatedly, "Blue Skies" holds a special place as one of the few that Goodman programmed for his legendary Carnegie Hall concert in January 1938; and it is the one he singled out for demonstration later that year when he invited Henderson on to his radio program, the *Camel Caravan*, to explain arranging. "Blue Skies" was "probably his [Goodman's] all-time Fletcher Henderson favorite," according to Loren Schoenberg, the tenor saxophonist and bandleader who played as Goodman's sideman in the 1980s and led the band after Goodman's death. Goodman continued rehearsing and performing it with his band to the end.[21]

The Details in "The Devil"

In "Between the Devil and the Deep Blue Sea," Henderson takes a similar approach to a vocal arrangement. Before considering it in detail, we might reflect on the vocalist's role in the emerging swing style. By now, singers, especially women, had become a standard feature in big bands. Singers, in fact, had been featured in some of the era's first racially integrated bands. Sometimes disdained and patronized as "girl singers" and "canaries," female vocalists were grudgingly tolerated by male musicians as a necessary part of the business, a commercial "concession" that helped support the purely instrumental numbers. Although Firestone notes that Helen Ward's vocals "became one of the band's strongest assets," Ward herself accepted that, for Goodman, vocalists were "a necessary evil." Goodman "didn't like singers, period. Commercial music, you know. Benny was strictly a jazz hound. But he felt he had to have them." John Hammond stands behind that attitude. Hammond disdained singers (although he was certainly a champion of Billie Holiday, among others) and urged Goodman to omit the vocal refrains of many arrangements. Goodman himself claimed that finding and keeping a singer, male or female, who could swing posed a formidable challenge, and his band became a revolving door for a parade of singers.[22]

Nevertheless, singing stood as the most commonly accepted way in which women regularly appeared in male swing bands. Henderson's arrangements reflect the singer's important but secondary role. Roughly one-third of Henderson's arrangements include a vocal part, to judge from the 225-odd surviving scores and parts in the Benny Goodman collections at the Yale Music Library and New York Public Library. Almost all of them feature the vocalist in just one chorus of the arrangement, usually the middle of a three-chorus arrangement. They show that the vocal-refrain format, which Henderson's own band had explored during its Connie's Inn run five years earlier, had now become standardized and, in fact, ideally suited to the three-minute form of radio and record arrangements. Indeed, Goodman's distaste for singers never seems to have gotten in the way of his hard-headed programming sense. His radio programs gradually became standardized with about three vocal numbers per set. But initially, during the run of *Let's Dance*, the band tended to feature more vocals, comprising half or more of the entire program. And two vocalists began as the norm: one woman and one man. Goodman, like most bandleaders, preferred the women.

Helen Ward recalled that Goodman "kept shuttling the male vocalists in and out—giving most of their tunes to me to sing." On record, women sing almost all of the band's vocal arrangements; yet none of them stayed for very long. After Helen Ward left at the end of 1936, the band saw a quick succession of singers for the next seven years, none staying for even two years—including Martha Tilton (August 1937–May 1939), Louise Tobin (May–October 1939), Mildred Bailey (October–December 1939), Helen Forrest (December 1939–August 1941), and Peggy Lee (August 1941–March 1943). Singers posed a dilemma: they added necessary variety to a program and helped hold an audience, but they detracted from Goodman's musical ideal (for him, "jazz" was instrumental music). They also took some of the spotlight from the bandleader. This may be the reason that Goodman always had a female singer but never had a particular one for very long. As long as singers came and went quickly, none could become irrevocably identified as the voice of the Benny Goodman Orchestra and challenge the leader's supremacy.[23]

Goodman preferred Helen Ward because she stood out as an exception to the "rule" that female singers could not swing. Thus Henderson wrote many of his earliest vocal arrangements for her. In his book *Jazz Singing*, Will Friedwald calls Ward "the archetype of the early canaries" for "her exuberant, toe-tapping approach" that proved highly influential in the mid-1930s. It did not hurt, of course, that Ward was extremely attractive. When she began working with Goodman she was a mere eighteen years old. She was "so beautiful," said trumpeter Jimmy Maxwell. "She came out in a white nightgown [that] fit her ... like it was painted on her, and you're just standing there with your favorite fantasy, and say[ing] 'Sing to me, baby, sing to me!' " Romances between band members and singers were commonplace. In fact, in Ward's two years with the band, she dated Goodman "off and on." At this point, Goodman's courtship technique mixed personal and musical motives, shifting between solicitous and blunt. In the "on" periods, Goodman would buy a gardenia for Ward every night. During an "off" period, however, Goodman saw Ward with another man and abruptly asked her to marry him. "I really believe Benny liked me a lot," she recalled. "But I have to think the real reason he proposed was to keep me from leaving the band. After all, I did sing every other tune." Ward did stay with the band, but the proposal otherwise resolved nothing: Ward and Goodman continued off and on for a while. Finally, in October 1936, Ward met Goodman at a restaurant to tell him she was leaving the band to marry another man. Goodman took his dinner menu and "flung it across the table in my face."[24]

Despite their romantic tension (or perhaps because of it), Goodman and Ward's musical rapport flourished, as in Henderson's arrangement of the 1931 rhythm song "Between the Devil and the Deep Blue Sea," by Harold Arlen and Ted Koehler. Koehler's lyrics inadvertently strike the keynote of the Ward–Goodman romance: "I should hate you, but I guess I love you," she sings, "You've got me in between the devil and the deep blue sea." No wonder composer-critic Alec Wilder calls it the "definitive performance" of the tune. If Berlin's "Blue Skies" melody had a deliberately nonjazz "straightness" in its rhythmic style, Arlen's "Devil" was custom-made for swinging. In fact, swing is built into the song, albeit with Tin Pan Alley's awkward approximation: dotted sixteenth-notes. It was one of the first Henderson vocal arrangements Goodman played on the air, appearing on the January 5, 1935, *Let's Dance* broadcast. The arrangement quickly won a niche in Goodman's book, as he featured it again on the following week's broadcast, and yet again on February 2. Goodman first recorded it on the legendary mammoth session of June 6, 1935, when the band made about fifty sides in one day—substituting instrumental solos for the vocals. He recorded it as a vocal just four weeks later, on July 1, 1935. Over the years, Goodman returned to it many times, perhaps more frequently than any other Henderson vocal arrangement, and it was among the core Henderson arrangements that Goodman rehearsed with his last band in 1985.[25]

Indeed the arrangement is another exemplar of how a Henderson score "really hung together and sounded unified." The cornerstone is a motif based on the chain-of-syncopation device, even more systematically applied than in "Blue Skies." Henderson announces the syncopated idea in the first bar with an ensemble shout in block voicing followed by a softly gliding saxophone phrase (ex. 9.8).

Ex. 9.8. "Between the Devil and the Deep Blue Sea" (1935), introduction. MSS 53, The Benny Goodman Papers in the Irving S. Gilmore Music Library of Yale University.

In the first chorus, under Goodman's solo melodic paraphrase, Henderson creates a bubbling simmer in the underscoring, rising to a syncopated brass climax into the bridge. The chorus ends with a long-link chain of syncopations in the saxophones and second trombone (ex. 9.9). As in "Blue Skies," Henderson punctuates the first chorus—and announces the impending second chorus—with single-note "stinger" in the first trombone.

In the second chorus, the vocal refrain, Henderson supports Ward's singing with a variety of saxophone figures—smooth chords, biting syncopated figures, and eighth-note chatter. At each seam in the vocal line, however, Henderson stitches a bar of shouting chains of brass syncopation derived from the first bar of the introduction.

Ex. 9.9. "Between the Devil and the Deep Blue Sea," chorus 1, ending and transition to vocal refrain. MSS 53, The Benny Goodman Papers in the Irving S. Gilmore Music Library of Yale University.

In the final chorus, Henderson himself begins to "improvise on the melody," as Goodman put it. Here Henderson truly takes the tune over from Arlen and makes it his own, as he now dramatically develops the syncopated motif. Henderson sparks the chorus with an accented full ensemble chord, followed by a rolling figure that flows into a brief chain of syncopation (ex.

Ex. 9.10. "Between the Devil and the Deep Blue Sea," chorus 3, mm. 1–8. MSS 53, The Benny Goodman Papers in the Irving S. Gilmore Music Library of Yale University.

9.10). The pattern repeats in the next two bars, then extends the chain of syncopation across three measures, capped by a soloistic rip. Henderson tapers the effect with a diminuendo as the ensemble descends to its lowest pitches of the passage (mm. 5–6).

As in "Blue Skies," the last section of the chorus is Henderson's coup de grace (ex. 9.11). The brass enters shouting for a call-and-response dialogue with the saxophones for four bars. In the last four bars, Henderson brings the entire band together playing on-the-beat block chords in a thundering crescendo. The chains of syncopations, which had accumulated thematic prominence throughout the arrangement, are now "straightened out" in the score's climactic moment.

Although less well known than Henderson's "big arrangements" (for reasons to be discussed later), "Blue Skies" and "Devil" encapsulate the key elements of Hendersonese in the popular-song repertory that formed the foundation of his work for Goodman. They begin with a purposeful introduction—pictorial in "Blue Skies" and motivic in "Devil." Omitting the song's verse, they proceed with three or four choruses of a thirty-two bar AABA popular song. The brass and reed sections are harmonized with enriched chords in tight, block voicing. A trombone "stinger" signals the second chorus. Sections of the band are featured in call-and-response patterns. The lead soloist or section stands out over a rich foundation of riffs and other background figures. Such figures tend to suggest instrumental stylizations of vocal effects, conjuring metaphors such as "humming,"

Ex. 9.11. "Between the Devil and the Deep Blue Sea," chorus 3, mm. 25–32. MSS 53, The Benny Goodman Papers in the Irving S. Gilmore Music Library of Yale University.

"chatter," and "banter." Along the way, the arrangements modulate to different keys—another feature that characterized Henderson's approach. Moreover, both arrangements feature unifying devices, most notably an increasingly prominent chain-of-syncopation pattern that "resolves" in the final chorus in a sequence of straight quarter notes.

Road Trips and Records

Henderson arrangements such as "Blue Skies" and "Devil and the Deep Blue Sea" became fixtures in Goodman's repertoire not simply because of their intrinsic artistry but also because they survived a series of rigorous tests imposed by the bandleader. The first test for most tunes, as Helen Ward pointed out, came before they even got into the hands of an arranger. Goodman, sometimes with Ward, would rifle through the professional copies supplied by publishers and give arrangers only the ones he believed had a chance. But that was just the beginning. After Henderson submitted an arrangement, the chart would undergo a three-phase rite of passage to earn a place in Goodman's book. Ward described the method by which Goodman winnowed his repertoire. Goodman would take the arrangements and first "try them out on the road," Ward recalled. "The ones that seemed to work would be played on *Let's Dance*. The best ones, the ones he really believed in, would eventually be recorded." We might call this rite of passage the "three R's": Road, Radio, and Recording.[26]

Since the mid-1920s, these three arenas had developed a symbiotic relationship in the hands of such entrepreneurs as Irving Mills, but now they functioned even more systematically to give dance music unprecedented national range and exposure. Goodman's weekly radio exposure on *Let's Dance* led to two other prizes in the music business—road tours and records—and they further enhanced the impact of Henderson's arrangements. The Road opened up thanks to the representation of the Music Corporation of America (MCA). It was highly unusual for a fledgling jazz-oriented band like Goodman's to sign with MCA. Founded in 1924 in the infancy of dance-band management, MCA had become by 1935 a nationwide industry giant, and its chief clients were well-established "sweet" bands led by the likes of Guy Lombardo and Bernie Cummins, dominant figures in white dance music in the early 1930s. (These were the bands that Goodman had been emulating when he led the "smooth and soporific dance combination" that so irritated Hammond.) Jazz did not have the commercial clout to attract MCA's sponsorship, and bands such as Goodman's that had enjoyed only modest, short-term success did not recommend themselves to MCA's agency. In fact, even after *Let's Dance* was renewed for a second thirteen-week run in February 1935, Goodman approached MCA for representation and was turned away. Soon after that, however, MCA hired a new agent who had been following Goodman's development on *Let's Dance*: Willard Alexander, a twenty-five-year-old musician who had honed his skills on both sides of the bandstand—as a bandleader and agent—during his college years at the University of Pennsylvania, from which he had graduated in 1930. As an agent, Alexander went against type: he loved music and showed a genuine interest in the professional welfare of his clients. If John Hammond "reawakened [Goodman's] musical conscience," as Firestone writes, Alexander created his business conscience. In Hammond's words, "he became as important in Benny Goodman's career as anyone." Alexander taught Goodman to shift his outlook from one of an independent freelance to one of a businessman responsible for meeting a payroll.[27]

Moreover—and this connects Alexander's impact more directly to Henderson—it was Alexander who urged Goodman to get his band "out of the studio, play for dancers, and really find its groove." Helen Ward recalled that going out on the road during the *Let's Dance* period was crucial to the band's success. Playing in public became the way to "break-in new tunes." On the road, "we learned a whole new book of arrangements," so that "each Saturday night we were able to belt them out with great confidence!" Such trips, far from the high life of New York, were rough and grinding. Ward described them as "a series of one-nighters up and down the East Coast ... on a rather ancient bus rented from an off-season amusement park in Coney Island, Brooklyn, [that] was slow, cold, and just plodded along out of habit." Yet the road trips were worth it, according to Ward, because they allowed the band to rehearse and perfect many new arrangements and to test them in front of real dancers, getting a sense of an arrangement's effectiveness that would have been impossible in Studio 8H with only one or two pairs of professional dancers. Thanks to Alexander and MCA, Goodman took his band on a national tour in the summer of 1935, extending the Kingdom of Swing's national reach. Indeed, Alexander deserves the chief responsibility for arranging the tour and for urging Goodman (and other doubtful MCA executives) to continue after his band's infamously poor reception at Denver's Elitch Gardens, leading finally to its historic appearance at the Palomar Ballroom in Los Angeles on the night of August 21, 1935.[28]

MCA's agency led to a third pillar of Goodman's budding career: Recording. Some time in the early spring of 1935, Victor records executive Ted Wallerstein signed Goodman to an unusual contract. Wallerstein, already a Goodman fan, offered terms that included granting Goodman royalties on the sales of his records. Goodman remained with Victor for four years and made more than two hundred recordings for the label. This brought unprecedented stability and productivity to Goodman's recording career, for Victor, like NBC, was owned by corporate giant RCA. Goodman's chroniclers tend to bracket 1935–39 as a distinct period of Goodman's career—such as the "Victor period" or simply the "Benny Goodman era." That these are precisely the years of Goodman's most intensive collaboration with Henderson is no coincidence. The collaboration—and Henderson's art—thrived on a foundation of consistent support by a network of agents in the music industry. In sum, commercial and artistic impulses, habitually seen as opposing forces in jazz history, merged in Goodman's rise to become "King of Swing."[29]

Stomping at the Palomar

Understanding that integration of commercial and artistic impulses invites a reconsideration of the most celebrated products of the Goodman-Henderson collaboration: "King Porter Stomp." For this arrangement, the three R's meshed so perfectly that the music appears in retrospect to have transcended the commercial circumstances surrounding it, making it a prime candidate for inclusion in the "jazz tradition"—a phrase connoting a musical lineage constructed to emphasize the music's autonomy from the marketplace.

"King Porter Stomp" was the first arrangement that Henderson gave to Goodman (along with his brother's "Big John Special"). Radio and Records had paved the Road for "King Porter Stomp." The piece appeared on *Let's Dance* several times and was recorded twice by Victor in June and July 1935. Along the way, the band had tried it out before dancers during its one-nighters between radio broadcasts. Then the Goodman band went on its lengthy, and ultimately legendary, tour across the United States culminating in a historic success at the Palomar Ballroom.

Any sense that the tour's culmination was somehow predestined, however, should be dispelled with a few facts about the band's vicissitudes in the spring and early summer. NBC failed to renew *Let's Dance* after its second thirteen-week run because a strike had put Nabisco in jeopardy. MCA then installed Goodman's band at one of its standard venues, the Roosevelt Hotel, an intimate restaurant where dinner audiences had grown accustomed to soft, elegant background music from MCA's sweet bands such as Guy Lombardo's orchestra. In that context, Goodman's radio-shaped "hot" orientation collided with the new venue's "sweet" aura. Helen Ward summed up the problem by asking, "how softly can you play 'King Porter Stomp'?" The answer was, you can't. Goodman got his two-week notice after the first night. The Roosevelt Room "horror," as saxophonist Hymie Schertzer called it, raised doubts that Goodman's brand of dance music had legs beyond its brief run on the radio.[30]

With Goodman's band expelled from MCA's flagship venue, Willard Alexander then tried something different: a cross-country tour, through Ohio and Michigan and extending across Colorado and Utah, ultimately to California. The band's reception along the way had been mildly enthusiastic, but not terribly encouraging, and the grinding life on the road exacerbated Goodman's doubts about the band's potential. Goodman had almost given up the band in Colorado. At Denver's Elitch Gardens, the band reached a low ebb, playing for minuscule huddles of dancers at a venue where the manager urged the band to play waltzes and do comedy. In Utah, Goodman fired his talented but undependable trumpet star Bunny Berigan, but then rehired him the next day.[31]

Then the California audience, first in Oakland, then in Los Angeles, showed a new receptivity to the music. When Bunny Berigan stood up and played "Sometimes I'm Happy" and "King Porter Stomp," Goodman recalled, "the place exploded." "From the moment I kicked them off," Goodman wrote, the band showed "some of the best playing I'd heard since we left New York. To our complete amazement, half of the crowd stopped dancing and came surging around the stand. . . . That was the moment that decided things for me. After traveling three thousand miles, we finally found people who were up on what we were trying to do. . . . That first big roar from the crowd was one of the sweetest sounds I ever heard in my life."[32]

The Palomar explosion and its aftershocks have led some historians to cite it as the birth of the swing era. Marshall W. Stearns, for example, after tracing jazz's development in 1930–34, could simply assert, "The Swing Era was born on the night of 21 August 1935." More than four decades after it was published, Stearns's formulation still echoes through the jazz literature, as in Gary Giddins's extension stressing swing's "birth" as a social phenomenon more than a musical one: "On that night, August 21, 1935, the swing era was born, because on that night middle-class white kids said yes in thunder and hard currency." Indeed, what Goodman's Palomar appearance revealed—as it grew from that first night into a three-month run—was not a new musical style but a new cultural "coalition" energized by white teenagers, who would comprise swing's most potent and unified audience. Social historians David W. Stowe and Lewis A. Erenberg both stress that youth was not a passive, hypnotized audience, but rather an active, empowered group who expressed that empowerment above all through dancing. These were the "jitterbugs" and "ickies" whose zeal and jerky movements startled older observers as well as the musicians themselves, and they created a subculture never envisioned by musicians such as Goodman, who was initially baffled by celebrity and sometimes puzzled by and even contemptuous of his fans.[33]

After the Palomar run, swing also became a kind of musical symbol of New Deal America. Cultural historians have emphasized swing as a model of populist pluralism and as such "the preeminent expression of the New Deal." Like Roosevelt's New Deal, swing crossed and blurred lines of class, ethnic, racial, and regional separation. Indeed, Goodman's arrival in California in August 1935 coincides with four new initiatives in the Second New Deal passed by Congress, including the Social Security Act, passed on August 14, 1935. Later, a ballroom manager, asked if attendance had risen because of swing's popularity, said, "Not at all—you can give much more credit to the present administration in Washington and to the morale of the nation in general."[34]

One of the paradoxes of the first night at the Palomar was that what signaled the band's effectiveness was not vigorous dancing, but its opposite, as "half of the crowd stopped dancing and came surging around the stand." Another is that one of the key pieces that Goodman singled out for its effect on the crowd was a complete anomaly in his book: "King Porter Stomp." "King Porter Stomp" was one of the oldest pieces in Goodman's book, dating back at least a quarter of a century. Moreover, it was one of Jelly Roll Morton's pieces, which were rarely played by bands other than Morton's, although a few had been issued in stock arrangements by the Melrose Brothers. It was a multistrain blues-inflected ragtime-based piece at a time when ragtime and blues were thoroughly out of fashion. In addition, the arrangement has an expandable form, whose final sections, the trio and "stomp" strains, could be extended indefinitely for a sequence of solos. The "stomp" genre itself was outdated, having been a popular marketing category in the 1920s when Henderson's band also recorded "Carolina Stomp," "Henderson Stomp," "Variety Stomp," "Whiteman Stomp," and of course, "Sugar Foot Stomp." "King Porter Stomp" could never belong among the "regular sequence of numbers" that Goodman played on a radio show; next to the popular songs that formed the core of Goodman's book and the majority of Henderson's charts, "King Porter" stood out as distinctively different.

Yet it has become a normative piece in jazz history, allowing historians to trace jazz's evolution through the various adaptations of "King Porter Stomp" from Morton's piano solo, to the Elmer Schoebel stock arrangement, to Henderson's head arrangement, to his revised and written-out score for Goodman. Gunther Schuller has called "King Porter Stomp" one of the "dozen or so major stations in the development of jazz in the twenty years between 1926 and 1946." The Palomar event signaled "a happy and rare coincidence: a large segment of the public seemed to prefer the best and most advanced arrangements the band had to offer, not, for once, the worst." And Goodman's recording of "King Porter Stomp" "was largely responsible for ushering in the Swing Era"—an assertion supported by the sheer number of bands that thereafter made the piece a staple in their books and imitated its call-and-response climax. Thus, the piece has been thoroughly assimilated into jazz history, but it actually serves as a reminder that swing's assimilation into jazz history requires some effort.[35]

When Goodman heard that "first big roar from the crowd" he heard the echo of the music coming out of Berigan's trumpet, which in turn echoed phrases that went back to Bobby Stark in Henderson's 1928 recording. The arrangement, too, was unmistakably based on the head arrangement that Henderson's band had developed over several years, including three recordings and countless nights on the bandstand. But the piece had to be reinvented for Goodman—that is, for a band that formed a whole greater than the sum of its parts, whose chief power lay in unified ensemble playing. Henderson's head arrangement grew within his own band and little or nothing had been written down. Now, however, for Goodman, Henderson finally put the arrangement on paper. Yet he did not simply provide a transcription of the head arrangement. For example, Henderson enhanced the riff accompaniment in the opening strain to include incisive exchanges between the brass and saxophones (ex. 9.12b), where before there had been only saxophones (ex. 9.12a).

In addition the revised arrangement for Goodman also restores Morton's trio melody to the foreground in the first trio; the melody retains the syncopated character that Henderson's band had brought to it in its earlier recordings, but it no longer accompanies a trumpet solo. The change is significant: it brings the saxophone section into the foreground, emphasizing written ensemble music over the improvised solo.

Henderson also recast the penultimate chorus. In 1933, Henderson had featured a rippling, triplet saxophone riff against piquant brass dissonances (ex. 9.13a). The 1935 arrangement, however, has a full-band chorus based on a climbing syncopated figure that demands a unified approach to phrasing (ex. 9.13b).

All of Henderson's changes to "King Porter Stomp" reflect a shift in emphasis toward ensemble precision, from a band that excelled in loose, solo-based, playing-in-the-mud head arrangements to a band that had fewer exciting improvisers but played together like a well-oiled machine. John Hammond recognized Goodman's version as "something of a landmark in white jazz circles. It is the first time, to my knowledge, that a large white orchestra has succeeded in capturing the attack and freedom of the best colored bands."[36]

Ex. 9.12. "King Porter Stomp," strain 1, mm. 1–8

Ex. 9.12a. Henderson recording (August 18, 1933) (transcribed by James Dapogny and Dave Jones)

Ex. 9.12b. Goodman recording (July 1, 1935). MSS 53, The Benny Goodman Papers in the Irving S. Gilmore Music Library of Yale University.

Ex. 9.13. "King Porter Stomp," penultimate strain riff

Ex. 9.13a. Henderson recording (1933) (transcribed by James Dapogny and Dave Jones)

Ex. 9.13b. Goodman recording (1935). MSS 53, The Benny Goodman Papers in the Irving S. Gilmore Music Library of Yale University.

From the Top: Rehearsing Henderson's Arrangements

Working from written music, the Goodman band captured the fiery abandon of "King Porter Stomp" only after extensive and disciplined preparation. Indeed, before any arrangement got performed on the Road, Radio, or Recording, it had to be assessed and perfected in the realm of a fourth "R": Rehearsal. Goodman particularly relished rehearsing Henderson's arrangements. "[I]t was one of the biggest kicks I've ever had in music to go through these scores and dig the music out of them, even in rehearsal." Rehearsals revealed Goodman's intensive concern for the written elements of an arrangement. He paid particular attention to the sectional brass and reed parts. In other words, Goodman structured his rehearsals in a way that emphasized Henderson's strengths. For Goodman, only intensive rehearsals could pull the "art" out of Henderson's arrangements.[37]

Accounts of Goodman's legendary rehearsals, ranging across a half century from the mid-1930s to the mid-1980s, evoke the image of an Old-World conductor leading a major orchestra through a symphony. Chris Griffin, a member of the trumpet section between 1936 and 1940, dubbed Goodman a "hard taskmaster." "Benny wanted perfection, and he got it," Helen Ward recalled. By the 1980s, rehearsals became "little daily psychodramas," Loren Schoenberg told Firestone. In "Blue Skies," Goodman "made us keep going over and over those opening figures. . . . It wasn't that the band wasn't playing the right notes, but it wasn't playing them precisely the way he wanted them played, with the exact nuances of phrasing." Schoenberg continued, and his illuminating statement conflates Henderson and Goodman into a single ideal embodied by Mozart: "We had always talked about those Fletcher Henderson arrangements, but once we started rehearsing them, I really began to understand Benny's stature as a band-leader and the real worth of those arrangements. . . . Playing those charts with Benny Goodman was like playing a Mozart quintet with Mozart there. The care and precision with which he could dissect them and put them back together again was truly remarkable." Nowhere in accounts of Goodman's rehearsals do observers mention improvised solos. What mattered to Goodman above all was tight, well-rehearsed ensemble and section playing.[38]

Goodman approached each arrangement in a systematic and hierarchical way far from the looser, collective construction of Henderson's head arrangements, where the leader delegated more authority to the sidemen. Chris Griffin gave a vivid description of Goodman's methodical approach. A typical rehearsal moved through four distinct phases. First, the band would "run the chart down as a group." Next, Goodman would ask the rhythm section to sit out while the brass and reeds rehearsed independently. Then, Griffin continues, "the two sections would rehearse the number together, over and over, without the rhythm section," because Goodman believed that without the rhythm section, the "band would swing better and have a lighter feel." Finally, the rhythm section returned. Goodman's view, in Griffin's words, was that "if you didn't depend on the rhythm section to swing, you would swing that much more when the rhythm section finally was brought in."[39]

"That was Benny's way," Helen Ward affirmed, "because any flaw, any weakness, is going to stand so revealed. You don't have a cushion." Alto saxophonist Hymie Schertzer related what could happen in such an exposed situation. One night, he recalled, he "added an eighth note by mistake. It was the first time it ever happened to me. I couldn't tell you how or why. I do know it hit the band like a tank charge. . . . It was that unexpected from any member of the band." Henderson appears to have agreed with Goodman's rehearsal style. When Goodman brought Henderson on to his radio program in September 1938 to explain his arrangement of "Blue Skies," Henderson "borrows" the band and runs through a passage using exactly the same four-step method that marked Goodman's rehearsals. Goodman's rehearsal style and Henderson's sectional writing went hand in glove. Soon, the sections of the band developed identities, and as personnel changed, so did the character of the band. Goodman aficionados can speak knowingly about the tone quality of specific sections. Loren Schoenberg, for example, noted the "unique blend of the Schertzer-led reed section."[40]

A particular vivid example of that quality can be heard in the rhythmless introduction of "Sandman." Here, Henderson writes a four-bar introduction for saxophones alone, moving in tight, block voicing. The original score reveals Henderson's elegant hand and dramatizes the transparency of the saxophone writing (see ex. 9.14).

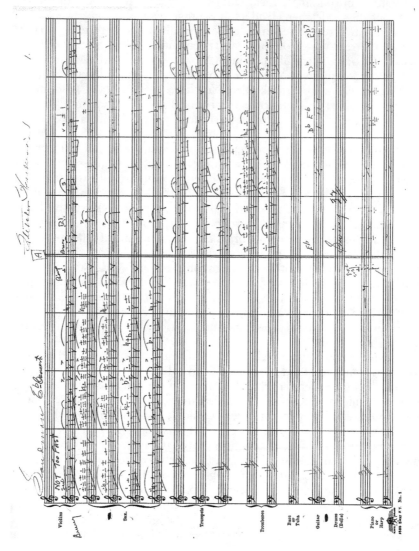

Ex. 9.14. "Sandman" (1935), first page of full score in Henderson's elegant hand. MSS 53, The Benny Goodman Papers in the Irving S. Gilmore Music Library of Yale University.

The saxophone players—altos Hymie Schertzer and Bill DePew, tenors Art Rollini and Dick Clark—phrase as if they were a single musician playing a four-voice chord, and the precision of their attacks and cutoffs far exceeds what Henderson indicated on paper. The introduction's six quarter notes—all appearing between the beats—receive two distinct kinds of articulation, observed unanimously by the four saxophone players. For example, while the players phrase through the quarter note in m. 1, they cut off the tied notes in m. 2, treating them like eighth notes, and thus subtly accentuating their syncopation. Further, although the offbeat quarter note in m. 3 gets held for its full length, the quarter note in the same spot of m. 4 gets truncated. Only intensive rehearsal could produce such an effect.

Paradoxically, the rehearsal process tended to transform the band's early star, drummer Gene Krupa, into an afterthought. Krupa added spark to the band. Lean and dashing with dark hair that brushed his forehead as he played, Krupa appeared to be doing magic tricks with his drumsticks. He was fun to watch, and his style packed a punch. Helen Ward called him "a revelation." John Hammond confirmed Krupa's arrival in the band as a "musical turning point" in the Goodman organization. Goodman himself saw Krupa as the only drummer who could give the rhythm section a "lift" and praised his "tremendous instinct for music." On record, however, the delicate interplay of brass and reeds sometimes gets overwhelmed by Krupa's aggressive pounding. By early 1937 Krupa had emerged as the biggest star of the Benny Goodman orchestra. Fans craved Krupa's showmanship and driving beat, but his style increasingly stood at odds with Goodman's musical vision of his band. While recognizing Krupa's impact, critics have tended to steer toward Goodman's taste. Gunther Schuller summed up the conventional wisdom on the band's sound when he called it "topheavy." In other words, the strong, unified ensemble playing lacked the supportive depth of a solid, integrated rhythm section. The Goodman band's abiding paradox, he continued, consisted in "a brilliant brass and reed ensemble . . . constantly trying to support itself on a rhythmically and harmonically weak foundation." If, as Helen Ward said, "the band breathed together," then sometimes the rhythm section, led by its drummer, could be suffocating.[41]

Goodman's and Krupa's competing visions of the band might be summed up as a conflict between a "top down" view favoring the melodic sections, brass and reeds, and a "bottom up" view, favoring the rhythm section, with a spotlight on the drummer. Henderson's charts focused on precise notation of the "top" parts; they provide only chords and other short-hand symbols for the "bottom." (A typical drum notation for a single chorus reads simply "Swing 32.") It was in rehearsal where Goodman and Henderson's priorities became most explicit. In fact, the rhythm section's sound and its relationship to the rest of the band is directly related to Goodman's rehearsal style, although it is unclear whether the rehearsal style caused the perceived problem or represented an adaptation to it. Perhaps for Goodman drumbeats left dents in the sleek surface of Henderson's swing scores. If "Blue Skies" and "Devil and the Deep Blue Sea" have not had the staying power of "King Porter Stomp" or "Sometimes I'm Happy," it may be because of the recorded performances, especially the drumming, not the arrangements per se. Despite intense conflicts, something about Krupa stuck in Goodman's mind. Nearly half a century after the Palomar breakthrough, Andre Previn asked Goodman, "Who was your favorite drummer?" Goodman answered, "Gene Krupa, without a doubt."[42]

The Ballad Style

A well-rehearsed band like Goodman's could excel in ballads, as ballad arrangements stand among Henderson's most transparent scores—music where the slightest miscue could send a shock wave through the band. And although Goodman's band defined its identity with hot jazz numbers, ballads to which dancers could fox-trot always held a distinctive place in the band's repertory. With the half-hour radio show as Goodman's basic programming unit, the idea was to fit the maximum variety of moods, styles, and instrumental combinations into every program. Ballads comprised an essential part of the program.

The band usually played at least one instrumental ballad in a radio program. An arrangement's score and parts usually reveal at a glance whether or not Henderson conceived it as a ballad: slow arrangements have only two to two-and-a-half choruses instead of the standard three. As a result, Henderson rarely needed to provide a tempo indication for such pieces. Among the scores and parts, ballad tempos appear only on such charts with more than two choruses, as in "Out of Nowhere" ("Medium slow," a three-chorus arrangement), "Sweet and Slow" ("Slow," three choruses), "Thanks for Everything" ("Slow-swing," two-and-a-half choruses), and the more ambiguous "Sandman" ("Not too fast," two-and-a-half choruses). In contrast, none of the two-chorus arrangements include a tempo marking. In other words, Henderson tends to write the indication when a glance at the arrangement might not immediately recommend it for ballad treatment.

"Rosetta," one of Henderson's earliest ballad arrangements for Goodman, provides an excellent example of Henderson's normative ballad style. It was first recorded in the marathon Victor record session of June 6, 1935; then again on January 14, 1937. It is a two-chorus arrangement with an eight-bar coda. Henderson begins with an intimate, brassless introduction featuring Goodman in a low, gently syncopated clarinet solo above placid saxophone harmony and a light, four-beat foundation in the rhythm section. The introduction flows into the first chorus for a straight, smooth melody rendition by a cup-muted trombone soaring above a soft bedding of saxophones, which play creamy triplets—marked "very legato" in Henderson's score—between the melody phrases. A trombone melody crystallized the ballad sound; and smooth saxophone triplets marked a distinctive element of Hendersonese in ballads.

Except for Goodman's three-note pickup, all of that, including Goodman's introductory solo and the trombone melody statement, is completely notated in Henderson's score. Space for improvised solos (marked "ad lib" in this and most of Henderson's other scores) is limited to one eight-bar bridge each for Goodman and guitarist Allan Reuss, plus a two-bar passage for tenor saxophone in each of the "A" sections of the second chorus. The guitar solo passage adds a particularly intimate touch and unique color combination: Goodman's guitarists rarely got a solo spot, and this one is accompanied by a sotto voce trio of clarinets.

In ballads, the brass provide color instead of power, and Henderson exploits a variety of coloristic possibilities by specifying passages for hat mutes and cup mutes, and for "open" (unmuted) brass. Henderson's mute indications tend to be varied and precise, creating an array of shades. Thus, in "Rosetta"'s first chorus the brass play a two-bar phrase in hat mutes; the trumpets alone provide cup-muted background figures for Goodman's bridge solo. In the second chorus, they play brief, two-bar responses to melodic variations in the saxophones. They shift to hat mutes for a pair of long tones behind the tenor solo spots, then take out the mutes for a phrase-ending turnaround. Henderson does not mark "open" for the beginning of the second chorus, but it seems to be implied and, on the recording, the brass certainly sound brighter from here to the end as their melodic participation becomes more prominent.

Goodman's best-known Henderson ballad arrangement was "Sometimes I'm Happy." The piece begins with one of Henderson's rhythmless introductions: two bars of brass and saxes without piano, bass, guitar, and drums. (In the score, there appears a single, bowed, long tone in the string bass, which is inaudible, if even played, on the recording.)[43] In one of Henderson's most transparent and delicately scored moments, the saxophones, marked pianissimo, launch the piece with a soft puff on the tonic chord (Ab), followed by cup-muted brass playing a legato phrase over saxophone harmony.

Also as in a typical ballad, the first chorus features a nearly note-for-note rendering of the melody, by the still cup-muted brass. What makes Henderson's setting memorable is the way he uses the melody's gaps for subtle saxophone punctuations, thereby developing the call-and-response pattern begun in the introduction's last four bars—an excellent stylization of the churchy, shouting climaxes of "King Porter Stomp" and "Sugar Foot" (ex. 9.15).

During Bunny Berigan's beefy trumpet solo, Henderson writes smooth, soft humming for the saxophones. (In a 1958 on-location recording in Brussels, these long tones, fortified by a baritone saxophone, wrap a bear hug around an elegantly understated and muted trumpet solo by Taft Jordan, a sharp contrast to Berigan's style—and a reminder that Henderson shaped his charts to specific musicians. By the late fifties, Goodman's saxes had a big, broad warmth in contrast to the laser-clarity and elegance of his mid-thirties saxophone quartet sound.)

Henderson himself "improvises" on the melody, as Goodman would say, in the last chorus and a half, with an arranger's variation, which, according to Horace, represents one of the brothers' collaborations in crisis. "Fletcher was so swamped," recalled Horace.

> Sometimes he said to me, "I just can't do it. Can you make something for Benny?" I was tickled to death to think that Fletcher asked me to write something for Benny Goodman. It was an honor. "Sometimes I'm Happy"—there's a beautiful thing he and I made together. The reed chorus was a legend, the way it flowed. Fletcher wrote this early in the morning,

Ex. 9.15. "Sometimes I'm Happy" (1935), introduction and chorus 1, beginning. MSS 53, The Benny Goodman Papers in the Irving S. Gilmore Music Library of Yale University.

and then he called me downstairs. I was asleep. He asked if I'd come down and finish the arrangement. I wrote the brass chorus—that's me. This happened many times.[44]

Many subtle details in the scoring belie the sweatshop atmosphere in which the brothers created it. The hallmark and most famous arranged passage in Henderson's ballad style is the sixteen-bar passage for saxophones in block voicing that opens the third chorus—the passage that Horace called "a legend, the way it flowed" (ex. 9.16).

The full ensemble plays a long pickup that swells and subsides as it glides gently into the downbeat of the new chorus. Henderson constructs most of the passage in four-bar units, with a two-bar phrase as the model for a repetition or slight variation to complete the four-bar unit. Despite the duple meter context and four-bar phraseology, however, each unit in mm. 1–12 grows from an idea based on groupings of three. In the first four bars, the gently swaying triplets impart the "flow" that Horace noted and smooth out the unexpectedly irregular 3+3+2 rhythmic pattern that Henderson introduces here. In the next four bars (mm. 5–8), Henderson creates a gentle secondary-rag effect—a calling card of the 1920s—with groups of three eighth notes (mm. 5–6), varying the pattern slightly in the next phrase. Next (mm. 9–12), Henderson builds a pattern based almost entirely on triplets, rising an octave, topping off in the next bar (m. 10), then rising and falling again in a comparable way. The final unit marks a departure from the previous three: triplets and other three-beat patterns relent to more straightforward rhythm, partly borrowed from mm. 5–8 (as in mm. 13–14).

Ex. 9.16. "Sometimes I'm Happy," pickups and chorus 3. MSS 53, The Benny Goodman Papers in the Irving S. Gilmore Music Library of Yale University.

Goodman's alto saxophones, playing here in their highest register, combine relaxed serenity and an intensely focused, unified tone. The leader of the saxes was the sweet-toned alto, Toots Mondello. No wonder that when Mondello announced he was leaving the band after the "Sometimes I'm Happy" recording session, "Henderson chased him around the studio to try to get him to stay."[45]

Horace's brass passage flows out of what preceded it, including figures that his brother had written for the saxophones. The passage has the quality of a subdued stylization of a Louis Armstrong solo, with its "rips" in mm. 20 and 21, its syncopated pickups to m. 25, the high-range syncopated leaps in m. 27, and the rising and falling triplet figures in preparation for the final cadence. (It might sound even more like Armstrong if a solo trumpet played the top staff at a faster tempo.)

Whether Fletcher or Horace wrote the final half-chorus is anyone's guess, but if Fletcher did indeed wake Horace up to "finish the arrangement" (and not just to write the "brass chorus," as Horace called it), then we have to assume the ending is Horace's work as well (ex. 9.17). Here, the brass and saxophones come together for the first time, a kind of shout-chorus effect adapted for the ballad style. Block voicing remains the rule here as the nine-voice texture (including considerable doubling) moves in syncopated patterns into the high register then closes with a triplet flourish related to the end of Horace's brass passage and to Fletcher's emphasis on patterns of three in the saxophone chorus. The four-bar passage repeats, followed by a

Ex. 9.17. "Sometimes I'm Happy," chorus 4, beginning. MSS 53, The Benny Goodman Papers in the Irving S. Gilmore Music Library of Yale University.

solo from Goodman backed by accented trombone and saxophone chords. The arrangement ends with an octave "ding" in the piano and a full ensemble cadence.

In its merging of African-American oral tradition practice, elegant sectional writing, and subtle unifying effects, "Sometimes I'm Happy" became a model for ballad arranging in the swing era and beyond. Goodman recognized it as an especially fine example among Henderson's— he should have named both Horace *and* Fletcher—arrangements of "melodic" tunes and singled it out, along with "King Porter Stomp," as one of the key numbers that ignited the Palomar Ballroom crowd on the evening of August 21, 1935.

Going to Chicago

Once his band was established on both coasts, Goodman moved on to the heartland and his home town. Capitalizing on the extended Palomar engagement, Willard Alexander arranged for Goodman's band to go east for what turned out to be another unusually long stint—a six and a half-month residency—at Chicago's Congress Hotel, from November 1935 to May 1936. Here, Goodman made the unprecedented move of hiring pianist Teddy Wilson to play in the band. Although Goodman's motivations were musical, not social, he had nevertheless made a social statement to the white dancers that packed into the Congress: now racial integration was a fact on the bandstand as well as in the recording studio. Meanwhile, NBC created a weekly sustaining program from the Congress that led to another commercially sponsored show, the *Elgin Revue,* sponsored by the Elgin Watch Company. Constant exposure on the airwaves required new arrangements and led to regularly recording for Victor. As the three R's continued to spur and support the band, Goodman's Chicago period saw many new Henderson arrangements.

On November 22, 1935, soon after opening at the Congress Hotel, Goodman led his band into a recording studio for the first time since the Palomar Ballroom run. The session was unusually fruitful, producing seven sides instead of the usual four. Four of them were Henderson arrangements. They show Henderson extending the elements of "Hendersonese" in new directions with particular emphasis on the strengths of the ensemble more than on the soloists.

"When Buddha Smiles," for example, features solos by Goodman and tenor saxophonist Art Rollini, but it is really a showcase for sectional unity and full-band cohesiveness in a slow-building swinger. The song itself dates from the "oriental foxtrot" craze of the early twenties, and it is one of the Paul Whiteman hits from the previous decade that Henderson practically reinvented for the swing era. ("Whispering" and "Changes" are the others.) Henderson brings it up to date in many ways. Perhaps the arrangement's most unusual feature is its through-composed quality. Although "Buddha" features a conventional thirty-two-bar AABA structure, Henderson artfully disguises the form through constant variation and a gradual build across four choruses to the final climax. The third chorus reveals a rare instance of Henderson writing across the seams of the pop song's eight-bar phrases. Here, Rollini's tenor sax solo spans ten bars that straddle the first two "A" sections. Throughout Henderson constantly varies the principal melody so as to obscure its identity. Although he had demonstrated this kind of internal variation in "Blue Skies" and "Devil and the Deep Blue Sea," he takes the procedure further in "Buddha."

Meanwhile, the arrangement shows imaginative recycling of proven elements of Hendersonese. The second chorus bridge (ex. 9.18) introduces an idea derived from the Armstrong-inflected melody from Henderson's own "Wrappin' It Up."

Ex. 9.18. "When Buddha Smiles" (1935), chorus 2, bridge. MSS 53, The Benny Goodman Papers in the Irving S. Gilmore Music Library of Yale University.

Two choruses later, Henderson transforms it into a call-and-response passage (ex. 9.19) harking back to his now-famous "King Porter Stomp" climax.

Ex. 9.19. "When Buddha Smiles," chorus 4, bridge. MSS 53, The Benny Goodman Papers in the Irving S. Gilmore Music Library of Yale University.

And in the two-bar lead-in to the final chorus, Henderson adopts a climactic effect from "Devil and the Deep Blue Sea" in a new guise: a sequence of on-the-beat quarter notes that "straighten out" the rhythm (ex. 9.20). Here, however, he reinforces the effect by increasing harmonic density during a crescendo, so that a chord cluster appears at the peak of loudness. It's a fascinating effect: Henderson creates a modulation by gradually amassing pitches that transform the chord from a tonic (G♭ in m. 97) to a densely enriched dominant (m. 100, beats 1–2) to a clarified dominant-seventh pickup (m. 100, beat 4) to the new key, D.

Ex. 9.20. "When Buddha Smiles," transition to final chorus. MSS 53, The Benny Goodman Papers in the Irving S. Gilmore Music Library of Yale University.

"When Buddha Smiles" became a regular radio feature and Goodman continued to play it into the 1980s.

"Breakin' in a Pair of Shoes" stands out for a different reason in Goodman's post-Palomar Chicago period. Unlike "Buddha," "Shoes" was a brand-new tune from publisher Leo Feist, a Tin Pan Alley stalwart for nearly half a century. The song's lyrics, by Ned Washington and Dave Franklin, mark it as a member of the "steppin' out" vein of popular song, popularized by Irving Berlin in such tunes as "Puttin' on the Ritz." But the lyrics could hardly match Berlin at his best, as a phrase from the bridge reveals: "Should I dance, take a chance, 'Ouch, my tootsies!' " With that line, perhaps there was no way Henderson could have arranged this as a convincing vocal number. Yet the music by Sam H. Stept is another story. It represents a fine example of how Tin Pan Alley could absorb the swing style in an unforced way. Like "Devil and the Deep Blue Sea," the melody is laced with swing-inflected dotted rhythms. The harmony of the principal phrase features a recycling two-bar chord progression that had been Henderson's bread-and-butter in the post-Connie's Inn period: a slightly enriched I–ii–V–I progression; in other words, a rhythm-changes progression. (The song's bridge, however, does not resemble Gershwin's.)

All together, the song lends itself naturally to a swing arrangement, so Henderson creates a clear and streamlined arrangement in his standard mold: an eight-bar introduction, three choruses of the thirty-two-bar AABA tune, and a brief coda. The band launches the arrangement with shouting chords in call-and-response with elegant solo lines from Goodman. As the chart moves on, the brass and saxes engage in the kind of fluent give-and-take that marked "Blue Skies." Henderson modulates from A♭ to D♭ for the final chorus featuring a tenor sax solo backed by brass figures played "open-in-hats," as marked in the original parts. For the coda (more than a perfunctory tag-ending), Henderson ratchets the key up to B♭ and writes a climactic ensemble variation on the principal tune (ex. 9.21).

Ex. 9.21. "Breakin' in a Pair of Shoes" (1936), coda. MSS 53, The Benny Goodman
Papers in the Irving S. Gilmore Music Library of Yale University.

In the last bar, pencil marks in all parts indicate a characteristic change:
Henderson's final beat-and-a-half chord becomes a quick eighth-note bite.
(Such changes comprise the written legacy of Goodman's rehearsals.) In the
recording, with Krupa sustaining light but active support throughout,
"Shoes" stands out as an unpretentious, simple-but-perfect swing chart that
must have been ideal for moderate-tempo dancing.

The *Camel Caravan*

Goodman's Chicago residency ended in May 1936 when the *Elgin Revue*
moved to New York. Back at the band's home base, Goodman's career flourished on all fronts. In fact, radio work would become an even more central
part of his band's activity. In June, the band began performing on another
commercially sponsored show called the *Camel Caravan*, sponsored by the
R. J. Reynolds Tobacco Company. Like *Let's Dance*, the *Camel Caravan* was
a weekly show featuring dance music and required Goodman's band to
perform a half-hour set. But the similarities ended there. The *Camel
Caravan* appeared on the CBS radio network for an hour on Tuesday
evening. Goodman's band initially split the hour with one other band; later
the show's format changed to a single half-hour featuring only Benny
Goodman and His Orchestra. Moreover, to suit Goodman's punishing road
schedule, the program was broadcast not from a single studio, but from the
CBS affiliate nearest to the venue where the band happened to be
performing. Radio and Road worked hand in glove. *Camel Caravan* was
broadcast not only from New York but also from Los Angeles, San Francisco, Chicago, Washington, DC, Philadelphia, Boston, Indianapolis, Kansas
City, Minneapolis, Louisville, Detroit, Cleveland, Pittsburgh, and many
others, including smaller cities such as Akron, Ohio; Asheville, North

Carolina; and Fort Wayne, Indiana. And unlike the mere twenty-six-week run of *Let's Dance*, the *Camel Caravan* continued uninterrupted for three-and-a-half years, from mid-1936 through December 1939 for a total of 182 programs. It became "the longest running commercially sponsored series featuring one orchestra continuously."[46]

And that was not all. In two extended stints totaling ten months from October 1936 to January 1938 at the Madhattan Room of New York's Pennsylvania Hotel, Goodman's band also held forth in frequent sustaining programs. In fact, during the second stint (October 1937 through January 1938), the band could be heard *at least once a night* on sustaining programs. Such intensive, indeed unprecedented, radio exposure forced Goodman to refresh his repertoire constantly. Naturally, along with many other arrangers, Henderson was called on again and again to produce new scores. Meanwhile, as he played earlier arrangements night after night over many months, Goodman brought them as well to the Victor studio for recording. Thus, the *Camel Caravan* period features recordings of many of Henderson's most exciting arrangements.

During this period of greatest radio exposure, Goodman's band made two public appearances in New York that matched the Palomar Ballroom breakthrough in their symbolic importance or visceral crowd reaction. The first was a brief run at the Paramount Theatre in March 1937 when crowds of teenagers lined a New York City block waiting for tickets and, once inside, danced in the aisles, thrilled at the sight of their heroes rising from the pit in the dark, their faces illuminated only by the reflected glow of their stand lamps. The second was the Carnegie Hall concert of January 16, 1938, a landmark presentation of swing for a strictly listening audience in a concert format. The perceived incongruity between style and function inspired Harry James's famous quip that "I feel like a whore in church." In 1937–38, Goodman's band reached its peak of popular success and media exposure. The period marks a watershed in music history for the way media saturation fueled public interest and sustained a musical style whose artistic legitimacy appeared to be crowned by the concert appearance at Carnegie Hall.

Several Goodman records capture the band in the first months of the *Camel Caravan* and show Henderson keeping his arranging style fresh and vital. Good examples are "(I Would Do) Anything for You," "Love Me or Leave Me, " and "I've Found a New Baby." If three minutes marked a normative performance, then any significant expansion of Henderson's typical three-chorus structure would dictate a rise in tempo. "Anything for You" offers a case in point. The arrangement itself dates from the *Let's Dance* period, but now Goodman brought it back to the recording studio after a year of rehearsal, public performance, and, most likely, radio exposure. Henderson expands the typical form to five choruses—only four got recorded—and opens up an unusually long stretch for improvised solos by Goodman and his sidemen. He parcels out solos for five different musicians (clarinet, trumpets 1 and 2, tenor sax 2, and piano) over the three internal choruses. Framing the solo choruses are two ensemble-dominated sections featuring a constantly evolving sequence of variations on the Claude Hopkins tune. As a result the arrangement matches the expandable "jamming" structure of the heads Henderson's own band had developed since the late 1920s.

Henderson scores the first chorus almost entirely in full-ensemble block voicing, including a few slicing chains of syncopation. (Ex. 9.22 lines up two versions of the melody in the first chorus, showing only saxophones. Measures 1–4 show only three saxophones because Henderson's score had called for alto saxophone 2 to double on baritone saxophone in the introduction just preceding this passage, so the rest allows the musician to put down one instrument and pick up the other.) Yet the polished playing—thanks undoubtedly to tireless rehearsal—sustains remarkable lightness and drive and keeps the eight-part, then nine-part, stack of sound from becoming a turgid, chunky mass.

Ex. 9.22. "I Would Do Anything for You" (1935), chorus 1 melody variants. MSS 53, The Benny Goodman Papers in the Irving S. Gilmore Music Library of Yale University.

Henderson ends the arrangement with a cadential flourish that would become his signature sign-off: a climactic build up, interrupted by solo breaks—fully composed, for Goodman—and a final full-band cadence (ex. 9.23)

On "Love Me or Leave Me," Henderson leaves much to the soloists but underscores each of them with distinctive, contrasting backgrounds: syncopated, pulsating saxophone figures for Goodman; long tones for tenor saxophonist Vido Musso; light figures for pianist Jess Stacy; soft, smooth chords behind guitarist Allan Reuss; and a lightly chanting riff behind trumpeter Chris Griffin. Matching an apt background to each soloist had been a trademark of Henderson's own band, often in the context of head arrangements; now with Goodman, he develops the procedure in written practice, and in the precision of Goodman's sectional and ensemble work, such figures emerge with sharply etched vitality.

Goodman takes the tempo up several notches for "I've Found a New Baby." Playing at 276 beats per minute ("probably the band's fastest arrangement," according to Loren Schoenberg[47]), Goodman probably could have fit yet another chorus into the recorded version, which clocks in at just two minutes and ten seconds. The sixteen-bar introduction (Henderson's longest) presents a striking full-band scalar rise and fall on whole notes. Like the climactic on-the-beat figures heard in "Devil" and "Buddha," the effect gains drama precisely because it does not swing. What follows is all swing, however, as Henderson proceeds with a four-chorus sequence in which, once again, ensemble statements, veering further and further from the melody, frame the internal solo choruses supported by a network of riffs. Under Goodman's solo in the second chorus, for example, the saxophones render with fierce precision a simple two-bar riff. Chris Griffin's third-chorus solo has all the earmarks of a swing trumpet player who has absorbed Armstrong. Launched by a smear up to a high note and marked by fat vibrato,

Ex. 9.23. "I Would Do Anything for You," ending. MSS 53, The Benny Goodman Papers in the Irving S. Gilmore Music Library of Yale University.

the solo skates over the fast tempo with a few choice pitches soaring over a foundation of riffs and rhythm. As if responding to Griffin's flares, Henderson's ensemble variations (which of course preceded—and shaped—the solo) follow with broad, dramatic figures bursting out above their rhythmic support—like an Armstrong solo written down and harmonized in block voicing.

"Orchestrated Armstrong": Jazz critic Gary Giddins has claimed that much of big-band music in the 1930s can be summed up in that phrase—a provocative idea that calls for both elaboration and qualification.[48] In swing arrangements, certain rhythms and pitch sequences echo figures that Armstrong played in solos with Henderson in the mid-1920s and beyond: syncopated double leaps, blues inflections, a sense of cohesion and development, an impression of floating above the beat. But what a band arrangement cannot really capture is Armstrong's rhythmic elasticity and timbral variety: those can only come from soloists. Armstrong appears to glide across the beat, now anticipating it, now lagging behind it, but always playing with an unerring sense of the actual pulse. So any claims that a passage sounds like "orchestrated Armstrong" must be qualified, because a group of musicians cannot play with the rhythmic or timbral freedom of a soloist. Henderson's arrangements offered a stylized interpretation of Armstrong, not a precise orchestral rendering of all facets of Armstrong's unique style. Orchestrating Armstrong, in effect, required filtering out some of the qualities that made Armstrong's playing so powerful.

With that condition in mind, however, Henderson wrote many passages that sound not only like an "improvised solo," as Goodman had pointed out, but like Armstrong in particular. In the final chorus of "Alexander's Ragtime Band," for example, Henderson's writing departs radically from the original tune in favor of a soloistic line, harmonized in block voicing and featuring several Armstrong-like devices (ex. 9.24): the opening phrase's syncopated skipping through the first two bars with the prominent blue notes (the flat seventh in m. 1 and the flat third in mm. 3 and 12), a syncopated figure on a repeated note (C) in m. 4 (as in the opening of Armstrong's famous "Potato Head Blues" solo), a couple of syncopated double leaps (mm. 9–10 and 13–14), a dramatic octave leap between mm. 10 and 11, and the final leap up to a high note to finish the section. Looking at the line without its block voicing helps to throw its Armstrong-like nature into relief. Meanwhile, the revised melody captures that Armstrong effect of floating over the beat.

Ex. 9.24. "Alexander's Ragtime Band" (1936), final ensemble chorus (top line only)

Henderson even applies Armstrong's language to slow fox-trots. Taking the chestnut "Whispering," popularized by Paul Whiteman back in 1920, Henderson gives it the full ballad treatment, with a soaring trombone solo playing the first chorus melody over suave saxophone riffs. In the final chorus, however, Henderson develops a climax with a full-band variation that likewise deploys Armstrong's leaping fourth figure (ex. 9.25). Henderson's arrangement of "Whispering" marks a medium through which the tune passed from 1920s Whitemanesque fox-trot music to 1940s bebop standard in the form of Dizzy Gillespie and Kirby Stone's contrafact "Groovin' High."

"Orchestrated Armstrong" is not the only way Henderson's arrangements hark back to their roots in his own band. The arrangements contain many other revealing glimpses of the past. For example, Henderson's tag ending of "Between the Devil and the Deep Blue Sea" comes from his 1933 piece "Can You Take It?" His arrangement of "St. Louis Blues" adopts the format and riff foundation from his own band's 1927 recording, itself based on a Redman-doctored stock. His arrangement of "Somebody Loves Me" features a Benny Carteresque saxophone chorus clearly derived from Carter's 1930 arrangement of the tune for Henderson's band. And for Goodman's solo in the central blues section of "Basin Street Blues," Henderson revives the famous stoptime chorus played by Johnny Dodds on "Dipper Mouth Blues"—and revisited in Redman's "Sugar Foot Stomp"— more than a decade earlier. In the film *Hollywood Hotel*, moreover, Goodman plays a solo on a rhythm changes tune called "I've Got a Heartful

Ex. 9.25. "Whispering," chorus 3, mm. 1–8

of Music" that echoes Horace's arranged brass bridge—itself based on a Red Allen solo—from "Hotter than 'Ell." Along with the "In the Mood" riff that passed through Henderson's band in Horace's tune "Hot and Anxious," these passages collectively reinforce the notion that Goodman and Henderson built the Kingdom of Swing partly from recycled shards of earlier black jazz and dance music.

Meanwhile, of course, Henderson also adapted several complete arrangements for Goodman's band. Along with "King Porter Stomp," these were among the first pieces Goodman played, including "Down South Camp Meeting," "Wrappin' It Up," "Sugar Foot Stomp," and "Honeysuckle Rose"—all recorded in 1935, played repeatedly, and recorded again before the decade was out. Goodman also played Henderson's "Stealin' Apples" and the 1920s blockbuster "Henderson Stomp." In "Camp Meeting" and "Wrappin' It Up," we hear the effects of Goodman's rehearsal process on two Henderson originals, the unified articulation and smooth blend of the sections far exceeds Henderson's own band; but the tempos seem deliberate, almost sluggish, next to the Henderson band's bright pace, and, except for Goodman, the soloists cannot match the imaginative, vibrant playing of Red Allen and Hilton Jefferson that had formed an integral part of Henderson's original conception of "Wrappin' It Up." On radio, however, "Wrappin' It Up" became a familiar closer for Goodman in 1938–39, apt for the spot not just for its hot jazz quality but also its title. "King Porter Stomp" and "Sugar Foot Stomp" served the same purpose on other broadcasts in 1939.

In "Sugar Foot Stomp" (which Goodman recorded September 1937) and "Honeysuckle Rose" (November 1939), Henderson introduces more changes to the versions his own band had played. "Sugar Foot Stomp" had undergone several phases of development and now solidified into a score that built up through an extended series of riffs into a carefully calibrated climax. "Honeysuckle Rose" marks the most dramatic difference between an earlier head arrangement and a later scored one. In this rare mixed-race big-band recording, we can hear some of Henderson's greatest backgrounds behind some outstanding solo work by an all-star lineup of Goodman, Charlie Christian, and Cootie Williams. Here, the backgrounds are notable for their variety, vitality, and dialogic interaction with the solos and with each other.

In the Cootie Williams solo, for example, the brass and saxophones engage in a shouting call and response that forms a supportive gauntlet. The rest of the arrangement is a model of seamless, riff-based swing, unusual for its dynamic effects. The saxophones emerge from the bridge to take the final eight of the penultimate chorus with a riff figure played in a finely tapered diminuendo. That passage moves seamlessly into the final riff chorus derived from Henderson's 1932 head, now featuring the brass and reeds together in a figure that grows louder through the eight bars of the song's "A" section. In the final "A" section, the principal riff returns, now growing softer and softer until the final cadence ends with uncharacteristic understatement.

A few weeks after Goodman recorded "Honeysuckle Rose," the *Camel Caravan* concluded its three-and-a-half year run. The show's end punctuates the first and most important phase of Goodman's bandleading career.

A Kingdom in Decline?

Well before the last *Camel Caravan* broadcast on December 30, 1939, Goodman's band had been in transition. A flurry of personnel changes made Goodman's 1939 band an almost entirely different group from the one that had built the Kingdom of Swing with Henderson's arrangements four years earlier. Gene Krupa had left back in March 1938 after an acrimonious dispute. Another celebrity, trumpet star Harry James, left on better terms in January 1939. Then, as Firestone put it, a "massive exodus of sidemen" began in the spring of 1939, leaving only trombonist Red Ballard, saxophonist Art Rollini, and pianist Jess Stacy as the surviving members of the Palomar Ballroom band of August 1935. Meanwhile, since Helen Ward's departure toward the end of 1936, many vocalists had come and gone.[49]

Goodman's predicament in 1939–40 conjures an image of Wile E. Coyote, powered by the Acme jets of Henderson's charts, running off the cliff of his New-Deal era, prewar cultural foundation and popularity, and spinning his legs in a frantic effort to stay aloft. In Jess Stacy's view, "the band was on the wane. The same interest wasn't there. Benny could see what was happening, and he was desperately trying to get back on top." Then Goodman even changed pianists, replacing Stacy with Fletcher Henderson himself. A gentle Missourian, Stacy reflected on the incident from Goodman's point of view: "Fletcher Henderson's arrangements had really made Benny's band," he recalled, "and he probably thought that if he could have Fletcher with him, he could bolster the band." By spring of 1939, some of Goodman's competitors had caught up, including Artie Shaw, whose star rose in 1938 with his hit record of Cole Porter's "Begin the Beguine," and especially Glenn Miller, who used the three R's to great advantage in his dominance of big-band music beginning in the spring of 1939. Miller enlisted in the army in September 1942, and, far from dropping out of the scene, became defined by the war as America's leading swing man, a reputation that survived his death in December 1944. Indeed, Goodman's "wane" marks a shift in American culture from the inward-looking Depression years to the outward-looking war years. The Goodman-Henderson heyday of 1935–39 created a populist sound with a youth-oriented blend of black and white in New Deal America. The new generation of bandleaders represented by Glenn Miller offered polish without the underlying energy of racial amalgamation at a time when war demanded American unity at the expense of racial equality.[50]

Meanwhile, Goodman too started de-emphasizing the racialized sound of his Henderson years. He was exploring new directions. Even as he continued a demanding schedule of road tours, radio appearances, and recordings with his big band and small groups, his fascination with European composers outside the domain of dance music peaked in 1939 with the premiere performance of a piece he had commissioned: Béla Bartók's *Rhapsody for Clarinet and Violin*. The next year he recorded the *Rhapsody*, retitled *Contrasts*, with Bartók at the piano and Josef Szigeti on violin.

While Goodman endured changing personnel, tried to fend off the competition, and pursued classical music interests, he saw two pillars of his early success dislodge under the structure of his professional activity. Willard Alexander left MCA in early 1939. Goodman remained with MCA but now lacked the agency's support. Meanwhile, Ted Wallerstein, who had signed Goodman to Victor in 1935, was now working for Columbia Records, and John Hammond went to work for him. So in May 1939 the band made its last record for Victor and two months later began a new phase of its recording career under Wallerstein's auspices at Columbia.

At precisely this moment, Goodman started playing charts by a new arranger: Eddie Sauter. Sauter built a style that could be construed as counter-Hendersonian, with its more "linear," sometimes contrapuntal conception of texture; its rich, unusual harmonic palette abetted by a larger band (Goodman now carried a third trombone and would soon add a baritone saxophone, giving the band a thicker, meatier sound); and its unique instrumental colors resulting from cross-sectional blends never heard in Henderson's block voicing and sectional choirs. Band members who had mastered Hendersonese took some time to adjust to Sauter's style. "His charts were so difficult and so involved, ... they didn't sound like Benny's band," according to saxophonist Jerry Jerome, who had actually been one of the band members who'd suggested that Goodman hire Sauter. In contrast, "Fletcher wrote in a very understandable, nice, easygoing style.... It just rolled." Even as he played more and more of Sauter's charts, Goodman seems to have remained ambivalent about them. "Benny used to edit his arrangements brutally—just brutally," according to Jimmy Maxwell. But Goodman rarely made changes in Henderson's arrangements, as the surviving band parts show. The changes he did make tended to be cuts for radio performance, changes in the choice of soloist, removal of a vocal—mostly changes brought about by things having nothing to do with the arrangement per se. In short, the kinds of cuts Goodman made in Henderson's arrangements were "pragmatic" cuts, whereas the cuts he made in Sauter's arrangements were "aesthetic" cuts.[51]

Finally, Goodman's medical problems capped a two-year period of growing instability. Sciatica forced him to disband and seek surgical relief at the Mayo Clinic in July 1940. Four months later, he reformed his band with new personnel and a new style marked by less emphasis on the Henderson arrangements on which the Kingdom of Swing had been built. Goodman would later whimsically commemorate his back problems with a sextet record he punningly called "Slipped Disc," based on the chords of a tune that recalled happier days: "King Porter Stomp."

Over a period of five years, the Kingdom of Swing had been built from a unique convergence of elements. Musically, it encompassed a repertoire consisting mainly of current popular songs, an arranging style that both revealed the tune and elegantly concealed it with swing variations, and a performance style founded on carefully rehearsed scores. Socially, the music got disseminated and popularized through an integrated network of those three R's: Road tours, Radio play, and Records. And it was eagerly absorbed by a fan-base consisting mainly of teenagers inspired and empowered by the music not just to listen but to dance. Above all, it consisted in a delicate consensus joining teenagers and adults, black and white, oral and written music, Tin Pan Alley and jazz. Henderson himself, however, never fully reaped the benefits of that consensus.

10.

Never Say "Never Again"

HENDERSON'S REMAINING LIFE may be seen as a cycle of fulfillment and frustration. His association with Goodman revived his bandleading career in 1936; the band intermittently flourished and fizzled. Later Henderson bands boasted an impressive roster of talent, for whom the band was "like going to school," but they had mixed success before listeners and dancers. In 1936, Henderson also had a hit song, "Christopher Columbus," but failed to capitalize on its success. Henderson was by turns generous and open, cheap and dishonest. Count Basie called Henderson "the only leader in the business that ever went out of his way to help me"; and indeed "dozens" of Henderson arrangements, according to John Hammond, formed the cornerstone of Basie's repertoire in the late 1930s. In the same period, a wide-eyed high-school student named Charles Anderson introduced himself to Henderson at the Vogue Ballroom in Los Angeles and got several tutorials in arranging. "A wonderful person," Anderson recalled, "Fletch wouldn't take a penny for all of his help." On the other hand, Garvin Bushell, who had been Fletcher's friend since meeting him at Penn Station on arrival in New York in the summer of 1920, was repeatedly underpaid—he once caught Henderson with much more money than he had claimed to have—and Bushell bitterly noted in 1989 that Henderson died owing him two to three thousand dollars. Many other musicians shared a similar complaint, but when the band was good, it seemed to matter less. "Almost each individual musician had money coming," Duke Ellington observed of the 1934 band, "and nothing ever happened." Yet musicians who recognized all of Henderson's faults still prized their time in his band, claiming it as "my biggest kicks" and "a great kick."[1]

As Henderson enjoyed greater financial security, he also suffered from increasingly poor health. Through the 1940s, Henderson intermittently suffered a variety of ailments, including an eye infection, dizziness, exhaustion, sciatica, high blood pressure, and, finally, a series of strokes that led to his death in 1952 at the age of fifty-five. The very work that helped sustain a steady income was also "a great strain," he confessed. "It was good money, but just too much for me to do." A naïf once asked Henderson, "Does Benny Goodman still arrange for you?" and he calmly responded, "No, I was working him too hard. His eyes went bad on him and he had to give it up."[2]

If the last sixteen years of Henderson's life—really, the last half of his professional career—reveal such mixed fortunes, they also reveal that, despite incredible success as an arranger for Goodman, Henderson's musical identity remained rooted in leading a band. Goodman tried to convince him to be a full-time arranger, and critics wondered why Henderson would continue struggling as a bandleader when he could be working full-time for the King of Swing. There is no question that working for Goodman would have brought greater fame and fortune, as well as the aesthetic satisfaction of hearing his scores expertly played by a renowned band.

That band, however, was not his own. So Henderson doggedly persisted, despite some volatile ups and downs. During a successful stint in Chicago in 1936, Ed Fox, the dictatorial manager of the Grand Terrace Café, fired a singer in what John Hammond called an "abusive tirade before a large crowd of onlookers," but Henderson did nothing, and John Hammond laid part of the blame on the bandleader. "It is certainly tragic that colored performers are so subject to exploitation," reflected Hammond, "but it is even sadder when they are themselves to blame." In another jam in early 1942, Henderson fired his entire band and re-formed with new personnel. Henderson expanded the band to seventeen, but by then, "the war was on and the draft took its toll on the band," according to George Floyd, a singer who fronted the Henderson band for the next three years. "Fletcher was a gentleman through it all," Floyd noted. "He would take a lot before he would fire a musician. I would complain about a musician not playing his part, and Fletcher would shrug it off and comment that, because of the war and the draft, he could not be too choosy." Sidemen came and went, the best of them both stoked by the heady experience of playing with a big-band legend and constrained by the musical format he had developed. Drummer Art Blakey, for example, roused the ire of Horace Henderson. "Art was playing bebop drums, dropping bombs with his bass drum," recalled Floyd, "and Horace could not stand that. In fact, they had a little skirmish over the situation." Meanwhile, as the national passion for swing cooled, a sibling rivalry heated up. Floyd said that "Horace and Fletcher . . . fought like cats and dogs."[3]

The early 1940s also featured some unusual experiences on the road. Henderson led his new orchestra on a tour featuring a celebrity "Swing Battle of the Sexes" against the all-female International Sweethearts of Rhythm, who, according to Sherrie Tucker, "enjoyed an enormous following . . . on the black theater circuit." A couple of years later, Henderson hired three white musicians to play in his band, and during a late-1943 tour of the South faced a series of problems when he tried to play in public. In one instance, like a negative photographic image of earlier discrimination, the musicians union insisted that, in order to conceal the sight of a mixed-race band in public, the whites perform in blackface.[4]

To many, Henderson seemed to lack some essential qualities that made for a good bandleader. Bushell, a careful and usually dispassionate observer, was particularly harsh on that point: "he was such a big coward . . . a nice mama's boy, like a baby." (Bushell quit the band without notice in Chicago. Substituting briefly was none other than Benny Goodman, whom Bushell refers to simply as "[o]ne of the world's worst saxophone players!") At some points, the backbone of the "Fletcher" Henderson band was really Horace. During trumpeter Roy Eldridge's stint with the band in 1936, it was Horace not Fletcher who "took care of business, worked the band into shape," according to Eldridge. "I really dug Horace."[5]

Yet Henderson liked being a bandleader because it was the job that allowed him the most autonomy, which in turn stoked his abiding taste for the road and its opportunities for extramarital liaisons. That affected both his career and his marriage. In fact, his marital problems appear to have guided some professional choices. John Hammond recalled that "[a]s Fletcher spent more and more time on the road, and with the news of other 'Mrs. Hendersons' in places like Chicago and Los Angeles filtering in, Miss Lee [as Hammond and others called Leora] took refuge in eating and grew to a formidable size." In 1941, Henderson's marriage appears to have been at a low ebb, and when his band had a chance to return to the Roseland Ballroom—"The manager came to Pittsburgh and begged Fletcher to come back"—Henderson opted to remain on tour. "He wasn't too happy home," according to Sandy Williams, "and when he was on the road he could play around." The choice inspired Williams and another band member, Peanuts Holland, to do some productive griping by writing a tune called "Let's Go Home," which naturally found its way into Benny Goodman's book. Later, Henderson's band settled in for a fifteen-month run at the Club DeLisa in Chicago, but for some reason, Henderson simply gave up the band and "disappeared," according to one band member. He headed west to Los Angeles, and made a few more arrangements, probably his last, for Benny Goodman.[6]

Henderson ultimately returned to New York, and there in his last years teamed up with former colleagues, such as Ethel Waters. After deteriorating health forced an extended break in late 1949 and the first half of 1950, Henderson came back to music and again wanted to form a band, which played brief runs at the Savoy Ballroom and in the East Village. He then composed music with J. C. Johnson for a revue called the *Jazz Train*, which portrayed the history of jazz. The collaboration led to the publication of an intimate ballad with a touch of whimsy called "Superstitions Never Worry Me." For the revue, Henderson "worked so hard," recalled Leora. "He was really trying to make a comeback—workin' days and nights on arrangements and rehearsals. But all of it was for nothing." Fletcher Henderson's last band was a sextet in residence at the Café Society, beginning December 7, 1950. The group was heard on radio broadcasts heralded by a tune that had been associated with Henderson for nearly fifteen years: "Christopher Columbus."[7]

At the Grand Terrace

"Christopher Columbus" had its origins in Henderson's revitalized band of 1936, sometimes called the "Grand Terrace band," after the south-side Chicago venue in which it played. It is likely that Goodman, who was at this point ensconced downtown at the Congress Hotel, had a hand in getting Henderson the job. The ensemble rivaled any group of musicians that ever performed under Henderson's name. Its two solo stars, tenor saxophonist Leon "Chu" Berry and trumpeter Roy Eldridge, not only shone in Henderson's band; stylistically speaking, they set the stage for Charlie Parker and Dizzy Gillespie, respectively. (Parker even gave his first son, born in January 1938, the middle name of Leon, after his idol.)

The Grand Terrace was a hot spot, packed with fans and musicians alike, including "armies of white musicians" who showed up to listen and learn.

The Grand Terrace band made several records. They offer the usual potpourri of styles, new and old tunes, pop songs and Henderson originals, and a mix of vocals and instrumentals. In other words, the recorded repertoire paints the profile of a band in residence at a swanky venue with floor show and a radio wire, like the Connie's Inn band. In this case, the repertory and style were restricted by the Grand Terrace's brutish manager, Ed Fox, who plugged material published by his own company at the expense of arrangements the band preferred.[8]

Yet in the record studio the Grand Terrace band clearly stretched beyond standard Tin Pan Alley-style fare. Two of the most remarkable tunes were blues-based: "Grand Terrace Stomp" and "Jangled Nerves." "Grand Terrace Stomp" represents a revised and utterly transformed version of Henderson's 1928 "'D' Natural Blues." The first notes of the introduction establish a relaxed swing groove, far from the mechanical, rigid phrase on the 1928 recording. Meanwhile, if Count Basie's book relied on Henderson's arrangements, "Jangled Nerves" sounds as if the influence went the other way. As a high-speed, riff-based blues head arrangement, with spectacular solos by Chu Berry and Roy Eldridge, it has all the key traits of the so-called Kansas City style as it emerged in the mid-1930s in the Bennie Moten and Basie bands. All traces of Henderson's "symphonic" blues have evaporated.

These recordings capture the Grand Terrace band's outstanding and unique qualities, but it was "Christopher Columbus" that became more closely associated with the band, and with Henderson in particular, than any other. "Christopher Columbus" represents a familiar musical phenomenon: a tune for which Henderson receives both too much credit and too little. It became a hit record for Henderson's band, and in fact, became Henderson's theme song, framing his performances up to his last appearance in the early 1950s. But this "Henderson" tune became better known and better played in Goodman's band, which in turn also made its main riff even more famous as a passage in one of Goodman's most popular flag-wavers: "Sing, Sing, Sing," arranged not by Henderson but by Jimmy Mundy. And, following another pattern in his career, when Henderson had a chance to build on the tune's success, he failed to do so.

On top of that, the tune leaves a confusing legacy of conflicting attributions. According to Allen, the tune originated as a "bawdy song" called "Cristoforo Columbo," but the popular instrumental version began with a saxophone riff developed by Chu Berry, to which Horace Henderson added a brass countermelody—or was it Roy Eldridge? Fletcher's band then began playing an arrangement at the Grand Terrace—the arrangement that Goodman soon picked up and played across town at the Congress Hotel. Solicited for a written version by Chicago publisher Joe Davis, Fletcher asked Horace to prepare a stock arrangement based on the version Fletcher's band was playing at the Grand Terrace. Horace apparently submitted a version crediting himself and Berry as co-composers. Davis then published the arrangement under the names of Leon Berry, as sole composer, and Larry Clinton, as arranger, with lyrics by Andy Razaf, the lyricist of "Honeysuckle Rose" among other hit songs. Horace received no official credit. "Chu got $300," Allen writes, "Fletcher got $100, but poor Horace got NOTHING." Nor did Roy Eldridge, who said the "brass parts" were his idea. Meanwhile, bandleader Jimmie Lunceford claimed that the tune's original riff developed within his own band. Others have made similar claims for parts of the tune. The problem remains that Walter C. Allen, who has traced the tune's origins and attributions in some detail, does not cite the sources of his information, although certain details point to Horace himself. Indeed, Horace's own account names Berry and himself as the creative forces behind the riffs, with Horace alone claiming credit for crafting the musical material into a complete piece. As so often happens in attempts to come to grips with Henderson's work, Fletcher Henderson himself remains an essential but shadowy figure in the moment and material form of musical creation.[9]

Another musical mystery of "Christopher Columbus" is how a piece whose two-voiced theme contains bone-jarring dissonances could sound so natural and become so popular (ex. 10.1). On paper, "Christopher Columbus" looks unpromising, with its jauntily rising and falling bass line (saxes and trombones) set against a simple four-note descending figure played by the trumpets. These opposing lines clash on strong beats: a major ninth on the third beat of the first measure followed on the next downbeat by a minor ninth (E♭ and E♮)—one of the most grating dissonances in western tonal music. "Weird," Horace Henderson called it with evident relish.[10]

Ex. 10.1."Christopher Columbus" (1936), chorus 1, beginning

Yet the harmonic plan and song form were familiar to Henderson and his musicians, because "Christopher Columbus" is a modified rhythm-changes tune. That is, it is yet another jazz standard based on the chords of the refrain of Gershwin's "I Got Rhythm," which had formed the basis of Henderson's earlier (and also somewhat confusingly attributed) "Yeah Man!" and "Hotter than 'Ell." While its principal melody (the "A" section of the AABA form) is grounded on alternating tonic–dominant harmony simpler than its source, the bridge ("B") comes straight from Gershwin.

"Christopher Columbus" occupied a central place in his repertory after the band took up residence at the Grand Terrace. In the summer of 1936, the Grand Terrace show featured singer Babe Matthews, who had replaced Billie Holiday after Holiday came to blows with the club's dictatorial manager Ed Fox. ("I picked up an inkwell and bam, I threw it at him and threatened to kill him," in the words of Holiday's as-told-to autobiography *Lady Sings the Blues*.) For the show's finale, the band played "Christopher Columbus" as several showgirls entered one by one and declared their vote for "king of swing." The first girl would come out and nominate Duke Ellington. Another would enter and say, "I nominate Cab Calloway for king of swing." A third would walk out and name Jimmie Lunceford. Finally, Matthews would come on and say, "I nominate Fletcher Henderson who made Christopher the thing. I think he should be crowned king of swing."

As the band continued to play, Matthews "would back up to the bandstand and get Fletcher, take him by the arm and ... come down front." At the time, Matthews had a lisp, meaning that the climactic word in her announcement came off as "thwing." Much to her dismay, this attracted the derision of Henderson's sidemen, including her childhood friend Roy Eldridge and the man who would later become her husband, trumpeter Joe Thomas. But the combination of hit song, feminine pulchritude, and a dramatic build-up of great names—all of which evoked the production values of the *Ziegfeld Follies*—proved to be a surefire closer that brought down the house. Other parts of the show came and went, according to Matthews, but the "Christopher Columbus" finale remained because it "stopped the show stone cold."[11]

"Christopher Columbus"'s wide appeal beyond the Grand Terrace can be measured by several means. Several bands—and record companies—recognized the tune's potential: Within a five-month span of 1936, thirteen bands recorded the piece on ten different labels, including one each in Paris and London. Five of those recordings ranked among the best-selling records of 1936 (by Henderson, Andy Kirk, Benny Goodman, Teddy Wilson, and Louis "King" Garcia). The piece thereafter became the Henderson orchestra's theme song, beginning and ending its radio sets from the Grand Terrace. Allen cites a 1937 article claiming that "thanks to 'Christopher Columbus,' he [Henderson] has commanded as high as $2,000 for one night." The piece became a economic boon for Henderson in a more unexpected way. A Chicago mugger released Henderson upon realizing he had held up "the man what plays Christopher Columbus."[12]

Besides being the Grand Terrace's finale and a hit record, "Christopher Columbus" also inspired new songs. Two spinoffs capitalized on its success. One was Horace Henderson's call-and-response tune, "Chris and His Gang," in which variations on the two countermelodies can be heard in dialogue, spiked with an apt, witty quotation from "Columbia, the Gem of the Ocean." The other was Jimmy Mundy's famous arrangement of Louis Prima's "Sing, Sing, Sing," into which the Goodman band incorporated an accelerated, minor-mode version of "Christopher Columbus" with yet a third countermelody laced in by Mundy. The arrangement, with Gene Krupa's primal pounding and Jess Stacy's elegant piano solo, proved to be a highlight of the 1938 Carnegie Hall concert, and the piece became as closely associated with Goodman as anything he ever played.

The fortunes of "Christopher Columbus" could have paved the way for further success for Henderson's band. Joe Thomas recalled that "Fletcher was hot. Everyone was asking for him. Duke came by one night and told him. Fletcher should have gone out on the road then, [but] by the time he got ready ... somebody else had something big, and Fletcher couldn't get started." Eldridge disdained Henderson for sharing his book, including "Christopher Columbus," with Goodman. "If it had been me Benny Goodman wouldn't have been broadcasting the same book," Eldridge said. "Don't forget that Henderson didn't spend as much time rehearsing the band as Benny did."[13]

"Christopher Columbus," then, makes an apt musical symbol for Henderson's career. The tune emerged from a collaboration of musicians whose specific individual contributions remain obscure. It became popular, linked to Fletcher Henderson's name, for many years. Benny Goodman, by then the "King of Swing" for most of the American public (despite what the

Grand Terrace show might have claimed), adopted it and gave it a more polished rendering in an arrangement credited to Fletcher, although Horace played a key role in putting the arrangement on paper. The tune's success offered Fletcher Henderson an opening through which to sustain and magnify his band and bandleading career. But at a moment when, for the first time, Henderson had found dual success as an arranger and a bandleader, he failed to jump on the opportunity, held back by what appeared to many to be an inscrutable passivity. It forms a moment of fulfillment that became another focal point of frustration to those around him.

Legacies

After suffering at least three strokes in two years, Henderson died on December 29, 1952. He had been born and married in December, had his car accident and first stroke in December, and now his death followed suit— a coincidence he had apparently predicted. "The day Fletcher died he had one of his biggest audiences out here on the street what with ambulances and the oxygen tanks," recalled Leora. "Louis Armstrong sent the most beautiful floral arrangement I've ever seen—shaped like an organ, pipes and all." The funeral took place on January 2, 1953. Several notables showed up to pay their respects, according to the *New York Age* obituary, including Count Basie, Benny Goodman, Don Redman, Andy Kirk, John Hammond, and comedian Pigmeat Markham, with whom Henderson had performed on vaudeville bills in the 1930s. Along with Goodman and Hammond, honorary pallbearers included former sidemen Red Allen, Dicky Wells, Irving Randolph, and Garvin Bushell. "Louis and Joe Glaser [Armstrong's manager] came to the funeral," recalled Leora, "and, you know, the people from Roseland sent a man up here to see how I was gettin' on."[14]

John Hammond remained loyal to "Miss Lee" until her death. Writing in the early 1960s, he described her as "an embittered though philosophical widow. A great lady, she had as many mourners as her more celebrated husband." Leora's twenty-eight-year marriage (her second) had revolved around her husband's career, and in it she had earned the respect of musicians in Fletcher's orbit by performing many crucial roles: booker, straw boss, copyist, talent scout, auditioner, and even substitute trumpet player. She probably had a hand in some arranging as well during that desperate period of late 1934. Leora died in early March 1958, and her funeral register includes the signatures of John Hammond, Walter Johnson, and Hilton Jefferson.[15]

Less than two months after Fletcher's death, Goodman organized a recording session of Henderson arrangements with the goal of compiling an entire long-playing record in tribute. Helen Ward, all of thirty-six years old, returned to sing a couple of the vocal arrangements. Among them was "I'll Never Say 'Never Again' Again," an arrangement from the 1930s that Goodman had never recorded. Knowing Goodman's strict guidelines for recording, we can only surmise that he had found something unsatisfactory about it. But now, with Ward back for a reunion with the band, Goodman dusted off the chart and found new value in it. With its rippling saxophone figures, sharply etched riffs, suave backgrounds behind Ward's swinging vocal, and a climactic ensemble variation in the final chorus, a fine new Henderson arrangement had had its premiere. In many ways, it marks the beginning of a posthumous legacy that musicians and listeners continue to absorb a half century later.

In 1957–58, the "Fletcher Henderson Reunion Band" performed at the Great South Bay Jazz Festival on Long Island, an event spearheaded by Rex Stewart. The enterprise attracted many former Henderson sidemen, including Don Redman, Coleman Hawkins, Buster Bailey, J. C. Higginbotham, Benny Morton, Garvin Bushell, Hilton Jefferson, Bernard Addison, and Joe Thomas. The program included Henderson originals and tunes on which Henderson's band had put its unique stamp: "Down South Camp Meeting," "Chinatown, My Chinatown," "Honeysuckle Rose," "Wrappin' It Up," "Shanghai Shuffle," and "King Porter Stomp." Martin Williams reviewed a return engagement in 1958 and heard in it a reaffirmation of "how much every arranger in jazz owes to Henderson and how much there is still to be learned from his terseness, directness, variety, and relating of soloists and ensemble."[16]

One member of that band was a reed player named Bob Wilber. Wilber knew Benny Goodman and played briefly in his band in the 1950s. In 1984, as Wilber was preparing a tribute concert to honor Goodman on his seventy-fifth birthday, Goodman gave him access to a cache of arrangements, among which were many unrecorded Henderson charts ranging from 1935 to 1947—the entire span of Henderson's work for Goodman. Later, in an effort to record many of these arrangements, Wilber found a band sympathetic to his cause: the Tuxedo Big Band from Toulouse, France. A compact disc titled *Bob Wilber and the Tuxedo Big Band: Fletcher Henderson's Unrecorded Arrangements for Benny Goodman* was released in 2000. Several other bandleaders and bands continue to perform Henderson's arrangements, reflecting a classicizing impulse that brings new vitality to the music. The Smithsonian Jazz Masterworks Orchestra, led by David Baker, has several Henderson arrangements in its sizeable book, including "King Porter Stomp," "Wrappin' It Up," "Hotter than 'Ell," and "Christopher Columbus." Under the direction of Wynton Marsalis, Jazz at Lincoln Center has also played many Henderson pieces. Loren Schoenberg, whose band Goodman hired en masse in the mid-1980s, continues to lead bands through performances of Henderson's charts and has been a key figure in both the Smithsonian and Lincoln Center enterprises. Bandleaders such as Vince Giordano (in New York) and James Dapogny (in Michigan) bring astonishing verve and precision to Henderson's earlier work from the 1920s and early 1930s.

John Hammond's *A Study in Frustration* record anthology, released in 1962 at a time when Hammond was cultivating the careers of folk musicians, including Bob Dylan, set a tone for Henderson's posthumous reputation and suggested the size and scope of the Henderson canon. It was clearly a key source for Gunther Schuller when writing *Early Jazz*. It included extensive liner notes by Frank Driggs reviewing Henderson's life and musical career, the most detailed account of Henderson's entire career to that date, preceded by Hammond's provocative essay ending with the famous line "no doubt about it, he was frustrated."

Whether or not Henderson was frustrated in life, his posthumous legacy shows no signs of fading away. No musician carried the torch for Henderson more than Benny Goodman, who continued to perform his arrangements for the rest of his life. Goodman's last years, in fact, reveal a concerted effort to restore the musical conditions of his initial success. By the mid-1980s, Goodman had winnowed his band's book into a core repertory of mostly Henderson arrangements, which he led through some of the most intensive, painstaking, and compulsive rehearsals ever. Along the way he pared down his band to its original 1935 size, to the point of firing three musicians, one each on trumpet, trombone, and saxophone, so that he had precisely the same numbers on reeds and brass that he had had in the *Let's Dance* band. In effect, he was doing what musicologists would call "historically informed performance practice" of Henderson's music. For Goodman this was not an archeological exercise but a restoration of his musical identity. As record producer George Avakian reported, Goodman "thought of the return to his Fletcher Henderson roots as 'being himself,' and I did, too."[17]

Within a few years of Henderson's death, rock and roll would become America's most popular music, and Elvis Presley assumed a role analogous to Benny Goodman's as the white "king" of a style saturated in African-Americanism. Meanwhile, musicians who had cut their teeth in the swing bands went on to rhythm and blues, like Louis Jordan, or bebop, like Parker and Gillespie. (Gillespie's first recorded solo in 1937, incidentally, had been on a modified version of Henderson's "King Porter Stomp" in Teddy Hill's orchestra.) Henderson, however, was not forgotten. His style of block voicing and sectional separation had already shaped Glenn Miller's book, though Miller's band developed a rich, voluptuous sound in sharp contrast to the lean, taut Goodman approach. Duke Ellington, who had claimed that upon arriving in New York in the early 1920s he had wanted nothing more than to sound like Henderson's band, continued to echo Hendersonese. Perhaps the most fascinating story of Henderson's influence relates to "Take the 'A' Train," composed for Ellington by Billy Strayhorn in 1941. Strayhorn almost destroyed the piece before even showing it to Ellington. Ellington's son Mercer recalled discovering the manuscript during a visit to Strayhorn. "I pulled a piece of his out of the garbage," Mercer noted. "I said, 'What's wrong with this?' And he said, 'That's an old thing I was trying to do something with, but it's too much like Fletcher Henderson.' I looked it over— it was '"A" Train'—and I said, 'You're right.' It was written in sections, like Fletcher Henderson. But I flattened it out anyway and put it in the pile with the rest of the stuff."[18] The piece would become the Ellington band's theme song for more than three decades.

Henderson's influence also saturates film-musical scores from the 1930s and 1940s. In the mid-1930s, Irving Berlin—a songwriter always tuned to the latest trends—laced his Fred Astaire songs "Check to Cheek" and "I'm Putting All My Eggs in One Basket" with prominent chains of syncopations. Bing Crosby's opening ballyhoo in *The Road to Zanzibar* ("You Lucky People You," 1941) is likewise accompanied by a taut swing arrangement unmistakably inflected with Hendersonese. In the next year's *Holiday Inn*, Crosby sings a blackface number called "Abraham" in front of a swing band evoking Henderson's style. No wonder the style has been called the "lingua franca" of big-band arranging.[19]

Several modern jazz musicians acknowledged and developed Henderson's legacy. An intriguing blend of Hendersonese and bebop can be heard in bop trombone pioneer J. J. Johnson's composition "Rambo," recorded by Count Basie's band in 1946. Art Blakey, the drummer whose bombs had so annoyed Horace, went on to become an influential bandleader in his own right, making his Jazz Messengers a "school" for young, ambitious players, much like Henderson had done with his band. Among the most devoted former sidemen was Herman "Sonny" Blount, who served a brief stint as Henderson's pianist in 1946–47 and went on to lead his own "arkestra" under the name of Sun Ra, playing several pieces identified with Henderson.

"King Porter Stomp," in particular, has become a touchstone for Henderson's legacy. Composer-arranger Gil Evans, who as a California teenager had absorbed Henderson's style through Goodman's Palomar broadcasts, made a modern jazz arrangement of "King Porter Stomp" that encapsulates the piece's history, alluding to Jelly Roll Morton's original as well as to Henderson's arrangement for Goodman. Composer-pianist John Lewis of the Modern Jazz Quartet wrote at least two original compositions based on the chords of "King Porters" 's stomp section: "Golden Striker" and "Odds Against Tomorrow." The chords are Morton's, but when asked what he found intriguing about a piece that dates back to the century's first decade, Lewis said, "What made 'King Porter Stomp' interesting to me was not a performance by Jelly Roll Morton or what I heard from him, but what Fletcher Henderson did. He recomposed the piece. That's what's important."[20] Singer and lyricist Jon Hendricks set lyrics—a vocalese—to Goodman's 1935 recording of "King Porter Stomp" that also playfully convey some of the piece's history dating back to Morton. Hendricks, in effect, unites the tune's three principal legends: Morton, Henderson, and Goodman. The vocal group Manhattan Transfer included Hendricks's version on its album *Swing*, issued at the height of the swing revival of the 1990s.

That revival began in southern California, so it should come as no surprise that in recent years, Henderson's arrangements—and Goodman's recordings of them—can be heard in Hollywood films evoking the 1930s and 1940s. In *Barton Fink*, for example, the struggling screenwriter celebrates his finished script by dancing to Henderson's "Down South Camp Meeting." Hendersonese also appears to be useful in conjuring the Prohibition-era underworld, as in *Miller's Crossing*, which uses "King Porter Stomp," and *The Road to Perdition*, in which a "King Porter" knockoff blares in a speakeasy while two gangsters engage in a tense back-office confrontation. The call-and-response climax accompanies a gruesome murder. Later in the film, Henderson's 1933 recording of "Queer Notions" haunts a diner scene. I have heard Henderson arrangements, usually in Benny Goodman recordings, woven into the playlists of canned music piped into bookstores and cafés and used as segue music during National Public Radio's *Morning Edition*. Henderson's music never again found the broad national following it had enjoyed for a brief period in the 1930s, but in the early twenty-first century, his legacy continues to inflect the soundtrack of American life.

Frustration or Fulfillment?

With Henderson's last years and his legacy now in view, the notion of consensus that concluded chapter 9 may seem pat. As compelling as it may be, it does not resolve the moral ambiguity in Henderson's career, in particular his famous collaboration with Benny Goodman and its aftermath. On one hand, there is something uniquely and satisfyingly American about a musical success story that brings together, during a desperate period of the nation's history, a Vanderbilt scion and two sons of America's historically most restricted and abject groups: former slaves and Russian-Jewish immigrants. On the other hand, between the key musical players, Henderson saw the greater disparity among creative effort, financial reward, and public recognition.

To conclude that Henderson's story thus forms "a study in frustration," as Hammond did, perhaps too easily casts Henderson as a victim in a familiar ritual of white-guilt expiation. To conclude, as others have, that Henderson's musical goals somehow became fulfilled in Goodman's performances, places the story in another uncomfortably familiar plotline: white agents appropriate African-American music and create a national (and international) phenomenon—which may be *the* story of twentieth-century American vernacular music. Recognizing how Henderson's story links up with such larger historical narratives makes it more than a compelling episode in American music history. It becomes a subject that we may still debate on a continuum between frustration and fulfillment.

Exploring—even living—that tension requires transcending guilt and blame. Two seemingly incompatible commentators have attempted to do that in strikingly different ways. Martin Williams's influential notion of a jazz tradition, described in this book's introduction, has tended to eclipse his more exploratory musings—his boldness in posing unanswerable questions. In an essay called "Just Asking," Williams wonders why

> a young man growing up in Chicago in the teens of [the twentieth] century, the son of Russian Jewish immigrant parents, would want … to form an orchestra that played like that of an American mulatto from Georgia named Fletcher Henderson? And stake his career in music on doing that? And after he had done that, why would the world make him a celebrity and one of the most famous musicians of the century?

Williams carries no disdain for Goodman, nor does he gloss over the asymmetries in the Henderson-Goodman collaboration. He emphatically declares his "respect for what Goodman did" and recognizes the best—and worst—of what each man brought to the music:

> it seems quite wrong to me to say that Goodman was exploiting Henderson's music.… He was playing it and conducting it with dedication and responsibility—and more precision and technical care than Henderson's own orchestra played it. Goodman was playing some of the best American music he could find in the best way he knew how.… If I do not hear the depth in Goodman's versions of "Wrappin' It Up" or "Down South Camp Meeting" that I do in Henderson's originals … I should confess such reactions. But I could not thereby accuse Goodman of deliberately popularizing or debasing the music.[21]

For Williams, the moral issue boils down to aesthetic results, and from that perspective frustration arises from a sense that neither man fully realized the music's potential, while fulfillment comes from having the comparison to make thanks to the material legacy of sound recording.

For another critic, Amiri Baraka, the moral issue hinges on social justice. Writing in *Blues People*, Baraka makes a resonant claim about the Henderson-Goodman collaboration without naming names: "The ease with which big-band jazz was subverted suggests how open an expression Negro music could become. And *no* Negro need feel ashamed of a rich Jewish clarinetist."[22] Baraka's authority would be easier to accept without its anti-Semitic overtones, for he has touched on a tradition of commentary exploring the complex and freighted interdependence of black and Jewish artists, entertainers, and expressive forms.[23] He labels Goodman the "rich Jewish clarinetist" instead of naming him so that his sociological point resonates more clearly. Like Williams, he doesn't blame Goodman, but he does disdain the social conditions that gave rise to his success. Behind the ethnically charged anger in its foreground, however, the statement embodies another delicate balancing act on the line between frustration and fulfillment: frustration that Goodman's wealth derived from playing music with African-American roots, and fulfillment in the music's power to survive and even thrive in social conditions rewarding its transformation.

Williams and Baraka face the same issue and come to opposite conclusions. For one, treating the music and musicians with honesty and respect requires discussing musical style with intelligence, knowledge, and taste. For the other, musical questions form the means to address larger social patterns, because in music he hears not just artistic expression but how people live their lives. Yet both writers recognize the Henderson-Goodman collaboration as an important intersection of social and musical currents. Both project their own feelings of frustration and fulfillment onto that collaboration and its results. Together, they remind us that, as twenty-first century observers trying to make sense of Henderson's legacy, the frustration and fulfillment are no longer Henderson's, but ours.

APPENDIX

Fletcher Henderson's Arrangements for Benny Goodman

HENDERSON'S ARRANGEMENTS for Goodman survive primarily in two collections created from bequests by Goodman: one at the Yale Music Library (Yale-BG) and the other at the New York Public Library for the Performing Arts (NYPL-BG). In a few instances, Goodman is known to have played (and even recorded) a Henderson arrangement that does not appear in any of the collections, such as "Alexander's Ragtime Band" and "I Want to Be Happy." In his book *Hendersonia*, Walter C. Allen lists several "Other arrangements not credited, but which should be investigated as possible FH arrangements" (see pp. 525–26), but only one of those, "Absence Makes the Heart Grow Fonder," is among the material Goodman bequeathed to Yale and the NYPL. The exact scope and contents of Henderson's work, then, remain elusive. Yet since Goodman's death, we have a clearer picture of Henderson's vast output than ever before.

Three resources provided valuable models and information: *Yale University Music Library Archival Collection MSS 53: The Papers of Benny Goodman,* compiled by David A. Gier with the assistance of James John and consultant Loren Schoenberg; an unpublished list compiled by Andrew Homzy; and Andrew Homzy and Ken Druker's *Jazz Orchestrations: A Resource List.* As these sources profile the physical makeup of the material (such as the precise number and nature of the instrumental parts), the following focuses more on musical contents.

The list of arrangements provides the following information:

Title: The title is given as it appears on the arrangement. When the actual song title is known to differ, the discrepancy is noted in brackets.

Songwriters: Songwriter names have been gleaned chiefly from Connor and through ACE title searches at the ASCAP website (http://www.ascap.com/ace/ACE.html).

Location: An arrangement's current location is given in abbreviated form, almost always either Yale-BG or NYPL-BG, followed by the box and/or folder number.

Date: Dates for most arrangements have been determined or estimated in the lists by Yale University, Andrew Homzy, and Ken Druker; Connor's bio-discography also helps establish dates by showing when arrangements were played in public, on radio, or on record. Internal evidence includes: the copyist's stamp on the manuscript, showing the current year through which union dues have been paid; the number of parts, since Goodman gradually added more musicians to his band over the years of Henderson's involvement; and paper types, which often help to corroborate dates found otherwise, especially when at least one manuscript in that paper type has a union copyist's date stamped on it. (No systematic study of paper types has been attempted.) Knowledge of the year in which the song was published can also be helpful in establishing at least an approximate date for an arrangement.

Form: The arrangements' formal outlines are based on the following key:

I = Introduction

A, B, C = principal formal divisions of arrangement (usually thirty-two-bar song form, sometimes twelve-bar blues or sixteen-bar strain)

a, b, c = subsections of chorus, usually four or eight bars in length

X = transition, or interlude

T = tag ending

Numbers in parentheses indicate number of measures in each section.

Keys: This item shows the progression of keys from chorus to chorus, separated by commas (for example, D, G, E♭); an en-dash indicates a modulation within a chorus (for example, E♭–A♭). One of Henderson's distinguishing marks as an arranger was his tendency to write in unusual keys and to include one or more modulations in a piece.

Vocal: The words "yes" or "no" indicate whether or not the arrangement includes singing. Although Goodman reportedly disdained singers and saw purely instrumental music as more jazz worthy, roughly one-third of Henderson's arrangements include at least one chorus for a singer.

Solos: Instrument names indicate the order in which solos appear. Henderson's arrangements designate instrumental solos usually with the phrase "ad-lib" or "solo" written above a staff showing the original melody to be improvised upon.

Notes: This item provides miscellaneous information gleaned from the scores and parts and from Connor's information about performances. Connor's book and my own listening have been the sources for notes about documented performances. The phrase "no documented performances" does not mean the arrangement was never played, but its perhaps surprising frequency does suggest that much of Henderson's work for Goodman remains virtually unheard.

Absence Makes the Heart Grow Fonder
(Sam M. Lewis, Joe Young,
  Harry Warren)
Yale-BG 1/1
Date: ca. 1939
Form: I(4) A(35, aaba) A(32) A(32)
Keys: A, Db
Vocal: yes
Solos: clarinet, trumpet
Notes: The final eight bars comprise a pattern that became a familiar sign-off in Henderson's 1940s arrangements: a sectional (or ensemble) soli variation, followed by a brief Goodman solo, and punctuated by a full-ensemble cadence (cf. "Behave Yourself," "Birds of a Feather," "Blue and Broken Hearted," "Every Sunday Afternoon," "I May Be Wrong"). Connor documents a single performance, on radio, in October 1939.

After I Say I'm Sorry
(Walter Donaldson, Abe Lyman)
Yale-BG 1/7
Date: ca. 1945
Form: I(6) A(32, abac) X(3) A(32) A(16)
Keys: A, D
Vocal: yes
Solo: clarinet
Notes: Goodman performed this song more in small groups than with big band.

After You've Gone
(Henry Creamer, Turner Layton)
Yale-BG 1/8A
Date: 1939
Form: I(4) A(40, abacd) A(38) A(38)
  A(22)
Keys: Db, F
Vocal: no
Solos: trombone, trumpet
Notes: No "Benny" part included, but several parts indicate, in pencil, a clarinet solo in the third chorus, which was repeated. Connor documents several performances, but only one recording, in 1942.

Ain't She Pretty
Yale-BG 1/10
Date: 1947?
Form: I(4) A(32, abac) X(5) A(32) A(32)
Keys: C, Db
Vocal: yes
Solos: clarinet
Notes: No documented performances.

All My Life
(Sidney D. Mitchell, Sam T. Stept)
Yale-BG 1/16
Date: 1936

Form: I(4) A(36, aabac) A(36) A(16)
Keys: Ab, Bb, G
Vocal: yes
Solo: clarinet
Notes: First recording by Bob Wilber and the Tuxedo Big Band, 2000.

Allah's Holiday
(Rudolf Friml, Otto Harbach)
Yale-BG 1/23
Date: 1940
Form: I(4) A(33, aaba) A(32) A(32)
Keys: E, Ab, Db
Vocal: no
Solos: clarinet, tenor sax
Notes: No documented performances.

Am I Blue?
(Harry Akst, Grant Clarke)
Yale-BG 1/27, 1/28, 1/28A
Date: 1935 (rev. 1946)
Form: I(4) A(34, aaba) A(35) A(34)
Keys: Ab, Bb, Ab (rev. Db)
Vocal: yes
Solos: clarinet, trumpet
Notes: 1946 revision features just two choruses (one vocal) in Db. Four documented performances in the 1935–49 period, and in rehearsal during Goodman's final year, when he revisited and intensely rehearsed many of Henderson's arrangements with his last band.

Baby
(Dorothy Fields, Jimmy McHugh)
NYPL-BG 69
Date: 1947
Form: I(4) A(32, aaba) X(4) A(32) X(4)
  A(32) T(10)
Keys: Db, Bb, Eb
Vocal: no
Solos: clarinet, trombone, tenor sax,
  trumpet
Notes: No documented performances.

Baby, Won't You Please Come Home?
(Charles Warfield, Clarence Williams)
NYPL-BG 70
Date: 1945?
Form: I(4) A(18) X(3) A(18) X(3) A(18)
  A(16 + 5)
Keys: C, Eb, Bb
Vocal: no
Solos: clarinet, trombone, trumpet
Notes: Solos written out; parts marked up with articulations, dynamics, and tied notes to be shortened. Recorded in 1945.

Back in Your Own Backyard
(Billy Rose, Al Jolson, Dave Dreyer)
NYPL-BG 375
Date: 1947
Form: I(4) A(34, aaba) A(32) X(4)
　A(32)
Keys: D♭, F, B♭
Vocal: yes
Solo: clarinet
Notes: Recorded in 1947 and 1958.
Connor shows no vocal used in
performances.

Basin Street Blues
(Spencer Williams)
Yale-BG 2/26
Date: 1935
Form: I(2) A(16) B(16) C(12) B(16)
　B(14) A(8)
Key: B♭
Vocal: yes
Solos: clarinet, trombone, trumpet
Notes: Folder includes parts only, in
Leora Henderson's hand. Most parts
have pencil-marked cuts for intro-
duction (marked "optional") and for the
last "B" section—cuts that Goodman
makes in the band's November 22,
1935, recording. Goodman recorded
the arrangement again in 1951 for
an LP record dedicated
to Henderson.

Basin Street Blues
(Spencer Williams)
Yale-BG 2/27
Date: 1935
Form: A(16) B(16) C(12) C'(12)
Key: B♭
Vocal: no
Solos: none
Notes: Folder includes score only,
but it is a different arrangement
from 2/26. Appears to be in
Henderson's hand.

Begin the Beguine
(Cole Porter)
Yale-BG 2/32
Date: 1939
Form: I(4) A(96, aa'bacc') T(6)
Key: D♭
Vocal: no
Solos: clarinet, tenor sax
Notes: Only one documented
performance, on radio in 1939. Given
Porter's extended refrain—three times
the conventional length—Henderson
arranges just one complete statement.
The alto sax 1 part contains evocative
marking in pencil over a six-bar phrase:
"a deep beauty of a breath."

Behave Yourself
(Alex Kramer, Joan Whitney)
Yale-BG 2/33
Date: 1947
Form: I(4) A(32, aaba) X(4) A(32) A(33)
Keys: B♭, F, D♭
Vocal: yes
Solo: clarinet
Notes: No documented performances.

**Between the Devil and the Deep
Blue Sea**
(Harold Arlen, Ted Koehler)
Yale-BG 3/10
Date: 1935
Form: I(4) A(32, aaba) X(4) A(32) A(37)
Keys: F, A♭
Vocal: yes
Solos: clarinet, trumpet
Notes: One of Goodman's most
frequently performed vocal charts over
fifty years (see chap. 9). This version,
"Transcribed by Sy Johnson 9/85 For:
Benny Goodman/PBS special."

Birds of a Feather
(Johnny Burke, Jimmy Van Heusen)
Yale-BG 3/16
Date: 1941
Form: I(8) A(32, aaba) X(4) A(32) X(4)
　A(32)
Keys: E♭, A, A♭
Vocal: yes
Solos: alto sax, clarinet, tenor sax
Notes: Recorded in 1941.

Blue and Broken Hearted
(Grant Clarke, Lou Handman,
　Edgar Leslie)
Yale-BG 3/20
Date: 1947
Form: I(4) A(32, abac) A(32) A(32)
Keys: D♭, D
Vocal: no
Solos: clarinet, trumpet, tenor sax
Notes: First recording by Bob Wilber and
the Tuxedo Big Band, 2000.

Blue Room
(Richard Rodgers, Lorenz Hart)
Yale-BG 3/27, 3/27A
Date: 1938
Form: I(4) A(32, aaba) X(4) A(32) X(4)
　A(35)
Keys: A♭, D♭, B♭
Vocal: no
Solos: clarinet, trumpet (alternative to
　clarinet in final chorus bridge)
Notes: Recorded in 1938. Several parts
suggest that Harry James set the tempo for
this arrangement, with penciled phrases
such as "Harry," "James Beat," and (on
trumpet 1 part) "Me Doctor the first."

Blue Skies
(Irving Berlin)
Yale-BG 4/2, 4/6A
Date: 1935
Form: I(8) A(32, aaba) A(32) A(32)
  A(32)
Keys: D, G, E♭
Vocal: no
Solos: trumpet, clarinet
Notes: One of Goodman's favorite
Henderson arrangements (see chap. 9),
performed frequently from 1935
onward, including the 1938 Carnegie
Hall concert. Parts contain many pencil
notations, including specific dynamic
and articulation marks, cuts in chorus 3
(probably for radio performances),
and the phrase "*pp* soft for announce-
ment" above the introduction of
trumpet 1 part, also suggesting radio
accommodation.

The Blues Jumped Up and Got Me
(Edward James Davis, Jack Hoffman)
Yale-BG 4/11
Date: 1946
Form: I(4) A(32, aaba) A(32) A(17)
Key: G
Vocal: yes
Solos: clarinet, tenor sax
Notes: Recorded in 1947.

Bolero
(Maurice Ravel)
Yale-BG 4/14, 4/15
Date: 1939
Form: A(33) B(26) C(35)
Key: C
Vocal: no
Solo: clarinet

Breakin' in a Pair of Shoes
(Ned Washington, Dave Franklin,
  Sam H. Stept)
Yale-BG 4/24
Date: 1936
Form: I(8) A(32, aaba) A(32) A(32)
  A(8)
Keys: A♭, D♭, B♭
Vocal: no
Solos: clarinet, tenor sax, trombone
Notes: See chap. 9.

Buds Won't Bud
(Harold Arlen, E. Y. Harburg)
Yale-BG 4/30
Date: 1940
Form: I(4) A(32) X(4) A(35) A(33)
Keys: G, C, A♭
Vocal: yes
Solos: clarinet, tenor sax
Notes: Recorded in 1940.

Can't Get Out of This Mood
(William W. Wolfer)
Yale-BG 5/11
Date: ca. 1939
Form: I(6) A(35, abab') A(32) X(5) A(17)
Keys: D♭, G
Vocal: no
Solos: none
Notes: No documented performances. A
typical ballad treatment, with muted
brass, soft saxes, and no solos.

Can't We Be Friends
(Paul James, Kay Swift)
Yale-BG 5/12, 5/12A
Date: 1935
Form: I(4) A(32, aaba) A(32) A(32)
Keys: B♭, E♭, F–D♭
Vocal: no
Solos: clarinet, alto sax
Notes: One of Henderson's earliest
arrangements for Goodman, recorded in
1935 and 1937, and revisited regularly by
Goodman over the next fifty years.

Careless
(Lew Qualding, Eddy Howard,
  Dick Jurgens)
Yale-BG 5/16
Date: 1940
Form: I(4) A(34, abac) A(32) A(32)
Keys: D♭, B♭
Vocal: yes
Solos: clarinet, tenor sax
Notes: No documented performances,
but parts indicate substantial cuts in first
and last choruses, suggesting a perfor-
mance emphasizing the second chorus
vocal.

Chicago
(Fred Fisher)
Yale-BG, 5/24, 5/24A
Date: 1935
Form: I(4) A(34, abac) A(32) A(34) A(16)
Keys: F, A♭, G
Vocal: no
Solos: clarinet, trumpet, alto sax
Notes: Credited to Horace Henderson in
Connor (pp. 47, 76), but score (5/24)
appears to be in Fletcher's hand.
Featured early in the *Let's Dance* run;
recorded in 1937.

Ciribiribin
(Alberto Pestalozza)
Yale-BG 5/28
Date: 1938
Form: I(4) A(34, abac) A(34) A(12)
Keys: G, B♭
Vocal: no

Ciribiribin *(continued)*
Solos: clarinet, tenor sax
Notes: Score is incomplete. Featured on radio, then recorded in 1938.

Clap Your Hands
(George and Ira Gershwin)
Yale-BG 5/29
Date: 1936
Form: I(4) A(32, aaba) X(4) A(34) A(33)
Keys: A♭, C
Vocal: no
Solos: clarinet, tenor sax
Notes: One documented radio performance, 1939.

Close as Pages in a Book
(Sigmund Romberg, Dorothy Fields)
Yale-BG 6/7
Date: 1945
Form: I(6) A(35, abac) A(32) T(5)
Key: B♭
Vocal: yes
Solos: trombone, clarinet
Notes: Structure and markings indicate high-class ballad conception, with vocal dominant and parts saturated with dynamic nuances as soft as *pppp*. Radio performances in 1945.

Coquette
(Gus Kahn, Carmen Lombardo, Johnny Green)
NYPL-BG 392
Date: mid-1939–mid-1940
Form: I(4) A(32, aaba) A(32) X(4) A(32)
Keys: E♭, D♭, G♭
Vocal: no
Solos: clarinet, alto sax, trombone, trumpet
Notes: With three trombone parts, the arrangement dates from between August 23, 1939, when Ted Vesely started as third trombone, and July 3, 1940, when BG orchestra disbanded due to Goodman's sciatica problem and operation at Mayo Clinic. Parts labeled with band members' names: Ziggy [Elman], Jimmy [Maxwell], trumpets; Red [Ballard], Ted [Vesely], and Vernon [Brown], trombones. The only documented performance dates from Feb. 1986, four months before Goodman's death.

Crazy Rhythm
(Irving Caesar, Joseph Meyer, Roger Kahn)
Yale-BG 6/31
Date: 1939
Form: I(4) A(34, aaba) A(32) A(32) A(32)

Keys: B♭, E♭, D♭
Vocal: no
Solos: clarinet, piano, tenor sax, trumpet, trombone
Notes: Solo-dominated "hot" arrangement recorded in 1940.

Daddy's Boy
Yale-BG, 6/35
Date: 1935
Form: I2 A(32, aaba) X(4) A(32) X(4) A(24)
Keys: E♭, D♭–C
Vocal: yes
Solos: trumpet, trombone, tenor sax
Notes: Score appears to be in Henderson's hand, but messier, possibly hurried: it has no meter marking, no "Benny" part, and only one trombone part. First chorus features rare clarinet soli. No documented performances.

Don't Blame Me
(Jimmy McHugh, Dorothy Fields)
Yale-BG 7/22
Date: 1945
Form: I(4) A(32, aaba) X(4) A(32) A(18) T(4)
Keys: D, A♭
Vocal: no
Solos: tenor sax, clarinet
Notes: Features elegant variations on the melody; never recorded.

Double Trouble
(Ralph Rainger, Leo Robin, Richard Whiting)
Yale-BG 7/33
Date: ca. 1936
Form: I(4) A(32, aaba) A(30) X(4) A(32) T(8)
Keys: E♭, G
Vocal: no
Solos: clarinet, trumpet, alto sax
Notes: Uptempo swinger with highly syncopated theme. No documented performances.

Down South Camp Meeting
(Fletcher Henderson)
NYPL-BG 26, 27 and Yale-BG 8/1, 8/1A
Date: 1936
Form: I(4) A(24, aba) A(24) X(8) B(32, aaba) B(32) X(4) C(32) C(17)
Keys: C, A♭, D♭
Vocal: no
Solo: clarinet
Notes: One of Henderson's "big arrangements," as Goodman called them, which Goodman played throughout his career. NYPL-BG 26 contains score "taken from record by Bill Fontaine—March 1953."

All other folders contain parts. See chaps. 8 and 9.

Every Sunday Afternoon
(Richard Rodgers, Lorenz Hart)
Yale-BG 8/25
Date: 1940
Form: I(4) A(31, aaba) X(3) A(32) A(32)
Keys: A, D♭, G♭
Vocal: yes
Solos: clarinet
Notes: Features brass variations based on chain of syncopation device; three brief clarinet solo passages are fully composed. Recorded in 1940.

Everything Is Okey Dokey
(John Jacob Loeb)
Yale-BG 8/31
Date: 1936
Form: I(4) A(32, aaba) A(31) X(4) A(32) A(16)
Keys: E♭, C, F, A♭
Vocal: yes
Solos: clarinet
Notes: Sprightly pop arrangement that names the singer Joe Harris for the vocal chorus. No documented performances.

Fascinatin' Rhythm
(George and Ira Gershwin)
Yale-BG 8/41
Date: 1939?
Form: I(4) A(32, abac) A(34) A(32)
Keys: E♭, A♭, F
Vocal: no
Solos: clarinet, trumpet, alto sax
Notes: Solo-dominated arrangement. Not recorded until 1945, but parts suggest earlier origins (with four instead of five saxes, and three instead of four trumpets).

Five O'Clock Whistle
(Josef Myrow, Kim Gannon, Gene Irwin)
Yale-BG 9/11
Date: 1940
Form: I(4) A(36, aaba) X(4) A(32) A(32)
Keys: B♭, E♭, D♭
Vocal: yes
Solos: clarinet
Notes: No documented performances.

Fletcher's Tune
(Fletcher Henderson)
NYPL-BG JPB 80–37 82
Date: 1940
Form: I(8) A(32, aaba) A(32) A(32) X(8) A(32)
Keys: D♭, G, C
Vocal: no
Solos: clarinet, trombone
Notes: No documented performances.

Frenesi
(Alberto Dominguez, Leonard Whitcup)
Yale-BG 9/25a
Date: 1941
Form: I(4) A(32, aaba') A(32) X(4) A(32)
Keys: D♭, D
Vocal: no
Solos: clarinet, trombone

From Another World
(Richard Rodgers, Lorenz Hart)
NYPL-BG 33, 34
Date: 1940
Form: I(4) A(32, aaba) X(4) A(32) A(16)
Keys: G, E♭
Vocal: yes
Solos: clarinet
Notes: Ballad treatment featuring constant variation of main melody ("a"). No documented performances.

Get Rhythm in Your Feet
(J. Russel Robinson, Bill Livingston)
Yale-BG 10/4 and NYPL-BG 34
Date: 1935
Form: I(4) A(31, aaba) X(5) A(30) X(4) A(32)
Keys: G, B♭
Vocal: yes
Solos: clarinet
Notes: Taut, syncopated vocal arrangement similar to "Between the Devil and the Deep Blue Sea." Recorded in 1935.

Goody Goodbye
(James Cavanaugh, Nat Simon)
Yale BG 10/25
Date: 1939?
Form: I(4) A(36, abac) A(30) X(5) A(34)
Keys: F, C, E♭
Vocal: yes
Solos: alto sax, clarinet
Notes: No documented performances.

Gotta Get Some Shut Eye
(Walter Donaldson, John H. Mercer)
Yale-BG 10/32
Date: 1939
Form: I(4) A(34, aaba) A(32) A(32)
Keys: G, A♭
Vocal: yes
Solos: clarinet, trumpet, tenor sax
Notes: Features animated dialogue of brass and saxes in melodic and accompanimental textures. No documented performances.

Great Day
(Vincent Youmans, Edward Eliscu, Billy Rose)
NYPL-BG 85

Great Day *(continued)*
Date: 1947
Form: I(7) A(32, abca) A(32) X(6) A(32)
    T(4)
Keys: D♭, B♭
Vocal: no
Solos: clarinet, tenor sax
Notes: Recorded in 1964.

Hallelujah!
(Vincent Youmans, Clifford Grey,
    Leo Robin)
Yale-BG 11/3
Date: 1935
Form: I(4) A(36, aaba) X(4) A(32) A(16)
Keys: F, E♭
Vocal: no
Solos: clarinet
Notes: "Dancers" written on "Benny"
part after first chorus (cf. "I Found a
New Baby"), suggesting action in the
Let's Dance studio. Recorded in 1937.

Have You Forgotten So Soon
(Dana Suesse, Leo Robin, Nat Shilkret)
Yale-BG 11/12
Date: 1938
Form: I(4) A(36, aaba) X(5) A(39)
Keys: G, B♭
Vocal: yes
Solos: clarinet
Notes: No documented performances.

Honeysuckle Rose
(Fats Waller, Andy Razaf)
Institute for Jazz Studies
Date: 1939
Form: I(4) A(32, aaba) A(32) A(32)
    A(32) A(32) A(32) A(32)
Key: D♭
Vocal: no
Solos: clarinet, trumpet
Notes: Transcription, but not of Good-
man's 1939 recording. See chaps. 8 and 9.

How High the Moon
(Morgan Lewis, Nancy Hamilton)
Yale-BG 11/31
Date: 1947
Form: I(4) A(32, abac) A(34) A(32)
Keys: B♭, D♭
Vocal: no
Solos: trumpet, clarinet
Notes: No documented performances.

Howd'ja Like to Love Me
(Burton Lane, Frank Loesser)
Yale-BG 11/34
Date: 1938
Form: I(4) A(38, aabac) A(44) A(20)
Keys: B♭, F, B♭
Vocal: "optional"

Solos: trombone, tenor sax, trumpet
Notes: Radio performance in 1938. Parts
bear union stamp of Leora Henderson.

Humoresque
(Antonin Dvořák)
Yale-BG 11/36
Date: 1941
Form: I(4) A(16) B(16) C(16) D(16)
    E(16) F(18)
Keys: G♭, F♯ min, A
Vocal: no
Solos: clarinet, tenor sax
Notes: First recording by Bob Wilber and
the Tuxedo Big Band, 2002.

**I Can't Believe That You're in Love
With Me**
(Jimmy McHugh, Clarence Gaskill)
NYPL-BG 175
Date: 1935
Form: I(4) A(32, aaba) A(34) A(32)
Keys: D♭, A♭
Vocal: no
Solos: clarinet, trumpet, tenor sax,
    drums
Notes: One of Henderson's earliest
arrangements for Goodman's *Let's
Dance* band, and a particularly vivid
example of Leora's loopy hand.
Performed on radio, but never recorded.

I Can't Give You Anything But Love
(Jimmy McHugh, Dorothy Fields)
NYPL-BG 383, 384
Date: 1935
Form: I(4) A(32, abac) X(4) A(32) X(6)
    A(32) X(4) A(32)
Keys: A♭, C, A♭
Vocal: yes? (crossed out on score)
Solos: trumpet, piano, clarinet
Notes: Effective exemplar of a Hender-
son trademark: creating rhythmic tension
by alternating between straight quarter
notes and chains of syncopation.
Recorded in 1935.

I Can't Love You Anymore
(Herb Magidson, Allie Wrubel)
Yale-BG 11/45
Date: 1940
Form: I(4) A(16) X(4) A(16) X(4) A(16)
    A(16) A(16) A(19)
Keys: G, C, A♭
Vocal: yes
Solos: clarinet, alto sax
Notes: Recorded in 1940.

I Got Rhythm
(George and Ira Gershwin)
Yale-BG 12/12
Date: 1935

Form: I(4) A(33, aaba) X(4) A(34) A(34)
A(34) A(34)
Key: B♭
Vocal: no
Solos: clarinet, trumpet
Notes: Goodman tended to feature the
tune in small-group performances, but
one full-band version appeared on radio
in summer 1937. Henderson's arrangement is an uptempo, five-chorus hot
number with several intricate variations
on Gershwin's tune.

I Had to Do It
(Fats Waller, Andy Razaf)
Yale-BG 12/15
Date: 1938
Form: I(4) A(34, aaba) A(32) A(16)
Keys: A♭, D♭
Vocal: yes
Solos: clarinet
Notes: Recorded in 1938.

I Happen to Be in Love
(Cole Porter)
Yale-BG 12/16
Date: 1939–40.
Form: I(4) A(32, aaba) X(4) A(33) A(32)
T(4)
Keys: E♭, C, A♭
Vocal: yes
Solos: alto sax, clarinet, trumpet
Notes: No documented performances.

I Hate to Lose You
(Archie Gottler, Grant Clarke)
Yale-BG 12/17
Date: 1947
Form: I(4) A(32, abac) A(32) T(8)
Key: C
Vocal: yes
Solos: clarinet, tenor sax
Notes: Recorded in 1947.

I Have Eyes
(Leo Robin, Ralph Rainger)
Yale-BG 12/19
Date: 1938
Form: I(4) A(34, aaba) A(32) A(16)
Key: C
Vocal: yes
Solos: clarinet, tenor sax
Notes: Recorded in 1938.

I Haven't Time to Be a Millionaire
(James V. Monaco, Johnny Burke)
Yale-BG 12/20
Date: 1939
Form: I(4) A(36, abca') X(4) A(36) X(4)
A(36) T(12) [=a']
Keys: B♭, F, D
Vocal: yes

Solos: clarinet, trumpet, piano
Notes: Uptempo rhythm tune with vocal,
unusually, reserved for last full chorus.
No documented performances.

I Hear Bluebirds
(Charles Tobias, Harry M. Woods)
Yale-BG 12/22
Date: 1939
Form: I(4) A(32, aaba) A(32) X(4) A(35)
A(17)
Keys: G, C, A♭
Vocal: yes
Solo: clarinet
Notes: No documented performances.

I Know That You Know
(Vincent Youmans, Anne Caldwell)
Yale-BG 12/25
Date: 1936
Form: I(4) A(32, abac) B(32, aaba) A(32)
X(4) A(32)
Keys: D♭, E♭–A♭
Vocal: no
Solos: clarinet
Notes: A standard in Goodman's book,
recorded in 1935 and 1936 and played
many times thereafter. Baritone sax and
"Benny" parts include additional chorus
of telegraphic riffs to be inserted after
"B," suggesting post-1940 addition.

I May Be Wrong (But I Think You're Beautiful)
(Harry Ruskin, Henry Sullivan)
NYPL-BG 387
Date: 1946
Form: I(4) A(32, aaba) A(32) A(32)
Keys: A♭, D♭
Vocal: no
Solos: clarinet, trombone
Notes: One documented performance
on radio, 1946. Clarinet solo passages
marked by active, punchy figures, riffs,
and syncopated chains.

I Never Knew
(Gus Kahn, Ted Fiorito)
NYPL-BG 388
Date: 1935
Form: I(6) A(30, aaba) X(4) A(32)
A(32)
Keys: D♭, E♭–A♭
Vocal: no
Solos: trombone, clarinet, trumpet
Notes: Exemplar of Henderson's ballad
style, including rhythmless introduction
and solo trombone melody. The 1935
recording, however, adds drum brushes
in the introduction.

I Wish I Had You
(Bud Green, Al Stillman,
    Claude Thornhill)
Yale-BG 13/11
Date: 1938
Form: I(4) A(33, abac) A(32) A(33)
Keys: E♭, B♭
Vocal: yes
Solos: clarinet, tenor sax, trumpet
Notes: No documented performances.

I Would Do Anything for You
(Alex Hill, Roberto Williams,
    Claude Hopkins)
Yale-BG 13/18
Date: 1935
Form: I(4) A(32, aaba) A(32) A(32) A(32)
Keys: E♭, C
Vocal: no
Solos: clarinet, trumpets 1 and 2,
    tenor sax
Notes: A standard in Goodman's book,
first recorded in June 1935 and performed
many times thereafter. See chap. 9.

I'll Never Say "Never Again" Again
(Harry Woods)
NYPL-BG 46
Date: late 1930s?
Form: I(4) A(33, aaba) A(32) A(32) A(16)
Keys: A♭, D♭
Vocal: yes
Solo: clarinet
Notes: Goodman apparently did not
perform the arrangement until after
Henderson's death. See chap. 10.

I'm Comin' Virginia
(Donald Heywood, Will Marion Cook)
Yale-BG 13/29
Date: 1940
Form: I(4) A(24, abc) B(26) A(26) A(24)
    A(26)
Keys: D♭, G♭, E♭, A♭
Vocal: no
Solos: clarinet, alto sax, trumpet
Notes: Goodman performed this stan-
dard many times, but rarely, if ever,
Henderson's arrangement of it.

**I'm Gonna Sit Right Down and Write
Myself a Letter**
(Joe Young, Fred E. Ahlert)
Yale-BG 13/33
Date: 1946
Form: I(4) A(32, abac) A(34) A(32)
Keys: D♭, G
Vocal: no
Solos: clarinet, trumpet, tenor sax
Notes: Goodman solo in final chorus
spiked with chains of syncopations in
saxes. Recorded in 1952.

I'm in a Crying Mood
Yale-BG 13/36
Date: 1947
Form: I(4) A(32, aaba) A(32)
Key: C
Vocal: no
Solos: none
Notes: Parts for piano, guitar, bass, and
drums only.

I've Found a New Baby
(Spencer Williams, Jack Palmer)
Yale-BG 12/6
Date: 1935
Form: I(16) A(32, aaba) A(32) A(32)
    A(32)
Keys: E♭, G
Vocal: no
Solos: clarinet, trumpet, alto sax
Notes: "Dancers" written on alto sax
part, above mm. 3–4 of 2nd chorus
(cf. "Hallelujah"). See chap. 9.

I've Got a Feeling I'm Falling
(Fats Waller, Harry Link, Billy Rose)
Yale-BG 13/49
Date: 1935
Form: I(4) A(32, aaba) X(4) A(32) A(16)
Keys: A♭, B♭
Vocal: yes
Solo: clarinet
Notes: Documented performances
include only a radio broadcast early in
Let's Dance (January 1935) and one
recording after Henderson's death (1953).

I've Got a Heavy Date
(Johnny Green)
Yale-BG 13/50
Date: 1936
Form: I(4) A(35, aaba) A(32) A(33)
Keys: E♭, G
Vocal: yes
Solos: clarinet, tenor sax
Notes: No documented performances.

If I Could Be With You
(Henry Creamer, James P. Johnson)
NYPL-BG 390
Date: 1935
Form: I(4) A(18, aa') A(18) A(18) A(18)
    A(18)
Key: D♭
Vocal: no
Solos: clarinet, alto sax, piano
Notes: Recorded twice in 1935.
Arrangement's piano solo slot taken by
guitar on record.

If I Had You
(Ted Shapiro, Jimmy Campbell,
    Reg Connelly)

Yale-BG 14/8
Date: 1939
Form: I(4) A(32, aaba) A(34) A(34) A(32)
Keys: D♭, G, E♭
Vocal: no
Solos: clarinet, trombone, tenor sax,
    piano, trumpet
Notes: Goodman played the tune chiefly
in small-group formats.

If It's Good
Yale-BG 14/12
Date: 1938
Form: I(4) A(18, aaba) B(38, aaba) B'(41)
Key: A♭
Vocal: yes
Solo: clarinet
Notes: Rare arrangement that includes
song's verse (A).

In the Mood
(Joe Garland, Andy Razaf)
Yale-BG 14/28
Date: 1940
Form: I(4) A(12) A(12) B(16) B'(16)
    A(12) A(12) A(12) A(12 + 6)
Key: A♭
Vocal: no
Solo: clarinet
Notes: Similar in format and style to
Glenn Miller version. Performed on radio
in 1939–40 but never recorded.

In the Shade of the Old Apple Tree
(Egbert Van Alstyne, Harry Williams)
Yale-BG 14/29
Date: 1937
Form: I(4) A(32, abac) A(32) X(4) A(32)
Keys: A♭, C
Vocal: no
Solos: trumpet, clarinet
Notes: Unusual scoring features clarinet
solo accompanied by clarinets (second
chorus) and muted trumpet solo accom-
panied by chromatic slides in saxes (final
chorus). Occasional radio feature in late
1930s but never recorded.

Indiana
(James F. Hanley, Ballard MacDonald)
NYPL-BG 184
Date: 1935
Form: I(4) A(32, abac) A(32) A(32)
Key: B♭
Vocal: no
Solos: trombone, clarinet
Notes: Recorded in 1935.

It's an Old Southern Custom
(Jack Yellen, Joseph Meyer)
Yale-BG 15/1
Date: 1935

Form: I(4) A(30, aaba) X(4) A(32) A(34)
Keys: F, B♭
Vocal: yes
Solos: clarinet, trumpet
Notes: Dates from *Let's Dance* period
but never recorded.

It's Been So Long
(Walter Donaldson, Harold Adamson)
NYPL-BG 185, 186
Date: 1947
Form: I(4) A(32, abac) A(32) X(4) A(32)
Keys: A♭, B♭
Vocal: yes (on parts [186] only)
Solos: clarinet, tenor sax
Notes: Recorded in 1936 with Helen
Ward and revisited after Henderson's
death, including soundtrack for film *The
Benny Goodman Story* (1955).

It's Never Too Late
(John Jacob Loeb, Carmen Lombardo)
Yale-BG 15/9
Date: 1939
Form: I(4) A(34, abac) A(34) A(32)
Keys: C, B♭
Vocal: yes
Solos: clarinet, tenor sax, trumpet
Notes: In first chorus, Henderson un-
characteristically divides the trumpets
and trombones into discrete sections
instead of arranging them as one block
of brass. Radio performance in 1939 but
not recorded.

It's Wonderful
(Stuff Smith, Mitchell Parish)
Yale-BG 15/22
Date: 1937
Form: I(4) A(34, aaba) A(32) A(16)
Keys: F, C, A–A♭
Vocal: yes
Solos: clarinet, tenor sax
Notes: All parts marked in pencil to cut
the introduction and all but last eight
bars of first chorus. Two documented
performances, both in December 1937
(one recording, one radio).

Jumpin' Jive
(Cab Calloway, Frank Froeba, Jack
    Palmer)
Yale-BG 15/32
Date: 1939
Form: I(4) A(38, aaba') A(38) A(38)
Keys: E♭, B♭, A♭
Vocal: yes
Solos: clarinet, trumpet
Notes: Two documented radio
performances in September 1939;
no recordings.

Just Like Taking Candy from a Baby
(Fred Astaire, Gladys Shelley)
Yale-BG 15/36
Date: 1940
Form: I(4) A(32, abac) A(36) A(32)
Keys: D♭, F
Vocal: yes
Solos: clarinet, alto sax
Notes: Recorded performance (May 1940) follows arrangement for first chorus only and includes an additional chorus featuring Astaire tap dancing with riff accompaniment. Much of the recording features Goodman's sextet, not the full band.

Just You, Just Me
(Raymond W. Klages, Jesse Greer)
Yale-BG 15/42
Date: 1945
Form: I(4) A(32, aaba) A(32) A(32)
Key: C
Vocal: no
Solos: clarinet, trombone
Notes: The 1945 recording was included on the 1953 LP-record dedicated to Henderson's arrangements. "Radio cut" (so called on trombone 1 part) omits middle sixteen bars of first chorus in all parts. First trumpet part includes penciled note "Chris-Folly" and profile of face with large nose. Goodman revisited this arrangement in a 1985 rehearsal.

Keep Smiling at Trouble
(Lewis Gensler, B.G. DeSylva, Al Jolson)
Yale-BG 16/1
Date: 1939
Form: I(4) A(32, aaba) A(36) A(32)
Keys: D, F
Vocal: no
Solos: clarinet, tenor sax, trumpet, alto sax
Notes: Goodman recorded the arrangement in 1953 with Helen Ward vocal, but the recording was never issued. He rehearsed the arrangement in early 1986.

King Porter Stomp
(Ferdinand "Jelly Roll" Morton)
Yale-BG 16/5
Date: 1935, rev. 1946
Form: I(9) A(16) X(4) B(16) ...
(expandable sequence of solos ending with three ensemble sections)
Keys: A♭, D♭
Vocal: no
Solos: clarinet, trumpet, trombone
Notes: Introduction and first strain based on Bobby Stark solo, orchestrated for four trumpets; the word "stand" is

written in pencil above the first staff of music in trumpet 2 part (entire trumpet section probably instructed to stand and play the introduction). Parts for trumpets 1–4, baritone [sax], bass, and drum in Leora Henderson's hand and undated, but fourth trumpet and baritone sax indicates 1940s vintage. All other parts stamped "Harrison Cooper [copyist] ... Registered 1946."

King Porter Stomp
(Ferdinand "Jelly Roll" Morton)
Yale-BG 16/6
Date: [1935] 1940s?
Form: keys, and solos as above, except introduction is eight bars
Notes: Score for five saxophones, three trumpets, and three trombones (i.e., 1940s orchestration), but represents at least partial transcription of BG 1935 recording, including Bunny Berigan trumpet solo and incipit of trombone solo.

King Porter Stomp
(Ferdinand "Jelly Roll" Morton)
Yale-BG 16/7, 16/7A
Date: [1935] 1949, 1980s
Form, key, and solos as above
Notes: Parts (16/7) and score (16/7A); trumpet solo based on Bunny Berigan's 1935 recorded solos; "as played in the 1980s" (Andrew Homzy).

[Oh,] Lady Be Good
(George and Ira Gershwin)
Yale-BG 16/10A
Date: ?
Form: I(4) A(32, aaba) A(34) A(32)
Keys: G, B♭
Vocal: no
Solos: clarinet, trombone, tenor sax, trumpet
Notes: Parts prepared by Ken Williams, who worked for Goodman as an arranger, transcriber, and copyist in the 1980s.

The Lamp Is Low
(Maurice Ravel, Bert Shefter, Peter DeRose, Mitchell Parish)
Yale-BG 16/15
Date: 1939
Form: I(4) A(36) A(34) A(36)
Keys: B♭, D
Vocal: yes
Solos: clarinet, piano
Notes: Documented performances in 1939 on radio only; not recorded until 1964.

Let's Go Home
(Sandy Williams, Peanuts Holland)
Yale-BG 16/31
Date: 1938
Form: I(8) A(32, aaba) X(4) A(32) A(32)
    A(17)
Key: D♭
Vocal: no
Solos: clarinet, tenor sax, trumpet,
    trombone, bass
Notes: Williams and Holland, as
Henderson's sidemen in the late 1930s,
wrote this piece and dubbed it "Let's Go
Home" as a plea to the bandleader to
return to New York after a long road
trip. Henderson's band recorded it in
spring 1941. The final seventeen-bar
section, labeled pages A, B, and C,
appears to be added later.

The Little Man Who Wasn't There
(Harold Adamson, Bernard Hanighan)
Yale-BG 16/40
Date: 1939
Form: I(4) A(32, aaba) A(38) A(32)
    A(32)
Keys: A min, B♭ min
Vocal: yes
Solos: clarinet, tenor sax, trumpet
Notes: Never recorded but performed on
radio in 1939.

Liza
(George and Ira Gershwin, Gus Kahn)
NYPL-BG 240 (score), 241 (parts)
Date: 1947
Form: I(4) A(32, aaba) A(32) A(34)
Keys: E♭, A♭
Vocal: no
Solos: clarinet, piano
Notes: Goodman recorded this standard
many times, in small groups and big
bands, in arrangements by others, but
apparently did not record the Henderson
arrangement until late 1969.

Lost in Meditation
(Duke Ellington, Irving Mills,
    Louis C. Singer, Juan Tizol)
Yale-BG 16/55
Date: 1938
Form: I(4) A(32) A(38) A(13)
Keys: B♭, C
Vocal: ?
Solos: clarinet (?), trombone
Notes: Parts in Leora Henderson's hand
and with her union stamp. Bass part
labeled "Harry" (Goodman), Benny's
brother. Folder lacks the usual part for
"Benny," which may indicate a clarinet
solo in the first chorus, where no parts
sustain melodic material.

Lost My Rhythm
Yale-BG 16/56
Date: 1935
Form: I(8) A(34, aaba) X(8) A(34) X(5)
    A(36)
Keys: E♭, B♭, A♭
Vocal: no
Solos: clarinet

Louise
(Leo Robin, Richard A. Whiting)
Yale-BG 16/57
Date: 1938
Form: I(4) A(32, aaba) A(35) A(33)
Keys: B♭, D♭
Vocal: no
Solos: clarinet, trumpet, piano, tenor
    sax
Notes: Recorded in December 1938; a
1939 radio performance features "special
lyrics" sung by Louise Tobin.

Louisiana Hayride
(Howard Dietz, Arthur Schwartz)
Yale-BG 17/2
Date: 1939
Form: I(4) A(24, aba) A(28) A(28)
    A(26)
Keys: A♭, G, C
Vocal: no
Solos: clarinet, trumpet, tenor sax
Notes: No documented performances.

Lulu's Back in Town
(Al Dubin, Harry Warren)
Yale-BG 17/19 and 19A
Date: 1935
Form: I(4) A(32, aaba) X(4) A(31) X(5)
    A(32)
Keys: G, A♭
Vocal: no
Solos: trumpet, clarinet?
Notes: Parts folder lacks the usual part
for "Benny." Parts for saxophone 5,
trumpet 4, and trombone 3 added later
with AFM stamp 1942. Performed on
radio in late 1930s and 1940s but not
recorded until spring 1951. Goodman
rehearsed the arrangement intensively
with his last band in 1986.

Make with the Kisses
(Johnny Mercer, Jimmy Van Heusen)
Yale-BG 17/22
Date: 1939
Form: I(4) A(35, aaba) A(36)
    A(33)
Keys: A♭, D♭, B♭
Vocal: yes
Solos: clarinet, trumpet
Notes: Recorded in October 1939
with Mildred Bailey as vocalist.

Unusually, Henderson features clarinets, instead of saxophones, in the vocal accompaniment.

Mama, That Moon Is Here Again
(Leo Robin, Ralph Rainger)
Yale-BG 17/28
Date: 1937
Form: I(4) A(36, aaba) A(32) A(32) T(5)
Keys: G, B♭
Vocal: yes
Solos: clarinet, trumpet
Notes: The folder contains "final corrected copy" of sheet music, signed by songwriters, with the words "vocal in B♭" written in black pen. This would be the sheet music on which Henderson based his arrangement. The sheet music also identifies the song as being for the film *The Big Broadcast of 1938*, which was released in February 1938. By then, Goodman had already recorded the arrangement and played it at least four times on radio with vocalist Martha Tilton. The phrase "2 beats nose" appears in pencil on a few parts, indicating that a band member other than Goodman set the tempo (perhaps the large-featured tenor saxophonist Art Rollini?).

Marie
(Irving Berlin)
Yale-BG 17/35
Date: 1937
Form: I(4) A(32, abac) A(35) A(32)
Keys: G, B♭
Vocal: no
Solos: clarinet, trumpet, tenor sax
Notes: Recorded from radio broadcast in October 1937.

Mean to Me
(Roy Turk, Fred E. Ahlert)
Yale-BG 17/40A
Date: 1947
Form: I(4) A(32, aaba) A(32) A(32)
Keys: A♭, C
Vocal: no
Solos: clarinet, trombone
Notes: Recording of December 8, 1936, credited as Henderson arrangement in Connor, but no score or parts earlier than 1947 appear in folder. Goodman recorded it in spring 1951 and rehearsed it in January 1986.

Memphis Blues
(W. C. Handy)
Yale-BG 18/6 and 18/7
Date: 1938
Form: I(4) A(15) A(26) A(12) A(12) A(24) A(12)

Keys: B♭, E♭, A♭, D♭
Vocal: no
Solos: clarinet, tenor sax, trumpet
Notes: Score and parts marked "not too slow (about the tempo of Big John)," referring to the Horace Henderson piece "Big John Special." All parts are stamped "Leora M. Henderson / H382 / Local 802 / Registered 1938." Bass part labeled "Harry" (Goodman). Henderson recorded the tune in September 1934, about two months before his band broke up.

Milenberg Joys
(Paul Mares, Leon Roppolo, Ferdinand "Jelly Roll" Morton)
Yale-BG 18/16
Date: 1939
Form: I(4) A(16) A(16) X(4) B(32) B(32) A'(16)
Keys: A♭, D♭, G♭
Vocal: no
Solos: trumpet, trombone, clarinet
Notes: Henderson's band recorded the piece in 1931, but the version for Goodman was not recorded until 2000, by Bob Wilber and the Tuxedo Big Band.

Minnie the Moocher's Wedding Day
(Harold Arlen, Ted Koehler)
Yale-BG 18/17
Date: 1935
Form: I(4) A(36, aaba) A(32) A(32) A(32)
Key: A♭
Vocal: no
Solos: clarinet, trumpet
Notes: Another example of a piece that Henderson recorded then arranged for Goodman. Connor gives co-arranging credit to Horace Henderson. Goodman featured the chart several times on radio in 1937–40 and recorded it in 1937.

Mister Deep Blue Sea
(Gene Austin, James P. Johnson)
Yale-BG 18/26
Date: 1935?
Form: I(8) A(34, aaba) A(30) A(17)
Keys: C, B♭, G
Vocal: yes
Solo: clarinet
Notes: The tune is a partial contrafact of "Between the Devil and the Deep Blue Sea," a link reinforced by the arrangement's coda, adapted from Henderson's "Devil" ending, itself taken from Henderson's piece "Can You Take It?" No documented performances.

Moonlight Serenade
(Glenn Miller, Mitchell Parish)
Yale-BG 18/42
Date: 1939
Form: I(4) A(48, aaba) A(49)
Keys: F, B♭
Vocal: no
Solos: clarinet, trumpet, alto sax
Notes: A 1945 radio program devoted to
Glenn Miller includes piece, but although
Goodman announced it as Henderson's
arrangement, Connor claims it was
Miller's.

More Than You Know
(Vincent Youmans, William Rose,
   Edward Eliscu)
Yale-BG 18/43A
Date: 1937?
Form: I(8) A(32, aaba) A(32) X(4) A(32)
Keys: D♭, E♭
Vocal: no
Solos: tenor sax, trumpet, clarinet
Notes: Recorded radio performance
in 1937 now available on compact
disc "Benny Goodman on the Air (1937–
1938)." One page of the parts contains a
handwritten list of more than a dozen
tunes, probably a playlist for a radio
program or public performance in 1946.
(The name of vibraphonist Johnny White,
who played in Goodman's band that year,
appears on the tune list; the tunes
themselves reflect the band's repertory
that Connor lists for 1946.) Goodman
also regularly played the tune in his small
group, and Eddie Sauter made a big-band
vocal arrangement for him.

Muskrat Ramble
(Kid Ory)
Yale-BG 18/45A
Date: 1947
Form: I(4) A(16) B(16) A(16) A(16+4)
   A(16) B(20)
Keys: A♭, D♭, F
Vocal: no
Solos: clarinet, trumpet, tenor sax,
   trombone
Notes: This old standard by New Orleans
trombonist Kid Ory shows that the
traditional-jazz revival touched Good-
man's band. Goodman recorded it in
1947 and returned to it, along
with many other Henderson
arrangements, in early 1986.

My Honey's Lovin' Arms
(Herman Ruby, Joseph Meyer)
Yale-BG 18/55
Date: 1935
Form: I(2) A(32, abac) A(32) A(32)

Keys: G, D♭
Vocal: no
Solos: clarinet, tenor sax
Notes: Piano and tenor sax 1 parts
contain pen and pencil markings showing
that piano takes half of tenor sax solo.
"Dick" indicated on tenor sax 2 part,
dating from the period between January
1935 and August 1936, when Dick Clark
played the part. The phrase "Benny 2
beats" appears in pencil on several parts
(cf. "Mama, That Moon"). Goodman
recorded it in 1938.

My My!
(Jimmy McHugh, Frank Loesser)
Yale-BG 19/8
Date: 1939
Form: I(4) A(34, aaba) A(34) A(34)
Keys: C, D♭, G♭
Vocal: yes
Solos: clarinet, trumpet
Notes: No documented performances.

**[You Brought A] New Kind of Love
[to Me]**
(Sammy Fain, Irving Kahal, Pierre Norman)
Yale-BG 19/22–23 (score), 19/24–25 (parts)
Date: 1939
Form: I(4) A(32, aaba) A(32) A(32) A(16)
Keys: B♭, F
Vocal: no
Solos: piano, saxophone, clarinet
Notes: Parts, in the key of D♭, do not
correspond to score. Goodman performed the arrangement frequently in
1945–46, including a 1945 recording
with vocal, and returned to it several
times, especially in last several months
before his death, as in a PBS television
special of October 1985.

Night and Day
(Cole Porter)
Yale-BG 19/30–31
Date: 1939?
Form: I(4) A(52, aab) A(48) Coda(17)
   [=b]
Keys: E♭, A♭
Vocal: no
Solos: clarinet, tenor sax, trumpet
Notes: Parts are split between folders;
parts in 19/30 are entirely in A♭.
Goodman featured the arrangement on
radio and record in summer 1939.

Notes to You [a.k.a. Henderson Stomp]
(Fletcher Henderson)
Yale-BG 19/40
Date: 1947
Form: I(4) A(16) B(16) A(16) C(16)
   C(16) C(16) A'(16) B'(16) T(6)

Notes to You (*continued*)
Keys: A♭, D♭
Vocal: no
Solos: clarinet, piano, vibraphone,
    trumpet
Notes: The folder contains only parts for
"Benny" (including trumpet cues) and
piano, bass, drums, and guitar.

Oh Boy
Yale-BG 19/46
Date: ca. 1938
Form: I(5) A(32, aaba) X(4) A(34)
    A(34)
Keys: E♭, B♭, A♭
Vocal: yes
Solos: clarinet, trumpet, tenor sax
Notes: As he did on some late 1930s
arrangements, Henderson wrote out the
two-bar clarinet solo preceding the final
cadence. No documented performances.

Oh! Look at Me Now
(Joe Bushkin, John DeVries)
Yale-BG 20/2
Date: 1941
Form: I(4) A(32, aaba) A(34) A(32)
Keys: C, G
Vocal: yes
Solos: clarinet, tenor sax
Notes: An Eddie Sauter arrangement also
dates from 1941, and Connor credits his
version, not Henderson's, as the one
Goodman performed that year on radio
and record.

Oh, You Crazy Moon
(Johnny Burke, Jimmy Van Heusen)
NYPL-BG 396
Date: 1939
Form: I(4) A(30, aaba) X(4) A(32) X(4)
    A(18)
Keys: D, E♭, D♭
Vocal: yes
Solos: clarinet, trumpet
Notes: For vocal refrain, trombone 1
part notes "solo" and four pitches in
pencil, possibly indicating the option for
the October 7, 1939, instrumental
version. Various cuts marked in pencil
for first and last choruses, adding up to a
half-chorus cut and resulting in a typical
ballad structure of two choruses.
Arrangement featured on radio, with and
without vocal, in fall 1939.

[Down by the] Old Mill Stream
(Tell Taylor)
Yale-BG 20/9
Date: 1938
Form: I(4) A(32, abac) A(34) A(34)
    A(16)

Keys: D♭, B♭, D
Vocal: no
Solos: clarinet, alto sax, trumpet
Notes: The tune, a Tin Pan Alley
standard from the early 1900s, was
among the oldest in Goodman's vast
book. The first page of parts bears
Henderson's union stamp: "Fletcher
Henderson / H380 / Local 802 /
Registered 1938"; second page bears
union stamp of familiar copyist for
Henderson's late-1930s arrangements:
"Morris Feldman / No. 93 / Local 802 /
registered 1939." Goodman featured the
arrangement on radio and record in
summer and fall of 1939.

On a Slow Boat to China
(Frank Loesser)
Yale-BG 20/13–14
Date: 1947
Form: I(4) A(34, abac) A(32) A(32)
Keys: D♭, G
Vocal: yes
Solos: trumpet, clarinet, tenor saxophone
Notes: Folder 20/14 contains a
shorter version of the arrangement.
The arrangement was recorded in 1947
and featured on a television appearance
the following year.

One Sweet Letter from You
(Harry Warren, Sidney Clare,
    Lew Brown)
Yale-BG 20/27
Date: 1939
Form: I(4) A(34, aaba) A(32) A(32)
Keys: F, A♭
Vocal: no
Solos: clarinet, piano, tenor sax, trumpet
Notes: Recorded in September 1939.

Ooh! Look-a There, Ain't She Pretty?
(Carmen Lombardo, Clarence Todd)
Yale-BG 20/30
Date: 1947
Form: I(4) A(35, abac) A(32) A(32)
Keys: C, D♭
Vocal: yes
Solos: saxophone, clarinet
Notes: Recorded in October 1947.

Opus Local 802
(Benny Goodman)
Yale-BG 20/39
Date: 1939
Form: I(6) A(32, aaba) A(36) A(32)
    A(34)
Keys: C, A♭
Vocal: no
Solos: clarinet, trumpet, string bass

Notes: The title refers to the New York musicians union, Local 802, and echoes several other "opus" tunes circulating in the swing era. The piece was originally played by sextet on a September 1939 radio broadcast. On the 1939 recording of Henderson's arrangement, Goodman takes the last eight measures of the trumpet solo.

Out of Nowhere
(Johnny Green, Edward Heyman)
Yale-BG 21/7
Date: 1945
Form: I(4) A(30, abac) X(5) A(32) A(32)
Keys: A, D♭
Vocal: yes
Solo: clarinet
Notes: First recording by Bob Wilber and the Tuxedo Big Band, 2000, without vocal.

[It's Only a] Paper Moon
(Harold Arlen, E.Y. Harburg, Billy Rose)
Yale-BG 21/14
Date: 1945
Form: I(4) A(35, aaba) A(32) A(19)
Keys: B♭, C
Vocal: yes
Solo: clarinet
Notes: Featured on radio and record in 1945; played on television in 1950.

Poor Butterfly
(John Golden, Raymond Hubble)
Yale-BG 21/32
Date: 1947
Form: I(4) A(34, abac) A(36) A(33)
Keys: B♭, A♭, D♭
Vocal: no
Solos: tenor sax, clarinet, piano, trumpet 2
Notes: This old Tin Pan Alley tune was one of Goodman's perennial small-group features (in duet, quartet, quintet, sextet, and octet), but there appears to be no record of him performing Henderson's arrangement with a full band. Its first recording was by Bob Wilber and the Tuxedo Big Band, 2000.

Poor Loulie Jean
(Willard Robison)
Yale-BG 21/34
Date: 1939
Form: I(4) A(34, aaba) A(32) A(17)
Keys: G, E♭, D♭
Vocal: yes
Solo: clarinet
Notes: Henderson wrote out the clarinet solo in the final eight bars. No documented performances.

Put That Down in Writing
(Harry Warren, Al Dubin)
Yale-BG 21/38
Date: 1939
Form: I(4) A(32, aaba) X(5) A(34) A(34) T(10) [=a]
Keys: D♭, E♭
Vocal: yes
Solos: clarinet, trombone
Notes: Unusually, the vocal appears in the last, instead of middle, chorus. Featured on radio in September 1939, but no other documented performances.

Remember
(Irving Berlin)
Yale-BG 22/9
Date: 1935
Form: I(9) A(34, aaba) A(35) A(34)
Keys: D, A
Vocal: no
Solos: trombone, clarinet, tenor sax
Notes: Following swing era custom, Henderson converted this waltz into duple time. Goodman played it in several documented radio and recorded performances in 1935–37.

Rhythm Is Our Business
(Jimmie Lunceford, Sammy Cahn, Saul Chaplin)
Yale-BG 22/14
Date: 1936
Form: I(4) A(16) A(16) A(15) X(4) A(16) [:B(16):] A(17) A(16)
Keys: E♭, B♭
Vocal: yes
Solos: clarinet, trumpet
Notes: "Conductor's note: 'E' [=B section] should be repeated with each instrument taking breaks according to lyrics in 3rd and 4th and 7th and 8th bars." Song lyrics appear in pencil on first and second trombone parts: "He's the leader man of the band / He plays the clarinet simply grand / When he starts swingin' we never get enough / Come on Benny, strut your stuff." No documented performances.

Rosalie
(Cole Porter)
Yale-BG 22/34
Date: 1938
Form: I(4) A(32, abac) A(32) A(34)
Keys: D, G
Vocal: no
Solos: clarinet, trumpet, piano
Notes: First recording by Bob Wilber and the Tuxedo Big Band, 2000.

Rose of the Rio Grande
(Harry Warren, Ross Gorman,
   Edgar Leslie)
Yale-BG 22/35
Date: 1947
Form: I(4) A(32, abac) A(34) A(32)
Keys: A♭, C
Vocal: no
Solos: trombone, piano, clarinet
Notes: First recording by Bob Wilber and
the Tuxedo Big Band, 2000.

Rose of Washington Square
(James F. Hanley, Ballard MacDonald)
NYPL-BG 197, 198
Date: 1947
Form: I(4) A(32, abac) A(32) A(32)
Keys: F, G♭
Vocal: no
Solo: clarinet
Notes: Jimmy Mundy claimed to have
arranged the recorded version of April
1939, but Goodman credited Henderson
(see Allen, 521; Connor, 98).
Considering that the record precedes the
material at NYPL, there may have been
two different arrangements, but only one
exists among the Goodman collections at
NYPL and Yale.

Rosetta
(Earl Hines, Henri Woode)
Yale-BG 22/37, 37A
Date: 1935
Form: I(4) A(32, aaba) A(32) T(8) [=a]
Keys: B♭, E♭, F
Vocal: no
Solos: clarinet, trombone, tenor sax
Notes: A classic ballad arrangement
recorded by Goodman in 1935 and 1937
(see chap. 9). Horace Henderson claimed
that he made this arrangement; the score
at Yale is signed by Fletcher Henderson.
Although Goodman had been
performing this arrangement since 1935,
the parts bear a later copyist stamp:
"Harry Wuest, Jr., ... 1942"—
suggesting a well-used arrangement
needing frequent recopying. Folder 37A
contains recopied parts from the 1980s,
probably the ones used for Goodman's
final concert in 1986.

Sandman
(Ralph Freed, Bonnie Lake)
Yale-BG 23/13
Date: 1935
Form: I(4) A(32, aaba) A(32) A(16)
Keys: E♭, A♭
Vocal: no
Solos: clarinet, trumpet

Notes: Introduction features unusual
effect of pure saxophone texture without
rhythm section (see chap. 9); second
chorus features unusual pairings of
trombones/tenor saxes and trumpets/alto
saxes. Goodman featured the arrangement on record and radio in late 1935
and early 1936.

S'posin'
(Paul Denniker, Andy Razaf)
Yale-BG 23/1
Date: 1947
Form: I(4) A(32, abac) A(32) A(16)
Keys: G, C, D♭
Vocal: no
Solos: piano, clarinet, tenor sax
Notes: Radio performance in 1948; first
recording by Bob Wilber and the Tuxedo
Big Band, 2000.

St. Louis Blues
(W. C. Handy)
Yale-BG 23/7
Date: 1936
Form: A(16) B(12) B(12) A(16) C(12)
   C(12) C(14) B(24) B(24) B(12) B(12)
Key: B♭
Vocal: no
Solos: clarinet, trumpet, piano
Notes: Score and parts appear to be
based on a transcription. The final
seventy-two bars, which sound like a
blues head arrangement with a climactic
riff from Count Basie's "One O'Clock
Jump," are not played on the 1936
recording but can be heard on an
aircheck of the 1937 radio performance
(from an on-location broadcast where
the band could extend well beyond the
usual three-minute limit). Goodman had
several different arrangements of the
piece. In 1935 his band played a different
arrangement, and it had a vocal version
as well. Yale-BG also has a 1961
arrangement by Wes Hensel. Goodman
often featured the tune as a small-group
number.

Seven Come Eleven
(Benny Goodman, Charlie Christian)
Yale-BG 23/26
Date: 1939
Form: I(12) A(32, aaba) A(34) A(32)
   A(32) A(16)
Keys: A♭, C, A♭
Vocal: no
Solos: drums, clarinet, tenor sax,
   trumpet, bass, trombone
Notes: Goodman had several versions
of this tune, created with guitarist
Christian mainly as a small-group

showcase. Allen notes that most of Goodman's full-band performances of the piece are of Henderson's arrangement, but Connor shows that several are of Eddie Sauter's arrangements. The Henderson arrangement opens with a rare drum solo, continues with an eight-bar vamp borrowed from "Christopher Columbus," and includes an unusual number of solos for a full-band arrangement in Goodman's book.

[In a Shanty in Old] Shanty Town
(Jack Little, Ira Schuster, Joseph Young)
NYPL-BG 201, 202
Date: 1947
Form: I(4) A(32, abac) A(32) A(32) T (4)
Keys: A♭, D♭
Vocal: no
Solos: clarinet, trumpet
Notes: A recorded radio performance dates from March 1947.

She's Funny That Way
(Richard A. Whiting, Neil Moret)
Yale-BG 23/37
Date: 1938
Form: I(4) A(32, aaba) A(35) A(35)
 A(17)
Keys: E♭, C, G
Vocal: no
Solos: trumpet, alto sax, clarinet, tenor sax
Notes: First recording by Bob Wilber and the Tuxedo Big Band, 2000.

Should I
(Nacio Herb Brown)
Yale-BG 23/45
Date: 1947
Form: I(8) A(32, aaba) A(32) A(32) T (8)
Keys: E♭, F
Vocal: no
Solos: clarinet, piano, tenor sax
Notes: No documented performances.

Show Your Linen, Miss Richardson
(Johnny Mercer, Bernie Hanighen)
Yale-BG 24/2
Date: 1939
Form: I(4) A(23, aab) A(20) B(16) A(12)
 A(20)
Keys: E♭, C, G, C
Vocal: yes
Solos: clarinet
Notes: Lyricist Johnny Mercer sings in the arrangement's two documented performances, on radio and record, in April 1939.

Sing an Old-Fashioned Song
(Joe Young, Fred Ahlert)
Yale-BG 24/8

Date: 1938
Form: I(4) A(36, aaba) A(32) X(4)
 A(33)
Keys: A♭, C
Vocal: no
Solos: clarinet, trumpet
Notes: No documented performances.

The Sky Fell Down
(Edward Heyman, Louis Alter)
NYPL-BG 204
Date: 1940
Form: I(4) A(32, abac) A(32) A(16)
Keys: G, C, A♭
Vocal: yes
Solos: alto sax, clarinet
Notes: Typical vocal ballad treatment; recorded in March 1940.

Small Fry
(Hoagy Carmichael, Frank Loesser)
Yale-BG 24/27
Date: 1938
Form: I(8) A(8) X(2) B(32, aaba) X(4)
 A(32) A(22)
Keys: D, B♭
Vocal: yes
Solos: clarinet, "Tenor [sax]-optional" for vocal chorus
Notes: A 1938 radio performance features the Kate Smith trio, with full band in coda only (Connor, 92). No other documented performances. Parts in Leora Henderson's hand include performer names "Benny [Goodman]," "Harry [James]" (trumpet 1), " 'Chris' [Griffin]" (trumpet 2), "Ziggie [Elman]," (trumpet 3), and "Harry [Goodman]," (bass). Several parts are included in two handwritten originals.

Some of These Days
(Shelton Brooks)
Yale-BG 24/46
Date: ca. 1939–40
Form: I(4) A(32, aaba) A(34) A(32)
 A(16)
Keys: C, D
Vocal: yes
Solos: clarinet, tenor sax
Notes: No documented performances.

Somebody Loves Me
(George Gershwin, B.G. DeSylva, Ballard MacDonald)
Yale-BG 24/49
Date: 1936
Form: I(4) A(32, aaba) A(30) X(6)
 A(32)
Keys: B♭, A♭
Vocal: no
Solos: clarinet, tenor sax, trumpet

Somebody Loves Me *(continued)*
Notes: The fluid, soloistic saxophone
phrases in the second chorus come from
Benny Carter's earlier version, which
Henderson's band recorded in 1930.
Goodman more often played the tune in
small groups, but he recorded the
Henderson arrangement in November
1936 in a fine performance featuring an
easy, relaxed precision at a slower-than-
usual tempo.

Somebody Stole My Gal
(Leo Wood)
Yale-BG 24/50; NYPL-BG 403
Date: 1940
Form: I(4) A(42, abacd) A(40) A(40) A(24)
Keys: A♭, D♭, E♭, A♭
Vocal: no; but Yale score includes vocal
    insert
Solos: clarinet, tenor sax, trumpet
Notes: Goodman featured the arrange-
ment regularly in the 1940s, especially in
the 1945–46 period. The NYPL parts
reflect heavy use, including marked cuts
in second and third choruses, and
multiple numbers.

Someday Sweetheart
(John Spikes, Benjamin Spikes)
Yale-BG 25/3 and 25/3A
Date: 1936
Form: I(4) A(35, aaba) A(30) X(4) A(32)
Keys: D♭, F, A♭
Vocal: no
Solos: clarinet, trumpet
Notes: The parts are in Leora
Henderson's hand, with tempo indication
"Not-Too-Slow-(Swing)." The word
"Nose" appears in light pencil above the
first measure of the second alto and first
tenor sax parts, suggesting once again
that another musician set the tempo (cf.
"Mama, That Moon"). The smooth,
gentle sax soli variation in the second
chorus is reminiscent of the famous
chorus of "Sometimes I'm Happy."

Sometimes I'm Happy
(Vincent Youmans, Irving Caesar)
Yale-BG 25/8
Date: 1935
Form: I(8) A(30, abac) X(4) A(32) A(32)
    A(32)
Key: A♭
Vocal: no
Solos: trumpets (1 and 2), clarinet
Notes: The arrangement stood out as one
of Henderson's most famous ballads,
made in collaboration with his brother
Horace, and it became a standard in
Goodman's book over his half-century of

bandleading (see chap. 9). The scholar
looking for evidence of two hands in the
score—Fletcher's and Horace's—is disap-
pointed. The Yale-BG score reflects a later
transcription, by someone else (its cover
is stamped "Bill Kratt Music Copying Service"), of the 1935 recording, including
the solos. Two sets of parts are included,
one stamped by a familiar copyist "Harry
Wuest, Jr./ W1563/Local 802/Registered
1942," and the other dating from the
1950s or 1960s. Bunny Berigan's famous
trumpet solo, labeled "Bunny's solo," is
on a separate sheet.

Song of the Wanderer
(Neil Moret)
Yale-BG 25/18
Date: 1947
Form: I(4) A(32, aaba) X(2) A(32) A(35)
Keys: G, A♭
Vocal: no
Solos: clarinet, trumpet, alto sax
Notes: First recording by Bob Wilber and
the Tuxedo Big Band, 2000.

South of the Border
(Jimmy Kennedy, Michael Carr)
NYPL-BG 144
Date: 1947
Form: I(4) A(32, abac) X(8) A(32) A(32)
    T(8)
Keys: A♭, E♭–C
Vocal: no
Solos: clarinet, trumpet
Notes: A recording was made in spring
1951 during a pair of sessions devoted
entirely to Henderson's arrangements a
few months after Henderson's stroke in
December 1950.

Spanish Town
Yale-BG 25/25
Date: ca. 1938
Form: I(4) A(34, abac) A(34) A(32)
Keys: D♭, E♭, C
Vocal: no
Solos: trombone, piano, clarinet, trumpet
Notes: No documented performances.

Spring Song
(Felix Mendelssohn)
Yale-BG 25/32
Date: 1939
Form: I(4) A(16) B(34) A'(41)
Key: A
Vocal: no
Solos: alto sax, clarinet?
Notes: After the introduction, Henderson
precisely maintains the length, structure,
and key of Mendelssohn's piece. An
exemplar of the swinging-the-classics

phenomenon, the arrangement was featured on radio and record in late summer 1939 and again in 1945.

Squeeze Me
(Fats Waller, Clarence Williams)
Yale-BG 26/1
Date: 1939
Form: I(4) A(20, aab) A(20) B(16) A(20) A(18)
Keys: C, D♭, B♭
Vocal: no
Solos: clarinet, tenor sax, trombone
Notes: Tempo indication: "Not fast" on clarinet and alto sax 1. Goodman recorded it in January 1940.

Star Dust [first version]
(Hoagy Carmichael, Mitchell Parish)
Yale-BG 26/5A
Date: 1936
Form: I(7) A(32, abac) A(32) A(16)
Key: D
Vocal: no
Solos: trumpet, clarinet
Notes: Goodman had at least four different full-band arrangements of "Star Dust" through his career, two by Henderson and one each by Spud Murphy and Gordon Jenkins. Henderson's first version displaced Murphy's, which Goodman had played in 1935. Henderson's arrangement then became a standard in Goodman's book, played regularly from 1936 to the mid-1940s. Like many of Henderson's earliest arrangements, Goodman rehearsed it intensively with his last band, and he performed it in his final concert. Top of trumpet 1 part features penciled profile of face with large nose.

Star Dust [second version]
(Hoagy Carmichael, Mitchell Parish)
Yale-BG 26/3 and 26/5
Date: 1946
Form: I(7) A(31, abac) A(32) A(16)
Keys: A♭, D♭
Vocal: no
Solos: trombone, clarinet
Notes: "New on 1/24/46" written on score cover; The "Benny" part indicates, in ink, that "This was the one recorded in 1951," as part of a pair of sessions devoted to Henderson's arrangements after Henderson's stroke.

Stealin' Apples
(Fats Waller, Andy Razaf)
Yale-BG 26/9, 26/10, 26/11
Date: 1939
Form: I(8) A(32, aaba) A(32) A(32) A(32) A(32)

Keys: D, A
Vocal: no
Solos: piano, trumpet, clarinet
Notes: Henderson's own band featured this tune from 1936 onward, and like many of his arrangements from that period, it became a standard in Goodman's book as well. The third trumpet part features a penciled profile of a face with large nose (cf. "Star Dust"); the third trombone part shows the word "nose" partially erased at the top (cf. "Mama, That Moon"). Several parts also reveal the phrase "Red Horse Fanfare" written in pencil at the end, indicating a piece played on Armed Forces Radio, sponsored by Mobil Gas Co., whose trademark was a red horse.

Stop Kicking My Heart Around
Yale-BG 26/21
Date: 1938
Form: I(4) A(35, abac) A(35) A(32) A(17)
Keys: B♭, D
Vocal: yes
Solo: clarinet
Notes: Parts in Leora's hand; no documented performances.

Stop Look and Listen
(Ralph Freed, George van Eps, John van Eps)
Yale-BG 26/23
Date: 1936
Form: I(4) A(32, aaba) X(8) A(32) A(32)
Keys: G, A♭
Vocal: no
Solos: tenor sax, clarinet
Notes: The score is not in Henderson's hand, and it contains several polished caricatures in pencil, including images of Duke Ellington, Cab Calloway, and Goodman. A note above m.9 of final chorus reads: "Mouses riff."

Strange Fruit
(Lewis Allan)
Yale-BG 26/25
Date: 1939
Form: I(4) A(33, aaba) X(8) A(32) A(32)
Keys: D/Bmin
Vocal: no
Solos: saxophone 3, trombone 2 (labeled "soli" to play melody, not improvisation)
Notes: Taking up this anti-lynching song that became a standard for Billie Holiday, Henderson created unusually smooth, quiet nonvocal arrangement. There are no documented performances; the lack of parts suggests it was never played.

Sugar
(Maceo Pinkard, Edna Alexander,
    Sidney D. Mitchell)
Yale-BG 26/27
Date: 1947
Form: I(4) A(32, aaba) A(32) A(34)
Keys: Db, D
Vocal: no
Solos: tenor sax, clarinet
Notes: First recording by Bob Wilber and
the Tuxedo Big Band, 2000.

Sugar Foot Stomp
(Joe Oliver, Louis Armstrong)
NYPL-BG 404
Date: 1935
Form: I(4) A(12) A'(12) B(16) C(36)
    C(24) D(12) D'(12)
Key: Bb
Vocal: no
Solos: trumpet, clarinet
Notes: Miscellaneous parts from three
different copyists, from 1940, 1951, and
later, with several marked cuts. The
arrangement had undergone a gradual
transformation in Henderson's band;
Goodman's version was based on the
Henderson band's 1931 revision of Don
Redman's 1925 arrangement of "Dipper
Mouth Blues" (see chaps. 4 and 7) and
frequently performed and recorded by
Goodman.

Sunday
(Ned Miller, Jule Styne, Bennie Krueger)
Yale-BG 26/32
Date: 1939
Form: I(4) A(34, aaba) A(34) A(32) A(33)
Keys: Eb, Db, F
Vocal: no
Solos: clarinet, tenor sax, alto sax,
    trombone
Notes: First recording by Bob Wilber and
the Tuxedo Big Band, 2000.

Sunrise Serenade
(Frankie Carle, Jack Lawrence)
Yale-BG 25/33A
Date: 1939
Form: I(4) A(16) B(16) B(16) B(16)
Key: Ab
Vocal: no
Solos: clarinet, piano
Notes: This arrangement represents one
of several derived from other big bands
(in this case, Glenn Miller's) that
Henderson did in the 1939–40 period.

Swanee River [Old Folks at Home]
(Stephen Foster)
Yale-BG 27/2
Date: 1939

Form: I(4) A(32, aaba) A(32) A(34) A(32)
Keys: G, Ab, Bb
Vocal: no
Solos: clarinet, piano, trumpet, tenor sax
Notes: Recorded from radio broadcast in
1946.

Sweet and Lovely
(Gus Arnheim, Harry Tobias,
    Jules Lemare)
Yale-BG 27/6
Date: 1947
Form: I(4) A(34, aaba) A(32) A(33)
Keys: D, G
Vocal: no
Solos: tenor sax, clarinet

Sweet and Slow
(Al Dubin, Harry Warren)
Yale-BG 27/9
Date: 1935
Form: I(4) A(30, abca) X(4) A(30) X(4)
    A(32)
Keys: Eb, F, Db
Vocal: yes
Solos: clarinet, tenor sax
Notes: Rare tempo indication "slow."
Band members' names appear on some
parts: "Benny," "Shertzer [sic]" (alto sax),
"DePew" (alto sax), and "Jess [Stacy]"
(piano). First recording by Bob Wilber
and the Tuxedo Big Band, 2000.

Sweet as a Song
(Mack Gordon, Harry Revel)
Yale-BG 27/10
Date: 1938
Form: I(4) A(34, abac) A(32) A(18)
Keys: Eb, Bb, G
Vocal: yes
Solo: clarinet
Notes: Each trumpet part labeled with
band member's name: "Cris [sic]
[Griffin]" (1st), "Harry [James]" (2nd),
"Ziggy [Elman]" (3rd). Bass part labeled
"Harry [Goodman]." One documented
radio performance, 1938.

Sweet Lorraine
(Cliff Burwell, Mitchell Parish)
Yale-BG 27/23
Date: 1941
Form: I(4) A(32, aaba) A(35) A(33)
Keys: A, C
Vocal: no
Solos: clarinet, trombone
Notes: First recording by Bob Wilber and
the Tuxedo Big Band, 2000.

Swingin' a Dream
(Jimmy Van Heusen, Eddie DeLange)
Yale-BG 27/32

Date: 1939
Form: I(4) A(35, aaba) A(32) A(36) A(33)
Keys: D♭, A♭, G
Vocal: yes
Solos: clarinet, trombone, trumpet
Notes: Song for swing adaptation of *Midsummer Night's Dream*, featured on radio, 1939.

Swinging Down the Lane
(Gus Kahn, Isham Jones)
Yale-BG 27/37
Date: 1938
Form: I(4) A(32, abac) A(34) A(32)
Keys: A♭, C
Vocal: no
Solos: clarinet, trumpet, tenor sax
Notes: One documented radio performance, 1939.

Thanks for Everything
(Isham Jones, Ed Stone)
Yale-BG 28/18
Date: ca. 1937
Form: I(4) A(36, abac) A(32) A(16)
Keys: E♭, A♭
Vocal: yes
Solo: clarinet
Notes: Rare tempo indication "(Slow-swing)." No documented performances.

That Lucky Fellow
(Jerome Kern, Oscar Hammerstein II)
Yale-BG 28/19
Date: 1939
Form: I(4) A(34, abac) A(32) A(32)
Keys: F, C
Vocal: yes
Solo: clarinet
Notes: Recorded in 1939.

That's What You Think
(Pinky Tomlin, Raymond Jasper,
   Coy Poe)
Yale-BG 28/27
Date: 1941
Form: I(4) A(32, aaba) X(4) A(33)
   A(32)
Keys: F, C, A♭
Vocal: yes
Solos: clarinet, trumpet
Notes: No documented performances.

Them There Eyes
(Maceo Pinkard, William Tracy,
   Doris Tauber)
Yale-BG 28/28
Date: 1938
Form: I(4) A(32, abac) A(36) A(32)
Keys: G, A♭
Vocal: no
Solos: clarinet, trumpet, tenor sax

Notes: In early 1939, featured on radio, then recorded by Johnny Mercer.

There'll Be Some Changes Made
(William Higgins, W. Benton Overstreet)
Yale-BG 28/33
Date: 1938
Form: I A(22) A(18) A(21) A(18)
Keys: E♭, C, D
Vocal: no
Solos: clarinet, alto sax, trumpet
Notes: Manuscript score paper labeled "Radio station W.B.B.M.—Columbia Broadcasting System."

Thou Swell
(Richard Rodgers, Lorenz Hart)
Yale-BG 29/9
Date: 1939
Form: I(4) A(32, abac) A(34) A(34)
Keys: G, A♭
Vocal: no
Solos: clarinet, tenor sax
Notes: First recording by Bob Wilber and the Tuxedo Big Band, 2000.

Trees
(Oscar Rasbach, Joyce Kilmer)
NYPL-BG 216
Date: 1939?
Form: I(6) A(24, abc) [:A(26):] A(26)
   A(24)
Key: D
Vocal: yes
Solos: drums, tenor sax, clarinet
Notes: "Zigg" [Ziggy Elman] written on 2nd trumpet part. First chorus marked to be cut in many parts.

Truckin'
(Rube Bloom, Ted Koehler)
Yale-BG 29/33
Date: 1936
Form: I(8) A(30, aaba) X(6) A(32) A(32)
Keys: C, F, A♭
Vocal: no
Solos: clarinet, alto sax?
Notes: incomplete set of parts (missing 1st alto, drums, and "Benny" part).

Tuxedo Junction
(Buddy Feyne, Erskine Hawkins,
   William Johnson, Julian Dash)
Yale-BG 29/35
Date: 1939
Form: A(16) B(32, aaba) B(40) B(32)
   A(16)
Key: C
Vocal: no
Solos: trumpet, alto sax, clarinet
Notes: Quiet (*pp*) ending (rare).
No documented performances.

Walkin' By the River
(Una Mae Carlisle, Robert Sour)
NYPL-BG 219, 220
Date: 1941?
Form: I(4) A(36, aaba) A(32) A(16)
Keys: D, A, D
Vocal: no
Solo: clarinet
Notes: Score signed "F. Henderson,"
but may be earlier than 1941, as it
includes Goodman original 1935
instrumentation (4 saxophones, 3
trumpets, and 2 trombones). Only
documented performances date from
1941, the arrangement for which
Connor credits Eddie Sauter (p. 119).

Warm Tropics
Yale-BG 30/3
Date: before mid-1939
Form: I(4) A(32, aaba) A(30) X(10)
   A(32) T(4)
Keys: F, D♭
Vocal: no
Solos: clarinet, bass, tenor sax
Notes: Score not in Henderson's hand;
no parts: possibly never played.

Way Down Yonder in New Orleans
(Henry Creamer, Turner Layton)
Yale-BG 30/8, 30/9
Date: 1947
Form: I(4) A(31) A(28) A(28) A(28)
Keys: G, D♭
Vocal: no
Solos: clarinet, trombone, alto sax
Notes: Arrangement ends unusually with
saxophone "pyramid" effect followed by
quick shifts between brass and saxes and
culminating in full-ensemble tutti (all
instruments playing same material).
Recorded from radio broadcast in 1947.

We Go Well Together
(Arthur Kent, Sid Robin)
Yale-BG 30/10
Date: 1941
Form: I(4) A(35, aaba) A(34) A(32)
Keys: G, A♭, D♭
Vocal: yes
Solos: clarinet, tenor sax
Notes: No documented performances.

We'll Never Know
(Irving Berlin)
Yale-BG 30/11
Date: 1938
Form: I(4) A(34, aaba) A(32) A(32)
Keys: B♭, C, D
Vocal: yes
Solo: clarinet
Notes: Recorded in 1938.

Well All Right
(Frances Faye, David Kapp, Don Raye)
Yale-BG 30/13
Date: 1938
Form: I(4) A(38) B(46) A(24)
Keys: G, C, G
Vocal: yes
Solo: clarinet
Notes: "A" section comprises consecutive
twelve-bar blues choruses. Vocal chorus
features lots of call and response with
band members, both singing ("well
alright" [sic]) and playing. One docu-
mented radio performance, 1939.

What a Little Moonlight Can Do
(Harry Woods)
Yale-BG 30/17, 30/18, NYPL-BG 242
Date: 1935
Form: I(8) A(32, aaba) A(32) A(32)
   A(32)
Keys: E♭, A♭
Vocal: yes
Solos: none, except for clarinet fills
   between vocal phrases
Notes: Goodman's band did not record
the arrangement until after Henderson's
death, during the 1953 sessions orga-
nized as a memorial for him, and
featuring Helen Ward.

What Have You Got That Gets Me?
(Leo Robin, Ralph Rainger)
Yale-BG 30/22
Date: 1938
Form: I(4) A(42, aaba) A(40) A(20)
Keys: B♭, C
Vocal: yes
Solos: clarinet, tenor sax
Notes: Recorded in 1938.

What'll They Think of Next?
(Hoagy Carmichael, Johnny Mercer)
NYPL-BG 224
Date: 1940
Form: I(8) A(36, aaba) X(4) A(36) X(4)
   A(22)
Keys: D, G, E♭
Vocal: no
Solo: clarinet
Notes: Taking a ballad tempo,
Goodman's January 1940 recording cuts
half of the first chorus and substitutes a
Helen Forrest vocal for the clarinet solo
in the second chorus.

What's New?
(Johnny Burke, Bob Haggart)
Yale-BG 30/27
Date: 1939
Form: I(4) A(35, aaba) A(32) A(16)
Keys: D, G

Vocal: yes
Solo: clarinet
Notes: Recorded in 1939.

What's the Matter with Me?
(Sam M. Lewis, Terry Shand)
Yale-BG 30/28
Date: 1939
Form: I(4) A(32, abac) A(36) A(36)
A(16)
Keys: A♭, D, C
Vocal: yes
Solos: trumpet, clarinet, alto sax
Notes: Goodman's January 1940
recording omits second chorus (featuring
all instrumental solos).

**What's the Reason [I'm Not Pleasin'
You]?**
(Earl Hatch, Pinky Tomlin, Coy Poe,
Jimmie Grier)
Yale-BG 30/29
Date: 1935
Form: I(7) A(32, aaba) X(4) A(34) A(30)
Keys: C, A♭, D
Vocal: yes
Solo: clarinet
Notes: Written for *Let's Dance*; featured
once again on radio in 1939.

When Buddha Smiles
(Arthur Freed, Nacio Herb Brown)
Yale-BG 30/29A and NYPL-BG 226
Date: 1935
Form: I(4) A(34, aaba) A(32) A(34)
A(33)
Keys: G♭, D
Vocal: no
Solos: clarinet, tenor sax
Notes: Yale parts combine copies from
1951 and the early 1980s, a sign of a
regularly used arrangement. See chap. 9.

When Dreams Come True
(John Murray Anderson, Carey Morgan,
Arthur Swanstrom)
Yale-BG 30/30
Date: 1938
Form: I(4) A(32, abab') A(32) A(32)
Key: D♭
Vocal: no
Solos: clarinet, trumpet, tenor sax
Notes: Score marked "Medium Swing—
Not Too Fast"; introduction features
unusual scoring of cup-muted brass and
clarinets. No documented performances.

When I Grow Too Old to Dream
(Sigmund Romberg,
Oscar Hammerstein II)
Yale-BG 30/31, 30/32
Date: 1938

Form: I(4) A(36, abcb) A(32) A(32)
Keys: D♭, A♭, C
Vocal: no
Solos: clarinet
Notes: Yale-BG 30/31 contains a six-page
sketch showing that Henderson began
arranging the tune in its original form: a
waltz in F major.

Where Do I Go from You?
(Allie Wrubel, Walter Bullock)
Yale-BG 31/2
Date: 1938
Form: I(4) A(32, abac) A(32) A(32)
Keys: D, A♭
Vocal: yes
Solo: clarinet
Notes: Intimate arrangement (the brass
shift between cup and hat mutes) with
unusually soft ending (*pp*) seems ideal
for the only documented public perfor-
mances, on radio: in the Peacock Court
of San Francisco's Mark Hopkins Hotel,
May and June 1940.

Whispering
(John Schonberger, Richard Coburn,
Vincent Rose)
NYPL-BG 227
Date: 1938
Form: I(4) A(34, abac) A(34) A(32)
Keys: A, D♭, B♭
Vocal: no
Solos: trombone, clarinet, trumpet,
tenor sax

Wrap Your Troubles in Dreams
(Harry Barris, Ted Koehler, Billy Moll)
Yale-BG 31/37
Date: 1947
Form: I(4) A(32, aaba) A(32) A(34)
Keys: G, F
Vocal: no
Solos: clarinet, piano, tenor sax
Notes: Recorded in 1947.

Wrappin' It Up
(Fletcher Henderson)
Yale-BG 31/39, 31/40
Date: 1935
Form: I(8) A(32, abac) A(32) A(32)
Key: D♭
Vocal: no
Solos: alto sax, trumpet, tenor sax
Notes: A standard in Goodman's
book (see chaps. 8 and 9); final chorus,
mm. 17–25, originally intended as
ensemble variation as on Henderson's
recording of 1934, but crossed out in
favor of tenor sax solo (see second alto
and first tenor parts, the oldest saxo-
phone parts).

Yankee Doodle Never Went to Town
(Ralph Freed, Bernie Hanighen)
Yale-BG 31/42
Date: 1935
Form: I(4) A(32, aaba) A(32) A(35)
Keys: C, G–D
Vocal: yes
Solo: clarinet
Notes: Arrangement sometimes attrib-
uted to Spud Murphy (e.g. Connor), but
parts are in Leora Henderson's hand,
with the phrase "arr. by Fletcher
Henderson" or "FHH Jr." written on
each part. Four-bar phrase of clarinet
solo in final chorus is entirely composed,
but Goodman instead quotes "Yankee
Doodle" on November 1935 recording.

**You Took the Words Right Out
of My Heart**
(Leo Robin, Ralph Rainger)
NYPL-BG 425
Date: 1937
Form: I(4) A(24, aba) X(4) A(24) X(4)
A(26)
Keys: D, C, G
Vocal: yes
Solos: clarinet, trombone
Notes: NYPL folder actually contains
two different arrangements in score,
one by Henderson (and in his hand), the
other not.

You Turned the Tables on Me
(Sidney Mitchell, Louis Alter)
Yale-BG 32/17
Date: 1936
Form: I(4) A(32, abac) X(4) A(32) T(8)
Keys: F, D♭, B♭
Vocal: yes
Solos: clarinet
Notes: Score in Henderson's hand, but
Yale catalog credits Jimmy Mundy, who
claimed the arrangement as his own
(see Schoenberg liner notes, *Benny
Goodman: The Birth of Swing
[1935–1936]*).

You Was Right Baby
(Peggy Lee, Dave Barbour)
Yale-BG 32/19
Date: 1945
Form: I(8) A(32, aaba) X(4) A(32) A(18)
Keys: F, A♭
Vocal: no
Solo: clarinet
Notes: Although written arrangement
lacks vocal part, Connor lists tune with
vocal by Liza Morrow in November/
December 1945 recorded radio perfor-

mance (Connor, 164). The songwriters
were singer and guitarist, respectively, in
Goodman's band in the early 1940s and
were married soon after Barbour left the
band in early 1943 (Connor, 142).

You'd Be So Nice to Come Home To
(Cole Porter)
NYPL-BG 426, 427
Date: 1943
Form: I(5) A(37, abac) A(32)
Key: D♭
Vocal: no
Solos: none?
Notes: Score and parts lack the
"Benny" part, but Henderson might
have intended the requisite clarinet solo
in the second chorus. That chorus
features the saxophone section but does
not appear to be a full melodic variation,
as it contains passages of long tones
typically found in accompaniments.
Unusually, the brass shift frequently
among three tone qualities: hat-muted,
fiber-muted, and "open" (unmuted).

You're a Heavenly Thing
(Joe Young, Little Jack Little)
Yale-BG 32/25
Date: 1935
Form: I(4) A(30, aaba) X(4) A(32)
A(32)
Keys: C, F, E♭
Vocal: yes
Solo: clarinet
Notes: One of the first Henderson
arrangements that Goodman recorded,
with Helen Ward, in April 1935.

You're a Sweetheart
(Jimmy McHugh, Harold Adamson)
Yale-BG 32/26
Date: 1937
Form: I(4) A(32, aaba) A(32) A(18)
Keys: G, D, B♭
Vocal: yes
Solos: none?
Notes: Parts labeled "Ziggy [Elman]"
(trumpet 1), "New Guy" (trombone 1),
"Red [Ballard]" (trombone 2). No
documented performances.

You're Driving Me Crazy
(Walter Donaldson)
Yale-BG 32/32
Date: 1938
Form: I(8) A(32, aaba) A(32) A(32)
Keys: C, B♭
Vocal: yes
Solos: clarinet, trombone

Notes: Featured on radio in 1938 and recorded from 1943 radio broadcast.

You're Tough on My Heart
NYPL-BG 429
Date: 1946
Form: I(4) A(8) A(32, aaba) A(16)
Keys: G, B♭
Vocal: yes
Solos: clarinet
Notes: Rare arrangement in which the vocal dominates (with a full chorus plus eight bars at the end). No documented performances.

You've Got Me This Way
(Jimmy McHugh, Johnny Mercer)
Yale-BG 32/44
Date: 1941
Form: I(6) A(34, aaba) A(34) A(32)
Keys: A♭, D♭, B♭
Vocal: yes
Solos: clarinet, tenor sax
Notes: End of score in Henderson's hand is note, probably to copyist: "Rock: Be sure and bring the professional copy to rehearsal / Thankx!" No documented performances.

Young Ideas
(Morris I. Charlap, Charles F. Sweeney, Jr.)
Yale-BG 32/46
Date: 1935
Form: I(5) A(36, abac) A(33) X(4) A(34) T(5)
Keys: D♭, F
Vocal: no
Solos: clarinet, tenor sax

Notes: One of the very few surviving Henderson arrangements from 1935 that Goodman never seems to have played. No parts exist, and Connor documents no known performances.

Yours Is My Heart Alone
(Franz Lehar, Harry B. Smith, Ludwig Herzer, Roger Casini, Beda Fritz Loehner)
Yale-BG 32/49
Date: 1939
Form: I(4) A(36, aaba) A(32) A(32)
Keys: A♭, F, D♭
Vocal: yes
Solos: clarinet, trumpet
Notes: Recorded in 1940.

Yours Truly Is Truly Yours
(J. Fred Coots, Ted FioRito, Benn Davis)
Yale-BG 32/50
Date: 1936
Form: I(4) A(30, abac) X(4) A(32) X(4) A(34)
Keys: C, E♭
Vocal: no
Solos: clarinet, trumpet
Notes: Unique score in which all parts are labeled by band members' first names in red pencil: saxophones Hymie [Schertzer], Bill [DePew], Dick [Clark], Arthur [Rollini]; trumpets Pee Wee [Erwin], Nate [Kazebier], Harry [Geller]; trombones Joe [Harris] and Red [Ballard]; bass Harry [Goodman]; guitar Allan [Reuss]; drums Gene [Krupa]; and piano Jess [Stacy]. No documented performances.

NOTES

Abbreviations

Amerigrove	The New Grove Dictionary of American Music
EJ	Gunther Schuller, Early Jazz: Its Roots and Musical Development
Jazz Grove	The New Grove Dictionary of Jazz
JOHP	National Endowment for the Arts/Smithsonian Institution's Jazz Oral History Project, housed at the Institute of Jazz Studies, Rutgers University, Newark, NJ
SE	Gunther Schuller, The Swing Era: The Development of Jazz, 1930–1945

Notes

Introduction

1 *"an autonomous art form"*: DeVeaux, The Birth of Bebop, 13.

2 *"The war against"*: Williams, ed., The Art of Jazz, 202.

3 *"was liberal in giving"*: Quoted from a 1943 interview, in Allen, 503.

4 *"In the '20s"*: Hammond, liner notes, 16.

5 *"extremely talented"*: Wilson, Teddy Wilson Talks Jazz, 48.
"Fletcher'd take these heads"; "to take improvised licks": Allen, 501.
Meanwhile, as a corollary: For two recent examples, see Sudhalter, Lost Chords; and Lees, Arranging the Score, whose introduction mentions several key black arrangers while each chapter focuses on the work of an important white arranger.

6 *"while half the band"*: Chilton, Song of the Hawk, 95.
"aloof": Procope, interview with Chris Albertson, JOHP transcript, II:22.
"removed" and "inaccessible": Ferguson, 57.
"Mona Lisa smile": Quoted in Allen, 236.
"depression": Saxophonist Billy Ternent, quoted in Shapiro and Hentoff, 218.

7 *He stood over six feet tall*: George Hoefer notes, Institute for Jazz Studies, Fletcher Henderson file. *The nickname "Smack"*: Various reasons have been put forth to explain the nickname—that it rhymed with his roommate's nickname ("Mac"), that it described the sound of his kisses, and that it was the sound he made in his sleep. All of them appear to date from his university years. See Allen, 6.

8 Stewart, Jazz Masters, 21–23.

9 *"car crazy"*: Wells/Dance, 51.
"a predilection for rose": Stewart, Jazz Masters, 26.

10 *Once he began writing:* Dance, *The World of Swing,* 352; and Allen, 302.

    Clarinetist Russell Procope: Procope, JOHP transcript, 2:36–37.

11 *The image inspired:* Gioia, "Jazz and the Primitivist Myth."

    Before that, social historians: Shih, "The Spread of Jazz and the Big Bands"; Hennessey, "From Jazz to Swing." This landmark dissertation was revised in 1994 as a book titled *From Jazz to Swing: African American Jazz Musicians and Their Music, 1890–1935.*

    On the other hand: See Baraka [Jones], *Blues People,* chap. 9, for a provocative discourse on black middle-class mentality.

    "a fraction of what their white counterparts earned,": DeVeaux, *The Birth of Bebop,* 50.

12 *"the blending . . . of class and mass":* Baker, 93 (emphasis original). Long interpreted as a chiefly literary phenomenon, the Harlem Renaissance has been traced in a variety of musical contexts in recent years. See, for example, Floyd, *Music and the Harlem Renaissance;* Ramsey, *Race Music,* 111–17.

13 Schuller, *SE,* 15.

14 *"learned two things at once":* Dodge, *Hot Jazz and Jazz Dance,* 101.

15 *Some of the earliest commentary:* For representative writing by white commentators, see Osgood, *So This Is Jazz;* Seldes, *The Seven Lively Arts,* both discussed in chap. 5 of this book. For a discussion of black writing, see chap. 2.

16 *"The radio made audiences":* Dance, *World of Swing,* 38.

    "Tours produced new markets": Stewart, *Jazz Masters,* 25–26.

    "best advertisement": Hammond, with Irving Townsend, *John Hammond on Record,* 67.

17 *"the golden, seething spirit":* Hobson, "Memorial to Fletcher."

    Meanwhile, jazz scholars have challenged: See the essays by Krin Gabbard, "The Jazz Canon and Its Consequences," and Jed Rasula, "The Media of Memory: The Seductive Menace of Records in Jazz History," in Gabbard, ed., *Jazz Among the Discourses.*

18 *"[o]ne of the most striking aspects":* DeVeaux, 12.

19 *"the public in general":* Panassié, *Hot Jazz,* xiii.

    "the artistry of ritual": Floyd, *The Power of Black Music,* 22. Floyd repeatedly stresses the integration of movement and music, since the foundation of his theory lies in the centrality of the ring shout, which "fused the sacred and the secular, music and dance" (p. 6). See also Olly Wilson, "The Association of Movement and Music as a Manifestation of a Black Conceptual Approach to Music Making," 98–105; Small, 28–29; Murray, chap. 10; and Marshall and Jean Stearns, esp. 315–34.

    "choreographed swing music": Stearns and Stearns, 325.

    "art form": Olly Wilson, "Black Music as an Art Form," in *Black Music Research Journal* 3 (1983): 1–22.

20 *"perhaps others will find":* Allen, viii.

1. A New Negro from the Old South

1 *"Fletcher Henderson came to New York":* Allen, 6; Bushell/Tucker, 15. In a phone conversation on July 20, 1992, Theresa Henderson Burroughs, Fletcher's niece, reported that the Hendersons had no relatives in New York when her uncle arrived there. The woman Bushell recalled, she said, may have been Emma Wallace, "a very close family friend" of the Hendersons who had moved to New York about that time. Before coming to New York, Wallace had taught at Howard Normal School in Cuthbert, Georgia—where Henderson's father and mother served as principal and teacher, respectively—and lived in the "teacher house" adjoining the Henderson home. According to Mrs. Burroughs (with her mother's concurrence in the background), it is "quite likely" that Fletcher lived with Wallace when he first arrived in New York. Wallace later married a man with four children, one of whom was actress Ruby Dee.

2 *"formative years"*: Osofsky, 17. E. Franklin Frazier, quoted in Osofsky (123), called 1920 Harlem "the Mecca of the colored people of New York City."

3 *"into a higher civilization"*: Quoted in Lewis, *When Harlem Was in Vogue*, 7.

4 *"the 1920s were the decade"*: Douglas, 77. Examining the transition between "Victorianism" and "modernity" (the terms he uses in his afterword, 399), May finds black culture to have been a catalyst. See May, 88.

5 *"all of the big hotels"*: Fletcher, *100 Years of the Negro in Show Business*, 261.

   "he did as much": Quoted in Kellner, *The Harlem Renaissance*, 117.

6 *"strong personality"*: Dews, *Remembering*, 1–3.

7 *"were constantly agitating"*: Washington, *Up From Slavery*, 71.

8 *"a cultural anomaly"*: Dews, "Young Fletcher Henderson," 65.

   "in what was later": Meier, 210.

   Wright's political activities: Dews, *Remembering*, 10.

9 *"largely on foot"*: The story may well be more fact than legend. According to Dews, who interviewed Irma Henderson Jacobs, Fletcher Sr. himself told the story to his children forty years after it happened (Dews, *Remembering*, 7). For Washington's account of his five-hundred-mile trip to Hampton, finished mostly "by walking" and "begging rides," see Washington, *Up From Slavery*, 53–55.

   Atlanta University's president: See Dews, *Remembering*, 7, 11, and Bullock, 32.

   "leading colored school": Dews, *Remembering*, 16, 21, 25.

10 *"battlegrounds for rival forces" to "disgusting"*: Harris, 3, 4, 8.

    By separating: Meier, 49.

    "State Education Evangelist": "Papers of the Fletcher Hamilton Henderson Family," in *Amistad Log* 2 (February 1985): 9.

11 *"ideal maker"*: Harris, 9–10.

    "He was the boss": J.C. Higginbotham, JOHP transcript, 35.

12 *"Anybody who thought"*: Author interview with Fletcher Muse, Cuthbert, Georgia, August 1992.

13 *Booker T. Washington*: Washington, 49.

    "represented more than": Dews, *Remembering*, 41–42.

    "used to lock Fletcher up": Horace Henderson, JOHP transcript, I:3–4. Horace (b. 1904) would not have been born yet when his brother was six or seven; he probably received the story from his parents. Irma attested that her parents' efforts to instill musical discipline included corporal punishment and she confirmed her parents' strict musical tastes (see Allen, 3).

14 *"phoenix-like" rise*: Russell, *Atlanta 1847–1890*, 116–18; Meier, 156.

15 *"bought a Winchester"*: Quoted in Litwack, 317.

    "negroes of the criminal type": Ray Stannard Baker, "The Atlanta Riot," booklet "republished" from *The American Magazine* (n.p., Phillips Publishing Co., 1907).

    Such sharp distinctions: See, for example, Harris, chap. 2, and St. Clair Drake and Horace R. Cayton, *Black Metropolis: A Study of Negro Life in a Northern City* (Rev. ed., New York: Harcourt Brace, 1970). Drake and Cayton's detailed study of Chicago's black community led them to describe a class dichotomy whose elements they characterize as "respectable" and "shady." For a discussion of how the terms reflected Fletcher Henderson's New York, as well as black Chicago, see Hennessey, *From Jazz to Swing*, 22, 68–69, and 82–83.

16 *"represented archetypal" to "pianists avoided"*: Harris, 27, 39, 48–49.

17 *"At the time his name was James"*: Bushell/Tucker, 15. As evidence of the name change, Allen (9) reprints an article with the byline "F. H. Henderson, Jr." that appeared in a January 1917 edition of *The Scroll*, Atlanta University's student newspaper. Three years later, "Mr. Fletcher H. Henderson" appears on the list of cast members in the program for the Atlanta University Senior Class production of Richard Brinsley Sheridan's play *The Rivals* (performed February 20, 1920). For a

copy of this program, I'm grateful to Josephine Harreld Love, whose father, Professor Kemper Harreld, played violin during the performance.

18 *"brought up"*: Dews, "Young Fletcher Henderson."

"had a little band": Horace Henderson, JOHP transcript, I:2. Unfortunately, Horace never mentions any of the pieces his brother played, and his comments on Fletcher's style of playing at these ad hoc performances, though provocative, seem filtered through the thick lens of the later history of the jazz piano: "it had a beat, and of course it had that stride, you know, like the late and great Thomas 'Fats' Waller ... Earl Hines, and James P. Johnson."

19 *"the mandatory-attendance chapel services"*: All quotations on Henderson at Atlanta University appear in Dews, "Young Fletcher Henderson." See Dominique-René De Lerma, "Harreld, Kemper," in *Amerigrove*, 2:327–28. An oral history of Atlanta offers a telling glimpse of Harreld's character. As professor at Morehouse College, Harreld "shrewdly worked out a way" for his students to see the city's annual performance of the Metropolitan Opera "by having them serve as ushers" (see Clifford M. Kuhn, Harlon E. Joye, and E. Bernard West, *Living Atlanta: An Oral History of the City, 1914–1948* [Atlanta: Atlanta Historical Society, and Athens: The University of Georgia Press, 1990], 285.)

20 *Although he never*: Allen, 6, 7. For more on Johnson, who was Clef Club president in 1915–19, see Kellner, 194. "I first met Fletcher," Leora recalled, "when we were playing a dance on a Hudson River boat." See Shapiro and Hentoff, 218. Marriage certificate dated December 25, 1924, in the Fletcher Henderson Family Papers, Amistad Research Center, Tulane University, Box 1A, File 6.

21 *close-knit spirit*: In an interview on June 27, 1989, Josephine Harreld Love talked of the "close circle" that Atlanta's network of alumni had formed. "Probably," she said, "Pace knew when Fletcher came to New York." Likewise, Dews describes the Atlanta alumni as "tight-knit group, with chapters in cities throughout the country." She adds that "It was natural for Henderson ... to consult Pace when he needed a part-time job." Moreover, it was Pace, she writes, "who dissuaded Henderson once and for all from a career in chemistry" ("Young Fletcher Henderson").

22 *"primitive"*: See Handy, 194.

His story of composing: Ibid., 118–21.

favorable reviews: See William Ferris's introduction to *Blues: An Anthology*, ed. W. C. Handy (1926; rpt. of revised edition [1972], New York: Da Capo Press, 1990), 2.

23 *"devoted disciple" to "sharp business side"*: Author interview with Love, March 24, 1989.

"an unusually progressive black enterprise": Alexa B. Henderson, 101.

"took charge of the arranging": Handy, 197.

"while Henderson played ballads": Handy, letter to Marshall Stearns, August 24, 1953. Thanks to Elliott S. Hurwitt for bringing this letter to my attention.

24 *The record, an audition*: Allen, 8.

25 *"the responsibility"*: Meier, 193.

26 *"one of the few"*: See Lewis, caption on photo of advertisement between pp. 144–45. The real estate office of Nail and Parker, on West 135th Street, stood just a few blocks from the Black Swan studio on West 138th Street. James Weldon Johnson dedicated his book *Black Manhattan* (1930) to Nail.

27 *"I never saw Pace"*: Bushell/Tucker, 31.

"to listen to the singers": Allen, 11. All the partners in Black Swan are listed in Sampson, 52.

28 *Kemper Harreld*: Allen (60) could not confirm Henderson's presence on the Kemper Harreld recording, but Josephine Harreld Love owns a rare copy of the record and remembers being in the recording studio with her father and Henderson that day (interview on March 24, 1989).

29 *Notably absent*: Albertson, 37.

30 *"the Black Swan company"*: See McGinty, 91.

31 *Black Swan's biggest hit*: Allen, 13–14.

"*It proved a great success*": Waters/Samuels, 141.

32 "*Remember those class distinctions*" to "*look me over*": Ibid., 141–42.

33 *Titled "Silas Green"*: Box 1A, File 12.

34 "*I kept having arguments*": Waters/Samuels, 146–47

35 "*didn't sing real blues*": Bushell/Tucker, 32.

36 Waters/Samuels, 147.

37 "*Conditions of traveling*": Bushell/Tucker, 36.

   Thanks to reports: See Allen, 25–32, for ample quotations from the *Defender*.

38 "*In those days*": Bushell/Tucker, 34, 38, 39.

   "*I heard this young man*": Quoted in Allen, 30. Note the use of the term *trumpet* in Henderson's statement, even though Armstrong is known to have played the cornet until at least 1924 or 1925. The jazz literature continues to reveal considerable confusion about who played which instrument and when. Thus, for convenience and consistency—and because it is nearly impossible for most people to hear the difference—*trumpet* will be used throughout the book to identify the soprano brass instrument in jazz and dance bands, unless referring to a known cornet player or to a published use of the term. The differences were slight but notable. Although many cornet models existed, the cornet tended to have a broader bore, a "squatter" shape, and a "mellower" tone than the trumpet. (See Clifford Bevan and Alyn Shipton, "Cornet," in *Jazz Grove*). Like many New Orleans players, inheriting the Crescent City's French traditions, Armstrong followed his mentor King Oliver in taking up the cornet. Among non–New Orleans players, Bix Beiderbecke stood as the most famous cornetist of the era, sticking with the instrument until his early death in 1931.

39 Allen, 45.

2. The "Paul Whiteman of the Race"

 1 Quoted in Allen, 113.

 2 "*commercial concessions*": Panassié, *The Real Jazz*, 198.
    "*erratic path*": Schuller, *EJ*, 257.

 3 "*True and False Jazz*": is the title of the first chapter of Panassié's *The Real Jazz*.
    "*hot*" and "*commercial*": Goffin, 2.
    "*black*" jazz, "*the primitive art*": Sargeant, 201.
    "*natural*," "*vibrant, spirited playing*" to "*carefully rehearsed*": Hobson, *American Jazz Music*, 15, 136–37.

 4 "*when I first*": Ellington, 419.

 5 "*disciplinary matrix*": DeVeaux, *The Birth of Bebop*, 44.
    "*new jazz history*": Erenberg, xvi–xvii.
    "*merely the sign*": Stowe, 9.

 6 "*Harlem talks American*": James Weldon Johnson, "Harlem: The Culture Capital," in Locke, 309.
    "*a case of complete acculturation*": Melville J. Herskovits, "The Negro's Americanism," in Locke, 360.
    "*inequities due to race*": Huggins, 3.
    "*mastery of form*": Baker, 15.

 7 Quoted in Hennessey (1994), 95.

 8 Howard Scott, JOHP transcript, 13 and 15.

 9 *Cultural historians:* Shih, "The Spread of Jazz and the Big Bands," in *Jazz,* ed. Hentoff and McCarthy, 173–74; and Hennessey, 82–83.

10 *four-tiered caste system:* Stewart, *Boy Meets Horn,* 90–91.

11 "*straw boss—and a worrier*": Bennie Morton, quoted in Dance, *The World of Swing,* 289.

12 *"had most of the work"*: Howard Scott, JOHP transcript, 4–5.

13 *"a cocky youngster"*: Quoted in John Chilton, *Song of the Hawk*, 9.

14 *"played a most important role"*: Stewart, *Jazz Masters*, 22.

15 Stewart, *Boy Meets Horn*, 93.

16 On Peyton and the recurring themes in his writing, see Hennessey, "From Jazz to Swing," 319–28.

17 *"has come to stay"*: J. A. Rogers, "Jazz at Home," in Locke, 221.
    "famous jazz orchestras": Rogers, 224.

18 *One well-documented factor*: See Sanjek, *From Print to Plastic*, 13. The first half of Sanjek's title sums up the change.

19 *"major white dance bands"*: Rust, *The American Dance Band Discography, 1917–1942.*

20 *The variety of record companies*: For information on record companies and labels, see Rust, *The American Record Label Book*. Henderson's recordings were also issued on two other Plaza satellites, Domino and Oriole, the latter specifically designed for sale in McCrory's stores for a quarter (Rust, 220).
    "graduated to Columbia": Driggs, 8.

21 *Club Alabam*: Sam Wooding, JOHP transcript, 144–45. Wooding's band succeeded Henderson's at the Club Alabam.
    standards of performance: See Tucker, *Ellington*, 91.
    "the Cotton Club of that era": Redman, quoted in Driggs, 8. Sam Wooding went even farther than Redman: "Well, the Cotton Club was only the echo from the Club Alabam." (Wooding transcript, 149.) For a perspective on the Alabam from one of Wooding's sidemen, see Bushell/Tucker, 51–53.

22 *Variety* 76, no. 7 (October 1, 1924): 34.

23 *"the elite level" to nickel, per dance*: Hennessey, "From Jazz to Swing," 242, 249–50.

24 *"wholesome entertainment"*: Allen, 113.

25 *"is one of the best"*: Allen, 114, quoting from *Variety*, July 30, 1924.
    most black musicians were excluded: Spring, "Changes in Jazz," 50.

26 *"From $300 to $1,200"*: Quoted in Hennessey, *From Jazz to Swing*, 93.

27 All publisher information has been gleaned from copyright cards, filed by song title, housed in the copyright office of the Music Division of the Library of Congress.

28 See Melnick, *A Right to Sing the Blues*.

29 Information on publishers in Jasen, *Tin Pan Alley*, 114–17. On Down South, see contemporary reports quoted in Allen, 63.

3. Inside the Strain: The Advent of Don Redman

1 *"the new demand"*: See Whiteman and McBride, *Jazz*, 219.
   Whiteman's own arranger: James Lincoln Collier, "Grofé, Ferde," in *Jazz Grove*.

2 *"At that time"*: Sam Wooding, JOHP transcript, 141.

3 *"the first master"*: Robert Kenselaar, "Redman, Don(ald) Matthew," in *Jazz Grove*, 1035.
   "the most outstanding": Schuller, "Arrangement," in *Jazz Grove*, 33.
   "no-nonsense": Stewart, *Boy Meets Horn*, 117.
   Recent scholars: Spring, "Changes in Jazz," 4–5.

4 *"architect"*: Schuller, *EJ*, 267.
   "restless curiosity": Schuller, *SE*, 845.

5 *"overwritten arrangement"* and *"baroque doodling"*: Gary Giddins, *Satchmo*, 81.

"a tendency to create": Olly Wilson, "Black Music as an Art Form," 3. See also Floyd, *The Power of Black Music*, 262.

6 *"resemblance ... by dissemblance"*: Gates, 104.

7 This basic theme, with its rising minor-key arpeggio falling hard on the flat-sixth degree and resolving to the fifth, can be heard in Bessie Smith's "Haunted House Blues" (recorded for Columbia with Henderson and Redman accompanying, on January 9, 1924), "Sing Sing Blues" (December 6, 1924), and "Blue Spirit Blues" (October 11, 1929). A similar idea forms part of the first-strain melody of "She's Cryin' for Me," by Santo Pecora, trombonist of the New Orleans Rhythm Kings, as played by NORK on a March 26, 1925, recording for Victor, reissued on New World Records 269.

8 *"the arranger's chorus"*: Lange, *Arranging for the Modern Dance Orchestra*, 207–12.

9 *"Arr. by Don Redman"*: Allen, 53.

10 *"When Smack heard Louis"*: Stewart, *Jazz Masters*, 22.

11 *In chorus 2:* This chorus, and in fact the entire Henderson band recording, seems to have no link to the stock arrangement issued by the Berlin company. Even the key scheme is different. The recording alternates between B♭ and E♭; the stock shifts from G to C to E♭ and back to C. Berlin claimed the song's publication copyright on May 10, 1923 (E564047), a few days before the recording, which suggests that Henderson's recording was responding to a publication. Irving Berlin, "When You Walked Out Someone Else Walked Right In," arrangement by Mornay D. Helm (New York: Irving Berlin, Inc., 1923).

12 *No chorus like this:* Paul Biese, James Altiere, and S. Walter Williams, "Chicago Blues," arrangement by William Grant Still (New York: Melody Music Co., 1924).

13 *"Special Chorus"*: Harry Owens and Vincent Rose, "Linger Awhile," arrangement by Frank E. Barry (New York: Leo. Feist, Inc., 1923).

14 For rare and provocative insights on Wiedoeft's "violin-based" style, "French school" tone, and vast influence on jazz reedmen, see Sudhalter, *Lost Chords*, 368 and 766. Samples of Krueger's rapid-fire obbligato playing can be heard on the ODJB's recordings of "Margie," "Broadway Rose," and "Home Again Blues," all from 1920–21. Other musicians felt Krueger's impact. Arranger-reedman Bill Challis, for example, claimed to have copied Krueger's lines from records when he was learning to play saxophone. See Challis, JOHP transcript, 5. Meanwhile, an obbligato by Otto Hardwick also resembles Redman's Kruegeresque runs, in Duke Ellington's "Choo Choo," transcribed in Tucker, *Ellington*, 144.

15 *"many bands continued"*: Tucker, *Ellington*, 140. Ronald Riddle, "Novelty Piano Music," in Hasse, *Ragtime*, 285.

16 *"blues novelty number"*: Allen, 89.

17 *"special phonograph record arrangement"*: Allen, 89. Still's stock arrangement merits some comment. Published in 1924, the stock calls for an artillery of percussion instruments: bells, "locomotive whistle," cymbal, gong, wire brush, and triangle, as well as conventional bass and snare drums. Twice the drummer even assumes the role of engineer calling out "Board" and "Next Stop Erie." Still wrote the arrangement within the brief period he studied with ultramodernist Edgard Varèse (1923–25), many of whose works feature imaginative uses of percussion.

18 *"electrical effects"*: A *Billboard* writer reported that "[After] the Storm" was one of the "high spots" of the Lafayette performance. Quoted in Allen, 92.

19 *"sobbing" effects"*: According to Russell Sanjek, the wah-wah effect was "responsible for its [the record's] large sales." See *The Popular Music Business*, 64.

20 *Redman must have been listening:* For a photo of the Little Ramblers with Rollini holding the goofus, see Charters and Kunstadt, 129. The group had begun recording on August 10 under the pseudonym "Goofus Five." Contact between Henderson's orchestra and the California Ramblers was unavoidable: In the Columbia studio on June 30, 1924, Henderson and Redman accompanied vaudeville singer George Williams on two recordings squeezed between sessions by the California Ramblers. See Allen, 111.

21 *an emissary for the blues:* There is abundant evidence testifying to Henderson's newly won reputation as a blues player, deserved or not. Allen has noted that Henderson's full name began to appear on the labels of records on which he appears as an accompanist, signifying increasing fame and marketability (Allen, 42). Moreover, by August, Henderson had been set up as the nominal head of Jack Mills's new race subsidiary, Down South Music Publishing Corporation.

22 *Turning a blues song:* See Tucker, *Ellington*, 299, n14, for one musician's testimony that recording studios dictated tempo and mood. James Dapogny, a jazz pianist and University of Michigan professor of music theory, told me that blues singer Sippie Wallace, who began her recording career in 1923 and with whom Dapogny performed before her death in 1986, made a distinction between the tempos of a sung blues and an instrumental blues performance: the latter was played faster than the former.

southern-style, gutbucket blues: Both "southern" and "gutbucket" carried specific stylistic connotations for 1920s jazz musicians. Garvin Bushell said that "there wasn't an Eastern performer who could really play the blues. We later absorbed how from the southern musicians we heard." See Nat Hentoff, "Garvin Bushell and New York Jazz in the 1920s," in *Jazz Review* (January 1959): 12. The term "gutbucket," current in the 1920s, connoted a rough, gritty playing style, often achieved with devices placed over the horn's bell, such as a hat, a plunger, or perhaps a small pail. See Bushell/Tucker, 19; Charters and Kunstadt, 192; and Gold, 116.

23 *"You didn't have written music":* Hentoff, "Garvin Bushell," 41. Clarinetist Buster Bailey, who joined Henderson in late 1924, spoke similarly about the band's session with Bessie Smith and other singers. "We didn't have any rehearsals for Bessie's records.... This, by the way, applied ... to almost all the blues singers," in Shapiro and Hentoff, 244. Bushell, however, later suggested that sometimes written music was used: "Often there were only two pieces of music, one for the piano and one for the trumpet (or violin). Sometimes everybody had a part," in Bushell/Tucker, 32.

24 *Another horn player:* Garvin Bushell suggested the extent of Dunn's influence, when, on hearing a recording from 1922 supposed to feature Dunn, he said, "I'm not too sure that's Johnny Dunn.... besides, by that time everybody was double-timing." See Bushell/Tucker, 157.

25 *bona fide hit:* Albertson, 33, 37–38.

"center tone": See Hadlock, 223–24. As Hadlock points out, the pitches F through A above middle C were Bessie Smith's "most powerful, ringing tones," and she often used one of them as a "center tone" in rendering a song. He cites "Down Hearted Blues" as an example.

26 *"one of the best informed":* Quoted in Allen, 63.

"rich negroes": Van Vechten, 77.

27 Quoted in Chilton, *The Song of the Hawk*, 9.

28 *the traits of Hawkins's early style:* Schuller, *SE*, esp. 426–30.

29 *several other musicians would echo it:* Mark Tucker has shown how large parts of Green's solo were transposed and rearranged by trumpeter Bubber Miley, in his famous 1926 solo from "East St. Louis Toodle-O." See Tucker, *Ellington*, 248–50. Later trombonists revisited the solo, including Dicky Wells in Lloyd Scott's 1927 recording of "Symphonic Scronch" (Tucker, 308), and Benny Morton in Henderson's 1931 recording of his brother Horace's piece, "Comin' and Going" (see chap. 7).

30 *"Paul Whiteman came himself":* Howard Scott, JOHP transcript, 12.

4. A New Orleans Trumpeter in a New York Band

1 *"He was big and fat":* Quoted in Driggs, 96.

2 *"an intricate, well-marked arrangement":* Quoted in Allen, 125. Henderson recalled the waltz medley (Allen, 125); Armstrong recalled the ballad, in Brothers, 93.

3 *"a good reader"*: Marshall, quoted in Allen, 125.
   "Louis, his style": Driggs, 96.
4 *"Louis played"*: Howard Scott JOHP transcript, 10.
5 *"is more than a historical event"*: Baraka [Jones], *Blues People*, 155.
   "The First Great Soloist" : Schuller, *EJ*, chap. 3.
6 *Like Beethoven:* See Burnham, *Beethoven Hero*.
   "appear painfully dated": Hadlock, 18.
   "shine like a solitary star": Panassié, *Louis Armstrong*, 60.
   "come from a different world": Porter and Ullman, *Jazz*, 61.
   "exists within his own": Bergreen, 249.
7 *"aural shift"*: Schuller, *EJ*, 263.
8 *"the House that Blues Built"*: See Kennedy, *Jelly Roll, Bix, and Hoagy*, 72–73.
   "a conscious effort": Allen, 139.
9 *"cause the listener"*: Schuller, *EJ*, 263.
10 *"ricky-tick"*: Harker, "The Early Musical Development of Louis Armstrong,"
   159–61.
11 *"stylistic tug-of-war"*: Schuller, *EJ*, 260.
   "deliberately banal figures": Collier, *Louis Armstrong*, 129.
12 *"the controversy"*: Shapiro and Hentoff, 205.
   "a heavy accented back beat": Stewart, *Boy Meets Horn*, 65. For more on the term
   Boston in early jazz, see Gold, *Jazz Talk*, 28, where it connotes both a hot solo, as
   in Stewart's usage, and "a piano style characterized by accented bass figures."
13 See Harker, " 'Telling a Story'," 46–83, for the most cogent analysis of the
   phenomenon.
14 Shapiro and Hentoff, 206.
15 Schuller, *EJ*, 262.
16 *"The first number"*: Shapiro and Hentoff, 206.
17 *Joe Smith's place:* According to Chris Albertson, she got Howard Scott fired
   "because she wanted Joe in the band." Russell Procope, JOHP transcript, II: 25–26.
   "Toots" to "Joe Smith was the Eastern": Shapiro and Hentoff, 205, 209, 221–22.
   "a considerable discussion": Quoted in Allen, 139, from *Variety*, October 7, 1925.
   "Bessie Smith was just crazy" and "the most soulful trumpeter": Shapiro and
   Hentoff, 210, 222.
18 *"key figure"*: The best assessment of Schoebel's work appears in Sudhalter, *Lost
   Chords*, 31 and chap. 2, passim.
19 *[Armstrong] showed a little book:* Allen, 134.
20 *"['Sugar Foot Stomp'] was the record"*: Allen, 134.
   It ranked among the best-selling: Whitburn, 208.
   Henderson himself: Unidentified published clipping in Fletcher Henderson file of
   the Institute of Jazz Studies, Rutgers Univ., Newark, NJ.
21 *"The whole association" to "semi-improvised passages"*: Schuller, *EJ*, 262–63.
22 *"old-time gospel music"*: Clark, 203.
23 *Redman's arrangement became the model:* Bands whose recordings of "Sugar Foot
   Stomp" are clearly based on the Redman arrangement (or its adaptation by
   Henderson for a 1931 recording) include those led by Merritt Brunies (Nov. 1925),
   Fred Hamm (Dec. 1925), Artie Shaw (Aug. 1936), Benny Goodman (Sept. and
   Nov. 1937), Larry Clinton (Aug. 1938), and Bob Crosby (Jan. 1942). See Crawford
   and Magee, 80–81, for a list of the bands that recorded the piece under one title or
   the other.
24 *And there were also continuous bookings:* See Allen, 129–64, passim.
   "I had 'Wedged' in there": Brothers, 94.
   "those fine boys": Shapiro and Hentoff, 206.
25 *"in the situation"*: Collier, *Louis Armstrong*, 127.

"all-too-brief solos": Bergreen, 250, 251.

"The stopper was still on": Giddins, *Satchmo*, 83.

26 *"Fletcher didn't dig me"*: Collier, *Louis Armstrong*, 133; Brothers, 64.

"cats" got "careless: Quoted in Allen, 140.

27 *"He used to write"*: Ibid.

"bands were always changing" to "He wasn't anxious to be a star": Berrett, 41; and Bergreen, 257. Both sources draw excerpts from a recorded interview released as *Satchmo and Me* (Riverside RLP 12–120).

"I had to choose": Brothers, 93.

28 *"All the boys"*: Ibid., 94.

29 *"the Talk of Chicago"*: Ibid.; Allen, 166.

5. A Paradox of the Race?

1 *From this perspective:* See, for example, Williams, liner notes for *The Smithsonian Collection of Classic Jazz*, 19.

"revue-derived variety entertainment format": Howland, 85 and 122.

2 *"improvisation and irresponsibility" to "no careless improvising"*: Osgood, 5–8. See also Seldes, *The Seven Lively Arts*. For an illuminating study of Seldes's life and work, see Kammen, esp. chap. 3, which discusses the book and the racial themes in its discussion of jazz.

3 *"If you didn't read"*: Bernhardt, 62.

4 *"this sense of always"*: DuBois, 215.

5 Hodeir, 25, 33.

6 "Clarinet Marmalade" became one of the most frequently recorded jazz standards before 1942. See Crawford and Magee, x, 14–15.

7 Eleven jazz recordings in 1921 followed quickly on the heels of Paul Whiteman's version in August 1920. From Oct. 1921 to Sept. 1926 no recordings of it are listed in Rust. See Crawford and Magee, 91.

8 *"the band tried hard"*: Schuller, *EJ*, 267.

9 *"ran across the floor"*: Horace Henderson, JOHP transcript, II:13–15.

10 *"astonished at the artistic rendition"* to *"blue syncopation"*: Quoted in Allen, 168.

"redeem us in the Loop": Allen, 214–15.

11 *"to incorporate elements"*: DeVeaux, *The Birth of Bebop*, 63.

12 *"something in the jungle beat"*: Quoted in Allen, 294.

"Students and their 'girls' ": Ibid., 292.

13 *The Savoy opened* to *Lindy Hop:* Stearns and Stearns, chap. 40; Spring, "Changes in Jazz," 99–118

"It was always inspiring": Wells/Dance, 35–40 passim.

14 *"Fletcher Henderson ('Himself')"*: Allen, 184, 211; see also Spring, "Changes in Jazz," 100.

15 *Don Redman is widely assumed:* See Allen, 194; Driggs, liner notes to *The Fletcher Henderson Story: A Study in Frustration* (CBS 66423); Rust, *Jazz Records*, 720; and Williams, liner notes, 46–47. Gunther Schuller calls "The Stampede" "one of Redman's best early arrangements," in *SE*, 430.

"to play like Louis": Stewart, *Boy Meets Horn*, 123.

16 *"brass hyperboles"*: Williams, liner notes, 47.

17 *Armstrong's openings:* Magee, 317–18.

"developing pattern of melody": Williams, liner notes, 47.

18 *even Roy Eldridge:* Chilton, *Song of the Hawk*, 44.

19 Rust, *Jazz Records*, passim, includes an impressive roster of bands making recordings of "The Stampede"—all of them white except for Henderson's and the Savoy Bearcats. They include ensembles led by key figures in 1920s jazz such as

Joe Candullo, Red Nichols and Miff Mole, Rube Bloom, Jean Goldkette, and Jack Hylton, the leader of Great Britain's premier dance orchestra.

20 *"Redman's prophetic ensemble background"*: Schuller, *EJ*, 265.

21 *"After a lot of top level"*: Stewart, *Boy Meets Horn*, 114 and 119. Stewart's story, it should be pointed out, contains some factual inconsistencies. Stewart writes that the band played a ballad called "Dear, on a Night Like This" for the "other side of the record," but both Rust and Allen date the band's only recording of that number on Nov. 26, 1927—more than six months later. Moreover, neither lists Stewart as a member of the band on either date. Nevertheless, Stewart's comments on "Whiteman Stomp" match up with what other black musicians have noted about the record industry, which tended to confine black bands to jazz and blues.
"The biggest thing Fletcher ever did": Judd, 7.

6. Beyond the Ballroom

1   *A band could still play:* See Spring, "Changes in Jazz," 75–83, on venues such as theaters; quote from Bushell appears on p. 29.

2   *"and through it all"*: New York *Amsterdam News* quoted in Allen, 221.

3   *announced as 150 performers:* Ibid., 228–30, cites press reports of *Great Day.*

4   *"we went further"*: Stewart, *Boy Meets Horn*, 106.
"known playing engagements": Allen, 241–43.

5   *"[T]he highways were bad"*: Williams quoted in Dance, *World of Swing*, 73.
"nice, clean looking place": Stewart, *Boy Meets Horn*, 74, 121.
"You could buy a gun": Wells/Dance, 50.

6   *"All the restraint"*: Stewart, *Boy Meets Horn*, 112.
"pecking order": Stewart, *Jazz Masters*, 152, 154.
"[e]verybody in the band drank": Higginbotham, JOHP transcript, 102.
"getting drunk with us": J. C. Higginbotham, as told to Ethel Klein, "Some of My Best Friends Are Enemies" (April 22, 1947): 7, unidentified clipping in Higginbotham file, Institute of Jazz Studies, Rutgers Univ., Newark, NJ.

7   *"Smack's band"*: Stewart, *Boy Meets Horn*, 106–7.
"If you own": Wells/Dance, 57.
Henderson drank, but only after: Higginbotham, JOHP transcript, 102.
not much of a "mixer": Procope, JOHP transcript, II:30–31.

8   *"cars, instead of buses"*: Shapiro and Hentoff, 217.
"modern New York": Douglas, 17.

9   *"in the early years"*: Dance, *World of Swing*, 289.

10 *"Fletcher was car crazy"*: Wells/Dance, 51.
"a real second line": Stewart, *Boy Meets Horn*, 107.
"Smack's guys": Quoted in Chilton, *Song of the Hawk*, 56.
"Those were the days": Stewart, *Boy Meets Horn*, 107–8.
Sandy Williams remembered: Dance, *World of Swing*, 73.

11 Stewart, *Jazz Masters*, 24–25.

12 *"a large-framed"*: Dews, *Remembering*, 47. According to Stewart, "the Hendersons wrote many letters, sent loads of telegrams, and telephoned all over the eastern seaboard to coordinate the trips and consolidate the bookings," *Jazz Masters*, 24.

13 *"gatekeepers"*: Hennessey, *From Jazz to Swing*, 123.
"Henderson might have": Stewart, *Boy Meets Horn*, 119, 120.

14 *"the Chicago counterpart"*: Ibid., 90.

15 *"Henderson never"*: Hadlock, 205.
"as architect": Schuller, *EJ*, 267.

"exchanging arrangements": Coleman Hawkins interview on Riverside LP 12–117/118 (1956).

16 *"careless"*: Leora Henderson, quoted in Shapiro and Hentoff, 222.

"the story about the head injury": Letter to the author from Theresa Henderson Burroughs, May 4, 1990. Mrs. Burroughs, although only three months old at the time of the accident, had heard the story from her mother and related the events with her mother's confirmation, in a phone conversation on June 4, 1992.

17 *"Fletcher's band had some"*: Hawkins interview and Hadlock, 203–6.

18 *"people who didn't hear"*: Stewart, *Boy Meets Horn*, 113.

"Don't let yourself": Hammond, quoted in Allen, 298.

"give anything like": to *"dionysiac heat"*: Hobson, "Memorial to Fletcher."

19 *"how far the soloists"*: Schuller and Williams, liner notes, 13.

20 *There is some question*: For discographical details see Allen, 244, and Rust, 722. Both suggest that Benny Morton might be the trombone player on the Paramount recording, and Jimmy Harrison has always been credited with the solo on the Columbia recording (see Allen, 245; Schuller and Williams, liner notes, 13–14, and notes for various LP reissues). The breaks are so similar, however, that they must have come from one man's horn, almost certainly Harrison's.

21 *the stock arrangement:* The stock itself is dated 1927, although Williams did not claim the copyright for "Hop Off" (in a piano solo version) until Jan. 23, 1928 (E 686068).

22 *Redman usually gets credit:* The arrangement's attribution to Redman seems to have begun with Frank Driggs, who assumed that the scat vocal in the coda of "Hop Off" was Redman, making "a brief final appearance" with the band. See Driggs's liner notes for *A Study in Frustration*. In fact, as Allen writes (p. 245) the vocal break is by Jimmy Harrison, who frequently sang with the band in public. The assumption that Redman made the arrangement, though he had not returned for a "brief final appearance," is repeated by Hadlock, 206; Schuller, *EJ*, 267; and Schuller and Williams, liner notes, 13.

23 Schuller, *EJ*, 268.

24 *"float against the rhythm"*: Dave Jones and James Dapogny, unpublished notes to a transcription of "King Porter Stomp."

25 *"I counted the choruses"*: Dance, *The World of Swing*, 69–71.

"bobbing in rhythm": Stewart, *Boy Meets Horn*, 102.

26 *"He [Morton] and Fletcher were great friends"*: Horace Henderson, JOHP transcript, 1:69.

27 Allen, 246, 529.

7. Connie's Inn Orchestra

1 *"almost every doorway"*: Russell Procope, JOHP transcript, I:27–28.

"Seventh Avenue, going north": Quoted in Shapiro and Hentoff, 167

2 *"Connie's Inn was in a different bracket"*: Procope, II:24. On Connie's Inn and the Lafayette, see also Anderson, 175; Lewis, *When Harlem Was in Vogue*, 210–11; and Kellner, 79, 214.

3 *"I remember seeing"*: Procope, JOHP transcript, II:24, 28.

"the Number One job": Quoted in Dance, *The World of Swing*, 353. In the era's informal hierarchy of Harlem jazz venues, "number three" would have been Small's Paradise, which accommodated a largely black audience, unlike the Cotton Club or Connie's Inn.

4 *"only colored band"*: quoted in Allen, 251.

"good deal": Ibid., 253.

"a great one": Ibid., 261.

5 *"some severe artistic lapses"*: Schuller, *SE,* 323.
   "backtrack": Chilton, *Song of the Hawk,* 67.
6 *"tangos, waltzes, foxtrots"*: Allen, 253; Procope, JOHP transcript, II:29.
   "I don't recall any 'desperation' ": E-mail correspondence with Benny Carter, mediated by Edward Berger, May 7, 2002.
7 *"growling stuff"*: Snowden, in Dance, *World of Swing,* 53.
   "there was an unwritten custom": Stewart, *Boy Meets Horn,* 113.
   "All the time": See Kirk/Lee, 73–74.
8 *"gentlemen"*: See Berger, Berger, and Patrick, I:17.
9 *"take care of business"* to *"The Big Trade"*: Procope, JOHP transcript, II:22–23, 38, 43, 46.
   The swap was remarkable: For quotation from the *New York Age,* see Allen, 254–55.
10 *"dignified" air* to *"intellectual ambitions"*: Ellington, 124–25.
11 *"bravura"*: Bob Zieff, "Stark, Bobby," *Jazz Grove.*
    "Mr. Bar and Mr. Grill": Williams, quoted in Dance, *World of Swing,* 68.
    "fired and hired": Stewart, *Boy Meets Horn,* 123.
12 *"Jimmy had soul"*: Dance, *World of Swing,* 284–85.
13 Bob Zieff, "Jones, Claude," in *Jazz Grove.*
14 *"[y]ou could play a solo"*: Quoted in Chilton, *Song of the Hawk,* 72–73.
15 Referred to as the "New Haven Conservatory of Music" in biographical sketches, it may have been the Neighborhood Music School, an academy created largely for immigrant children that enjoyed considerable support from the Yale University School of Music, beginning with the largesse of Yale's first music professor, composer Horatio Parker in the 1890s. See Grimes, *They Who Speak in Music.*
16 The following comes from Procope, JOHP transcript, I:1–16, 29.
17 *"a master"*: Ellington, 222.
18 *"way of accenting"*: Quoted in Chilton, *Song of the Hawk,* 69.
19 *"the real leader"*: Schuller, *SE,* 325.
    "simple, metrically accurate": T. Dennis Brown, "Johnson, Walter," in *Jazz Grove.*
    "sonically enveloped the band": Schuller, *SE,* 227.
    "They used to call Walter": Dance, *World of Swing,* 351.
20 *"nine-tenths Caucasian"*: For Stewart's colorful portrait of Kirby, see *Jazz Masters,* 151–59.
21 *"one of the finest"*: Schuller, *SE,* 325
22 *"warm B-flat baritone"*: Will Friedwald, *Jazz Singing,* chap. 2, "Mr. Satch and Mr. Cros." 32, 33. For a revealing cultural interpretation of popular singing in this period, with emphasis on how Bing Crosby supplanted Rudy Vallee as a "normative" model for male singing, see Allison McCracken, " 'God's Gift to Us Girls': Crooning, Gender, and the Re-Creation of American Popular Song, 1928–1933," *American Music* 17, no. 4 (Winter 1999): 365–95.
23 *"Fletcher used all sorts of arrangers"*: Procope, JOHP transcript, II:34–35.
    "I don't recall": E-mail interview with Benny Carter, mediated by Edward Berger, May 7, 2002.
    "would write skeleton things": Horace Henderson, JOHP transcript, 15.
24 *"made arrangements for Henderson like mad"*: Horace Henderson, JOHP transcript, 155.
    "a spectacular, out-of-this-world swinger": Stewart, *Boy Meets Horn,* 114.
25 *"When the long-awaited record date"*: Stewart, *Boy Meets Horn,* 114.
26 *"the one that brought"*: Horace Henderson, JOHP transcript, 155.
    "Chinatown" received no jazz recordings: Crawford and Magee, 14, which is based on Rust, *Jazz Records.*

27 *Schuller claims:* Schuller, *SE*, 634–37.
    Richard Sudhalter challenges: Sudhalter, *Lost Chords*, 341ff.
28 *"popular music, mostly bland":* Carter quoted in Berger, Berger, and Patrick, 1:59.
29 *"Stark's brief but spectacular":* Schuller, *EJ*, 268.
30 *"He would give me":* Carter interview, May 7, 2002.
31 *"the final key":* Schuller, *EJ*, 273.
32 *"When Henderson began":* Quoted in Lees, *Arranging the Score*, 155.
33 *"Ever hear him"* and *"Everybody memorized that solo":* Quoted in Porter, *Lester Young*, 34. The story about Young carrying the record around is told in Williams, liner notes, 46.
34 *"in the inflections":* Sudhalter, *Lost Chords*, 451. For Stewart's prose tribute to Beiderbecke, with whom he once shared a locker at the Roseland Ballroom, see *Jazz Masters*, 18.
    mallet-on-chimes tone: Carmichael's first memoir, *The Stardust Road* (1946), begins with memories sparked by Bix Beiderbecke's death, and he quotes himself describing Bix's sound: " 'Just four notes,' I said. 'But he didn't blow them—he hit 'em like a mallet hits a chime.' " See Carmichael, 7.
    "Admiring Bix as I did": Quoted in Allen, 255.
35 He is not listed in the *ASCAP Biographical Dictionary* of 1948, 1952, or 1966, and he does not figure in most histories of jazz, although Schuller refers to him as one of several "arrangers" working for the "Mills band . . . on an intermittent basis" in the early 1930s (Schuller, *SE*, 386).
36 *"haunt[ed] the Roseland":* Rex Stewart: *Jazz Masters*, 21.
37 *"household word":* Quoted in Berger, Berger, and Patrick, I:176.
    "the great Archie Bleyer": Horace Henderson, JOHP transcript, 22.
    "valuable technical reference works": Quoted in Berger, Berger, and Patrick, I:74.
    "Every professional musician": Quoted in ibid., I:177.
38 *Horace contributed two pieces:* Horace played piano on both records, whose labels credit Horace as the composer. "Comin' an' Goin' " [*sic*], however, was submitted for copyright eighteen months later as a melody only, and with Fletcher's name, not Horace's, on it (see Allen, 267 and 545). Perhaps the piece was a fraternal collaboration, or perhaps—given the time lag between recording and copyright—Fletcher saw some reason to protect the piece after his brother had moved on, and quickly jotted down the tune and claimed it as his own.
    "I had nothing but admiration": Horace Henderson, JOHP transcript, 14, 122.
39 *"the biggest and most outstanding"* and *"highly elated:* Press reports from Allen, 259, 261.
40 *"play[ed] like mad"* to *"he won many a battle like that":* Horace Henderson, JOHP transcript, II:13–15.
41 *"nothing but plain fun"* to *"about 7:30 or 8":* J. C. Higginbotham, JOHP transcript, 102.

8. Playing in the Mud

1 *"two musicians":* Hammond/Townsend, 67–68.
2 *"marble halls"* to *"I could think of ":* Ibid., 48–52. On inheriting his mother's reformer impulse, see p. 89.
3 *"aura of noblesse oblige":* Stowe, 63.
    "playing Pygmalion": to *"the greatest band in the country":* Hammond/Townsend, 67, 89.
4 *"problem with Fletcher":* Ibid., 53, and Allen, 275.
5 *"the men were incapable":* Allen, 275.
    "casual behavior": Hammond/Townsend, 67.
6 *"Fletcher was letting me down":* Ibid., 53 and 89.

7   *"they disliked John Hammond"*: Procope, JOHP transcript, II:32–33.

8   *"the Big Bringdown"*: Stowe, 58.
    "I don't think he dug me": Hammond/Townsend, 113.
    "[o]ften my help": Ibid., 89.

9   *"throng," "breakfast dance," "extended indefinitely"*: Press reports quoted in Allen, 276–77, 284.

10 *"Phoenix-like rise"*: Quoted in ibid., 297.
    "Mills turned band management": Hennessey, *From Jazz to Swing*, 125.

11 *"[t]hings are going badly"*: Quoted in Allen, 297; see also pp. 291–92.

12 *"bankruptcy blues"* to *"gaped in amazement"*: Quoted in ibid., 284, 289.

13 *"Smack had been having trouble"*: Quoted in Porter, ed. *Lester Young Reader*, 27.
    "[t]he band was so good": Quoted in Allen, 275.
    "That was the kind of spirit": Wells/Dance, 51.

14 *"the most disorganized"*: Quoted in Chilton, *Song of the Hawk*, 75.
    "Easygoing": See, for example, Stewart, *Jazz Masters*, 22; Lawrence Lucie, in Dance, *World of Swing*, 352; and Horace Henderson, JOHP transcript, II:11.
    "too phlegmatic": Hammond/Townsend, 67.
    "part of the whole thing": Quoted in Dance, *World of Swing*, 352.

15 *"They would seem"*: Horace Henderson, JOHP transcript, II:11.
    "[p]erhaps to make amends": Hammond/Townsend, 67.
    "gave his soloists": Quoted in Chilton, *Song of the Hawk*, 75.

16 *"what we call 'heads' "*: Quoted in ibid., 68.
    "knew his style": Horace Henderson, JOHP transcript, II:15.

17 Wells/Dance, 68–69.

18 *"Fletcher had to struggle"*: Stewart, *Jazz Masters*, 21.

19 Like the ideas in many head arrangements, the riff has unclear origins. It may have been developed by Henderson, or a member of his band, but Walter C. Allen also notes unidentified sources claiming that the riff originated in Claude Hopkins's band, which used the same riff in its "Honeysuckle Rose" recording of March 1933. The recorded legacy suggests Henderson's precedence but cannot prove it. Once Henderson wrote down the arrangement and gave it to Benny Goodman, however, idea became fixed in jazz history as the "Henderson riff." See Allen, 528.

20 *"the good head arrangements"*: Quoted in DeVeaux, *The Birth of Bebop*, 160.

21 *"People used to dance fast"*: Procope, JOHP transcript, II:8.

22 *"The guys in the band"*: Wells/Dance, 28.

23 Quoted in Chilton, *Song of the Hawk*, 68.

24 *"When you hear some"*: Wells/Dance, 42.

25 On the Yeah Man nightclub, see George Hoefer, liner notes for *The Sound of Harlem* (Columbia C3L 33), n.p. For a jazz discography of "I Got Rhythm" and its contrafacts, see Crawford, *American Musical Landscape*, 222–25. The list shows one "rhythm" contrafact that preceded "Yeah Man!" onto disk: Sidney Bechet's "Shag." The two earlier recordings of "Yeah Man!" were by Joel Shaw and His Orchestra (October 1932) and The King's Jesters (July 29, 1933). For conflicting attributions, see Allen, 310, 316, and 543.

26 *That new bridge*: Allen, 285.

27 Wells/Dance, 28.

28 *"weird keys"*: Horace Henderson, JOHP transcript, II:15.
    "scared": de Valk, 36.
    "you had to see": Quoted in Dance, *The World of Swing*, 22–23.
    "it meant less notes": Wells/Dance, 66.
    "oriental keys": For more on keys and their significance among professional jazz musicians, see DeVeaux, *The Birth of Bebop*, 214–17; and Allen, 503.

29 *"Cole Hawkins"* to *"featuring Henry 'Red' Allen"*: Allen, 304, 311.

30 *"prototype"*: Chilton, *Song of the Hawk*, 62.
   Hawkins told Russell Procope: Procope, JOHP transcript, II:8.

31 *Henderson was beginning to worry*: Chilton, *Song of the Hawk*, 76–85 passim.
   "Nobody made time": Higginbotham, JOHP transcript, I:102.

32 *"cut the Ellington band"*: Quoted in Dance, *World of Duke Ellington*, 77.
   "I was rooming": Quoted, from a 1956 interview, in Porter, ed., *A Lester Young Reader*, 160.

33 *"severe blow"*: Schuller, *EJ*, 278.
   "The audiences were real hip": Wells/Dance, 41.
   "[E]verybody agreed": Procope, JOHP transcript, II:40.

34 *"a one-man avant-garde"* and *"bassett melancholy"*: Balliett, 3, 5. Although Red Allen still remains in Armstrong's shadow, several books have given him his due. The best and most sustained musical analysis of his work appears in Schuller, *SE*, 617–31. For biography, see Chilton, *Ride, Red, Ride*. For critical appreciations, see Williams, *Jazz Masters of New Orleans*, and Balliett, *Improvising*.

35 *"the National anthem of Harlem"*: Quoted in Allen, 299.

36 See Whitburn, 15; Sanjek, *Pennies from Heaven*, 126–27; and Rust, *American Record Label Book*.

37 *Kapp has been reviled*: John Hammond takes special pride in having exposed Kapp's practices in 1937; see Hammond/Townsend, 145–46.
   "most innovative": Sanjek, *Pennies from Heaven*, 126.
   "is possibly the most controversial": Friedwald, 37.
   "in different ways": Kenney, *Recorded Music in American Life*, chap. 8. All together, the eighty-track Smithsonian anthology includes eighteen Decca records by ten different bands in the decade 1934–44.

38 *"crack the race barrier"*: Kirk/Lee, 84–85.

39 *"Big John Special"*: Horace Henderson, JOHP transcript, I: 63–64. On the warmth and generosity of Big John, see Wells/Dance, 25–26.
   jazz-Chinese connection: In a topic ripe for further research, jazz and entertainment memoirs contain provocative hints that jazz and Chinese cuisine went together to form a kind of hybridized exotic experience. According to Jimmy Durante, writing about a period in the late 1920s, "there was a Chinese restaurant every few doors along Broadway, each featuring a good band, revue, and dinner. They had control of some of the best spots in town." Durante/Kofoed, 223–24. On the 1930s, see, for example, Russell Procope, JOHP transcript, I:48, where Procope mentions Chinese food at the Ubangi Club (the former Connie's Inn) then acknowledges the interviewer's assertion that it was "common" to have jazz in places that served Chinese food.

40 *"Fletcher had a way of writing"*: Wells/Dance, 28.

41 *"marvelously light"*: Schuller, *EJ*, 281. See Schuller, *SE*, 426–39 (on Hawkins with Henderson), and 623–28 (on Allen with Henderson).

42 *"reportedly arranged"*: Allen, 316.
   "had an ear for uptown riffs": Quoted in Sudhalter, *Lost Chords*, 791, in an illuminating footnote that stands as the most trenchant account of Hudson's style and career.

43 *"Everybody loved Big John"*: Wells/Dance, 25–26.

44 Schuller and Williams, liner notes, 14.

45 *beautiful tone*: Procope, JOHP transcript, II:20. "Jeff had a better tone than I did," said Procope with typical modesty.
   "He was so good": Quoted in Shapiro and Hentoff, 222.

46 *"drew good business"*: Allen, 299–300.

47 *"did the unbelievable thing"* to *"Fletcher Henderson's band this week is 'hot,'"*: Ibid., 301–2.

9. Building the Kingdom of Swing

1 The principal source for this survey of Goodman's early years is Firestone, *Swing, Swing, Swing*.

2 *"another smooth"*: Quoted in Firestone, 78.
"If it gets around": Hammond/Townsend, 85.
"horrified" Hammond: Firestone, 80–82.
turning point: Ibid., 84.

3 *the record industry began to relax*: Goodman/Kolodin, 129.
"who really put me back in touch": Hammond/Townsend, 111.
father figure: See, for example, Firestone, 374.

4 *"some sort of a pinnacle"*: Goodman/Kolodin, 144.

5 *Network radio*: Smulyan, *Selling Radio*, 167. On network radio and swing, see Stowe, *Swing Changes*, 108–9.

6 *"for the* Let's Dance *party"*: Benny Goodman and His Orchestra 1935 from the "Let's Dance" Broadcasts (Circle CCD-50), recorded introduction to "I Got Rhythm," track 7. "Dancers" appears on parts for "Hallelujah" and "I've Found a New Baby." All parts for both arrangements are signed "Fletcher Henderson" in his own hand. The parts for "I Found a New Baby" are particularly old and worn looking.
"used to pair up": Helen Ward, liner notes to *Let's Dance* CD.
On *Let's Dance*, see also Firestone, 106.

7 *The program's format*: Hammond/Townsend, 108–9.
NBC's contract: Firestone, 109.
"this was what we needed": Goodman/Kolodin, 154.

8 *"an outstanding musician"*: Ibid., 139.
"swell arrangement": Ibid., 144.

9 *"But about the most important thing"*: Ibid., 156.
"I guess I didn't": Quoted in Allen, 323.

10 *"had to be convinced"*: Goodman/Kolodin, 161.

11 *"the regular sequence"* to *" turned out to be"*: Ibid., 161–62.

12 *"ground into a formula"*: Schuller, *SE*, 20.
"the first time": Hammond/Townsend, 109.
"Fletcher's ideas": Goodman/Kolodin, 162.

13 *"the only time"*: Schuller, *SE*, 6.

14 *"would sift through"*: Ward, liner notes for *Let's Dance* CD.
"Benny had a fantastic": Ward, quoted in Firestone, 125.

15 *"over-indulgence"*: Quoted in Dance, *World of Swing*, 261.
Teddy Wilson also discovered: See DeVeaux, *The Birth of Bebop*, 160.

16 *"first chorus emphasizing the tune"*: Hammond/Townsend, 109.
Goodman claimed agent Willard Alexander used it: Goodman/Kolodin, 152.
"horrible products of the tunesmiths": Russell, in Williams, *The Art of Jazz*, 202.

17 *"background figures"* to *"sounded unified"*: Goodman/Kolodin, 162.

18 *"Hendersonese"*: Schuller, *SE*, 22.

19 *Benny Goodman and His Orchestra, Complete Camel Caravan Shows* (Jazz Horn JH-1038), track 16. Connor, 310.

20 *"stinger"*: I borrow the term *stinger* from marching band music, where it describes an accented final chord to confirm the cadence. Here it denotes a single accented tone announcing a new phrase or section.

21 *"probably his [Goodman's] all-time Fletcher Henderson favorite"*: Quoted in Firestone, 447.

22 *"became one of the band's strongest assets"* to *"had to have them"*: Ibid., 128–29.
Goodman himself claimed: Goodman/Kolodin, 155.

23   *"kept shuttling"*: Ward, liner notes to *Let's Dance* CD.
24   *"the archetype"*: Friedwald, 94–95.
     "so beautiful": Jimmy Maxwell in *Benny Goodman: Adventures in The Kingdom of Swing* (Columbia Music Video, 1993).
     "off and on" to *"in my face"*: Ward in Goodman video and Firestone, 184–86.
25   *"definitive performance"*: Wilder, *American Popular Song*, 258.
     It was one of the first: See Connor, 309–12 passim, for dates of "Devil" performances.
26   *"The ones that seemed to work"*: Firestone, 125.
27   *"reawakened [Goodman's] musical conscience"*: Ibid., 85.
     "he became as important": Hammond/Townsend, 108.
28   *"out of the studio"*: Goodman/Kolodin, 157–58.
     "break-in new tunes" to *"out of habit"*: Ward, liner notes to *Let's Dance* CD.
29   *Goodman's chroniclers:* See Collier, *Benny Goodman*, 195, and Connor, 50.
30   *NBC failed to renew:* Firestone, 129.
     "how softly" and *"horror"*: Quoted in ibid., 130.
31   Goodman/Kolodin, 193–94, and Firestone, 146.
32   *"the place exploded"*: Quoted in Goode liner notes.
     "From the moment": Goodman/Kolodin, 198–99.
33   *"The Swing Era was born"*: Stearns, *The Story of Jazz*, 211.
     "On that night": Giddins, *Visions of Jazz*, 156. See also Erenberg, 3–4, for another echo of Stearns's statement.
     See Stowe, chap. 1, and Erenberg, chap. 2, esp. 36–41.
34   *"the preeminent expression"*: See Stowe, 13; and Erenberg, "Preface."
     "Not at all": Quoted in Stowe, 25.
35   *"dozen or so major stations"*: Ibid., 840.
     "a happy and rare coincidence": Ibid., 21.
     "was largely responsible": Schuller, "Morton, Jelly Roll," in *Amerigrove*.
36   *"something of a landmark"*: Quoted in Erenberg, 74, from Hammond article in *Melody Maker* on May 28, 1935.
37   *"[I]t was one of the biggest kicks"*: Goodman/Kolodin, 157.
38   *"hard taskmaster"*: Quoted in Deffaa, *Swing Legacy*, 45.
     "Benny wanted perfection": Quoted in Firestone, 173.
     "little daily psychodramas" to *"truly remarkable"*: Quoted in ibid., 447.
39   *"run the chart down"* to *"brought in"*: Quoted in Deffaa, *Swing Legacy*, 45–46.
40   *"That was Benny's way"*: Quoted in Firestone, 115.
     "added an eighth note": Quoted in ibid., 173.
     "unique blend": Schoenberg, liner notes.
41   *"a revelation"* and *"musical turning point"*: Quoted in Firestone, 120.
     "lift" and *"tremendous instinct for music"*: Goodman/Kolodin, 163–64.
     "topheavy" to *"weak foundation"*: Schuller, *SE*, 28.
42   *"Who was your favorite"*: Quoted in Connor, 307.
43   *In the score:* The parts and score held at Yale Music Library (box 25, folder 8) are not in Henderson's hand, but represent recopies from two different eras, a common phenomenon for Goodman's most often-played repertoire.
44   *"Fletcher was so swamped"*: Quoted in Firestone, 116.
45   *"Henderson chased him"*: ibid., 117.
46   *"the longest running"*: Connor, 109.
47   *"probably the band's"*: Schoenberg, liner notes.
48   *"Orchestrated Armstrong"*: Giddins, *Satchmo*, 81.
49   *"massive exodus"*: Firestone, 260.
50   *"Fletcher Henderson's arrangements"*: Quoted in Firestone, 261.
51   *"His charts were so difficult"* to *"Benny used to edit"*: Quoted in ibid., 262–63.

10. Never Say "Never Again"

1   *"like going to school"*: Jonah Jones, quoted in Allen, 406.

"the only leader" and "dozens": Allen, 341.

"A wonderful person": Letter to author, February 2, 1990.

he once caught Henderson: Bushell/Tucker, 87.

"Almost each individual": Quoted in Shapiro and Hentoff, 217.

"my biggest kicks" and "a great kick": Dance, *World of Swing*, quoting Sandy Williams, 77, and Lawrence Lucie, 351, both of whom had brief stints with Henderson in the early 1930s and returned to the band in the later 1930s or early 1940s.

2   *"a great strain"*: Quoted from *Baltimore Afro-American*, May 1942, in Allen, 380.

"Does Benny Goodman": Allen, 410.

3   *"abusive tirade"*: Quoted in Allen, 419.

"the war was on" to "cats and dogs": Charles Walton, "George Floyd: The Fletcher Henderson Chicago Connection," at http://jazzinstituteofchicago.org (accessed August 2003).

4   *"Swing Battle of the Sexes"*: Allen, 412, 414–15; Sherrie Tucker, *Swing Shift*, 165.

5   *"he was such a big coward"*: Bushell/Tucker, 86–87.

"took care of business": Quoted in Chilton, *Roy Eldridge*, 78

6   *"[a]s Fletcher spent more"*: Hammond, 16.

"The manager came": Quoted in Dance, *World of Swing*, 75.

"disappeared": Quoted in Allen, 456.

7   *"worked so hard"*: Quoted in Shapiro and Hentoff, 223. On Henderson's last musical activities and final illness, see Allen, 457–66 passim.

8   *"armies of white musicians"*: *Baltimore Afro-American* quoted in Allen, 333. See also Chilton, *Roy Eldridge*, 78.

9   Allen, 332. Chilton, *Roy Eldridge*, 71–72; Roy Eldridge, JOHP transcript, 87; and Horace Henderson, JOHP transcript, II: 76–77.

10   Horace Henderson, JOHP transcript, II: 77.

11   *"I picked up an inkwell"*: Holiday/Dufty, 64.

For the show's finale to "stone cold": Thomas, JOHP transcript, I:22–25.

12   *Within a five-month span*: Rust, *Jazz Records*.

best-selling records: Whitburn, 485.

"thanks to 'Christopher Columbus' ": Quoted in Allen, 348.

"the man what plays": Quoted in ibid., 336.

13   *"Fletcher was hot"*: Quoted in Firestone, 162.

"If it had been me": Quoted in Chilton, *Roy Eldridge*, 78.

14   *a coincidence* and *"honorary pallbearers"*: Allen, 474–75.

"The day Fletcher died" and *"Louis and Joe Glaser"*: Shapiro and Hentoff, 223.

Several notables: New York Age obituary in the Henderson Family Papers, Amistad Research Collection, Tulane Univ., Box 1A, File 8.

15   *"an embittered"*: Hammond liner notes, 16.

The funeral register exists among the Henderson Family Papers at the Amistad Research Center, Tulane University. It also includes the signatures and addresses of dozens of her Strivers' Row neighbors, including one Willie Mays, whose address, 231 West 139th Street, identifies him as one of Leora's closest neighbors. I have been unable to confirm whether this is the same Willie Mays who played major league baseball. In the early 1950s, Mays played for the New York Giants and lived in Harlem. By 1958, however, the Giants had moved to San Francisco, yet Leora's death preceded the beginning of the baseball season by at least one month, so Mays might have been still in New York.

16   *"how much every arranger"*: Quoted in Allen, 479.

17   *"thought of the return"*: Quoted in Firestone, 375. For personnel changes, see Conner, 311.

18 *"I pulled a piece"*: Quoted in Hajdu, 84.

19 *"lingua franca"*: Berger, Berger, and Patrick, I:110.

20 *"What made 'King Porter Stomp'"*: John Lewis, telephone interview with the author, 1987.

21 Williams, *Jazz Heritage*, 94–95.

22 Baraka [Jones], 177.

23 See, for example, Melnick, and Michael Rogin, *Blackface, White Noise: Jewish Immigrants in the Hollywood Melting Pot* (Berkeley: Univ. of California Press, 1996).

BIBLIOGRAPHY

"Papers of the Fletcher Henderson Family." In *Amistad Log* 2 (February 1985). Fletcher Henderson Family Papers, Amistad Research Center. Tulane Univ.

Albertson, Chris. *Bessie*. Revised and expanded edition. New Haven: Yale Univ. Press, 2003.

Allen, Walter C. *Hendersonia: The Music of Fletcher Henderson and His Musicians: A Bio-Discography*. Highland Park, NJ: published by the author, 1973.

Anderson, Jervis. *Harlem: The Great Black Way, 1900–1950*. London: Orbis, 1982.

Badger, Reid. *A Life in Ragtime: A Biography of James Reese Europe*. New York: Oxford Univ. Press, 1995.

Baker, Houston A., Jr. *Modernism and the Harlem Renaissance*. Chicago: The Univ. of Chicago Press, 1987.

Balliett, Whitney. *Improvising: Sixteen Jazz Musicians and Their Art*. New York: Oxford Univ. Press, 1977.

Baraka, Amiri [LeRoi Jones]. *Blues People: Negro Music in White America*. New York: Morrow, 1963.

Berger, Morroe, Edward Berger, and James Patrick. *Benny Carter: A Life in American Music*. 2 vols. Metuchen, NJ: The Scarecrow Press and the Institute of Jazz Studies, Rutgers Univ., 1982.

Bergreen, Laurence. *Louis Armstrong: An Extravagant Life*. New York: Broadway Books, 1997.

Berlin, Edward A. *Ragtime: A Musical and Cultural History*. Berkeley: Univ. of California Press, 1980.

———. *King of Ragtime: Scott Joplin and His Era*. New York: Oxford Univ. Press, 1994.

Bernhardt, Clyde E. B., as told to Sheldon Harris. *I Remember: Eighty Years of Black Entertainment, Big Bands, and the Blues*. Philadelphia: Univ. of Pennsylvania Press. 1986.

Berrett, Joshua, editor. *The Louis Armstrong Companion: Eight Decades of Commentary*. New York: Schirmer, 1999.

Brothers, Thomas, editor. *Louis Armstrong in His Own Words: Selected Writings*. New York: Oxford Univ. Press, 1999.

Bullock, Henry Allen. *A History of Negro Education in the South, From 1619 to the Present*. New York: Praeger, 1970.

Burnham, Scott G. *Beethoven Hero*. Princeton: Princeton Univ. Press. 1995.

Burroughs, Theresa Henderson. Telephone interviews with author. June and July 1992.

———. Letter to author. May 1990.

Bushell, Garvin, as told to Mark Tucker. *Jazz from the Beginning*. Ann Arbor: Univ. of Michigan Press, 1988.

Carmichael, Hoagy. *The Stardust Road and Sometimes I Wonder: The Autobiographies of Hoagy Carmichael*. 1946. Reprint. New York: Da Capo Press, 1999.

Carter, Benny. Interview by Morroe Berger. Princeton, NJ, October 13, 1976. JOHP transcript.

———. E-mail interview with the author, mediated by Edward Berger. May 2002.

Challis, Bill. Interview by Ira Gitler. Washington, DC, n.d. JOHP transcript.

Charters, Samuel B., and Leonard Kunstadt. *Jazz: A History of the New York Scene*. 1962. Reprint. New York: Da Capo Press, 1981.

Chevan, David. "Written Music in Early Jazz." Ph.D. diss., City Univ. of New York, 1997.

Chilton, John. *The Song of the Hawk: The Life and Recordings of Coleman Hawkins*. Ann Arbor: Univ. of Michigan Press, 1990.

———. *Ride, Red, Ride: The Life of Henry "Red" Allen*. New York: Cassell, 1999.

———. *Roy Eldridge: Little Jazz Giant*. London: Continuum, 2002.

Clark, John L., Jr. " 'Stock-In-Trade': Investigating the Role of Stock Arrangements in the Development of the Orchestral Repertoire of Fletcher Henderson and His Contemporaries." Ph.D. diss., Brandeis Univ., 2003.

Collier, James Lincoln. *Louis Armstrong: An American Genius*. New York: Oxford Univ. Press, 1983.

———. *The Reception of Jazz in America: A New View*. I.S.A.M. Monographs, no. 27. Brooklyn, NY: Institute for Studies in American Music, 1988.

———. *Benny Goodman and the Swing Era*. New York: Oxford Univ. Press, 1989.

Connor, D. Russell. *Benny Goodman: Listen to His Legacy*. Studies in Jazz, No. 6. Lanham, MD: The Scarecrow Press, Inc. and the Institute of Jazz Studies, 1988.

Crawford, Richard. "Notes on Jazz Standards by Black Authors and Composers, 1899– 1942." In *New Perspectives on Music: Essays in Honor of Eileen Southern*, edited by Josephine Wright with Samuel A. Floyd, Jr. Warren, MI: Harmonie Park Press, 1992.

———. *The American Musical Landscape*. Berkeley: Univ. of California Press, 1993.

Crawford, Richard, and Jeffrey Magee. *Jazz Standards on Record, 1900–1942: A Core Repertory*. C.B.M.R. Monographs, no. 4. Chicago: Center for Black Music Research, 1992.

Dance, Stanley. *The World of Swing: An Oral History of Big Band Jazz*. New York: Charles Scribner's Sons, 1974.

———. *The World of Duke Ellington*. 1970. Reprint. New York: Da Capo Press, 1981.

Deffaa, Chip. *Swing Legacy*. Metuchen, NJ: Scarecrow Press; New Brunswick: NJ: Institute of Jazz Studies, Rutgers Univ., 1989.

———. *Voices of the Jazz Age*. Urbana: Univ. of Illinois Press, 1990.

de Valk, Jeroen. *Ben Webster: His Life and Music*. Berkeley: Berkeley Hills Books, 2001.

DeVeaux, Scott. "Constructing the Jazz Tradition: Jazz Historiography." *Black American Literature Forum* 25 (Fall 1991): 525–60.

———. *The Birth of Bebop: A Social and Musical History*. Berkeley: Univ. of California Press, 1997.

Dews, Margery P. *Remembering: The Remarkable Henderson Family*. Chicago: Adams Press, 1978.

———. "Young Fletcher Henderson." *Jazz Magazine* 4 (Spring 1980): 65.

Dodge, Roger Pryor. *Hot Jazz and Jazz Dance: Roger Pryor Dodge Collected Writings, 1929–1964*. Selected and edited by Pryor Dodge. New York: Oxford Univ. Press, 1995.

Douglas, Ann. *Terrible Honesty: Mongrel Manhattan in the 1920s*. New York: Farrar, Straus and Giroux, 1995.

Driggs, Frank. "Don Redman: Jazz Composer-Arranger." *Jazz Review* 2 (November 1959): 6–12.

DuBois, W. E. B. *The Souls of Black Folk*. 1903. Reprint. *Three Negro Classics*. New York: Avon Books, 1965.

Durante, Jimmy, and Jack Kofoed. *Night Clubs*. New York: Knopf, 1931.

Eldridge, Roy. Interview by Dan Morgenstern. June 15, 1982, and June 22, 1983. JOHP transcript.

Ellington, Duke. *Music Is My Mistress*. 1973. Reprint. New York: Da Capo Press, 1976.

Erenberg, Lewis A. *Swingin' the Dream: Big Band Jazz and the Rebirth of American Culture*. Chicago: The Univ. of Chicago Press, 1998.

Ferguson, Otis. *The Otis Ferguson Reader*. Highland Park, IL: December Press, 1982.

Firestone, Ross. *Swing, Swing, Swing: The Life & Times of Benny Goodman*. New York: W. W. Norton, 1993.

Fletcher, Tom. *100 Years of the Negro in Show Business*. 1954. Reprinted with introduction and index by Thomas L. Riis. New York: Da Capo Press, 1984.

Floyd, Samuel A., Jr. *The Power of Black Music: Interpreting Its History from Africa to the United States*. New York: Oxford Univ. Press, 1995.

———, editor. *Music and the Harlem Renaissance: A Collection of Essays*. New York: Greenwood Press, 1990.

Foster, Pops. *Pops Foster*. Berkeley: Univ. of California Press, 1971.

Friedwald, Will. *Jazz Singing*. 1990. Reprint. New York: Da Capo Press, 1996.

Gabbard, Krin, editor. *Jazz Among the Discourses*. Durham: Duke Univ. Press, 1995.

Gates, Henry Louis. *The Signifying Monkey: A Theory of African-American Literary Criticism*. New York: Oxford Univ. Press, 1988.

Giddins, Gary. *Satchmo*. New York: Doubleday, 1988.

———. *Visions of Jazz: The First Century*. New York: Oxford Univ. Press, 1998.

Gioia, Ted. "Jazz and the Primitivist Myth." *Musical Quarterly* 73 (1989): 130–43.

Goffin, Robert. *Jazz: From the Congo to the Metropolitan*. 1944. Reprint. New York: Da Capo Press, 1975.

Gold, Robert. *Jazz Talk*. 1975. Reprint. New York: Da Capo Press, 1982.

Goode, Mort. Liner notes to *Benny Goodman: The RCA Years (Bluebird 5704–1)*, 1986.

Goodman, Benny, and Irving Kolodin. *The Kingdom of Swing*. 1939. Reprint. New York: Frederick Ungar, 1961.

Grimes, Clarence A. *They Who Speak in Music: The History of the Neighborhood Music School, New Haven, Conn.* New Haven: Neighborhood Music School, 1957.

Gushee, Lawrence. Liner notes to *Steppin' on the Gas: Rags to Jazz, 1918–1927*. New World Records NW 269 (1977).

Hadlock, Richard. *Jazz Masters of the 20s*. 1972. Reprint. New York: Da Capo Press, 1988.

Hajdu, David. *Lush Life: A Biography of Billy Strayhorn*. New York: Farrar, Straus and Giroux, 1996.

Hammond, John. Liner notes to *A Study in Frustration: The Fletcher Henderson Story*. Reprint 1961. Columbia/Legacy 57596.

Hammond, John, with Irving Townsend. *John Hammond on Record: An Autobiography*. New York: Ridge Press/Summit Books, 1977.

Handy, W. C. *Father of the Blues*. 1941. Reprint. New York: Da Capo Press, 1990.

Harker, Brian Cameron. "The Early Musical Development of Louis Armstrong, 1901– 1928." Ph.D. diss., Columbia University, 1997.

———. "'Telling a Story': Louis Armstrong and Coherence in Early Jazz." *Current Musicology* 63 (1999): 46–83.

Harris, Michael W. *The Rise of Gospel Blues: The Music of Thomas Andrew Dorsey in the Urban Church*. New York: Oxford Univ. Press, 1992.

Hasse, John Edward. *Beyond Category: The Life and Genius of Duke Ellington*. NewYork: Simon & Schuster, 1993.

———, editor. *Ragtime: Its History, Composers, and Music*. New York: Schirmer Books, 1985.

Hawkins, Coleman. Recorded interview by Paul Bacon and Bill Grauer. Riverside LP 12-117/118 (1956).

Henderson, Alexa Benson. *Atlanta Life Insurance Company: Guardian of Black Economic Dignity*. Tuscaloosa: Univ. of Alabama Press, 1990.

Henderson, Horace. Interview by Tom MacCluskey. 2 vols. Denver, Colorado, April 9–12, 1975. JOHP transcript.

Hennessey, Thomas Joseph. "From Jazz to Swing: Black Jazz Musicians and Their Music, 1917–1935." Ph.D. diss., Northwestern University, 1973.

———. *From Jazz to Swing: African-American Jazz Musicians and Their Music, 1890– 1935*. Detroit: Wayne State Univ. Press, 1994.

Hentoff, Nat. "Garvin Bushell and New York Jazz in the 1920s." In *Jazz Panorama*, edited by Martin Williams. New York: Crowell-Collier, 1962.

Hentoff, Nat, and Albert J. McCarthy, editors. *Jazz*. 1959. Reprint. New York: Da Capo Press, 1974.

Higginbotham, J.C. n.p., n.d. JOHP transcript.

Hitchcock, H. Wiley, and Stanley Sadie, editors. *The New Grove Dictionary of American Music*. London: Macmillan, 1986.

Hobson, Wilder. *American Jazz Music*. 1939. Reprint. New York: Da Capo Press, 1976.

———. "Memorial to Fletcher." *Saturday Review*, September 30, 1962.

Hodeir, André. *Jazz: Its Evolution and Essence*. Translated by David Noakes. New York: Grove Press, 1956.

Holiday, Billie, and William Dufty. *Lady Sings the Blues*. New York: Penguin, 1984.

Howland, John Louis. "Between the Muses and the Masses: Symphonic Jazz, 'Glorified' Entertainment, and the Rise of the American Musical Middlebrow, 1920–1944." Ph.D. diss., Stanford Univ., 2002.

Huggins, Nathan Irvin. *Harlem Renaissance*. New York: Oxford Univ. Press, 1971.

Jablonski, Edward. *Gershwin: A Biography*. 1987. Reprint. New York: Da Capo Press, 1998.

———. *Irving Berlin, American Troubadour*. New York: Henry Holt, 1999.

Jasen, David. *Tin Pan Alley*. New York: Donald I. Fine, 1988.

Johnson, James Weldon. *The Autobiography of an Ex-Colored Man*. 1912. Reprint. *Three Negro Classics*. New York: Avon Books, 1965.

Jones, LeRoi. See Amiri Baraka.

Jones, Max, and John Chilton. *Louis: The Louis Armstrong Story, 1900–1971.*
    Boston: Little, Brown, 1971.
Judd, Anne. "A Portrait of Russell Smith." In *Jazz Journal* 20 (April 1967): 5–9.
Kammen, Michael. *The Lively Arts: Gilbert Seldes and the Transformation of
    Cultural Criticism in the United States.* New York: Oxford Univ. Press, 1996.
Kellner, Bruce, editor. *The Harlem Renaissance: A Historical Dictionary for the
    Era.* New York: Methuen, 1984.
Kenney, William Howland. *Chicago Jazz: A Cultural History.* New York: Oxford
    Univ. Press, 1993.
———. *Recorded Music in American Life: The Phonograph and Popular
    Memory, 1890–1945.* New York: Oxford Univ. Press, 1999.
Kennedy, Rick. *Jelly Roll, Bix, and Hoagy: Gennett Studios and the Birth of
    Recorded Jazz.* Bloomington: Indiana Univ. Press, 1994.
Kernfeld, Barry, editor. *The New Grove Dictionary of Jazz.* 1988. Reprint, 1 vol.
    New York: St Martin's Press, 1994.
Kinkle, Roger. *The Complete Encyclopedia of Popular Music and Jazz,
    1900–1950.* 4 vols. New Rochelle, NY: Arlington House, 1974.
Kirk, Andy, as told to Amy Lee. *Twenty Years on Wheels.* Ann Arbor: Univ. of
    Michigan Press: 1989.
Lange, Arthur. *Arranging for the Modern Dance Orchestra.* New York: Arthur
    Lange, Inc., 1926.
Lax, Roger, and Frederick Smith. *The Great Song Thesaurus.* 2nd ed. New York:
    Oxford Univ. Press, 1987.
Lees, Gene. *Arranging the Score: Portraits of the Great Arrangers.* New York:
    Cassell, 2002.
Lewis, David Levering. *When Harlem Was in Vogue.* New York: Oxford Univ.
    Press, 1979.
Lewis, John. Telephone interview with the author. March 1987.
Litwack, Leon F. *Trouble in Mind: Black Southerners in the Age of Jim Crow.*
    New York: Alfred A. Knopf, 1998.
Locke, Alain, editor. *The New Negro: An Interpretation.* 1925. Reprint, with an
    introduction by Arnold Rampersad. New York: Atheneum, 1992.
Love, Josephine Harreld. Interviews with the author. Ann Arbor, March 1989; and
    Detroit, June 1989.
Magee, Jeffrey. "The Music of Fletcher Henderson and His Orchestra in the
    1920s." Ph.D. diss., Univ. of Michigan, 1992.
May, Henry F. *The End of American Innocence: A Study of the First Years of Our
    Own Time, 1912–1917.* 1959. Reprint, with a preface by David A. Hollinger.
    New York: Columbia Univ. Press, 1992.
McGinty, Doris Evans. "Conversation with Revella Hughes: From the Classics to
    Broadway to Swing." *The Black Perspective in Music* 16 (Spring 1988):
    81–104.
McNamara, Daniel I., editor. *The ASCAP Biographical Dictionary of Composers,
    Authors, and Publishers.* 2nd ed. New York: Thomas Y. Crowell, 1952.
Meier, August. *Negro Thought in America, 1880–1915.* 2nd edition. Ann Arbor:
    Univ. of Michigan Press, 1988.
Melnick, Jeffrey. *Right to Sing the Blues: African Americans, Jews, and American
    Popular Song.* Cambridge: Harvard Univ. Press, 1999.
Miller, Paul W., editor. *Atlanta: Capital of the South.* New York: Oliver Durrell,
    Inc., 1949.

Murphy, Greg. "The Forgotten Ones: Charlie Green." *Jazz Journal International* 39 (1986): 16.

Murray, Albert. *Stompin' the Blues.* 1976. Reprint. Da Capo Press, 1987.

Nicholls, David, editor. *The Cambridge History of American Music.* Cambridge: Cambridge Univ. Press. 1998.

Osgood, Henry O. *So This Is Jazz.* 1926. Reprint. New York: Da Capo Press, 1978.

Osofsky, Gilbert. *Harlem: The Making of a Ghetto.* 2nd edition. New York: Harper and Row, 1971.

Panassié, Hugues. *Hot Jazz: A Guide to Swing Music.* 1936. Reprint. Westport, CT: Negro Univ. Press, 1970.

———. *The Real Jazz.* Revised and enlarged edition. New York: A. S. Barnes, 1960.

———. *Louis Armstrong.* New York: Scribners, 1971.

Peretti, Burton W. *The Creation of Jazz: Music, Race, and Culture in Urban America.* Urbana: Univ. of Illinois Press, 1992.

Porter, Lewis. *Lester Young.* Boston: Twayne Publishers, 1985.

———, editor. *A Lester Young Reader.* Washington, DC: Smithsonian Institution Press, 1991.

Procope, Russell. JOHP transcript. Interview by Chris Albertson. 4 vols. March 6–13, 1979.

Rampersad, Arnold. *The Art and Imagination of W. E. B. Du Bois.* Cambridge: Harvard Univ. Press, 1976.

Ramsey, Frederic, Jr., and Charles Edward Smith. *Jazzmen.* 1939. Reprint. New York: Limelight Editions, 1985.

Ramsey. Guthrie P., Jr. *Race Music: Black Cultures from Bebop to Hip-Hop.* Berkeley: Univ. of California Press, 2003.

Riis, Thomas L. *Just Before Jazz: Black Musical Theater in New York, 1890–1915.* Washington, DC: Smithsonian Institution Press, 1989.

Russell, James Michael. *Atlanta 1847–1890: City Building in the Old South and the New.* Baton Rouge: Louisiana State Univ. Press, 1988.

Rust, Brian. *The American Dance Band Discography, 1917–1942.* New Rochelle, NY: Arlington House, 1975.

———. *The American Record Label Book.* New Rochelle, NY: Arlington House, 1978.

———. *Jazz Records 1897–1942.* 5th ed. Chigwell, Essex: Storyville, 1983.

Sampson, Henry T. *Blacks in Blackface: A Source Book on Early Black Music Shows.* Metuchen, NJ: The Scarecrow Press, 1980.

Sanjek, Russell. *From Print to Plastic: Publishing and Promoting America's Popular Music (1900–1980).* I.S.A.M. Monographs, no. 20. Brooklyn, NY: Institute for Studies in American Music, 1983.

———. Updated by David Sanjek. *Pennies From Heaven: The American Popular Music Business in the Twentieth Century.* New York: Da Capo Press, 1996.

Sargeant, Winthrop. *Jazz: Hot and Hybrid.* 1938. Reprint. New York: Da Capo Press, 1975.

Schoenberg, Loren. Liner notes to *Benny Goodman: The Birth of Swing (1935–1936).* Bluebird 07863 (1991).

Schuller, Gunther. *Early Jazz: Its Roots and Musical Development.* New York: Oxford Univ. Press, 1968.

———. *The Swing Era: The Development of Jazz, 1930–1945.* New York: Oxford Univ. Press, 1989.

Schuller, Gunther, and Martin Williams. Liner notes for *Big Band Jazz*. Washington, DC: The Smithsonian Collection of Recordings R 030 (1983).

Scott, Howard. Interview by Chris Albertson. Washington, DC, March 8, 1979. JOHP transcript.

Seldes, Gilbert. *The Seven Lively Arts*. 1924. Reprint. Sagamore Press, 1957.

Shapiro, Nat, and Nat Hentoff, editors. *Hear Me Talkin' to Ya: The Story of Jazz as Told by the Men Who Made It*. 1955. Reprint. New York: Dover, 1966.

Shih, Hsio Wen. "The Spread of Jazz and the Big Bands." In *Jazz*, edited by Nat Hentoff and Albert J. McCarthy, 1959. Reprint. New York: Da Capo Press, 1974.

Small, Christopher. *Music of the Common Tongue*. 1987. Reprint. Hanover: Wesleyan Univ. Press. 1998.

Smulyan, Susan. *Selling Radio: The Commercialization of American Broadcasting, 1920–1934*. Washington, DC: Smithsonian Institution Press, 1994.

Spring, Howard Allen. "Changes in Jazz Performance and Arranging in New York, 1929–1932." Ph.D. diss., University of Illinois at Urbana-Champaign, 1993.

———. "Swing and the Lindy Hop: Dance, Venue, Media, and Tradition." *American Music* 15, no. 2 (Summer 1997): 183–207.

Stearns, Marshall. *The Story of Jazz*. New York: Oxford Univ. Press, 1956.

Stearns, Marshall, and Jean Stearns. *Jazz Dance: The Story of American Vernacular Dance*. 1968. Reprint. New York: Da Capo Press, 1994.

Stewart, Rex. *Jazz Masters of the Thirties*. New York: Macmillan, 1972.

———. *Boy Meets Horn*. Edited by Claire P. Gordon. Ann Arbor: Univ. of Michigan Press, 1991.

Stowe, David W. *Swing Changes: Big Band Jazz in New Deal America*. Cambridge, MA: Harvard Univ. Press, 1994.

Sturm, Fred. *Changes Over Time: The Evolution of Jazz Arranging*. N.p.: Advance Music, 1995.

Sudhalter, Richard M. *Lost Chords: White Musicians and Their Contributions to Jazz, 1915–1945*. New York: Oxford Univ. Press, 1999.

Sudhalter, Richard M., and Phillip R. Evans. *Bix: Man and Legend*. New Rochelle, NY: Arlington House, 1974.

Thomas, Joe, and Babe (Matthews) Thomas. Interview by Stanley Dance. JOHP transcript.

Tucker, Mark. *Ellington: The Early Years*. Urbana: Univ. of Illinois Press, 1991.

Tucker, Sherrie. *Swing Shift: "All-Girl" Bands of the 1940s*. Durham: Duke Univ. Press, 2001.

Van de Leur, Walter. *Something to Live For: The Music of Billy Strayhorn*. New York: Oxford Univ. Press, 2002.

Van Vechten, Carl. *Nigger Heaven*. 1926. Reprint. Urbana: Univ. of Illinois Press. 2000.

Washington, Booker T. *Up From Slavery*. 1901. Reprint. *Three Negro Classics*. New York: Avon Books, 1965.

Waters, Ethel, with Charles Samuels. *His Eye Is on the Sparrow: An Autobiography*. 1950. Reprint. Westport, CT: Greenwood Press, 1978.

Wells, Dicky, as told to Stanley Dance. *The Night People: The Jazz Life of Dicky Wells*. 1971. Reprint. Washington, DC: Smithsonian Institution Press, 1991.

Whitburn, Joel. *Joel Whitburn's Pop Memories, 1890–1954*. Menomonee Falls, WI: Record Research, 1986.

Whiteman, Paul, and Mary Margaret McBride. *Jazz*. 1926. Reprint. New York: Arno Press, 1974.

Wilder, Alec. *American Popular Song: The Great Innovators, 1900–1950.* New York: Oxford Univ. Press, 1972.

Williams, Martin. *Jazz Masters of New Orleans.* New York: Macmillan, 1967.

———. *The Jazz Tradition.* 1970. Revised edition. New York: Oxford Univ. Press, 1983.

———. *Jazz Heritage.* New York: Oxford Univ. Press, 1985.

———. Liner notes for *The Smithsonian Collection of Classic Jazz.* Washington, DC: The Smithsonian Collection of Recordings R 033 (revised edition, 1987).

———, editor. *The Art of Jazz: Essays on the Nature and Development of Jazz.* New York: Oxford Univ. Press, 1959.

———. *Jazz Panorama.* New York: Crowell-Collier, 1962.

Wilson, Olly. "The Association of Movement and Music as a Manifestation of a Black Conceptual Approach to Music Making." In *International Musicological Society Report of the Twelfth Congress,* Daniel Heartz and Bonnie Wade, editors. Basel: Bärenreiter Kassell, 1981.

———. "Black Music as an Art Form." In *Black Music Research Journal* 3 (1983): 1– 22..

Wilson, Teddy, with Arie Lighart and Humphrey Van Loo. *Teddy Wilson Talks Jazz.* New York: Continuum, 2001.

Wooding, Sam. Interview by Chris Albertson. Washington, DC, April 22–May 8, 1975. JOHP transcript.

DISCOGRAPHY

FLETCHER HENDERSON'S MUSIC is more completely available and easily accessible than ever. Three collections represent efforts to survey Henderson's entire career on record. The most comprehensive remains the multi-record album produced by John Hammond in 1962, with sixty-four recordings on a set of three compact discs and titled *The Fletcher Henderson Story: A Study in Frustration* (Columbia 57596). The best single-CD anthology of Henderson's career is *Fletcher Henderson—Swing* (ABC 836 093-2), featuring sixteen recordings from the 1920s and 1930s carefully reproduced by Robert Parker with "new direct-from-disc-to-digital techniques" resulting in remarkable clarity and power. At this writing, the most widely available one-CD survey is *Ken Burns Jazz: Fletcher Henderson* (Columbia Legacy 61447).

The Classics series offers remarkably comprehensive coverage of key jazz figures in the 1920–45 period. Henderson stands among the best represented musicians in the series, with sixteen compact discs covering two decades of recording activity. The series, however, does not include alternate takes and rarely includes multiple recordings of the same arrangements (with the rare exception of such key pieces as "King Porter Stomp"):

- *Fletcher Henderson 1921–1923* (Classics 794)
- *Fletcher Henderson 1923* (Classics 697)
- *Fletcher Henderson 1923–24* (Classics 683)
- *Fletcher Henderson 1924*, vol. 1 (Classics 647)
- *Fletcher Henderson 1924*, vol. 2 (Classics 657)
- *Fletcher Henderson 1924*, vol. 3 (Classics 673)
- *Fletcher Henderson 1924–1925* (Classics 633)
- *Fletcher Henderson 1925–1926* (Classics 610)
- *Fletcher Henderson 1926–1927* (Classics 597)
- *Fletcher Henderson 1927* (Classics 580)
- *Fletcher Henderson 1927–1931* (Classics 572)
- *Fletcher Henderson 1931–1932* (Classics 546)
- *Fletcher Henderson 1932–1934* (Classics 535)
- *Fletcher Henderson 1934–1937* (Classics 527)
- *Fletcher Henderson, 1937–1938* (Classics 519)
- *Horace Henderson 1940, Fletcher Henderson 1941* (Classics 648).

Louis Armstrong's thirteen months in Henderson's band are definitively represented, with all alternate takes, on a three-disc set called *Louis with Fletcher Henderson, 1924–1925* (Forte F38001/2/3). Several of Armstrong's Henderson recordings can also be heard on *Louis Armstrong: Portrait of the Artist as a Young Man, 1923–1934* (Columbia/Legacy 57176), with thorough, insightful liner notes by Dan Morgenstern.

Other Henderson collections feature music from a specific period, label, or radio broadcast:

- *Fletcher Henderson: Tidal Wave* [1931–34] (Verve 643)
- *Fletcher Henderson: Under the Harlem Moon* [1932–37] (ASV/Living Era 5067)
- *Fletcher Henderson—Swing: Great Original Performances, 1929–1937* (ABC Records 836 093–2)
- *Fletcher Henderson and His Orchestra: "Live" at the Grand Terrace, Chicago, 1938* (Jazz Unlimited JUCD 2053)
- *Fletcher Henderson & His Orchestra: The Father of the Big Band* (EPM Musique 159352)
- *The Essence of Swing: Wild Party* (Our World 101067).

A fine re-creation of some of Henderson's best arrangements can be found on *Henderson Stomp: Keith Nichols and the Cotton Club Orchestra Play the Music of the Fletcher Henderson Orchestra, 1924–31* (Stomp Off CD 1275; 1994), including soloists who faithfully, but not slavishly, match their counterparts in Henderson's band.

Goodman's recordings of Henderson arrangements can be found on many compact disc collections, including the following:

- *Benny Goodman Plays Fletcher Henderson*, vol. 1 (HEP CD 1058)
- *Benny Goodman Plays Fletcher Henderson*, vol. 2 (HEP CD 1059)
- *Benny Goodman and His Orchestra, 1939–1940* (Classics 1098)
- *Benny Goodman Orchestra* (Laserlight 15 762)
- *Benny Goodman & The Rhythm Makers: Good to Go* (Buddha Records 7446599624 2)
- *The Yale University Music Library Benny Goodman* vols. 3–4 (MHS 522431L)
- *Benny Goodman: The Birth of Swing (1935–1936)* (Bluebird 07863) includes comprehensive and illuminating notes by Loren Schoenberg.

Many of Goodman's public and radio performances are now available on compact disc, offering a glimpse of how the band—and Henderson's arrangements—sounded outside of the record studio:

- *Benny Goodman and His Orchestra, 1935: Let's Dance* (Circle CCD-50)
- *Benny Goodman and His Orchestra: Complete Camel Caravan Shows, September 6, 1938–September 13, 1938* (Jazz Hour JH-1038)

- *Benny Goodman on the Air (1937–1938)* (Columbia/Legacy C2K 48836)
- *Benny Goodman: The Famous Carnegie Hall Jazz Concert* (Columbia/Legacy C2K 65143).

Many of Henderson's arrangements for Goodman remained unrecorded until 2000, when clarinetist Bob Wilber made a compact disc with the Toulouse, France-based Tuxedo Big Band, featuring seventeen arrangements on *Bob Wilber and the Tuxedo Big Band: Fletcher Henderson's Unrecorded Arrangements for Benny Goodman* (Arbors Records ARCD 19229).

ACKNOWLEDGMENTS

IF COLLABORATION FORMED A KEY ELEMENT of Fletcher Henderson's artistry, it also proved to be essential to the completion of this book. Years ago, when this book took root as a doctoral dissertation at the University of Michigan, Richard Crawford brought energy, enthusiasm, and editorial savvy to my writing about Henderson's music beginning with a simple walk around the block. From him, and from other members of the dissertation committee, including James Dapogny and Mark Tucker, I have continued to learn over the years. I regret that Mark Tucker did not live to see the final version, but his model of musicianship, scholarship, and writing remains as strong as ever. At Michigan I also formed enduring friendships with Jeffrey Taylor, Guthrie Ramsey, and Paul Austerlitz, all of whom read parts of the book and made useful comments. As I worked on the book, a new wave of scholars of early jazz—such as Howard Spring, Brian Harker, David Chevan, John Howland, and John Clark—found intersections between our interests, and I have benefited from talking about and reading their work. Teresa Nemeth, musician and editor, proved to be a lucky find, and she brought tough love to the manuscript and inspired substantial improvements. In the book's late stages, I had the great fortune to receive careful readings of a complete draft from Lewis Porter and Scott DeVeaux. Their own work had already made an impact on mine, and their copious commentary on large issues and small details in the manuscript have made this a much better book. Several others have my enduring gratitude for support and suggestions at various stages of the book's evolution, including Patricia Advaney, Matthew Balensuela, Geoffrey Block, Mark Burford, Samuel A. Floyd, Jr., Elliott Hurwitt, Marianne Kielian-Gilbert, Anne K. Magee, Stephen Meyer, Carol J. Oja, Ron Radano, Loren Schoenberg, Bill Schafer, and William Youngren.

At Indiana University, I have been fortunate to work among a legion of fine jazz musicians thriving under the energetic and omnivorous leadership of David Baker, who somehow found time to read the entire manuscript and offer valuable comments and support. Discussions with—and performances by—Luke Gillespie, Gary Potter, Pat Harbison, Tom Walsh, and the remarkable Caswell family (Austin, Judy, Rachel, and Sara) have also been helpful and inspiring. At Indiana, too, I have enjoyed the support of the musicology department, and I would like to single out the late A. Peter Brown for quietly guiding me toward and through the tenure process, which reached a positive

outcome just weeks after his death. I have also been fortunate to have graduate student assistants to do a variety of tasks along the way, including
Amy Bland, Kunio Hara, and especially Peter Schimpf, who, in the late
stages, assumed the important, demanding, and seemingly endless role of
what might be called master of musical examples. Outside the music school,
I have enjoyed exchanging and discussing writing with Ray Hedin, a key
figure in helping me get acclimated to life in Bloomington.

Invaluable supplies of source material came from the late Charles
Anderson, David Baker, James Dapogny, Andrew Homzy, and Mark Tucker.
I'm grateful to librarians and archivists who assisted me in many ways,
including Kendall Crilly and Suzanne Eggleston Lovejoy at Yale University
Music Library; Vincent Pelote and Edward Berger at the Institute of Jazz
Studies, Rutgers University; George Boziwick at the New York Public
Library for the Performing Arts, and Shugana Campbell at the Amistad
Research Center, Tulane University. Thanks to Hazen Schumacher at the
University of Michigan's WUOM for allowing me to explore his vast collection of 78-rpm and LP records before many of Henderson's recordings had
been reissued on compact disc. Frank Driggs and Duncan Schiedt made
their photograph collections available, and I'm glad to count Duncan as one
of the friends I've made through writing this book. Thanks, too, to Steve
Smith for sending tapes; and to Pyotr Michalowski (another helpful member
of the dissertation committee) for bringing back from his foreign travels
some otherwise hard-to-find recordings.

People who knew Henderson, now few and far between, have been
generous with their time, including Theresa Henderson Burroughs, the late
Benny Carter, Margery Dews, Josephine Harreld Love, and the late Fletcher
Muse. James T. Maher regaled me with uniquely informed perspectives on
the Henderson-Goodman collaboration. He proved to be exceptionally
generous, and I enjoyed many long exchanges with him. Thanks to him, I
also had the chance to meet and talk with Goodman's biographer, Ross
Firestone, a key source for chapter 9.

My research has been supported by grants from the University of
Michigan Office for the Vice-President of Research, the Indiana University
Office of Research and the University Graduate School, the American Musi-
cological Society, and the National Endowment for the Humanities.

The Oxford University Press staff has been patient, helpful, professional,
and efficient. Thanks especially to music editor Kim Robinson, production
editor Joellyn Ausanka, copy editor Mary Sutherland, and also to Eve
Bachrach, Jordan Bucher, Matthew Sollars, Maribeth Payne, and Sheldon
Meyer, who offered me a contract near the end of a remarkable career of
cultivating Oxford's jazz list.

Collaboration begins in the family. Together, my parents form an anchor
of love and support. Behind everything worthwhile I have written stands my
father, Richard, who applied his red pen to my earliest efforts and whose
own prose makes every word count. Behind my finished projects also stands
my mother, Joyce, a model of cheerful but quiet determination. (And it
seems appropriate to mention that she, like an important subject in this
book, was born on August 21, 1935.) Rich Magee, not just an older brother
but a great friend, was a rock to lean on when the going got tough, and I'm
grateful to him and his family, Dianne, Katie, and Kevin, for their generosity
and hospitality while the book developed. My daughter Ellen (born 1996)

has grown up with the book, challenged me to be a storyteller, and has become one herself. I'm sorry to report (as one of her favorite authors might say) that this is not the "kid book" she asked for, but there will be plenty of other stories to share. She and my new son Miles (born 2004)—a remarkably easygoing baby who sat patiently on my knee while his dad made some final changes to the book—remind me of greater things beyond the computer screen. Finally, thanks to Gayle—wife, mother, scholar, writer, editor, teacher, musician, advisor, friend, and confidante—for her love, support, and wisdom. As the ultimate collaborator, she earns the book's dedication with my love.

The book incorporates material from several previously published articles, including:

"Crossing the Tracks in Cuthbert." *Institute for Studies in American Music Newsletter* 23, no. 1 (Fall 1993): 6–7.

"Revisiting Fletcher Henderson's 'Copenhagen'," *Journal of the American Musicological Society* 48, no. 1 (Spring 1995): 42–66.

"Henderson, Fletcher Hamilton, Jr." In *International Dictionary of Black Composers*, edited by Samuel A. Floyd, Jr. Chicago: Fitzroy Dearborn, 1999.

"Fletcher Henderson, Composer: A Counter-Entry to *The International Dictionary of Black Composers*." *Black Music Research Journal* 19, no. 1 (Spring 1999): 61–70.

"Before Louis: When Fletcher Henderson Was 'The Paul Whiteman of the Race.'" *American Music* 18, no. 4 (Winter 2000): 391–425.

"'King Porter Stomp' and the Jazz Tradition." *Current Musicology*, nos. 71–72 (2001–2002): 22–53.

CREDITS

INDEX

CPSIA information can be obtained
at www.ICGtesting.com
Printed in the USA
BVHW040046040820
R11038500001B/R110385PG584564BVX3B/1